INTRODUCTION TO URBAN PLANNING

INTRODUCTION TO URBAN PLANNING

Edited by

Anthony J. Catanese
James C. Snyder

School of Architecture and Urban Planning
University of Wisconsin–Milwaukee

Architectural Drawings by Jeffrey E. Ollswang

McGraw-Hill Book Company

New York St. Louis San Francisco Auckland Bogotá Düsseldorf
Johannesburg London Madrid Mexico Montreal New Delhi
Panama Paris São Paulo Singapore Sydney Tokyo Toronto

INTRODUCTION TO URBAN PLANNING

234567890 HDHD 7832109

This book was set in Helvetica Light by A Graphic Method Inc.
The editors were Rose Ciofalo and David Damstra;
the designer was Merrill Haber; the cover was designed by Hermann Strohbach;
the production supervisor was John F. Harte.
Other drawings were done by J & R Services, Inc.
Halliday Lithograph Corporation was printer and binder.

Library of Congress Cataloging in Publication Data
Main entry under title:

Introduction to urban planning.

    Includes index.
    1. City planning. 2. City planning—United States.
I. Catanese, Anthony James. II. Snyder, James C.
HT166.I67   309.2′62′0973   78-13275
ISBN 0-07-010228-7

To Felicity Brogden-Ollswang

Contents

About the Contributors

Editors

ANTHONY J. CATANESE, AICP, is Dean, School of Architecture and Urban Planning, University of Wisconsin-Milwaukee. He received degrees in urban and regional planning from Rutgers University (B.A.), New York University (M.C.P.), and the University of Wisconsin-Madison (Ph.D.). He has worked as a planner for Middlesex County and the state of New Jersey, and he has had extensive consulting experience from Florida to Hawaii. In addition, Dr. Catanese has taught at Georgia Institute of Technology, University of Miami at Coral Gables, and at the University of Wisconsin-Milwaukee. He is the author or editor of seven books in the area of urban planning, including *Systemic Planning: Theory and Application* (1970), *New Perspectives in Transportation Research* (1972), *Scientific Methods of Urban Analysis* (1972), *Planners and Local Politics* (1974), and *Personality, Politics, and Planning: How City Planners Work* (1978). Long active in the American Institute of Planners, Dr. Catanese also has been involved in political campaigns as a policy analyst, and is a Commissioner, Milwaukee City Plan Commission.

JAMES C. SNYDER, AICP, is Associate Dean and Associate Professor of Architecture and Urban Planning, University of Wisconsin-Milwaukee. A graduate of the Ohio State University (B. Arch.) and the University of Michigan (M. Arch.; M. City Planning; Ph.D., Urban and Regional Planning), Dr. Snyder has taught at the University of Michigan, Georgia Institute of Technology, and the University of Wisconsin-Milwaukee. He is the author of *Fiscal Management and Planning in Local Government* (1977). In addition to teaching and research, Dr. Snyder has served as a planning and design consultant to numerous local governments and as president of the Wisconsin Chapter of the American Institute of Planners.

Contributors

ERNEST R. ALEXANDER is Associate Professor of Urban Planning, University of Wisconsin-Milwaukee, where he teaches planning theory, organization and decision theory, development planning, and policy analysis. Dr. Alexander has degrees from the University of Cape Town, South Africa (B. Arch.) and the University of California-Berkeley (M. Urban Planning; Ph.D., City and Regional Planning). He has extensive experience in teaching and research and authored, with A. J. Catanese and D. Sawicki, *Urban Planning* (1978), and with R. Beckley, *Going It Alone? A Case Study of Planning and Implementation at the Local Level* (1975).

WAYNE O. ATTOE is Associate Professor of Architecture, University of Wisconsin-Milwaukee, where he teaches in the areas of architectural design, architectural criticism, and historic preservation. Dr. Attoe has degrees from Cornell University (B.A.), the University of California-Berkeley (B. Arch.), and the Union Graduate School (Ph.D.). He is the author of *Architecture and Critical Imagination* (1978).

ROBERT M. BECKLEY, AIA, is Professor of Architecture, University of Wisconsin-Milwaukee, and has degrees in Architecture from the University of Cincinnati and the Graduate School of Design, Harvard University. He is a registered architect and has conducted extensive research and consulting work in urban design, urban redevelopment, transportation design, housing, and the relation between environment and behavior. He is the author of numerous consulting and research reports, and with Professors Alexander and Rapoport authored *Applied Design Sciences: The Application of Multidisciplinary Research Concerning Human Need to the Planning Process* (1973). Professor Beckley teaches courses in urban design, architectural design, and the environmental impacts of transportation.

EDWARD BEIMBORN is Professor and Director, Center for Urban Transportation Studies, College of Engineering and Applied Science, University of Wisconsin-Milwaukee, where he teaches in the areas of systems analysis, transportation planning, and municipal engineering. He has degrees from the University of Wisconsin-Madison (B.S.) and Northwestern University (M. Civil Engineering and Ph.D.). A registered engineer, Dr. Beimborn has extensive planning and research experience with the Urban Mass Transportation Administration, the National Sea Grant Program, and state and regional transportation and planning agencies.

W. PAUL FARMER, AICP, is Assistant Professor of Urban Planning, University of Wisconsin-Milwaukee, and has degrees from Rice University (B.A., B. Arch.) and Cornell University (M. Regional Planning). Professor Farmer teaches in the areas of urban law and land policy, comparative urban planning, and urban design. He edited, with A. J. Cantanese, *Personality, Politics and Planning* (1978), and currently serves as the President of the Wisconsin Chapter of the American Institute of Planners.

ABOUT THE CONTRIBUTORS

JULIE A. GIBB was formerly an Assistant Professor of Urban Planning, University of Wisconsin-Milwaukee. She has degrees from Mount Holyoke College (A.B.) and Washington University School of Law (J.D.). She teaches in the areas of urban planning and land development law, administrative law, and real estate transactions, and she has written in the areas of coastal zone management and differential housing code enforcement.

DAVID HOEH, AICP, is Executive Director, Park West Redevelopment Task Force, Inc., Milwaukee, Wisconsin. He has degrees from the University of New Hampshire (B.A.), Boston University (A.M.), and the University of Massachusetts (Ph.D.). Dr. Hoeh has taught at Dartmouth College, where he was Associate Director of the Public Affairs Center, and at the University of Wisconsin-Milwaukee. He has extensive experience in state, regional, and local planning.

AMOS RAPOPORT is Professor of Architecture and Anthropology at the University of Wisconsin-Milwaukee, where he was a Research Professor between 1974 and 1977. He has a B.Arch. and Postgraduate Diploma of Town and Regional Planning from Melbourne University, Australia, and M. Arch. from Rice University. He is a Fellow of the Royal Australian Institute of Architects, an Associate of the Royal Institute of British Architects, and a Registered Architect in Australia. He has taught at Melbourne and Sydney Universities in Australia, the University of California-Berkeley, and University College, London. Professor Rapoport has been involved in human environment studies and has written numerous papers and books, including *House Form and Culture* (1969), *The Mutual Interaction of People and Their Built Environment* (1976), and *Human Aspects of Urban Form* (1977).

DAVID S. SAWICKI is Associate Professor of Urban Planning, University of Wisconsin-Milwaukee, where he teaches in the area of methods for planning and policy analysis. Dr. Sawicki is currently Review Editor of the *Journal of the American Institute of Planners* and he wrote, with A. J. Catanese and E. Alexander, *Urban Planning* (1978). In addition, Professor Sawicki has been a consultant to government agencies in the United States and several developing countries.

SAMMIS B. WHITE is Chairman and Associate Professor, Department of Urban Planning, University of Wisconsin-Milwaukee. He has degrees from William College (B.A.) and the University of Pennsylvania (M.C.P. and Ph.D., City Planning). He teaches in the areas of housing and housing policy, and social and policy planning. Dr. White has been engaged in housing research with the Rand Corporation and the National League of Cities, and he coauthored *Rethinking Housing and Community Development Policy* (1977).

LARRY WITZLING is Assistant Professor of Architecture and Urban Planning, University of Wisconsin-Milwaukee, where he teaches in the areas of urban design, comprehensive community development, and planning methods. Dr. Witzling has degrees from Cooper Union (B. Arch.) and Cornell University (Ph.D.).

Preface

This book is an introductory survey of the built environment. The concern is primarily with the physical elements, with the realization that there are social, economic, and political elements that shape this environment as well. While this may seem limiting, it is a realistic constraint imposed in order to achieve certain pedagogical objectives. Design and planning are considered in this physical sense, however, in order to introduce the many facets of the built environment to entering archtecture and urban planning students as well as those seeking an introductory knowledge of these fields.

Architecture and urban planning are fascinating areas for professional practice. These two fields were once one, usually called architecture or master building. Within the last century, the increasing specialization of labor in our society has led to the formation of two distinct fields of study and practice. A principal distinction is that of scale. Architecture is primarily concerned with the built environment at three scales: smaller-than-buildings, buildings, and larger-than-buildings. Although there is sometimes an overlap at the last scale, urban planning is concerned with the built environment from the larger-than-buildings scale to the regional and national scale. While architecture is primarily concerned with physical manifestations of design, and urban planning is more concerned with policy formation and management, both fields are related to the natural environment within the social, economic, and political context of civilization.

There have not yet been any convenient textbooks for these two fields, especially textbooks which deal with the full range of the built environment or the relationships between each professional area. The objective of our two companion volumes, *Introduction to Architecture* and *Introduction to Urban Planning,* is to remedy this problem by incorporating the diverse components of both fields into two interrelated textbooks. By emphasizing the broad perspective and depth of architecture and urban planning, rather than accepting artificially restrictive disciplinary perspectives, we hope to fulfill this need.

The organization and substance of these two volumes was determined largely by the results of surveys undertaken by the editors during 1976 and 1977. Questionnaires were sent to members of every accredited and recognized university-based program in architecture and urban planning. These questionnaires dealt with the content, approach, and literature of introductory courses in architecture and urban planning.

Introductory level courses in architecture can occur at different levels. Entering students in architecture may be freshmen in preprofessional, paraprofessional, or nonprofessional two-year programs; freshmen or sophomores in four- or five-year professional or nonprofessional undergraduate degree programs; juniors or seniors in five- or six-year professional programs; first-year graduate students in two- or three-year professional programs; and even first-year doctoral students. The introductory level course may range from a two- or three-hour lecture course to a nine-hour studio. This variety provides a clue to why there have been so few previous textbooks for introductory courses.

Most of the reading lists for these courses are constructed from scattered text and journal readings dealing with similar subject matter and comprehensive sets of topics. There was sufficient convergence of subject matter and substance to allow us to synthesize a general outline of topics.

Introductory level courses in urban planning sometimes appear at the freshmen or sophomore level for nonprofessional undergraduate programs (only a few undergraduate professional programs exist). The more typical introduction to urban planning occurs in the first year of the two-year professional master's degree program. As with architecture courses, it was possible to synthesize an outline of the content and substance of introductory courses in urban planning. While there have been a number of attempts to create textbooks for certain aspects of urban planning (for example, methods), as well as attempts to provide guides for planning practice, there is no comprehensive treatment of the field that incorporates the range of subject matter being taught entry-level students. We hope this volume meets that need.

Most architecture curricula include introductory courses in urban planning, and many urban planning curricula allow for selection of courses dealing with\the design and development aspects of architecture. There has been much interest in recent years in both architecture and urban planning programs by nonmajors, especially students in fields that are intertwined in professional practice, such as economics, management, finance, political science, social work, law, history, and anthropology. We believe that the absence of introductory level textbooks for architecture and urban planning has impeded the development of such courses for nonmajors and may well have been a source of frustration for those students who did enroll in such courses. Again, we hope these two volumes will assist with the dissemination of knowledge of architecture and urban planning to these students.

Three guiding principles emerged from our interpretation of survey results (tempered by our own experience and judgment). There is a need for introductory textbooks in architecture and urban planning that:

1 Include those subject areas regularly covered in introductory courses in schools of architecture and programs in urban planning

2 Emphasize the broad perspectives and breadth of both fields rather than constrict substantive issues

3 Are aimed at the student with little or no previous experience in either field

Thus, these companion volumes (used separately or together) are designed to provide a convenient source of readings for the varied introductory level courses offered at the university level. Each volume is sufficient for the typical three-hour, one-semester lecture course. These volumes also can be used as a base of reading for more extensive introductory courses in the studio format. In addition, the breadth of coverage, synthetic nature, and coverage of contemporary subjects should appeal to professional practitioners.

Much credit must be given to the many contributors to these volumes—who have worked together in the best academic and professional tradition. Also, much credit must be given to Mary Eichstaedt and Bruce Thomson for invaluable assistance in production, and to David Damstra from the McGraw-Hill Book Company. The editors assume full responsibility for the texts. Each chapter was edited for organization, clarity, interrelationships with other chapters, sense, and style. In addition, each author worked closely with the editors to ensure an overall level of quality and cohesiveness.

Anthony J. Catanese
James C. Snyder

INTRODUCTION TO URBAN PLANNING

Part One
History and Cultural Context

The first part of this volume includes three chapters on the history, cultural origins, and design of urban areas as they provide a context for urban planning. Together, they involve a broad field of knowledge that helps us understand the physical manifestations of civilization. It is important to consider this body of knowledge since it is impossible to know where we are and where we should go without knowing where we have been and how we got here. If history repeats itself, urban planners should understand the successful planning responses to particular problems or situations. On the other hand, if the past is but prologue, then we might incorporate the more stable elements of culture and physical structure into those elements requiring change and replacement.

The context of reality for the practice of urban planning is made up of the economic, social, and physical aspects of civilization. These are understood best in the evolutionary framework of urban history, culture, and form.

CHAPTER 1

History and Trends of Urban Planning

Anthony J. Catanese

Most urban planning techniques rely on the extrapolation of past trends from historical sources. It follows, then, that an understanding of the rich history of urban planning is useful, even essential, for the serious student. Even those who insist that we must change the trends seen in the past recognize that using historical analysis as a predictive base is a reasonable and reliable approach.

In addition, this history is most fascinating. It reflects the evolution of humankind from cave dwellers and nomads to an urbanized society. It is the history of the rise of cities and their metropolitan areas.

PRECURSORS OF URBAN PLANNING

The Ancient World

Around 4,000 B.C., in the area known as the Fertile Crescent (corresponding roughly to the Nile Valley and Tigris and Euphrates alluvial plain), civilization began. Most striking was the development of city-kingdoms by the Sumerians of Assyria. These warrior-kings built cities that were both fortresses and marketplaces for the agricultural products of the surrounding lands. There was also some light manufacturing and craft making in these cities, typical of the Bronze Age.

These cities were *planned cities*. In most of them, the population was from 3,000 to 5,000. City life centered on 100-foot-high buildings called *ziggurats*, which were both temples and observa-

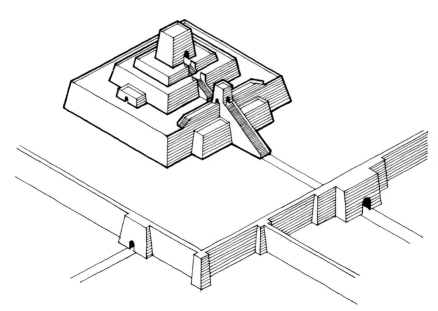

Ziggurat at Ur, Turkey.

tories. The basic plan used a massive wall surrounding the ziggurat, palace, and other buildings. There was much decoration of lower walls with painting on plaster or bas-reliefs.

One of the earliest of these cities was Babylon (about 55 miles south of modern-day Baghdad, Iraq). Originally built like other Sumerian cities, it reached its legendary greatness when Nebuchadnezzar had it rebuilt during the sixth century B.C. The new city followed a regular street plan, bisected by the Euphrates River. The temple and tower remained at the center, and the famous Hanging Gardens Palace was on the river by the north wall. At its height, as the capital of the Babylonian Empire, Babylon had as many as 10,000 people—probably the largest city of its time.

Egyptian civilization flourished at this time as well. Egypt was also city-oriented, but its cities were generally rather small. The exceptions were the cities built in conjunction with the construction of the pyramids. For example, one of the oldest cities was Kahun, which was built primarily to house the workers and artisans engaged in building the great

Illahun pyramid. There may have been up to 20,000 persons living in this city at times during the pyramid's construction. While there was a rectangular street system, the housing consisted of little more than a grouping of cells for slaves and a hierarchy of larger accommodations for artisans. Most of these cities, such as Giza, were abandoned after the completion of the pyramid. They were never considered permanent towns—indeed, the complex was more appropriately considered a *necropolis,* or city for the dead.

The only other known cities of the ancient world were planned and built along the Indus Valley in what is now Pakistan and the Yellow River Valley of China. These cities had some similarities with the Egyptian cities of the time. Clearly the transportation, agricultural, and defensive advantages associated with these great rivers were the primary factors in their location. Generally, however, little is known of the Asian city planners of the ancient world and of their influence on later cities.

Western civilization began on the islands of the Aegean Sea and grew with the settlement of Greece

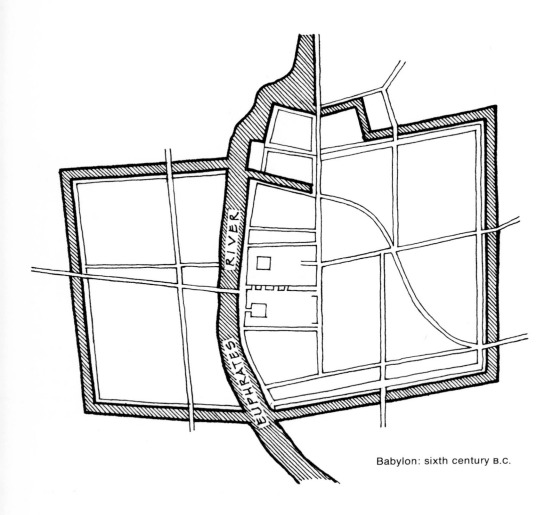

Babylon: sixth century B.C.

by northern peoples mingling with the southerners. During the fifth century B.C., Pericles led the establishment of a moral and political form of citizenship that was called *democracy*. The temple of Athena become a meeting place of the people. It, rather than the ruler's palace, was the center of the city. As democracy grew, the houses and facilities of the community became more important elements of the city plan.

With this increasing sense of order and structure in the fifth century B.C., there emerged a person who might well be considered the first city planner—Hippodamus. Trained as an architect, Hippodamus developed the first philosophical basis for physical planning in cities. Having observed Sumerian and Egyptian cities, he theorized the need for a rectangular street system (or *gridiron pattern*) to give a geometrical form to urban spaces. Residential blocks were designed to enable the houses to be serviced and related to public buildings and spaces. Houses were arranged to guarantee privacy—an essential element of Grecian democracy.

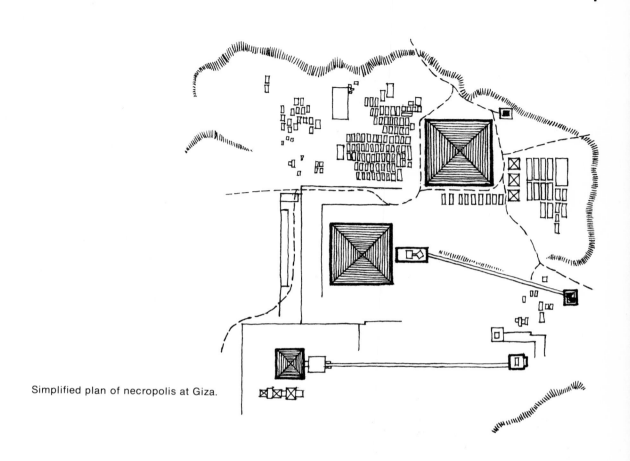

Simplified plan of necropolis at Giza.

The Acropolis, Athens.

8

Hippodamus developed the concept of an *agora*—a central marketplace laid out along rectangular lines. The agora was distinct from the political assembly area of the people—the *pnyx*—but often close to it. In this area, the business of the city was conducted. There is some evidence that building regulations were developed to prevent private encroachment upon public places and rights-of-way.

Hippodamus is believed to have planned the port of Athens (Piraeus) as well as Rhodes and Thurii. His planning philosophy and designs were used extensively in Greek colonial towns and city-states, such as Miletus and Priene. During this period, Athens grew to a city of 40,000 citizens, plus as many as 100,000 slaves and foreigners.[1] Yet Hippodamus theorized that only Athens, as the capital, should be this large, and that an ideal city would have no more than 10,000 residents. This theory was related primarily to hygienic beliefs and to the capability of such cities to provide food and water.

Many of the architectural plans and proportions of buildings in Greek cities during the last three centuries B.C., or Hellenistic period, are in what is called the *classical style*. Vitruvius was a Roman architect and engineer who assimilated the treatises written by his contemporaries and formulated a number of books on architecture. These theories and philosophies are evident in the design of many modern buildings and were extensively emulated until the twentieth century. The Hellenistic period was the classical age of architecture as well as a transition from Greek to Roman planning and building.

As Socrates warned, civilization must either grow or decline, but the Greeks found change difficult, especially as the citizens prospered and grew complacent. Plato and Aristotle had warned of the abuse of democracy by wealthy persons fleeing the city for their country estates and villas. Conditions in the cities worsened, and it became difficult for people to earn a living. Corrupt politicians plundered

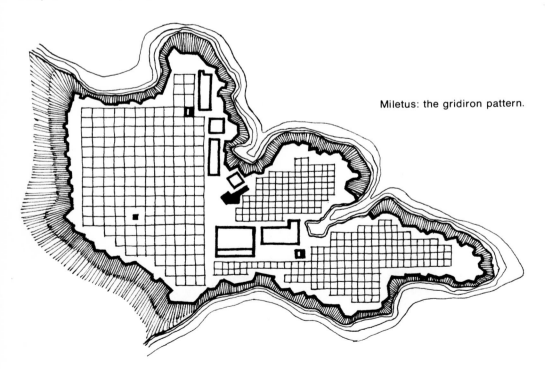

Miletus: the gridiron pattern.

the cities, and a disastrous series of wars reduced Greece to a mere Roman province by 146 B.C.

Rome never was a democracy. From the Etruscan kings of 500 B.C. to Julius Caesar in the first century B.C., the Romans accepted the notion of a god-like leader. Each succeeding emperor had to accomplish ever-greater conquests to establish the world order necessary for the Roman concept of one world composed of different peoples sharing the same laws and leader. The concept was embodied in the Roman Empire, which existed from 27 B.C. to A.D. 324.

Rome replaced Athens as the center of the world during this period. Unlike the Athenians, the Romans believed in bigness and accepted all strangers into their domain, as long as they were loyal. Growth was so rapid that over 45,000 apartment blocks and almost 2,000 private homes were built by the third century A.D. Eight-story buildings were erected before Augustus imposed a 70-foot height limit—the first example of *zoning*—in the first century A.D.

As the Roman Empire grew in power and wealth, the population of Rome greatly increased —estimates vary from 250,000 to 2,000,000 permanent residents. With this growth, severe housing shortages and transportation problems arose. Rome also suffered from an inadequate water supply, which led to the construction of massive aqueducts to bring in fresh water. Despite these conditions, Roman emperors and leaders were able to build huge monuments to the greatness of their empire and themselves. Each new emperor built a forum grander than the last. These fora served as the centers for the political and business life of the city.

The Romans understood the importance of transportation and emerged as the first regional planners in this sense. They planned and built roads throughout the sprawling empire, which ranged from Spain to Armenia and Britain to Egypt. These roads enabled communications and commerce to flow from Rome, and they also provided the most rapid means of transportation for imperial armies to maintain order and quell uprisings.

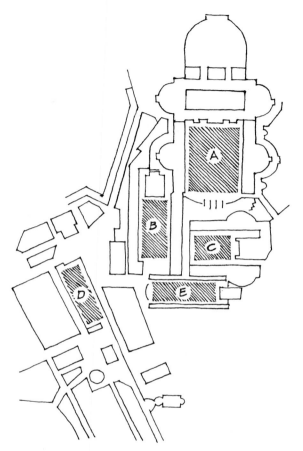

A FORUM OF TRAJAN
B FORUM OF JULIUS CAESAR
C FORUM OF AUGUSTUS
D FORUM ROMANUM
E FORUM OF NERVA

Imperial Rome: The Fora.

In an attempt to colonize new territories, siphon off some of the migration to Rome, and construct symbols of Roman law and order, the Romans built a number of military cities throughout the empire. Most of them followed a master plan that varied only

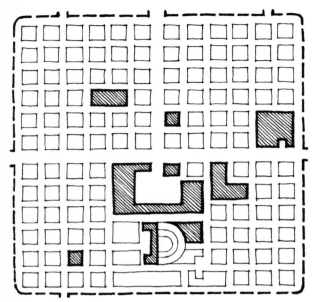

Roman camp at Timgad.

slightly and enabled rapid construction. Built in virtually a square pattern, these colonial cities were dominated by civic buildings at the intersection of the two main roads. Housing was predominantly small apartments, with atrium-style houses for the wealthy.

The fall of the Roman Empire was gradual. The people became hedonistic and indolent, and the leadership was divided by quarreling. Barbarian hordes began attacking, and, for the first time in five centuries, Rome had enemies at the walls. The growth of Christianity also eroded the base of Rome's power, and warring sects and parties from within contributed to her decline. The monuments of the caesars were quarried for building materials. Public places like the fora were dismantled by fighting masses. Rome collapsed by the end of the third century.

During the next 100 years, Constantine moved the capital to Constantinople and divided the empire, and the western part of the empire became

overrun by barbarians. By the fifth century, the Dark Ages had begun. Cities planned as great symbols of imperial might were replaced by medieval towns based upon the rule of feudal lords over their serfs rather than on principles of democracy or imperialism.

The importance of the ancient world is that it established a long-lasting pattern of planning for cities. This pattern held that cities are built upon four bases. The *physical* base of the city is the visible manifestation of buildings, roads, parks, and other features that give it *form*. The *political* base of the city is essential for its *meaning*. The *economic* base of the city provides as much of a *reason* for its existence as the other bases. And finally, a *social* base is essential for city *life*. The design of the cities of the ancient world was a precursor of what we now consider the urban pattern.

The physical base of cities was especially well defined in the classical cities of the ancient world. Regular street patterns were always imposed in contrast to the meandering and "extemporaneous" streets of nonclassical cities. The center was usually dominated by buildings devoted to worship, government, and business—in essence, power was based at the core of a classical city. Housing filled the remaining spaces; it rarely was responsible for the city's form. The planners of classical cities created their designs in order to fulfill the wishes of the ruling parties and leaders, not for their own personal artistic satisfactions or dreams. The planners were technicians working to find solutions to city problems, constrained by political, economic, social, and physical conditions.

Medieval to Renaissance

The major contribution of the Romans to urban planning, then, was planned city building as a symbol of governmental power and presence. After the fall of the Roman Empire, however, the barbarians either destroyed many of the Roman cities or used them as fortresses in their local wars. Urban life disin-

Carcassonne, France.

Mont St. Michel.

tegrated and a rural civilization reemerged. Central authority was replaced by an incredible assortment of local powers based in fortresses and castles and feudal city-states. Only in the monasteries did intellectual communities survive.

There was little need for urban planning again until the eleventh century, since there were no real cities built or rebuilt during the intervening period. By late in the tenth century, however, the countryside had become unsafe, and serfs demanded that their feudal lords protect them behind the walls of towns A reestablishment of the town as a business center began. Both feudal lords and church leaders saw advantages in such a role. As a result, many medieval towns were built during the eleventh, twelfth and thirteenth centuries, all concerned with trade and marketing as well as defense.

During the eighth to twelfth centuries, a considerable amount of the town building in the Western world was centered upon the church. These towns reflected the influence of Christianity upon Western thought. The style of architecture employed is often called *romanesque* because it used the arched building systems discovered by the Romans. To the

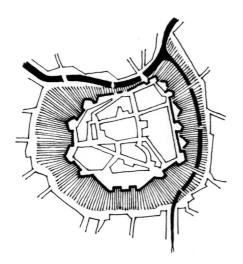

Medieval and contemporary Vienna.

serf of these times, the security of the church as a mystical force, coupled with the secular protection of the feudal lord in the walled town, was the essence of life and the reason for hard work and fealty.

By the thirteenth century, there were many towns in the Western world, but few had more than 50,000 inhabitants, and most had fewer than 1,000. The reasons were more practical than planned: because of the walled fortification systems, water supply problems, and sanitation considerations, few towns occupied more than 1 square mile. While often crowded, however, these cities mostly were clean and safe.

With the onset of the Middle Ages, a few cities grew to considerable size. Florence was the seat of much political power and grew to 90,000 population. Venice was the foremost world trading center of the Byzantine Empire and grew to 200,000. Paris was emerging as a major world trade center and had a population of 240,000 by the fourteenth century. London also was outgrowing its medieval form, which was not much different from a Roman camp city.

Two remarkable events marked the fifteenth century. The first was the discovery of gunpowder and its subsequent use in warfare. The immediate impact was the restructuring of walled cities. First, new outer walls were built at some distance from the cities to create a defensive buffer zone sometimes called "no-man's-land." Simultaneously, however, the new techniques of warfare led to a greater demand for soldiers, and for power, by the feudal lords. Cities began to grow in both population and area. Within a century, gunpowder made walls around cities useless. The medieval wall around Vienna, for example, was removed and replaced by a road—the Ringstrasse.

The second remarkable event of the fifteenth century was the flowering of the *Renaissance,* most evident in Italy. Mainly because of the largesse of the great ruling families of Florence, Venice, and Rome, but fully supported by the papal powers, an intensive preoccupation with the arts and humanities arose. However, the effect upon urban planning

Florence, Italy.

was more artistic than substantive. The basic form and pattern of cities remained unchanged, but there was more concern for beauty within. Palaces, churches, and public buildings had to be monuments of great beauty—for they represented the people who had ordered them built. Even more fascinating was the personal recognition afforded the architects and planners. Unlike their predecessors, Brunelleschi, Michelangelo, and Leonardo in Italy; Christopher Wren and Inigo Jones in England; and Mansart and Fontaine in France were recognized as great artists and given much creative freedom by their patron merchants, popes, and kings.

Some important concepts of urban planning emerged during the Renaissance. The axis style of city design was foremost; it meant that urban form now had an organizing centerline. The use of formal piazzas or squares was fostered by Michelangelo, Bernini, and others, culminating in the creation of one of the most beautiful piazzas, San Marco in Venice. The planners were opening up the cramped areas of the old walled cities. Bernini used open space symbolically, to represent the church reaching out to comfort her flock, in St. Peter's in Rome.

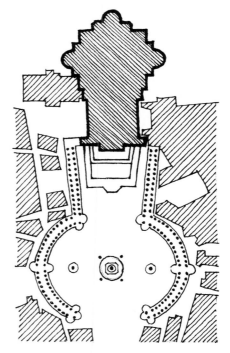

St. Peter's Cathedral and Piazza, Rome.

HISTORY AND TRENDS OF URBAN PLANNING

Versailles, France.

The transition from the Renaissance to the *baroque period* was orderly. The baroque period, during the seventeenth and eighteenth centuries, was marked by the monumentalism and grandeur of the reigning monarchs of the Western world, seen most vividly in France. The most important patterns of urban planning in the baroque period were essentially elaborations of Renaissance urban design. The city centerline or axis was embellished to symbolize the radiance of monarchs and rulers. The demand for larger open places was never-ending, and huge open spaces were created in cities.

Important patterns thus emerged from the return to cities that characterized the medieval, Renaissance, and baroque periods. Clearly, cities had become the places where trade and commerce occurred. This often meant the existence of a centralized physical space, related to the religious and secular areas of the city. The monumental designs for open spaces, boulevards, and dwellings that emerged in the late Renaissance and baroque periods, however, were indicative of more ominous signs. Hidden by the monumental creations were deprived and oppressed people; such people would revolt and burn those planned areas in the eighteenth century. This was an early sign that planning for the wealthy and powerful to the exclu-

sion of all others sows seeds of destruction. It also should have warned people that physical planning and design alone are not sufficient to meet societal needs. Yet this era left a lasting impression that all cities can be beautiful and inspiring—an idea that was altered by the industrial revolution.

The Industrial City

Just as the discovery of gunpowder had an immense impact on urban spaces, so did the invention of the steam engine in 1769. It signaled the beginning of an *industrial revolution,* because it meant that human labor could be supplemented or replaced by machines. Supported in addition by a philosophy of private enterprise, expressed in the writings of Adam Smith, among others, a period of intensive industrialization was well underway by the beginning of the nineteenth century.

The early impacts of the industrial revolution were increased congestion, new safety hazards, and air and water pollution. Transportation was the key to industrialization. Unless raw materials could be brought to the factories and finished products distributed to market areas, the industrial revolution could not happen. Thus, cities had imposed upon them new streets, railways, shipping lanes, and canals. Usually these transportation facilities were merely laid over existing patterns, often causing grave incompatibility.

With the industrial revolution came a new phenomenon of city life—the *journey to work*. Prior to the industrial revolution, work was carried on at home —in the so-called cottage industries—or in shops close to home. With mechanization, the means of production were centralized in factories, thereby physically separating workers from their places of work.

The industrial revolution spawned an even greater opening up of cities than the invention of gunpowder had. The increasing congestion and health hazards created a movement towards *suburbs* made possible by improved streets and urban railway systems. By the late nineteenth and early twentieth centuries, suburbs housing the more affluent were common at the periphery of cities, while lower-paid workers lived in the congested central areas. The patterns of urban flight and suburban sprawl so characteristic of contemporary American cities had their precursors a century ago. It took only the invention of the automobile to foster a massive sprawl of residential areas far from older central areas.

So rapid was the growth of cities and the problems of industrialization that a number of reform movements had emerged by the late nineteenth century. The first public health act, passed in England, dealt mainly with standards for housing. In the late 1800s, model housing units were built by the rulers of England, France, and Germany. Germany, Austria, and the United States began experiments with zoning to control land uses and building heights in cities. It became quite clear by the beginning of the twentieth century that the infrastructure of cities, water supply, transit, and streets, as well as health and sanitation services, would have to be planned and built by the city governments themselves.

Somewhat romantic precursors of urban planning evolved in the latter part of the nineteenth century. These were the anti–industrial revolution, anti-city *utopian* movements. Some of the earliest involved cooperative housing schemes, like Robert Owen's early plans for New Lanark in England.[2] Others were philosophical, like J. S. Buckingham's plan for an associated temperance community.

The titans of the industrial revolution, perhaps out of guilt or *noblesse oblige,* or perhaps out of societal concerns, created a number of new towns. One of the most famous was Sir Titus Salt's town,

London, by Gustave Doré.

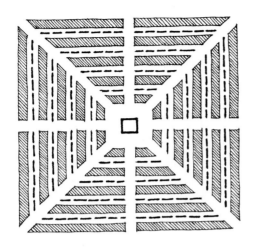

☐   CENTRAL SQUARE

---   MUNICIPAL AND COMMERCIAL

▨   HOUSING

Diagrammatic plan of Buckingham Terrace.

named Saltaire, built in England in 1852 to house 3,000 workers from his textile mill. Salt served as his own planner and designer. The Krupp family built a number of small towns near Essen, Germany for their arms and munitions factory workers. George Cadbury was a successful chocolate manufacturer who combined his practical needs for production with his Quaker social consciousness and moved his factory and workers from Birmingham, England to his new town of Bournemouth in 1879. There were numerous other examples in France, Germany, Italy, America, and elsewhere.

These new towns were quite modest solutions to the increasing congestion of industrial centers. They attracted much interest, however, and Ebenezer Howard solidified the concept of new towns as an urban planning movement. Howard was born in 1850 in London and emigrated to the United States at age 21 to try farming in Nebraska. Failing at that, he worked for a while in a Chicago office and then returned to London in 1876. Somewhat of an eccentric, he became a shorthand expert and inventor. In 1898,

Saltaire, England.

he published a book entitled *To-Morrow: A Peaceful Path to Social Reform,* in which he proposed the *garden city* as a solution to urban planning problems. Howard wanted to combat the crowding and congestion of industrial cities by building garden cities outside developed areas so that people could "return to nature." In a systematic urban planning program, garden cities could be used to prevent large cities, such as London, from becoming further congested.

There were four main components of Howard's invention:

1 All the land, about 1,000 acres, would be owned singly in the public trust.

2 Population and development would be staged until a maximum of 30,000 people were housed.

3 A greenbelt of 5,000 acres of agricultural land would surround the city.

4 There would be a mixture of land uses to insure social and economic self-sufficiency.

Howard's book appeared at the right historical moment. It enjoyed immense success, and he acquired a considerable following. In 1899, the Garden City Association was founded, and in 1903 it formed a unique limited-dividend company to build Letchworth. Following Howard's scheme, Letchworth grew to a community of 15,000 with shops and industries on 4,500 acres of land. Shortly thereafter, another limited-dividend corporation built Welwyn, which quickly reached a population of 10,000. Both of these new towns were within 33 miles of London, yet they became self-sufficient and, rather remarkably, were able to return limited dividends to stockholders and reinvest additional profit in community facilities. Unlike other utopians, when Howard died in 1929 he had seen his dream become a reality.

Whether or not these first two garden cities could be considered successes is at least debatable. More importantly, they provided practical illustrations for the development of a national urban poli-

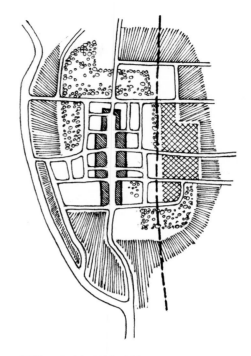

COMMERCIAL
INDUSTRIAL
AGRICULTURAL BELT
PARKLANDS
--- RAILROAD

Diagrammatic plan of a garden city.

cy in England. Over a period of years, especially after World War II, the British government used the concepts of greenbelts, garden cities, and communal trusts in building a series of new towns as a means of controlling urban growth. Most of these cities surrounded London, but there were others, near, for example, Edinburgh, Scotland. While it had become clear by the early 1960s that these towns of 20,000 to 50,000 population would not alone stem the flow of urban migration to the principal city of London, a sufficient number was built to improve

Cumbernauld, Scotland: a new town.

substantively the urban condition. New towns were also built in Sweden, Holland, Germany, Russia, and elsewhere along the lines of the English approach.

While Howard will be remembered as a man of vision and action, it was his Scottish contemporary, Patrick Geddes, who made the major philosophical contribution of this era. Geddes theorized that physical planning could not improve urban living conditions unless it were integrated with social and economic planning in a context of environmental concern. This integration should occur at a regional scale including both the city and its surrounding hinterland—in his words, the *urban connurbation.* Geddes insisted on complexity and diversity in planning and thereby set the stage for large-scale, comprehensive planning. Without his contribution, the evolution of urban planning beyond pat physical solutions would have been delayed.

EARLY PLANNING IN THE UNITED STATES

The early period of urban planning in the United States reflected a diversity of style and character.

The first agrarian colonies in North America were little more than forts to protect settlers from Indian attacks. Then there emerged the New England towns of the seventeenth century, which were remarkable for their simplicity. Modest houses for each family were grouped in a gridiron pattern around a park or *commons* that was usually next to a meeting place. The Southern settlers were more isolated and developed a plantation style of settlement. Those Southern cities that were planned, such as Williamsburg and Jamestown, Virginia, were more formal, with a market square as the center; they were reminiscent of English villages.

The Dutch settlement of New Amsterdam was quite a different development. It was more like a medieval town surrounding a castle—in this case, the Battery. When the area of Manhattan was planned, the gridiron pattern used was the one William Penn had developed for Philadelphia in 1682. James Oglethorpe's 1793 plan for Savannah, Georgia, partly imitated the Philadelphia plan, but Oglethorpe was far more generous with open spaces for squares.

The most notable exception to the gridiron approach in early American planning was the Pierre

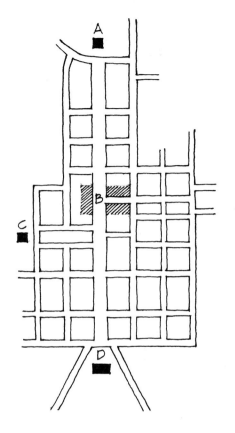

A   THE CAPITOL

B   MARKET SQUARE

C   GOVERNOR'S PALACE

D   THE COLLEGE OF
    WILLIAM AND MARY

The market square as town center: Williamsburg.

L'Enfant plan for Washington, D.C. A baroque-like plan of radial streets slashing through the gridiron, it was to be a monument to the new federal government, although it was reminiscent of Versailles or Napoleonic Paris.

Thus the pattern of early American planning, as would be expected, was not unlike European planning of the seventeenth and eighteenth centuries. The difference was that the colonists wanted more space and openness in their cities—when they wanted cities at all. The early settlers were not urban people. It was not until the middle of the nineteenth century that more than 20 percent of the U.S. population lived in cities. This precedent of anti-city sentiment greatly influenced American urban planning. Savannah may be the epitome of such planning—in the midst of the Georgia marshlands was set out an urban plan based upon open spaces as the organizing feature, with the country brought into the city.

The halcyon years of American urbanization saw the great industrialization and foreign immigration of the late nineteenth and early twentieth centuries. Adequate transportation, communications, cheap labor, resources, and open space made North America grow at an unprecedented rate. It was a chaotic growth, however. The industrial cities became drab, polluted, unsafe, and unhealthy. Greed and selfishness meant land was treated as a commodity to be traded for profit. Ugliness was accepted, and ruthless efficiency the planning goal.

The critics of this era were solidified by Lincoln Steffens, who prompted the name *muckraker* with his *Shame of the Cities* in 1904. He pointed out the horrors of late nineteenth-century urban life in industrial America. The muckrakers spurred a generation of social reformers and activists, yet it took a visionary architect-planner to capture fully the imagination of the people.

Daniel H. Burnham was the chief planner and architect for a World's Fair in Chicago in 1893. Called the *Columbian Exposition,* it was to commemorate the 400th anniversary of the discovery of America. Burnham chose to develop a "White City" as an antithesis of the dark American industrial centers. The fair was to honor the new industrial might of the country, yet Burnham used classical buildings and expansive esplanades, promenades, and open spaces on the Chicago waterfront. He in-

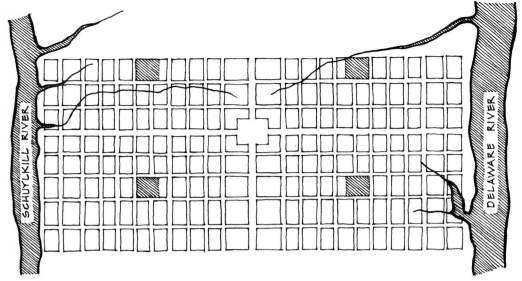

Diagram of Penn's 1682 plan for Philadelphia.

L'Enfant's plan for Washington, D.C.

The Columbian Exposition.

voked an adage that became a manifesto for planners and their patrons:

> Make no little plans, they have no magic to stir men's blood. Make big plans, for a noble document once recorded will never die.

The White City of the Columbian Exposition was a commercial success, but more importantly, it showed the populace what could be achieved by planning on a colossal scale.

So was the *city beautiful movement* of American urban planning ushered in. Burnham created plans for several cities, including San Francisco, Cleveland, and Chicago, and he revised the Washington plan. Scores of American cities commissioned other plans for landmarks, monuments, plazas, esplanades, and great avenues. Major buildings at the focal points of axes of streets were the common order. The *Ecole des Beaux Arts* in Paris was the mecca for architects designing these buildings. The *master plan* or grand design was the hallmark of a progressive city in America at the beginning of the twentieth century; the lack of such a plan was a sign of atrophy.

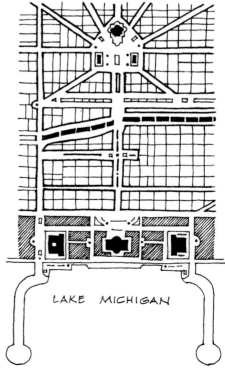

Burnham's plan for Chicago.

CONTEMPORARY PLANNING IN THE UNITED STATES

While the city beautiful movement was impressive, it was unrealistic. Trying to transform an industrial nation into Pericles's Athens or Caesar's Rome was somewhat fatuous; it was planning in a vacuum, by and for the privileged. Yet, the city beautiful movement was an essential precursor of contemporary planning in America, for it showed people that conditions could be improved.

Reform Movement

The roots of our contemporary planning practice can be traced to the union of the design professions with the social reformers of the early twentieth century. The architect and engineer joined with the lawyer and social worker to reform American cities. The concepts of Geddes were invoked as frequently as those of Burnham. Planning commissions were established throughout the country. Zoning was begun. Housing, subdivision, and public health codes were created. And, in 1917, a profession was created.

The American City Planning Institute, later the *American Institute of Planners,* was founded in Kansas City in 1917 at a conference of professional people concerned with urban planning. In November of that year, 52 men—14 landscape architects, 13 engineers, 5 architects, 6 lawyers, 4 realtors, 2 publishers, and 8 others—met in New York City to become the charter members of the Institute dedicated to the advancement of the art and science of planning. Design and reform interests merged to mold a new profession.

The growth of the profession was rapid. Meeting on its sixtieth anniversary in Kansas City in 1977, the Institute claimed a membership of more than 12,000 professional urban planners. In 1978, the AIP merged with the *American Society of Planning Officials* to form the 18,000-member *American Planning Association,* which in turn, includes the *American Institute of Certified Planners.*

A number of major reforms were quickly undertaken. In 1916 New York City adopted the first comprehensive zoning ordinance to control the use of land and the height and bulk of buildings. In 1922, the U.S. Department of Commerce, seeing land control as good for the economy, issued the first Standard State Zoning Enabling Act, by which states could grant such powers to cities. After the *Euclid v. Ambler Realty* case of 1926, in which the U.S. Supreme Court upheld the constitutionality of zoning, such ordinances became ubiquitous.

In the 1920s, regional planning, influenced by Geddes's concepts, began to grow. Regional planning authorities were first created in New York, Philadelphia, Chicago, and Washington. By 1931, there were over 67 such agencies.

By 1932, the growth in planning agencies in the United States appeared phenomenal. The reform movement had been so dramatic in its success that only a few areas in the South and Far West did not have planning or zoning agencies.

Depression and War Years

In the depths of the Depression in the 1930s, the over 800 planning commissions in the country felt the lack of funding severely. Planning commissions were among the first victims of economic hardship—perhaps reflecting a cynicism that planning was politically acceptable only as long as times were good. While many of the city planning commissions survived through volunteer labor and private funding, the responsibility for planning shifted to the national level.

Ironically, planning appeared to be a solution to the vagaries of a laissez-faire economic system. Planning was an integral part of the New Deal—Franklin Roosevelt believed that national planning could channel the investments of the government in order to end the Depression and stabilize the economy. The *National Resources Planning Board (NRPB)* was the central agency created to fulfill this mission. The NRPB offered financial and personnel resources as incentives to those states that created state planning agencies. These agencies were to plan for needed improvements that would be eligible for funding through the *Works Progress Administration* (WPA). By 1940 every state save three had created a state planning agency to prepare and implement comprehensive plans.

Much of this national-state planning effort was directed towards resolving urban problems. The theory involved was that a comprehensive plan would set the context for economic investment and resource utilization as part of a national effort. The NRPB published two reports, *Our Cities: Their Role in the National Economy* (1937) and *Urban Planning and Land Policies* (1939), which together comprised as much of a national urban planning policy as the country had ever had. Furthermore, the way was cleared for integrated planning from the top to bottom through intergovernmental coordination.

Other major planning projects emanated from the New Deal. The most interesting was the program of *greenbelt towns* carried forth by the Rural Resettlement Administration (RRA) under the leadership of Rexford G. Tugwell—a member of Roosevelt's Brain Trust and a foremost planning theoretician. The RRA built three greenbelt towns—Greenbelt, Maryland; Greenhills, Ohio; and Greendale, Wisconsin—which were roughly analogous to Howard's *Garden Cities* in their use of open space and greenbelts. However, they were dormitory suburbs of Washington, Cincinnati, and Milwaukee, rather than self-sufficient and balanced land use new towns like those in England While these greenbelt towns were not significant in terms of establishing new patterns of urbanization in the United States, they did serve as early models of what could be done. Unfortunately, the "foreign" feeling of the new towns coupled with a fear of

Greenbelt: Maryland

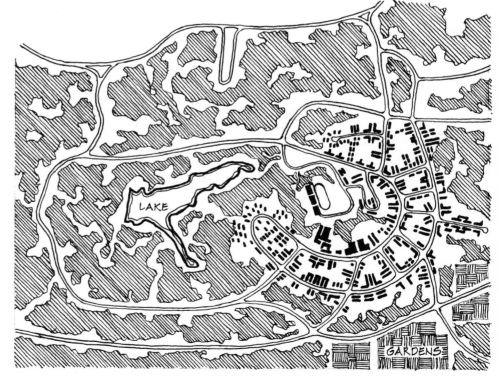

nationalization of residential community building was sufficient to seal their fate politically by the early 1940s.

Probably the most successful and significant achievement of the New Deal was the formation and development of an extensive system of flood control projects, reclamation programs, and economic and physical development by the *Tennessee Valley Authority (TVA)*. The TVA accomplishments include tangible projects like dams, reservoirs, power plants, and new towns, as well as a plethora of social, economic, and political programs that greatly improved the quality of life in a largely rural, underdeveloped area of the South. While the TVA remains unique in the United States, it has been emulated throughout the world. It was never replicated in the United States because of conservative fears of socialism and increased federal power in the states.

These national planning and other ancillary programs of Roosevelt's New Deal were formidable, but the major visible signs were the extensive public works projects and buildings in the cities. With the start of World War II, a recalcitrant Congress was able to shelve most of the controversial programs. The state planning agencies were converted to wartime emergency planning boards concerned mostly with conservation of scarce resources. This concern often produced important plans for transit programs and the redevelopment of cities in order to reduce automobile usage, but since they were emergency plans, the effects were only temporary. Also developed was a hasty program of emergency housing for defense plant workers, and this did establish a precedent for national involvement in dealing with housing problems. Overall, the urgency and uncertainty of the war made long-term planning somewhat difficult, and urban planning was more of a discussion item than an action program.

Postwar Growth to the Fifties
The immediate postwar years showed a pattern of urban planning oriented toward recovery and eco-

nomic development. As the economy gained momentum, cities began to reconsider their problems. Ironically, the movement toward national and state planning severely dissipated—national planning was abolished and state planning became primarily concerned with industrial location and job creation. The only significant national programs related to planning had to do with providing housing. Most prominent among these was the *National Housing Act of 1949,* which established public housing and assistance programs and provided aid for urban redevelopment. This encouraged cities to plan and resolve their own problems with federal financial assistance. Urban planning had returned to its pre-Depression stature in essence, with the addition of some national aid. The result was a predictable increase in the number of urban planning agencies.

The early part of the urban redevelopment movement lacked any sort of conceptual basis. From 1948 to 1951, Coleman Woodbury, with foundation funding and support from a consortium of professional societies, directed a massive study of cities and their future.[3] Many of the recommendations were incorporated into the *National Housing Act of 1954,* which established a basic approach to urban redevelopment. In the same year, the U.S. Supreme Court upheld the constitutionality of urban renewal as a manifestation of the police power of government.

The typical approach to *urban renewal* was simple. A city would clear a blighted area, rebuild the streets and utilities, and sell the area to private developers at a written-down cost. This would enable a developer to package an economically feasible project. The benefits to the city would be slum clearance and the addition of new ratables to the tax rolls.

To insure that the urban renewal and housing programs were well-planned, the federal government offered financial assistance through the so-called *Section 701 Program,* which provided matching grants to communities that produced comprehensive plans. This "carrot-and-stick" approach to urban renewal, housing, and planning was expanded and improved upon throughout the 1950s and early 1960s. It established a set of intergovernmental relationships that resulted in cities seeking more and more financial assistance from the federal government. The government used its funding as an incentive to get cities to undertake programs that Congress believed necessary. To become eligible for federal aid, the cities had to agree to certain guidelines.

Unfortunately, this approach caused certain problems. Urban planning was reduced to eligibility for federal aid. If a certain kind of housing were to be funded in a given year, a city's plans would reflect a need for such housing. In addition, the emphasis of many renewal programs tended to be entirely physical. Massive developments were seen as a panacea for the social and economic problems of the poor and disadvantaged.

The same sorts of problems occurred with other public works projects aided by the federal government—most clearly in the *Interstate Defense Highway Program*. The Interstate Program offered state and local governments 90 percent of the costs of building high-service, restricted-access freeways of four, six, or eight lanes to connect metropolitan areas. Congress approved the program in 1956 in

the name of defense—i.e., it would improve the logistics of military evacuation of cities—and authorized funding of $60 billion by creating a National Gasoline Tax Trust Fund. In view of that sort of money and the attendant jobs created, every city, with the support of states, began planning massive freeway systems. Within a decade, the now-familiar problems of devastated neighborhoods, suburban sprawl, and the energy demands of auto-dominant transportation began to emerge. The cities had reacted to the stimulus of federal aid at the expense of the quality of urban life.

Radicalism and Activism in the 1960s

Growing dissatisfaction with federal bureaucracy, discontent over the Vietnam War, the youth and drug cultures, and a national "loss of innocence" following the assassination of President Kennedy, all influenced the emergence of the *radicalism* and *advocacy movements* that marked the 1960s. Students and younger planners began to reject purely physical planning and design solutions to urban problems. Some advocated the *systems approach* developed by the aerospace-defense industries as a sub-

Urban Renewal: Washington, D.C.

stitute for physical planning. But most of the radical planners wanted a redefinition of planning and design that would include the goals of social justice, equality, and redistribution of wealth and power. Perhaps, as some have charged, this was a peculiarly American version of a socialist movement. Yet the planning side of the movement was more theoretical and procedural than revolutionary.

Springing from this movement were numerous approaches and techniques that have been loosely referred to as *social planning* or *advocacy planning*. This meant that urban planners were to represent the most disadvantaged groups and articulate their planning needs. Using planning techniques and skills, the advocate would represent a specific group's interests rather than a vague public interest. Thus these groups would be able to compete with traditionally powerful groups in the urban decision-making forum.

The movement received political support in the *War on Poverty* programs of President Johnson, most particularly through the incorporation of a "maximum feasible participation" requirement in the *Model Cities Program*. The Model Cities Program was an effort to combine physical, social, and economic solutions to the cities' problems under one planning and implementation authority. Subject to the rhetoric and unfounded promises of the times, the program quickly degenerated into a quagmire of corruption, bungling, and neighborhood squabbling. It did get poor people involved in government, but it led to a generation of socially conscious and often unskilled planners who had little to offer these people other than sympathy and time. Politicians quickly lost interest in the movement, and its credibility waned. With the election of Richard Nixon, the federal government abandoned any interest in such programs.

During the late 1960s and early 1970s, a major effort was launched to protect the natural environment from further degradation. The argument was made that untrammeled growth and proliferation of buildings, cars, and industrialization must be con-

trolled to prevent disasters to the natural environment. Eager to diffuse the energy of those concerned with social problems, the Nixon administration embraced environmental protection in its initial years. A series of important laws was passed, establishing tough standards for pollution control as well as processes for the analysis of negative impacts upon the natural environment.

The Realistic 1970s
The Nixon administration quickly and systematically dismantled the urban renewal, housing, and planning programs that had developed since the 1950s and replaced them with *revenue-sharing* programs in which cities were given blocks of financial aid according to a needs formula. These *community development block grants* were to be used in whatever way the city believed most appropriate, rather than according to a list of federal priorities. The concept of returning the decision making to cities was inherently sound; what was lacking was any planning capability on the part of the cities, since they had spent the previous quarter-century responding to the federal government's guidelines.

The early results of the revenue-sharing programs were unimpressive. Many cities spent the money on frills such as tennis courts and swimming pools, while others used the grants to support existing projects in order to hold down property tax levels in declining central cities. It also became clear that the distribution of funds was unfair, as wealthy suburbs were granted unneeded monies while poorer central areas received inadequate funds.

The Carter administration attempted to ameliorate some of these problems while supporting the basically sound theory behind the programs. It has become apparent, however, that the federal government no longer seems capable of handling the responsibility for solving urban problems that it began to assume during the Depression. The current trend is a return to state and local governmental responsibility for urban problem solving and a new awareness of the need for private investment in cities.

The most important pattern of the 1970s has been the coalescing of planning and management. Traditionally oriented toward design and reform, urban planners have not dealt extensively with budgeting, personnel, infrastructure, and other short-term aspects of management. Hence, plans have usually been turned over to other agencies for implementation. The new pattern holds that planning and management are essentially linked, so that planning is no longer separated from implementation.

MAJOR SUCCESSES AND FAILURES IN AMERICAN PLANNING

The history of urban planning in America has been disturbingly short on major successes. Critics of urban planning argue that there is little evidence that planning has made any difference in American cities. No classical Athens or imperial Rome has emerged despite major governmental involvement. There have been no real examples of self-sufficient

new towns although suburban satellites, such as Reston, Virginia, have been built along the lines of European models. Critics concede that the TVA has been a successful planning effort but feel that it is a unique case, not be be duplicated. American cities often look awful, and suburbs are dull, sterile enclaves. Critics argue, with some logic, that urban planning in America is a curious compromise of political, social, and economic objectives. The free market enthusiasts argue that cities would be better off if we left all planning to private entrepreneurs.[4] Social activists argue that only a redistribution of the wealth of this country can allow urban planning to be successful—they like cities in Great Britain and Sweden as planning models. Others argue that only a national economic plan could resolve the resources imbalance between cities and reduce the competition for jobs and facilities. And finally, some would prefer to preserve the present political climate surrounding planning, believing that the complexity of contemporary American cities and regions will only permit ad hoc, incremental improvements.

All of these views have some validity in that no one political, social, or economic structural change will guarantee success for urban planning. Certainly the slowing of the country's economic development

New Town: Reston, Virginia.

and the costs of existing cities make radical rebuilding plans seem foolish. Thus, the existing situation lends some credence to those who argue for realistic, incremental improvements in urban conditions; in essence, for a lessening of expectations.

One of the best defenses of urban planning is the argument that it is a continuous process that can aid in decision making in the contemporary world. As such, it has no real starting and stopping points and, hence, cannot be evaluated successful or unsuccessful. To deny the need for planning is universally considered narrow-minded; what is debatable is who should plan and how to do it. To expect the accomplishments of a Nebuchadnezzar in a modern U.S. city is foolish, but to learn from urban history what has worked and what has failed should be useful.

It has been said that not until the 1920s did the statistical probability that seeing a doctor would do more good for a sick patient than not seeing one became more than 50 percent. Medical knowledge had not progressed far enough to insure successful diagnosis and treatment. It may well be that the state of knowledge of urban planning in the United States is analogous. So little is known about how cities work and change that it is difficult to analyze the problems (let alone find the solutions). The time is near, however, when the possibility of having good cities will be correlated with urban planning.

RECENT TRENDS IN URBAN PLANNING

To conclude this chapter, it is worth reviewing some recent trends in urban planning in America—some of which are actually worldwide.

Growth Control and Decline Management

With increasing shifts of people and jobs away from the Snow Belt cities of the North and Midwest to the Sun Belt cities of the South and West has emerged a concern with either controlling growth or alleviating the problems of decline.

The growth control movement is most evident in Sun Belt cities or places such as resorts, mountain areas, and environmentally unique sites. Long-term residents of such areas tend to react negatively to a rapid influx of new residents. There is reason for this response, because of the loss of land and resources, rising public service costs, and the difficulty of protecting the amenities. The urban planning mechanisms employed have been land use and building regulations, settlement plans, and other controls to effectively slow in-migration. Most court decisions have upheld these devices, stating that they are not violating constitutional rights of individuals as long as there is some semblance of planning as a basis.

Urban planning practice has been drastically changed through this response to public reaction against rapid growth. Previous planning practice was more concerned with accommodating and guiding growth. Planners worked to insure that new residents would have access to all needed public services and could enjoy the amenities of urban life. Now planners are dealing with practices that overtly discourage new residents. This has raised basic questions about the fairness of the collective judgment of the public. In addition, it has invoked the specter of racism and prejudice since the poor and minorities are often the most unpopular of new residents.

The growth control movement has been strongest in suburban areas of large cities or in smaller cities. The largest cities of the North and Midwest are losing high numbers of residents. This is a new trend in the United States, as, until recently, cities had been growing since their incorporation. Consequently, urban planning had always been concerned with growing central cities. Now urban planning has been redirected towards preservation of existing central cities.

The preservation trend involves encouraging industries and services that are sound to remain in the central city. This is somewhat antithetical to the earlier urban renewal programs, which assumed that the old must make way for the new. Now urban planners seek to preserve the old—since there may not be anything to replace it.

Neighborhood Planning

Closely related to the preservation trend in older cities is neighborhood planning. Planning assistance is provided to neighborhood groups that are organized to preserve their neighborhoods and prevent decline. A planning department often supplies special staff and financial assistance to such groups. In some cases, planners themselves may actually be involved in organizing such neighborhood groups.

Even in growing cities, there is a trend towards neighborhood planning, which has resulted both from neighborhood demands and from recognition by planners that the modern city is an organism composed of individual cells, or neighborhoods. The trend clearly reflects the realism of the 1970s in which urban planners are addressing more manageable problems. The neighborhood offers an ideal unit in which to concentrate planning programs which are especially effective when there is an overall urban planning strategy. Recently, people like Geno Baroni, Carter's assistant secretary of Housing and Urban Development, have worked to provide federal financial incentives for these efforts. However, the basic thrust has come from the political leadership of large cities in response to constituent demands.

Adaptive Reuse and Conservation

Another trend in urban planning is the adaptive reuse of buildings and conservation of special areas. An inherent characteristic of American society has been to assume that buildings, like automobiles, have built-in obsolescence. In recent years, because of energy-conservation programs, European examples, and rising construction costs, the lasting value of older buildings and neighborhoods has been recognized. Reuse and conservation no longer are limited to historic preservation but now involve redesign and redevelopment of buildings and neighborhoods to handle new needs and demands. The urban planning process has been modified to reflect these trends.

CONCLUSION: BEYOND LEGITIMACY

It is clear that urban planning has a long history as a process and institutional endeavor. The legitimacy of urban planning appears to have been established—particularly if mere survival is the criterion. What seems most important now is to create more realistic planning so that implementation is more likely. While it is true that history shows the greatest implementation under authoritarian governments, contemporary times require more complex and subtle processes of debate, compromise, and agreement. Thus, the "new" urban planner must be reformer, designer, and politician.

NOTES

1. Athens was probably the largest city in the world at this time. There is some speculation, however, that Teotihuacan, located near modern-day Mexico City, had a population of 100,000 at the same time. The evidence is fragmentary—as are traces of the race that built the city.
2. Owens never built the New Lanark project; he emigrated to the United States and planned and built New Harmony, Indiana in 1825.

3. Coleman Woodbury et al., *The Future of Cities and Urban Redevelopment* (Chicago: University of Chicago Press, 1953).
4. Houston is often held up as a model for the no-controls approach, since it has no zoning in the normal sense but uses instead a legal contract approach employed by individuals.

FOR FURTHER READING

Anderson, Martin. *The Federal Bulldozer.* Cambridge, Mass.: M.I.T., 1964.

Bacon, Edmund. *Design of Cities.* New York: Viking, 1967.

Collins, George R., ed. *Planning and Cities.* 10 vols. New York: Braziller, 1968.

Doxiadis, C. A. *Ekistics: An Introduction to the Science of Human Settlements.* London: Hutchinson, 1968.

Gallion, Arthur B., and Eisner, Simon. *The Urban Pattern.* 3d ed. New York: Van Nostrand, 1975.

Golany, Gideon, and Waldon, David, ed. *The Contemporary New Communities Movement in the United States.* Urbana: University of Illinois Press, 1975.

Goodman, Robert. *After the Planners.* New York: Simon & Schuster, 1971.

Gutkind, E. A. *International History of City Development.* 8 vols. New York: Free Press, 1964-1972.

Hilberseimer, L. *The Nature of Cities.* Chicago: Paul Theobald, 1955.

Howard, Ebenezer. *Garden Cities of To-Morrow.* Cambridge, Mass.: M.I.T., 1965 (originally published in 1898 in England).

Kulski, Julian. *Land of Urban Promise.* South Bend, Ind.: University of Notre Dame Press, 1967.

Mumford, Lewis. *The City in History.* New York: Harcourt, Brace, 1961.

Pirenne, Henri. *Economic and Social History of Medieval Europe.* New York: Harvest Books, 1959.

Reiner, Thomas. *The Place of the Ideal Community in Urban Planning.* Philadelphia: University of Pennsylvania Press, 1963.

Reps, John W. *The Making of Urban America: A History of City Planning in the United States.* Princeton, N.J.: Princeton University Press, 1965.

Scott, Mel. *American City Planning: Since 1890.* Berkeley: University of California Press, 1969.

Sjoberg, Gideon. *The Pre-Industrial City.* New York: Free Press, 1960.

Spreiregan, Paul D. *Urban Design: The Architecture of Towns and Cities.* New York: McGraw-Hill, 1965.

CHAPTER 2

On the Cultural Origins of Settlements

Amos Rapoport

An important part of the history of cities and urban planning concerns human behavior. Through an examination of such behavior, with a cultural and anthropological approach, we can begin to understand some of the bases for urban settlements. The cultural analysis in this chapter is valuable for illuminating concepts that are clearly seen in history yet not fully explained. This examination of the cultural origins of urban settlements allows us to make a more detailed exploration of an important aspect of history and to understand more fully how human behavioral patterns resulted in subsequent urban settlement patterns. While this chapter deals only with settlement patterns, it is also enlightening about the broader concepts and techniques of such evaluation.

THE ORIGINS OF CITIES

The ability to make valid analyses and decisions depends on the existence of valid theory. So much has been written about cities and urbanism from all sorts of perspectives that without theory no one can possibly absorb more than a small portion of it. The use of a theory allows the vast amount of material on cities to be integrated into larger conceptual structures, providing better understanding of its value. Such integration can also result in knowledge becoming cumulative.

Such a theory, however, must be based on a very broad sample in order to be valid. Much of what passes for theory in planning, urban design, architecture, and even people-environment studies is based only on the *high-design tradition;* i.e., it concentrates on the work of planners and designers and ignores those environments created by the folk or popular tradition. Yet by far the larger percentage of all built environments belong to this latter category. Moreover, even the high-style components of cities—the acropolises, agoras, plazas, avenues, axes, and so on—can only be understood in the context of the vernacular matrix, infil, or what is being organized by these elements. Finally, when looking at the time when settlements began, it is difficult, if not impossible, to separate the two traditions.

The existing theories tend to be based on the Western tradition, neglecting the many others—African, Asian, Middle Eastern, pre-Columbian, and Latin American. They tend also to be based on recent developments and to overlook the historical dimension—particularly the remote past in general and the recent past in the nonliterate and non-Western tradition. Thus it is very important now to consider settlements both through time and *cross-culturally*.

The trouble with concepts based on the Western, high-style tradition of the recent past is that generalizations based on such a limited sample may be invalid. The broader our sample—in space and in time—the more likely we are to be able to see regularities in apparent chaos and to understand better the significant differences; i.e., the more likely we are to see *patterns* and *relationships*.

Being able to establish the presence of such patterns can help us deal with the problem of constancy and change and help us determine certain baselines to guide environmental design. Some of these baselines may be evolutionary.[1] If people as a species have certain characteristics, if human beings have done certain things for a very long time, there may be very good reasons for these traditions.[2] It is, therefore, important to understand constancies as well as change—particularly since our own culture stresses change to an inordinate degree.

If apparent change and variability are actually an expression of invariant processes, i.e., if the *reasons* behind apparently different ways of doing things remain the same, this too is extremely important. If we can understand these reasons and the processes they represent, we may find that apparently unrelated forms are in fact equivalent, in the sense that they achieve the same objectives, are the result of similar mental processes, or are transformations of each other.

For example, consider three urban forms—a dense city of courtyards; a low-density urban fabric of widely scattered houses; and a city made up of *urban villages* of highly homogeneous populations with strong social links. These forms appear very different, but they can all be shown to be mechanisms for controlling unwanted interaction, i.e., for reducing information overload and stress and achieving

desired levels of privacy.[3] This kind of approach is most important in dealing with major disagreements and differing views about cities, including the very definition of a city.

Different Views of Cities

French newspapers and books often make the point that U.S. cities have no structure or form. Clearly this is incorrect—they do have both.[4] The differences are in the nature of their order, their hierarchy (which places are important), and their morphology. The open-endedness and endlessness of U.S. cities are incomprehensible and disturbing, as are their sense of being unfinished and their process orientation. As both Sartre and Lévi-Strauss have commented, the streets of American cities seem to lead into infinity. There is no sense of containment as there is in European cities. The time dimension is also different: American cities do not age gracefully; they decay. All this, Europeans and American expatriates felt, leads to placelessness. Gertrude Stein's famous description of Oakland, California, illustrates the point: "When you get there, there is no there there."

This open-endedness and process orientation leads to the high value placed on mobility in U.S. cities. As a result, Americans have trouble understanding foreign cities, and they say that *those* cities have no form or structure. For example, Americans have said this about Moslem cities—i.e., about cities that have a structure that is in fact highly articulated but is antithetical to the U. S. form. The Moslem organization, rather than maximizing movement and accessibility, limits it and controls behavior by restricting mobility. Such cities contain a large number of specific districts—ethnic, religious, trade, or use—which are distinct, and the inhabitants of each tend to stay within it. The order and pattern may be incomprehensible, to Americans, but are definitely not absent.[5]

One generalization that cannot be applied cross-culturally is that of the city as a center of change. In the West it has been, but in China and Iran the city has been a center of stability.[6] Also invalid cross-culturally are generalizations based on the U.S. tradition that status goes up as we go outward from the center. In some cases there is no relationship at all between status and city center, and in many others the relationship is the opposite; i.e., status goes down as one moves outward from the center. More generally, then, environments that appear confusing or disordered are not necessarily random but usually represent a structure based on specific schemata and social orders.

Definitions of Cities

Traditional definitions of the city have been rather *ethnocentric*, based on the modern (i.e., medieval and later) Western city. For example, one classic definition states that a city is a "relatively large, dense, and permanent settlement of socially heterogeneous individuals." [7] Gordon Childe, who dealt with the origin of cities as the *urban revolution*, lists the criteria of urbanism as: a concentration of large numbers of people, craft specialization, a redistributive economic mode, monumental public architecture, developed social stratification, the use of writing, exact and predictive sciences, naturalistic art, foreign trade, and group membership based on residence rather than kinship.[8] Yet, as we shall see, examples can be found of major settlements violating these criteria. Both Jericho and Çatal Hüyük, as well as pre-Columbian settlements, predate writing.

Hardoy uses 10 criteria to define a city:

1 Large size and population for its time and place

2 Permanency

3 A minimum density for its time and place

4 Urban structures and layout as indicated by recognizably urban streets and spaces

5 A place where people live and work

6 A minimum of specifically urban functions, which may include a market, an administrative or political center, a military center, a religious center, or a center of intellectual activity with corresponding institutions

7 A hierarchical heterogeneity and differentiation of society

8 A center of urban economy for its time and place linking an agricultural hinterland and processing materials for a larger market

9 A center of services for neighboring areas

10 A center of diffusion, having an urban way of life for its time and place.[9]

These kinds of definitions have led to major arguments as to whether or not Mayan complexes in pre-Columbian Meso-America were cities and whether or not precontact African settlements, such as those of the Yoruba, were cities. Neither of these would fit the classic definitions, nor would major settlements in early China, Cambodia, Java, and Egypt; in pre-Chimu Peru; or in preclassical Greece.

Moreover, in different cultures different elements have been used as the minimum necessary for a settlement to qualify as a city. For example, in the Hellenistic world, these include a theatre, gymnasium, and *prytaneion;* in medieval Islam, a Friday mosque, permanent market, and public bath; in Mesopotamia, Cambodia, or among the Mayans, a temple; in Europe, fortifications, market, a court enforcing its own laws, and autonomy; in Carolingian Europe, a keep, church, and market; in India, a temple, palace, and market; and in early China, an altar to the god of the soil, walls, and a temple to the ruler's ancestors. In other words, what is regarded as a city varies in different cultures. In fact, the more one broadens one's sample in space and time, the more difficult it becomes to apply the definitions derived from Western forms.

However, working through this complexity eventually leads to an improved understanding of cities and urbanism so that a definition can be derived that can be applied to a larger range of settlements. Thus, a settlement can be defined as a city not in terms of particular morphological features, or even collections of features, but in terms of a particular function—that of organizing a region and creating effective space.[10] This view now seems generally accepted. Any definition of a city, to have cross-cultural significance, must be in terms of a unit of settlement that in some way organizes a broader hinterland or region.[11]

In this sense, ceremonial centers, such as in the Mayan area or elsewhere, qualify as cities, as do Yoruba settlements in Africa, and so on. In fact the organization of the larger environments may occur before the development of those types of settlements Westerners call cities. For example, the New Zealand Maori polity was hierarchical and organized, yet had no dominant settlements.

It is therefore likely that cities did not suddenly spring up. There was no *urban revolution*—they developed gradually as settlements gradually extended their organizing functions outwards. There is a progression from the house-settlement system to the settlement-settlement and settlement-region systems. In other words, since human activities tend to occur in organized settings, these form a system with continuity and commonalities extending from the dwelling to the region.

Thus in North America, in the Midwest (near the present city of St. Louis), Cahokia organized a very large region of about 400 square miles with smaller towns, villages, and so on. It had an east-west axis of 3 miles and a north-south axis of $2\frac{1}{4}$ miles. There were $6\frac{3}{4}$ square miles of pyramids and mounds, habitations, graves, circles of wooden posts, and so forth. The central parts of the site were enclosed by walls. At its height, somewhere between the thirteenth and tenth centuries B.C.E.,* Cahokia had between 10,000 and 30,000 residents but organized a much larger population.[12]

Organizing Functions

It is useful to discuss the various views about the origin of the organizing functions. In general they have been *ecological* (having to do with the setting; e.g., unusual fertility), *demographic* (having to do with populations; e.g., numbers), or *differentiational or*

*B.C.E. refers to Before the Common Era; C.E. refers to the Common Era. These terms are used here in place of the more familiar B.C. and A.D.

technological (having to do with the ability to do things).

None of these views seems adequate in itself, but they all play a role as aspects of increasing sociocultural complexity. This complexity, related to social differentiation, has been analyzed in tracing the origins of urbanism. Included in the analysis have been considerations of trade and/or marketing, irrigation, warfare, and religion. Of these it appears that religion may be the most important, for the origin of cities is related to *sacred symbols*.[13] In other words, the organizing function itself was symbolic, since religion and the sacred are central in all traditional cultures, which are the ones where cities and other settlements began. This approach does not, of course, explain the *need* for such larger organizations, but this is not central to the argument here. One view, often accepted, is that this need was a response to a common phenomenon—the increased complexity of settled life. But then, one could ask, why should people settle down? After all, the present view of hunter-gatherer nomads is that they were the original affluent society and were better off than most peasants, in terms of total food intake, protein intake, and leisure time.[14]

Cities, then, in this view begin with a ceremonial center having symbolic meaning. Thus the city can be seen as a particular type of cosmic symbol, powerful enough to organize larger areas.

But the symbolism of the city, its meaning as an idea expressed in physical form, powerful enough to organize regions and states, is a subset of the larger concept that cities, or *any* built environments, are embodiments or expressions of *cognitive schemata*. This idea embodies not only the different definitions of the city, but also the discussion of the different views of cities and their apparent lack of order (which is related to incomprehensible schemata). In fact, the purpose of our discussion was *not* to try and define cities or urbanism. Rather it was to show how by broadening the sample an apparently simple problem becomes more complex—but also much richer. Moreover it makes it possible to include many different kinds of settlements in a discussion of this sort, avoiding the issue of whether they are cities or not. In fact, it is *settlements* that we wish to discuss, whether they are cities or not, and more particularly, how they are organized, and what can be learned by studying these organizational patterns.

The question is really why people build environments. In order to understand built environments, one should understand how the human mind works. The human mind imposes an order on the world. The world is chaotic and disorderly; the human mind classifies, orders, and imposes cognitive schemata. Settlements, buildings, and landscapes are results of this activity. When the Neanderthals buried their dead with flowers, they were trying to impose an order reconciling life and death. The cave paintings of Europe mark complex ordering systems and define certain caves as sacred, humanized space. Symbolic notational systems—obviously efforts to impose a conceptual order on time and natural phenomena—existed remarkably early.

Giving ideas physical expression is useful; encoding them makes them into mnemonic devices that *reinforce behavior* by telling people how to act and what is expected of them. One can, therefore, look at built environments, including settlements, as one way of ordering the world. In the case of traditional cultures this way of ordering, as we shall see, is primarily sacred.

DESIGN, ORGANIZATION, AND SCHEMATA

Settlements, like all built environments, are designed in the sense that they embody human decisions, choices, and specific ways of doing things. Since there are now few places on this planet that human beings have not altered in some way, we could say that much of the earth is really designed. This tends to make us forget the original impact of a created environment contrasted with wilderness.

Designed environments thus include places that have been cleared or planted, areas where rivers have been diverted, and fields that have been fenced in certain patterns. The placement of roads, buildings, and cities has been designed. Roadside stands and used-car lots are as much designed environments as office buildings or new towns. The work of a tribesman burning off and laying out a camp or village is as valid an example of design as the work of any modern architect or planner. In fact many apparently commonplace activities have a greater impact on the earth than design in the traditional sense. The way cities, regions, and countries look depends, in the final analysis, on the design activity of many individuals and groups at different times.

What all these activities have in common is that each represents a choice out of all possible alternatives. The choice made tends to be lawful according to the culture of the people concerned. One way of looking at cultures is in terms of the most common choices made. It is the lawfulness of choices that makes places recognizably different from one another. It also decides how people dress, what they eat, and how they behave. It affects the way they interact and the way they structure space and time. These consistent choices result in a certain *style*, whether of built environments or life.

Certain values, norms, criteria, and assumptions are used in making choices. These are often embodied in ideal schemata. Built environments reflect and encode these schemata and order. The order expressed through the choice process, or the image that is to be encoded and given form, is a set of cognitive schemata and ideals. This means there is some vision of an ideal environment that built environments, however imperfectly, express. Such environments are conceptualized as settings for the kind of people a particular culture sees as normative and for the kind of life style that is regarded as typical of the group, distinguishing it from other groups. What we call culture can be seen in three major ways, the first two of which are included in the above: (1) as a way of life that typifies the group; (2) as a system of symbols, meanings, and cognitive schemata; and (3) as a set of adaptive strategies for survival linked to ecology and resources.

Thus culture is about a group of people who have a set of values and beliefs and a world view that embody an *ideal*. Their rules lead to systematic and consistent choices. Though settlements are determined by individual decisions and acts of numerous people, they become a recognizable whole of which one can say (if familiar with the code and ordering system), this is a Chinese or French city, a Peruvian or Indian landscape. Through such choices, habits, manners, roles, and behavior are formed as well as environments. They all should be mutually illuminating and should show regularities caused by the common underlying schemata.

These schemata represent one product of what seems a basic process of the human mind: the attempt to give the world meaning, to humanize it by imposing an order on it—a cognitive order often achieved through classifying and naming. One could say that the order is thought before it is built, and consequently it is possible to show how people like the Australian aborigines, who build little, impose an order through thinking it—i.e., conceptually, and through rituals.[15] In this way aborigines, through ritual movement to various sacred sites and through appropriate ceremonies at these sites, delimit, define, and order their territory.

In what way, then, does their type of ordering differ from that proposed as typical of cities? First, in the size of the group and the complexity of the system; second, in the absence of a permanent physical expression of the ordering principle as a mnemonic, which becomes necessary as population numbers and social complexity go up; and third, in that there is no single center dominating the system.

For example, while both aborigines and Maya use ritual movement in their settlement pattern, Mayan movements are related to permanent ceremonial centers.[16] In the case of the aborigines, their ritual sites and even camps show organization, but the movement system is the most significant aspect, because there is no single center. In the case of the Maya, we find a major and significant organization that also uses movement, but movement related to a powerful ceremonial center that can organize large regions and populations.

Thus settlements not only impose an order on the larger domain but are themselves organized. There is an ordering system both in the settlement, ceremonial center, or whatever, and at the larger scale; there are systems within systems. While all settlements (and all buildings—in fact, all environments) are ordered and organized, cities are distinguished by their organizing of larger and more complex areas.

Among settlements in traditional cultures, one can sometimes find differing orders according to the *degree* of sacredness. Thus, among the Gururumba in the highlands of New Guinea, one finds both living villages and ceremonial villages. The former consist of 25 to 30 circular houses arranged linearly, along a path, with the men's houses on the other side of the path. Sacred villages are arranged around an open space; one side consisting of a long shedlike, noncompartmentalized structure with many hearths and also a fenced enclosure which has religious significance. This ceremonial village is thus more complex than the living village, and it organizes the larger domain through rituals.

Organization of the Environment

Cities and other settlements are specific examples of built environments. One view of the organization of the built environment is that it is the organization of four things:

1 Space
2 Meaning
3 Communication
4 Time

Planners and designers have always dealt with

space organization. Space can be thought of in many different ways. This can be illustrated briefly by recalling that designers and the public have repeatedly attached different meanings to the concept of space, and that the built space of traditional cultures is sacred space rather than the geometric space of technological cultures.

The environment can be seen as a series of relationships among elements and people (between things and other things, things and people, people and other people). These relationships are orderly; i.e., they have a pattern and a structure. The environment is not a random assemblage of things. These types of relationships are primarily *spatial.* Basically, but not exclusively, objects and people are related through various degrees of spatial separation. The above mentioned city of courtyards is fundamentally different from a city where houses face, and are related to, streets. Such kinds of organization can also be seen as physical expressions of domains. In fact, design and planning, from landscapes of regions to the furniture arrangements of rooms, can be seen as the *organization of space* for different purposes, according to the various rules that reflect the culture of the groups or individuals involved. These designs and plans embody ideal images and represent the congruence (or lack of it) between physical space and social space. Thus we recall the example of status and its relation to the center or periphery.

This relationship is also an example of the *organization of meaning,* and the two can be separated conceptually. The same urban form can have three different meanings in this case: location close to center may indicate either high or low status, or it may have no special significance.[17]

While space organization itself does express *meaning* and has communicative and symbolic properties, meaning is often expressed through signs, materials, colors, forms, landscaping, and the like. Meaning may coincide with space organization —and usually did in most traditional settlements, so when we discuss them we will be able to concentrate on space organization. It may, however, also represent a separate symbolic system through which different settings become indicators of social position; a way of establishing social identity; and a way of indicating expected behavior. One example is the variation in planting, mailboxes, decoration, and levels of maintenance in Westchester. Other examples are the analyses of Las Vegas and Boston, which show that in modern U.S. cities neon lights, signs, pictorial and verbal messages, and the like may represent a meaning system independent of spatial organization.[18] But spatial organization still communicates meanings (although to a lesser extent than in traditional settlements), and, moreover, meanings are clearest and strongest when there is high redundancy, when spatial organization, activities, and other meaning systems are congruent and therefore reinforce each other.

Such congruence is important because the meanings conveyed by the environment, and by settings within it, can help social *communication* among people (whereas meaning is communication from the *environment* to people). Thus environments, spatially and through meanings, influence and reflect the *organization of communication.* Who communicates with whom, under what conditions, how, when, where, and in which context, are important ways in which the built environment and social organization are linked and related. Environments reflect and are ways of controlling interaction: its nature, intensity, rate, and direction. This control occurs through spatial organization of meaning when people notice and understand cues in the environment that signal to them how to behave appropriately, i.e., when the context is established. Of course, they must also be prepared to act accordingly. If the cues are not noticed or not understood, appropriate behavior is impossible, and the examples already given of misunderstood urban orders illustrate this.

Finally, the environment is also temporal and can be seen as the *organization of time,* i.e., as reflecting and influencing behavior in time. This idea may be understood in two ways. The first concerns large-scale, cognitive structuring of time. It refers to concepts such as linear flow versus cyclic time; future orientation versus past orientation; and the value of time, and hence, how finely it is subdivided into units. This latter concept relates to the second way in which the organization of time can be considered—the tempos and rhythms of human activities. Tempo refers to the number of events per unit of time, and rhythm to the distribution of activities in time.

It is possible to distinguish among groups in modern cities on the basis of their tempos and rhythms. For example, think of the work schedules of a university professor and a factory worker. The former has very irregular and flexible time use. He or she comes and goes at different times of day, works at home, attends conferences, spends long periods away during the summer or on sabbatical, and works evenings and weekends. The factory worker has a highly routinized and regular schedule, with specific starting and ending times, and work and leisure rhythms quite different from those of the professor. Their temporal *signatures* are different.

Tempos and rhythms may be congruent or incongruent with each other. People may be separated in time as well as, or instead of, in space, so that groups with different rhythms that occupy the same space may never meet. Clearly, spatial and temporal aspects interact and influence one another, and one should probably speak of space-time.

Once again, many of our assumptions about these variables are based on a very limited sample. If we look at traditional settlements, we find much greater uniformity of temporal organizations, based on natural cycles, whether of day and night or seasons, or on the ritual religious calendar accepted by most people. In terms of meanings, there was much greater sharing of the symbols and cues that communicated them. Most people agreed about them, and the environment and meaning congruence was strong and clear. Space organization was clearly related to meaning. Communication was much more predictable, being fixed and prescribed,

and related to membership in various groups. Such membership was easily read from clothing, hair styles, language, and place of residence. Today it is far more difficult to place people in social space.[19] Hence, communication becomes more difficult and, paradoxically, certain aspects of the environment more critical.

In the case of traditional settlements, it is possible, however, to concentrate on spatial organization as reflecting and influencing all the other types of organization to a much greater extent than is true currently in modern cities. This is fortunate since much of our evidence regarding early settlements is archaeological; i.e., it is largely in terms of space organization as revealing ordering systems.

Comparative Ordering Systems

To recapitulate: built environments represent physical expressions of ordering systems. The ordering systems are the result of a universal property of the human mind, the need to impose order on the world and make it meaningful; the individual *forms* of ordering are culturally specific. All built environments, and hence all settlements, show this ordering, but some settlements typically order extensive domains, and they can be defined as cities. The organization of the environment is more than spatial, but, when dealing with traditional settlements, spatial organization is the most useful concept (and often the only one in evidence). Finally, in traditional settlements, since religion and ritual are central, the organization is often based on the sacred, and it has been suggested that cities began as ceremonial centers.[20]

There is a major element of the sacred in all traditional settlements. If settlements are thought of as humanized environments, then for most traditional people they must be, by definition, sacred or sanctified environments. Why should this be? Different reasons can be given, but two seem most likely. First, the world view of traditional societies is religious, so that inevitably environments that encode world views and ideals must encode the sacred, since it represents the most significant meaning. A second, more pragmatic, view is that the sacred and the accompanying ritual can be most effective in getting people to do things, in legitimizing things.[21] In other words, cities as organizing elements work most efficiently when seen as sacred and, hence, of high legitimacy. Thus this interpretation of cities makes sense also in a larger anthropological perspective.

Ritual is a powerful way of both legitimizing and preserving culture.[22] Physical elements help in this process by reminding people of ritual, providing settings for it, being supportive of ritual, and expressing both ritual and its underlying schemata and cosmologies in permanent, and often impressive, form. It is interesting to note how many cities have encoded the center of the world, navel of the world, world axis, etc. and have also used this for the name of kings; e.g., in ancient Iran the royal title was "axis of the world."[23]

Any traditional culture will show a sacred order extending from the dwelling to the settlement and to the whole landscape. Thus, understanding traditional settlements requires that they be considered as physical expressions of sacred space.

The *Roman city* was an earthly representation of a heavenly image incorporating the world axis and the division of the world into four based on Rome. The city was sacred and set out in a definite way, with appropriate and rather complex rituals. A most important act was the plowing of the outline, i.e., a purifying enclosure of land, its division into four parts, and a bringing of these divisions together again by formula and gesture. The town was born when the site was purified and made sacred. This important act was to define the boundaries sharply. The most important part of the whole ceremony was the initial furrow made by the founder, using a bronze plow, a white ox, and a cow, starting at the southwest corner of the site, and moving in procession in a counterclockwise direction. The walls were sacred and the gates were in civil jurisdiction. This also was reflected in the details of the plowing. In effect, the settlement was made habitable and existed as a fully constituted entity at the end of the rit-

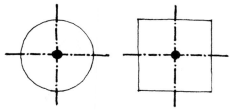

The idea of the center of the world in urban form (based on Muller, 1961; Rykwert, 1976).

uals. Once the sacred furrow defining the city was plowed, the essential city was there—it remained only to build it. The sacred space had been created in the image of the sacred model, and giving it physical form was a less important act. This same belief applied to Etruscan cities, which were also primarily religious. Founding a town was a recapitulation of a divine instituting of a center of the world.[24]

The *ancient Chinese city* has been described as a "cosmomagical symbol." The layout, gates, walls, street pattern, location of center, and its nature all were an aspect of astrobiology.[25] In this view, only the sacred is real, and certainly only the sacred is safe. Settlements (and buildings) imitate celestial archetypes. Before a place can be inhabited it must be made sacred, and this is done through allowing communication among heaven, earth, and the underworld. Cities are then both devices for maximizing this communication and machines for achieving it. Typical of such models of the universe are axiality, cardinal orientation, centrality, and a wall that is often more important as a sacred symbol than a defense mechanism. Obviously, one cannot understand settlements of this type in terms of geometric space but must see them as instances of sacred space; i.e., one must first understand the underlying paradigm.

In China, there were certain differences between the north and south. In the north the city walls were defined first and people moved in over time. The city and its rectangular form represented a self-sustaining cosmic symbol. In the south commercial and residential areas were established first, and the outer walls built later. They lacked the tradition of cosmic significance. Thus while the cities looked similar, their meanings were different.

In both cases, however, the wall was very important. The same word stood for wall and city, and a proper city could not exist without a wall. Within the city, position was related to social organization, so different neighborhoods housed different groups. At different periods, the degree of mobility and communication allowed varied greatly. In Han cities, the space was subdivided by walls with gates which were closed at night and illegal movement was severely punished. During other dynasties, other schemata obtained, and there was less rigid control and more liveliness and mobility.[26]

In the layout of northern cities (which are the earlier), we find geomantic precautions, axiality and cardinal orientation, the symbolism of the center, and a coincidence of *microcosmos* and *macrocosmos*. The microcosmos of the city represented an ordered and consecrated world separated by a wall from the disorderly and profane world beyond. As in Rome the act of founding was most important and consisted of complex rituals. The first and essential act was the definition. The walls were the first thing built, and thus the most sacred part of towns was built before there was anything to defend. After the walls, the ancestral temple and the altar of the earth were erected, all in accordance with prescribed rituals.

A Chinese royal city had to have walls, proper orientation, a square shape, and 12 gates representing the 12 months. The four quadrants of the heavenly vault were reflected in the four directions. Each side of the square was related to the four seasons and to positions of the sun in very complex ways. The two sacred places, the royal ancestral temple and the altar of the earth, were on either side of the main street, and the royal palace, residence, and audience hall were enclosed at the center. The royal complex dominated the city and thus the universe. The palace also separated the center of profane activity (the market, on the north of the inner enclosure)

from the centers of religious activity—the ancestral temple and the altar of the earth. The ruler faced south in the audience hall, with his back literally to the market.

The main street ran from the south gate of the city to the south gate of the palace and was an expression of the celestial meridian and polar star. The symbolism could be further elaborated, but the main point is that the city was to reflect cosmological beliefs, and the physical expression was to get as close as possible to the sacred beliefs. The city, founded as a religious act, enclosed within its walls a model of cosmic order and civilization, i.e., predictable and ordered life. The Chinese city was, in effect, a machine for capturing cosmic forces and distributing them to the country.

The *Khmer cities* of Cambodia, such as Angkor Thom, are a representation of Hindu cosmological myths. It covers an area of 6 square miles. The center of the city is the sacred temple-mountain, and the symbolism of wall and moat replicates the universe as conceived by the culture. This ordering system extends well beyond the city itself; through roads, causeways, and canals it tries to order the whole landscape and kingdom, incorporating smaller settlements, ceremonial centers, and temples in a grand pattern of sacred symbolism.

Indian cities, based on the same Hindu tradition, also represent sacred symbols. They incorporate social dimensions of sacredness through the relation of centrality and caste, with Brahmins at the center, lower castes closer to the edges, and untouchables at the periphery. Even here there is a *schema,* with the Brahmins seen as the head, Kshatryas as the heart, Vatshyas as the arms, and Sudras as the feet.

More generally Hindu cities reflect the notion that the sacred is manifested in space, time, and matter, so that manifest space and material things make visible unmanifest space. Any environment is created primarily to reflect cosmological models that must be scrupulously followed. Within such settings ritual purity must be maintained. Brahmins at the center are near the sacred temple. The rules for design and layout are laid down in books called the *Silpa Sastras.* Once again, boundaries, axial cosmology, and the center (*axis mundi*) are of great importance.

Religious symbolism governed the layout of all Hindu towns and villages, wards, streets, and the location of buildings, as well as open spaces, gates, and tanks (water pools). In the *silpa sastras,* various plans follow mystic figures, symbols, and images. Thus settlements may be laid out in the form of the body of Vishnu, or of the sacred bird, Guruda, or a mystic flower. All these have broad streets running east-west or north-south and intersecting at the center, where the temple is located. Other settlement forms may represent the eight-petalled lotus (*Padnaka*) or cosmic crosses. The site where a city is built is as sacred as an altar. The social space—areas of castes, kin groups, and occupations—is clearly specified and related to the sacred order.

The center of the town and its focus is the temple, whether the temple-mountain of northern India or the hollow space with gateways of southern India. From this square or oblong area with walls and streets, an order extends outwards to organize the whole landscape, including settlements, villages, and hamlets, in a rectilinear system based on a pair of intersecting straight lines oriented to the cardinal directions. Since this sacred order also incorporates all nature, it even helps explain the survival of plants and animals.[27]

Thus environmental order in India reflects the divine substance that permeates the world. The environmental order makes the divine substance real, so design is a spiritual science ("the science of the dwellings of the gods") that makes visible the divine order. Cosmology is the model for structuring all built environments. This type of design has been described as a *symbolic technology,* so that a form succeeds only if it harmonizes with the cosmic symbol. Clearly Indian design must be evaluated in quite different terms from our own environments.

Yoruba cities in Africa can only be properly understood as reflecting sacred schemata. The natural and supernatural worlds are *isomorphic,* the former reflecting the latter. Here again the center and the palace located there, the crossing of roads and the walls are only meaningful to the extent that they adequately reflect the cosmic order pervading all of traditional Yoruba life and culture.

The persistence of these various forms can be quite striking. Thus the *Aztec pattern* used at Tenochtitlán (see diagram on page 43) at the very large scale of an imperial capital (population 70,000 to 300,000 on 1,875 acres), is found in the village of Tlayacapan today.[28] Tenochtitlán, on islands in the middle of a lake and linked to the shore by causeways, was centered on the sacred temple compound, emperor's palace, and market, surrounded by residences of nobles. The two principal north-south and east-west axes intersecting at that center organized units (at least 69 of them) called *calpulli.* These were residential clusters of related groups; they were the basic units of Aztec society, comprising a social unit, kin unit, and territorial property unit. Each unit had its own chapels. This system also existed at the level of the smaller towns, villages, and the state. The social organization also related to these different scales—the emperor at the center, with the nobles around him, military chiefs in the quadrants, and elected chiefs in the calpulli.

Conceptions of time and space conformed to this cultural model of the clan-like groups of the calpulli. The image of society was that of a truncated, quadrilateral pyramid of seven levels. It is still visible in Tlayacapan, where there are chapels that reflect the original elaborate neighborhood and chapel complex traceable to the calpulli. This village, Tenochitlán, and the Aztec state were based on the same model at different scales. The system connected space, time, meaning, and communication. At its base were Aztec religious beliefs and ritual based on 26 clans arranged in a system of 7 facing 7 and 6 facing 6. The god Omete Clihtli gave birth to four sons who became the gods of the four world quarters. Time coordinates with this spatial dimension in a complex pattern.[29]

The *Mayan pattern,* although different in detail, is equally complex. In the case of the Maya, the centers were "empty" and linked through ritual and ceremonial movement at all levels—the house group of just two or three dwellings, among such groups within the cluster, the cluster group, the minor ceremonial centers, and, finally, the major center; i.e., there was a complex organization at many levels. These movements not only organized the units, and the larger areas of hundreds of square kilometers, but also ritually established and purified the boundaries.

The ceremonial centers themselves were different in detail but had characteristics in common. They all consisted of plazas, temple complexes on pyramids, palaces (larger buildings), and some dwellings scattered on hills in forest clearings. The dwellings, often linked by roadways and causeways, included altars, stelae, and ball courts.

It is interesting to note that among the Maya there were changes in the ordering schemata. It has recently been shown that at Cozumel, the decline in art did not mean decadence but rather a change in values. Art was no longer valued, and great importance was attached to trade. The result was the construction of vast causeways and storage platforms for goods (some of which were 20 feet high and 17 acres in area), field wall systems, and coastal defenses.[30] There was still an organizing schema, but it was not based on a sacred order.

Cosmic symbolism and sacrality usually have decreased in more recent periods, with other schemata substituting. However, it is quite possible to look at the medieval city in terms of sacred meanings. World views and buildings are certainly so structured.

Regarding the Renaissance, we can use an analogy based on the convincing argument that buildings, far from being designed according to aesthetic criteria, were cosmic symbols related to neo-Platonic philosophy. It may prove quite possible to show that Renaissance cities embodied cosmic symbols, particularly when we consider designs for ideal cities.

We find support for this hypothesis in studies of Filarete's and Campanella's designs. Filarete's design is based on "squaring the circle." The garden is like a map of the earth; flowing water like the veins and arteries of a human being. It is an identification of humankind with the universe represented microcosmically. Other diagrams and symbols are involved, e.g., the four elements (earth, fire, water, and air) circling around an altar in the center of a piece of ground divided into squares. The other four corners represent the four Aristotelian qualities of dryness, humidity, cold, and heat. Thus the two intersecting squares represent the four elements and four qualities, and Sforzinda, the city designed in this way, is an allegorical representation of the *city of man.* The circle is identified with virtues and the perfect Platonic shape. In his *city of the sun,* Campanella tried to represent both Dante and Copernicus and combine two schemata of cosmic order.[31]

The very fact that various secular and religious utopias are often expressed in terms of urban designs, and that one can discuss ideal cities, suggests the importance of schemata in urban form. It is useful to recall that the term *civilization* is closely related to the concept of the presence of cities and city life. Even after the Renaissance, beginning with Ledoux, a different schema was expressed—nature and the individual are all that count, and cities are evil. This is Rousseauism in urban form—a very different schema, but still a schema. Cities can become symbols of evil, and, finally, the schema of city as humanized space and wilderness as dangerous space actually reverses.

Schemata are basic to all settlements, and people design, react to, and experience environments primarily in terms of meanings and associational qualities rather than perceptual qualities. What changes are the meanings and the schemata in which they are encoded. One can therefore use this notion to study cultural change in settlements or to

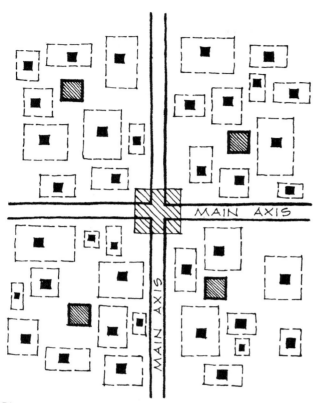

Diagrammatic plan of Tenochtitlán.

 MAIN CENTER WITH PRINCIPAL TEMPLE, PALACE, ETC.

 LARGE TEMPLE IN EACH QUADRANT

 CALPULLI, EACH WITH SMALL TEMPLE INSIDE

This distinction between sacred and profane and, hence, humanized and dangerous, or inside and outside, is a cognitive dichotomy that is crucial to an understanding of both settlements and buildings in traditional cultures. This system of binary oppositions is regarded as very basic by many scholars (for example, Lévi-Strauss and other structuralists, and cognitive anthropologists).[32] In reference to environments, one can conceptualize many such binary distinctions:

sacred - profane
center - periphery
inside - outside
town - wilderness
front - back
public - private
men - women
adults - children
us - them

Underlying a number of them, it has been suggested, is a very basic distinction between culture and nature.[33] Houses and villages belong to culture, to people, whereas the forest belongs to nature. It is interesting to note that cultivated fields represent an intermediate term, and extensions of the cultural domain into the domain of nature are accompanied by ritual. A similar middle term is found in the case of the *Fang village* in Africa, where the settlement is the domain of culture and is itself subdivided into men's and women's domains, fields are the middle term, and the bush is nature—the profane and dangerous realm.[34] This distinction with

compare indigenous and colonial components of cities in Africa, Asia, and elsewhere and show the very different schemata they express even though they are on the same site and in the same climate. One can look at French, English, Dutch, German, Portugese, and Spanish colonial cities and see how the various cultural schemata produce very different towns.

In the case of traditional, especially early, settlement, the schemata are primarily (although not exclusively) sacred. Only sacred places are meaningful, habitable, and humanized, and only they are places. When outside, one is in a profane, dangerous, nonhuman domain or realm. The specific ordering systems vary, but the approach does not.

ON THE CULTURAL ORIGINS OF SETTLEMENTS

a mediating term is found among the Zapotec Indians of Mexico, and probably in many other cases, but it is always related to philosophy and cosmology, so that settlements express belief systems of cultures (see diagram on page 45, top right).

A useful way, therefore, to study settlements and other environments is in terms of the schemata imposed on the world and given expression, the domains defined, the particular models used and the way they are given expression, and the ordering systems that distinguish and differentiate built environments. For example, dense, nucleated settlements relate the various domains very differently from diffuse settlements, where ritualized movement plays a major role in linking and integrating the system.

EXAMPLES OF SETTLEMENTS

We do not accept the view that cognitive ordering schemata show a developmental sequence, that they get more sophisticated through time. We can say that the technological and economic aspects of modern industrial states are at the most complex stage of development of any culture. Yet in terms of the ideology of belief systems, modern industrial societies are at a rather simplistic level compared to the Australian aborigines, the Temne of Africa, and many other peoples. The various schemata used in ordering settlements thus were not simpler in the past, but merely different; they emphasized other values related to the particular ideology. Understanding landscapes, settlements, or buildings involves understanding the underlying schemata in which the important elements are encoded.

It is certainly true that through time settlements show an increase in scale and extent of organization. (Recall that settlements can be defined as cities when they begin to organize relatively large areas.) However, the sophistication and conceptual complexity do not really show development. The following examples illustrate the different organiza-

tions of early settlements and the belief that from the earliest settlements known organizing schemata have existed. In fact, one cannot conceive of a settlement, or any built environment, without an underlying cognitive schema. Some *template* must exist so that a form can emerge. Such forms always represent some level of congruence between physical space organization and social space organization.

All settlements, like all built environments, essentially involve the making of places. Each place is a differentiated portion of the earth's surface of previously undifferentiated space, a portion that both is distinguishable from other such portions and has a specific meaning. Recall that places can be defined purely cognitively and that a nomadic camp is a place, or an *ethnic domain*.[35] What makes a place is always some schema, some ordering principle, which varies in different cultures. In most traditional cultures these schemata are related to the sacred so that a place is differentiated from the profane undifferentiated space around it. Other types of schemata also exist. However, in all cases the purpose of places is to create a space that is habitable and usable in terms acceptable to the culture.

At what point in history do we begin our study? One of the discoveries common to recent research on all topics is that everything had its beginnings earlier than was once thought. Sizable settlements go back quite a long time. Even if we disregard nomadic camps, which do show organization and the presence of underlying schemata, whether social or ritual, the antiquity of settlements is quite remarkable. It is important to remember that settlement size and density are relative; i.e., they must be seen in terms of overall population in an area and its density.

Antiquity also is relative, not absolute. Aborigines lived in Australia for over 30,000 years without developing permanent settlements. In the Middle East, large settlements go back at least 10,000 years, whereas it was believed until recently in the Americas that they only go back about 2,000 years. But even this date is being pushed back. Recent excavations in Ecuador suggest the presence of formally planned ceremonial centers, such as the one at *Real Alto,* by 3,000 B.C.E., and it is unlikely that Real Alto is the earliest. Thus very early we find lavishly constricted and carefully maintained public spaces for rituals. In Ecuador, villages tended to be circular, and this form was so important that as long as there was any vitality to the culture it was maintained—as late as 1924, in fact. The large ceremonial center, however, was strongly rectangular.[36]

Thus, in terms of the overall developmental sequence, relatively large and complex settlements occur as early in the Americas as in the Old World. The following examples are therefore not arranged chronologically, in order to avoid the idea of development. Neither are they ordered geographically.

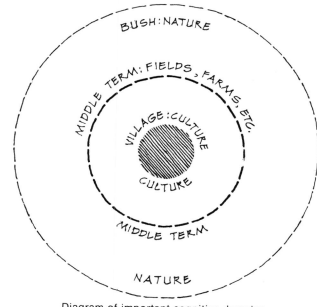

Diagram of important cognitive domains.

A FIESTA HOUSE
B CHARNEL HOUSE
[hatched] RESIDENTIAL AREAS

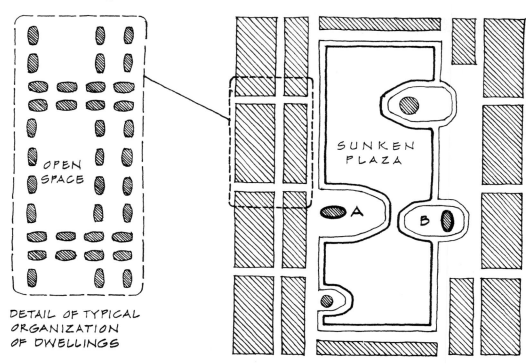

OPEN SPACE

DETAIL OF TYPICAL ORGANIZATION OF DWELLINGS

SUNKEN PLAZA

A

B

Diagrammatic plan of Real Alto, Ecuador, 3,100 B.C.E. This may have been even larger than shown, because part of the site has eroded. The permanent population is estimated at 1,500; the center organized a much larger area with many hamlets (based on Lathrap, 1977).

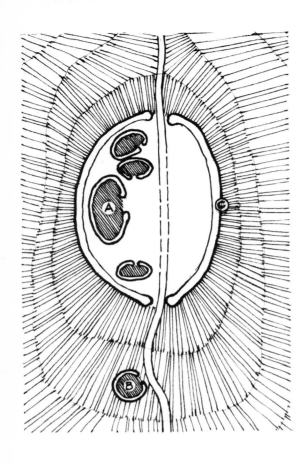

A   HUT, APPROX. 45 ft. × 27 ft. WITH FIVE HEARTHS

B   CIRCULAR, PARTLY EXCAVATED HUT, WITH STONE RETAINING WALLS AND CENTRAL OVEN. MANY CLAY ARTICLES NOT OF DAILY LIFE. PROBABLY A SACRED PLACE.

C   WALL, IDENTIFYING PLACE AND SOCIAL UNITY.

Dolni Vesconice, Czechoslovakia, 25,000 years ago. This settlement had a population of 80 to 125; comparable settlements in the area had populations up to 250. This was the winter settlement of people who were nomadic in the summer. Thus, there were probably migratory routes and territories arranged to reduce aggression; i.e., they were organized. Within the living compound there was a pit burial of a female with a crooked face, similar to statuettes. Burial within the compound suggests elements of ritual and the sacred (based on Klim, 1962, 1963).

Lepenski Vir, Yugoslavia, 6,500 to 5,600 B.C.E. The whole settlement, the marketplace, and the houses all have the same trapezoidal form, as if it "were the formula and essence of the universe." The organizing form is clearly essential and was retained over a period of 900 years, through six successive settlements. The settlement is conceived as the interior of a gigantic house related to the river: it is oriented and ordered by a system that has mathematical quality. It shows evidence of careful choice (based on Srejovič, 1974).

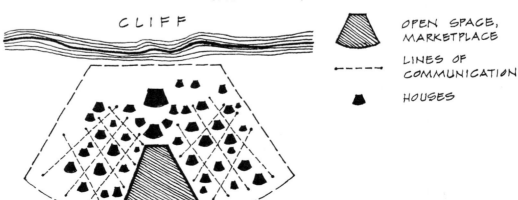

CLIFF

OPEN SPACE, MARKETPLACE

LINES OF COMMUNICATION

HOUSES

RIVER

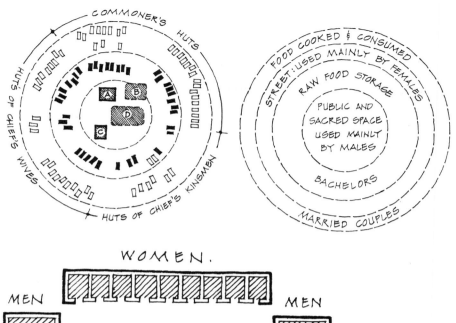

COMMONER'S HUTS

HUTS OF CHIEF'S WIVES

HUTS OF CHIEF'S KINSMEN

A
B
C
D

FOOD COOKED & CONSUMED

STREET: USED MAINLY BY FEMALES

RAW FOOD STORAGE

PUBLIC AND SACRED SPACE USED MAINLY BY MALES

BACHELORS

MARRIED COUPLES

A CHIEF YAM HOUSE
B DANCING GROUND
C CHIEF'S HUT
D BURIAL GROUND
▭ LIVING HUTS
▬ YAM STORAGE HUTS

Omarakama Village, Trobriand Islands. Described in the 1930s (Malinowski, 1935; Lévi-Strauss, 1967).

WOMEN.

MEN

OPEN SPACE

MEN

WOMEN

Plan of Fang Village, Africa (based on Fernandez, 1977).

Generalized plan of one type of village, Sepik River, New Guinea.

SMALL HOUSES

EMBANKMENT · PLANTED WITH PALMS

HOUSE TAMBARAN · MEN'S SACRED HOUSE · 60 FT. HIGH ELABORATELY DECORATED. SITED IN GROVE AT END OF GRASSED AVENUE

EMBANKMENT · PLANTED WITH PALMS

SMALL HOUSES

R I V E R

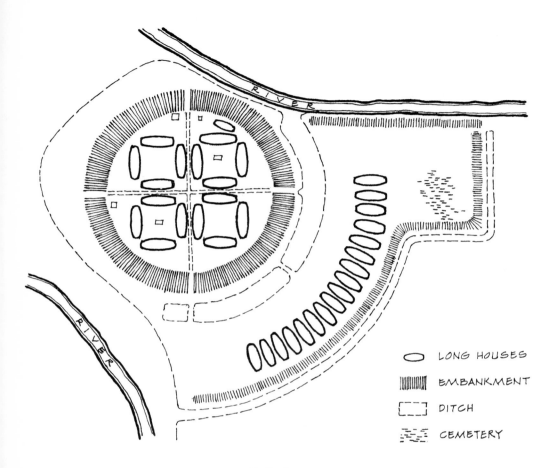

Simplified plan of fortified Viking settlement, Trellenborg, Denmark, tenth century B.C.E. The main embankment is 564 feet in diameter and 16 feet high (based on Hawkes, 1974; Muller, 1961).

Scandinavian 8-hufen village. Model related to the sun (based on Muller, 1961).

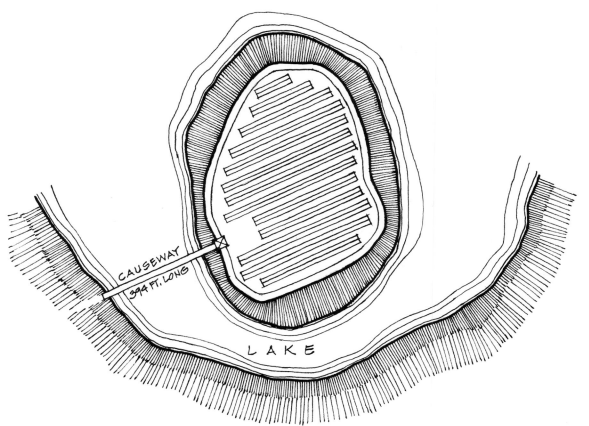

Fortified settlement on a 5-acre island. Biskupin, Poland, 550 to 400 B.C.E. Earth bank with timber palisades surrounded by breakwaters and wood-paved streets. At the gate was a market/meeting place. There were 105 dwellings in 13 rows, each with a single thatched roof (based on Hawkes, 1974).

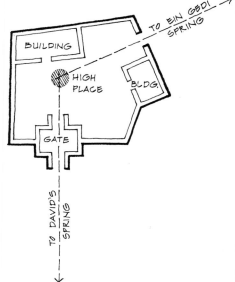

Ein Gedi, Israel, early Canaanite sanctuary, third millenium B.C.E.. This sacred enclosure sits on a hill terrace. The wall encloses a sacred precinct within which is a high place—a sacred center. The gates form transitions and face springs (scarce water in a desert environment). The conceptual ordering and the relating of the springs to the sacred central place are significant. There may have been permanent settlements, nomadic camps, or both at the springs (based on a model at Israel Museum, Jerusalem).

Nahal Oren, west flank of Carmel Range, Israel, eighth millenium, B.C.E. Small pre-pottery neolithic settlement. It includes 4 terraces, with 14 huts of large undressed stones, sharing walls 2½- to 3½-feet high. All doors face south, indicating a definite ordering system (based on a model at the Israel Museum, Jerusalem).

Wheel model of kingdom, ancient Ceylon. This was also used for settlements (based on Muller, 1961).

Ideal type of north Chinese city. While no actual city fully reflected this pattern, this schema is necessary to understand the actual cities (based on written descriptions by Tuan, 1968; Wheatley, 1971).

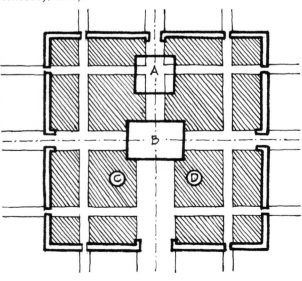

A MARKET
B PALACE
C TEMPLE OF ANCESTORS
D ALTAR OF THE EARTH

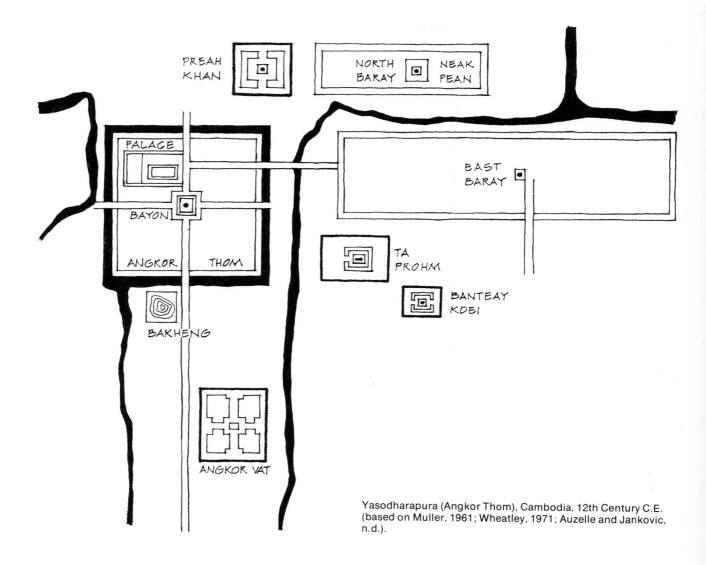

Yasodharapura (Angkor Thom), Cambodia, 12th Century C.E.
(based on Muller, 1961; Wheatley, 1971; Auzelle and Jankovic,
n.d.).

ON THE CULTURAL ORIGINS OF SETTLEMENTS

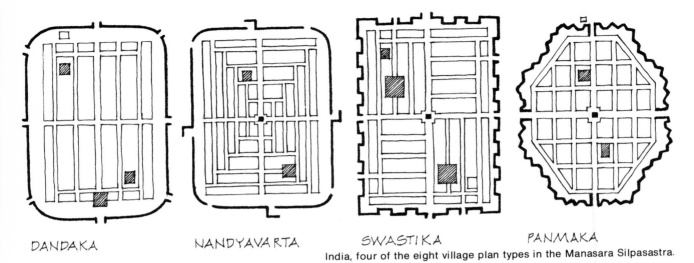

DANDAKA　　　NANDYAVARTA　　　SWASTIKA　　　PANMAKA

India, four of the eight village plan types in the Manasara Silpasastra.

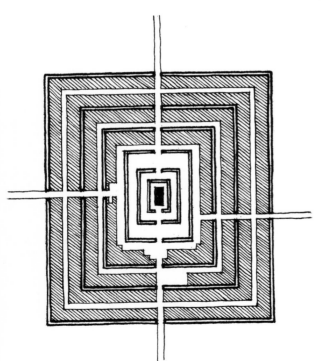

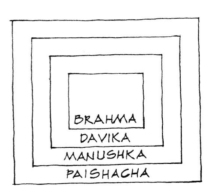

BRAHMA
DAVIKA
MANUSHKA
PAISHACHA

Conceptual plan of Sarvatobharda, sixth to ninth centuries C.E. (based on Mukerjee, 1961; Muller, 1961; Sopher, 1962; Wheatley, 1971; Ghosh and Mago, 1974; Rykwert, 1976).

Simplified plan of Srirangam (based on Sarvatobharda).

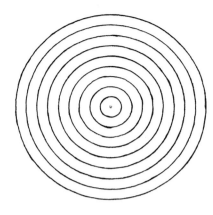

Renaissance: ideal city plans based on ideal and magical schemata: a search for all-embracing harmony. *Top:* Campanella's city of the sun based on a combination of Copernicus's model of the solar system and Dante's *Divine Comedy. Middle:* model on which Filarete's Sforzinda plan is based. *Bottom:* Filarete's plan of Sforzinda (all based on S. Lang, 1952; Morris, 1972).

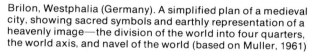

Brilon, Westphalia (Germany). A simplified plan of a medieval city, showing sacred symbols and earthly representation of a heavenly image—the division of the world into four quarters, the world axis, and navel of the world (based on Muller, 1961)

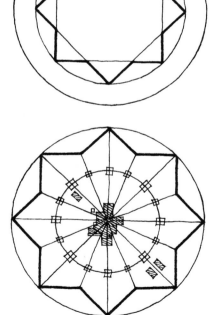

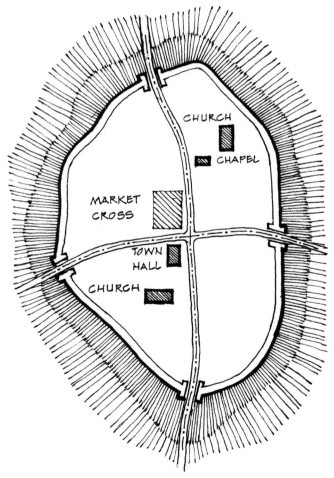

CHURCH

CHAPEL

MARKET CROSS

TOWN HALL

CHURCH

ON THE CULTURAL ORIGINS OF SETTLEMENTS

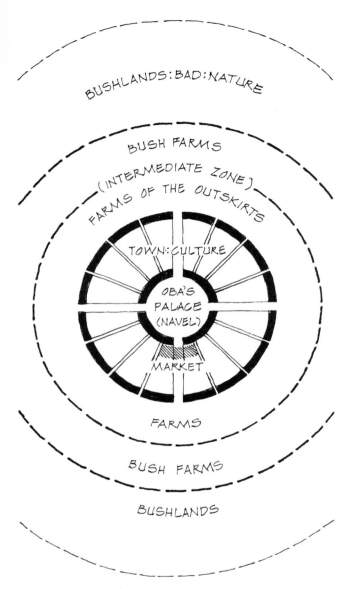

Ideal model of northern Yoruba city (Africa). This pattern is related to cosmology. The palace layout reflects the model more accurately than the town, but the town and the entire state try to replicate the cosmic schema. The town is divided into quadrants. The four-fold division is very important (e.g., the ancient city of Ife). Four of the quarters are at cardinal points with three inserted in between those; i.e., there are 16 quarters in all plus a central precinct (e.g., ancient Ibadan had 16 gates). The quarters and chief's compounds look towards the palace; other compounds are grouped around the chief's compound (based on Krapf Askari, 1969; Kamau, 1976).

Comparison of Nea Nokomedia, Northern Greece, seventh millenium B.C.E. with Çatal Hüyük, Anatolia, seventh millenium B.C.E. Very different traditions already existed over 8,000 years ago in Europe and the Middle East and still exist.

Typical European pattern, with individual houses 25 by 25 feet, spaced 6 to 15 feet apart. The sacred building is 40 by 40 feet. The settlement is built on a knoll with two concentric walls, which were replaced later by a deep, water-filled ditch. The overall shape of the settlement is not known.

Part of Çatal Hüyük, where a tradition of buildings tightly clustered against each other and around courts is found. It is an orderly plan with standardized sizes. (Nea Nokomedia based on Rodden, 1965; Çatal Hüyük based on Mellaart, 1964, 1967, and Todd, 1976).

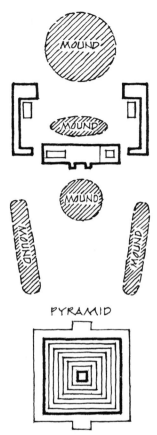

PYRAMID

La Venta (southern coast of Veracruz, Mexico) Olmec ceremonial center. Organizes a larger area of huts, farms, and villages (as in the case of the Maya). The basic schema persisted for the next 2,000 years on the central plateau of Mexico (based on Hardoy, 1973; north point not indicated).

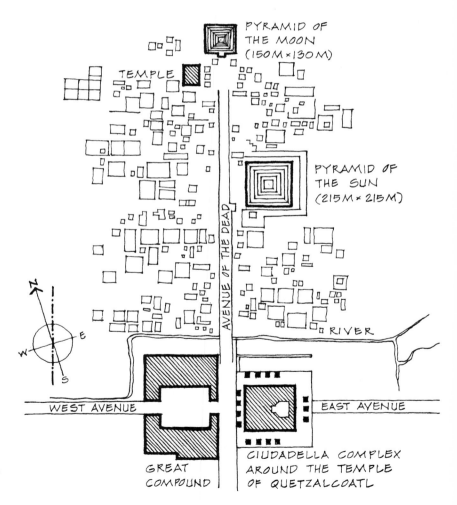

Teotihuacan, Mexico, 100 B.C.E. to 700 C.E.; peak 500 C.E. The overall city area includes 8 square miles, with a population of 50,000 to 100,000; it organized a vast region. The great pyramids came early in its history, 2,000 years ago. The general orientation of the center was carefully calculated. The city was built quickly and there was clearly an overall plan. The relatively impermanent residential compounds were gradually replaced by stone-walled apartment complexes within the overall guiding scheme. These compounds are organized enclaves and the city is an assemblage of these—organized by major axes and centers.

56

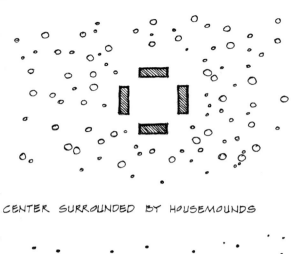

CENTER SURROUNDED BY HOUSEMOUNDS

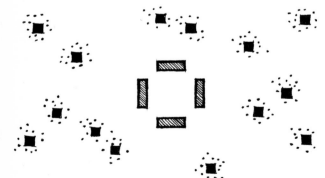

CENTER WITHOUT HOUSEMOUNDS, WITH SCATTERED SINGLE HOUSE UNITS

MAJOR CENTER, WITH NO POPULATION; SECONDARY CENTERS SURROUNDED BY HAMLETS OR VILLAGES, NOT INDIVIDUAL HOUSEMOUNDS.

Idealized patterns, Maya, Mesoamerica (based on Willey, 1956).

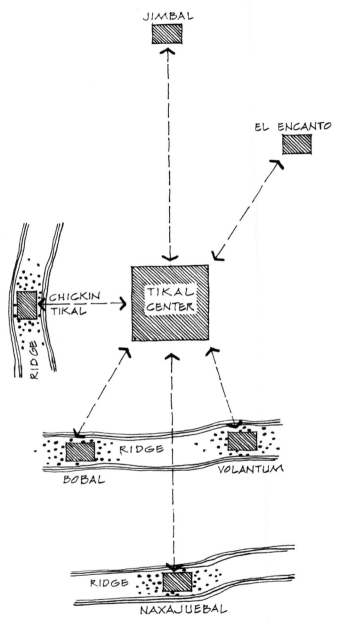

Conceptual plan of Tikal, Guatemala (based on Sanders, 1975).

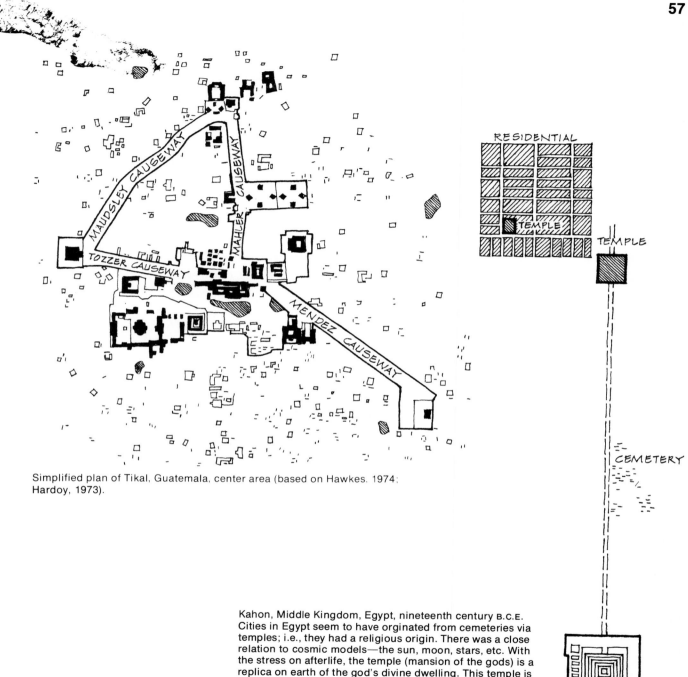

Simplified plan of Tikal, Guatemala, center area (based on Hawkes, 1974; Hardoy, 1973).

Kahon, Middle Kingdom, Egypt, nineteenth century B.C.E. Cities in Egypt seem to have orginated from cemeteries via temples; i.e., they had a religious origin. There was a close relation to cosmic models—the sun, moon, stars, etc. With the stress on afterlife, the temple (mansion of the gods) is a replica on earth of the god's divine dwelling. This temple is thought of as being founded on the primeval island or mound at the hub of the universe (based on Sée, 1973; Ucko et al., 1972).

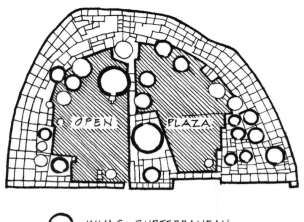

  KIVAS. SUBTERRANEAN

  DWELLING ROOMS IN MULTISTOREY BLOCKS

Pueblo Bonito, New Mexico, 350 to 1300 C.E.

Chan Chan, Peru, 1000 to 1476 C.E. The capital of the Chimu Kingdom had a total area of 15 to 25 square kilometers. The central area so far excavated is 4 km N-S by 4½ km E-W. The whole city was oriented 10 degrees east of north—corresponding to the setting sun at the winter solstice. The city consists of compounds, "wards," or "citadels." All of these, except *one*, have the same orientation. Some are almost square, but most are elongated rectangles. There is no city center or street pattern, just narrow lanes among the compounds. Streets, plazas, reservoirs, houses, and temples are within the compound walls. There are some houses scattered among the compounds; these are less regular—like an infil. This pattern is unique in pre-Columbian America (based on Hardoy, 1973; Hawkes, 1974).

CONCLUSIONS

What we have seen is that the human mind has a need to order the universe, and one manifestation of this is the ordering of the environment. All cultures have environmental ordering systems; i.e., they communicate symbolically through their environmental orders. All environments have meaning and communicate the schemata, priorities, preferences, and culture of the creators. Thus it is possible to compare all settlements, traditional and modern, indigenous and colonial.

In addition, schemata change over time and vary among cultures. Though they increase in scale, they do not necessarily follow a developmental sequence. The schemata and ordering systems of Australian aborigines are as sophisticated, in their own way, as those of modern peoples; in some ways they are more sophisticated. We also saw that the ordering of the environment began earlier than was once thought and its beginning is constantly being pushed back even further in time.

In traditional cultures, those with which we are primarily concerned in considering the cultural origins of settlements, the ordering was sacred. Its basic purpose was to order the earthly chaos by replicating an ideal order—the heavenly order and harmony.

Even though we have argued that ordering systems show no development, there still remains the question: what marks the development of those forms of settlements that can be called urban? One possible answer has been given: when they begin to order larger territorial units in certain ways. Another answer is also possible.

If we consider traditional cultures, there seem to be two major ordering systems. These are not mutually exclusive; in fact, they are often related. First is a geometric order related to the sacred and to cosmology, and second is an order related to social relationships, as in !Kung bushman, M'Buti pygmy, or Australian Aboriginal camps. In these camps, ritual grounds or centers are often separate, as is the cognitive ordering of the larger environment. However, there is still some correlation with the larger order through the intimate relationship between the social order and the sacred, so that even spatial relationships have more than social meaning. Generally such camps lack the strong cosmic significance of other settlements. The transition from these camps to settlements of cosmic significance is important and probably marks the beginning of those types of settlements that in some way can be seen as becoming urban.

In authentic traditional urban settlements, we can see both these orders closely coexisting, so that one additional, very important purpose of the sacred order is to establish, stress, and reinforce the social order. The cognitive elements in settlements both reflect and reinforce the social order. In some way

the development of modern urban settlements can be seen as a process whereby sacred ordering systems are, once again, replaced by social ones, so one can relate certain spatial and social orders in different cultures and show how they differ. For example, we can compare the very different character of Italian, English, French, U.S., and Japanese urban orders.[37] More recently, one can see the replacement of both by technological orders related to lifestyle and preferences, but out of control and at odds with human needs. We have already briefly addressed the question of the value of looking at the broadest range of environments in order to generalize validly and to trace patterns. There is another reason for doing so. There is still today a bewildering variety of cultures, subcultures, lifestyles, and cognitive styles. In order to design valid settings for them it is necessary to know how environments relate to these specifics. If underlying the differences there were regularities and constancies, we could reduce the degree and zone of variable elements and generalize the constants for Homo sapiens. This would make it much easier to analyze and understand, as well as to design, valid environments that are culture-supportive.

There is an interesting question with which to end our discussion of settlements: is there any relationship between constancy, variability, and scale? It could be suggested that whereas at the urban, metropolitan, and megalopolitan scales new patterns apply, at smaller scales there may still be lessons to be learned from the past. Perhaps we must go back to the dawn of settlements, to that remote past when people first imposed a visible physical order on the land to reflect their conceptual order, to fix that order, and to remind people of how they should act in settings.

NOTES

1. David A. Hamburg, "Ancient Man in the Twentieth Century," in V. Goodall, ed., *The Quest for Man* (New York: Praeger, 1975); Lionel Tiger, *Men in Groups* (New York: Random House, 1969); Lionel Tiger and Robin Fox, *The Imperial Animal* (New York: Delta Books, 1971); Robin Fox, "The Cultural Animal," *Encounter*, vol. 35, no. 1 (July 1970), 31–42; S. V. Boyden, "Conceptual Basis of Proposed International Ecological Studies in Large Metropolitan Areas," mimeo, 1974.

2. Amos Rapoport, "An Anthropological Approach to Environmental Design Research," in Basil Honikman, ed., *Responding to Social Change* (Stroudsburg, Pa.: Dowden, Hutchinson & Ross, 1975).

3. Amos Rapoport, *Human Aspects of Urban Form* (Oxford: Pergamon, 1977), p. 399.

4. Larry S. Bourne, ed., *Internal Structure of the City* (New York: Oxford University Press, 1971); Grady Clay, *Close-Up: How to Read the American City* (New York: Praeger, 1973); Robert Venturi, Denise Scott Brown, and Steven Izenour, *Learning from Las Vegas: The Forgotten Symbolism of Architectural Form* (Cambridge, Mass.: M.I.T., 1977).

5. Amos Rapoport, *Human Aspects of Urban Form* (Oxford: Pergamon Press, 1977).

6. Rhoads Murphy, "The City as a Center of Change: Western Europe and China," *Annals of the Association of American Geographers*, vol. 44 (1954); Paul W. English, *City and Village in Iran* (Madison, Wis.: University of Wisconsin Press, 1966).

7. Louis Wirth, "Urbanism as a Way of Life," *American Journal of Sociology* 44 (1938):1–24.

8. V. Gordon Childe, "The Urban Revolution," *Town Planning Review* 21 (1950): 3–17.

9. Jorge E. Hardoy, *Pre-Columbian Cities* (New York: Walker, 1973).

10. Paul Wheatley, *The Pivot of the Four Quarters* (Chicago: Aldine, 1971).

11. Peter J. Ucko et al., eds., *Man, Settlement, and Urbanism* (London: Duckworth, 1972).

12. M. Fowler, *Cahokia: Ancient Capital of the Midwest*, Addison-Wesley Modules in Anthropology, no. 48 (Reading, Mass.: Addison-Wesley, 1974).

13. Wheatley, *The Pivot of the Four Quarters*.

14. Richard B. Lee and I. Devore, eds., *Man the Hunter* (Chicago: Aldine, 1968).

15. Amos Rapoport, "Australian Aborigines and the Definition of Place," in William J. Mitchell, ed., *EDRA* (Los Angeles: University of California, 1972) vol. 1, pp. 3-3-1—3-3-14; expanded version in P. Oliver, ed., *Shelter, Sign and Symbol* (London: Barrie and Jenkins, 1975).

16. Evon Z. Vogt, "Some Aspects of Zinacantan Settlement Pattern and Ceremonial Organization," in K. C. Chang, ed., *Settlement Archaeology* (Palo Alto, California: National Press Books, 1968) pp. 154–173; Evon Z. Vogt, *Tortillas for the Gods* (Cambridge: Harvard University Press, 1976).

17. Amos Rapoport, *Human Aspects of Urban Form* (Oxford: Pergamon Press, 1977) p. 49.

18. James S. Duncan, Jr., "Landscape Taste as a Symbol of Group Identity," *Geographical Review* 63 (July 1973):334–555 Las Vegas: Venturi, Brown, and Izenour, *Learning from Las Vegas* (Cambridge, Mass.: M.I.T., 1977); Boston: Carr, *City Signs and Lights: A Policy Study* (Cambridge, Mass.: M.I.T., 1973).

19. Amos Rapoport, 1977; Lyn H. Lofland, *A World of Strangers* (New York: Basic Books, 1973); Paul Reed, "Situated Interaction," in *Urban Life and Culture*, vol. 2, no. 4 (January 1974), pp. 460–487.

20. Wheatley, *Pivot of the Four Quarters*.

21. Roy A. Rappaport, "Ritual, Sanctity and Cybernetics," *American Anthropologist* 73, no. 1 (1971): 59–76; and "The Sacred in Human Evolution," *Annual Review of Ecology and Systemics* 2 (1971): 23–44.

22. Evon Z. Vogt, *Tortillas for the Gods* (Cambridge: Harvard University Press, 1976).

23. Werner Müller, *Die Heilige Stadt: Roma Quadrata, Himmlisches Jerusalem und di Mythe des Weltnavbel* (Stuttgart: Kohlhammer, 1961).

24. Joseph Rykwert, *The Idea of a Town* (Princeton, N.J.: Princeton University Press, 1976); Müller, *Die Heilige Stadt.*

25. Wheatley, *The Pivot of the Four Quarters.*

26. Yi Fu Tuan, "A Preface to Chinese Cities," in *Urbanization and Its Problems*, ed. R. P. Beckinsale and J. M. Houston (Oxford: Blackwell, 1968), pp. 218–553.

27. Richard Lannoy, *The Speaking Tree: A Study of Indian Culture and Society* (London: Oxford University Press, 1971); David Sopher, "Landscapes and Seasons," *Landscape Thirteen* (Spring 1964) 14–19; Bijit Ghosh and K. C. Mago, "Sprirangam: Urban Form and Pattern of an Ancient Indian Town," *Ekistics* 38 (November 1974):377–384.

28. Hardoy, *Pre-Columbian Cities.*

29. John M. Ingham, "Time and Space in Ancient Mexico: The Symbolic Dimension of Clanship," *Man* 6 (1971):615–29.

30. J. A. Sabloff and W. L. Rathje, "The Rise of a Maya Merchant Class," *Scientific American* 233 (October 1975): 72–83.

31. S. Lang, "The Ideal City from Plato to Howard," *Architectural Review* 112 (August 1952): 91–101.

32. C. Lévi-Strauss, *Structural Anthropology* (Garden City, N.Y.: Doubleday, 1967).

33. Evon Z. Vogt and Catherine C. Vogt, "Lévi-Straus among the Maya," *Man* 5 (1970):379–92; Evon Z. Vogt, *Tortillas for the Gods: A Symbolic Analysis of Zinacanteco Rituals* (Cambridge, Mass.: Harvard University Press, 1976).

34. James W. Fernandez, *Fang Architectonics*, Working Paper No. 1 (Philadelphia: Institute for the Study of Human Issues, 1977).

35. Suzanne Langer, *Feeling and Form* (New York: Scribner, 1953).

36. Donald W. Lathrap et al., "Real Alto: An Ancient Ceremonial Center," *Archaeology* 30 (January 1977).

37. Martin Meyerson, "National Character and Urban Development," *Public Policy* 12 (1963):78–96.

FOR FURTHER READING

Bacon, Edmund N. *Design of Cities*. New York: Viking, 1967.

Bourne, Larry S., ed. *Internal Structure of the City*. New York: Oxford University Press, 1971.

Hawkes, Jacquetta, ed. *Atlas of Ancient Archaeology*. New York: McGraw-Hill, 1974.

Lévi-Strauss, C. *Structural Anthropology*. Garden City, N.Y.: Doubleday, 1967.

Meyerson, Martin. "National Character and Urban Development." *Public Policy* 12 (1963): 78-96.

Moore and Reginald G. Golledge. Stroudsburg, Pa.: Dowden, Hutchinson & Ross, 1976. Pp. 220-234.

————. *Human Aspects of Urban Form*. Oxford: Pergamon, 1977.

Morris, A. E. J. *History of Urban Form*. London: Goodwin, 1972.

Rapoport, Amos. *House Form and Culture*. Englewood Cliffs, N.J.: Prentice-Hall, 1969.

————. "Environmental Cognition in Cross-Cultural Perspective." In *Environmental Knowing,* edited by Gary T.

Moore and Reginald G. Golledge. Stroudsburg, Pa., Dowden, Hutchinson, Ross, 1976, p. 220–234.

Rykwert, Joseph. *The Idea of a Town*. Princeton, N.J.: Princeton University Press, 1976.

Sjoberg, Gideon. *The Preindustrial City*. Glencoe, III.: Free Press, 1960.

Venturi, Robert; Brown, Denise Scott; and Izenour, Steven. *Learning from Las Vegas: The Forgotten Symbolism of Architectural Form*. Cambridge, Mass.: M.I.T., 1977.

Weber, Max. *The City*. Translated and edited by D. Martindale and G. Neuwirth. Glencoe, III.: Free Press, 1958.

CHAPTER 3

Urban Design

Robert M. Beckley

Urban design is a bridge between the professions of urban planning and architecture. The primary concern of urban design has been with the physical form of the city. For most of recorded history, architecture and urban planning have shared a concern with the overall design of human settlements and the quality of the physical environment. In the twentieth century urban design has focused on the form of urban settlements and the cultural processes which affect those forms. The following discussion of urban design is organized in four parts: historic contributions to urban design, the elements of urban design, urban design and physical planning concerns, and mechanisms for implementing urban design.

HISTORIC CONTRIBUTIONS TO URBAN DESIGN

There is no single definition for urban design. Each age and culture has produced its own definition based on its own expectations and possibilities. Urban design is a phenomenon closely associated with both architecture and planning; it may manifest itself in the facade of a building, design of a street, or a plan for an entire town or region. Simply put, urban design is concerned with the *form of urbanized areas*. To gain a better understanding of urban design, we will begin by looking at its cultural context, its ideological principles, and some recent concerns of urban designers.

The Cultural Context of Urban Design

It is possible to put urban design in two categories; *self-conscious* and *un-self-conscious*. Self-conscious urban design is created by people who think of themselves as designers. Their interest is in using their design skills to create a pleasing urban setting. Un-self-conscious urban design is created by people who do not think of themselves as designers, but who do affect the form of the urban environment. A self-conscious design is usually based upon a set of clearly stated design ideas or principles; un-self-conscious design is based upon intuitions that are not clearly stated. Michelangelo's design for the Piazza di Campidoglio in Rome, in the sixteenth cen-

Self-conscious design: Piazza di Campidoglio, Rome, by Michelangelo.

tury, was carefully conceived, very self-consciously,
by a master of aesthetic principles. It remains one of
the finest squares in the world. An equally fine
square exists on the Greek island of Santorini, in
front of St. George's Church in the small town of Oia.
The people of Oia built this square using building
techniques and a respect for form that had been
passed down for generations. In the field of urban
design there have been major contributions made
by both self-conscious and un-self-conscious designers.

Un-self-conscious design: St. George's
Church, Oia, Greece.

For the architect, the simple act of locating a
building in an urban setting is an act of urban
design, because the new building transforms the
character of the environment. Because the architect
usually works within a specific formal context, a
choice is possible. The choice lies between accepting the existing context or making a statement that
alters it. This is perhaps the most important urban
design decision to be made. Other important decisions concern the program or purpose of a building
and its size. These decisions are often made by

URBAN DESIGN

someone other than the architect. The architect is in an ideal position, however, to note the aesthetic impact of those decisions on the form of the city.

The decisions of the planner also affect urban design. The location of roads, services (infrastructure), and activities is part of urban form. The urban planner's ability to control urban form is tempered by the regulatory power of government and by public and private attitudes towards development. In a society as complex as ours, hundreds of decisions made every day shape the design of the city. Because of the complexity of decision making that affects urban form there has been a growing interest among both planners and architects in the process that leads to changes in urban form. No one individual has enough authority, even in autocratic societies, to control the form of the urban environment. An understanding of cultural determinants that influence urban form is essential for the person who hopes to affect urban form in a positive manner.

Urban form and people's reaction to it are interactive. Reaction to the urbanized environment occurs at two levels: the *physical* and the *psychological* or *emotional*. The physical impact on human beings is fairly obvious. The physical form of a city determines how far away one lives from school, work, play, and friends. It determines the kind of recreational opportunities one has: parks, beaches, playgrounds. It affects the kind of dwelling one lives in, the amount of noise one is subjected to, and the amount of time it takes to go shopping. Psychological impact is less easily determined, although a great amount of research is currently being conducted on this topic.[1] We do know, for example, that excessive noise can cause anxiety as well as hearing impairment. We know that the appearance of the environment can affect one's sense of pride. We know also that the visual form of some cities makes them easier to understand— it is easier to create a mental map of certain cities.

The psychological needs the city fulfills are important. Civilizations throughout time have been sensitive to these psychological needs. As an illustration we can look at ancient settlements, which were often designed to give symbolic meaning to human existence. This was often achieved by the location of settlements at holy places or the incorporation of sacred forms in the layout of the town itself. The earliest urban designers were the wise men or religious leaders, the augurs, shamans, and priests who set forth the layout and boundaries of a settlement. Perhaps the high point of symbolic concerns was reached in Rome from 1586 to 1691, when a succession of popes, beginning with Sixtus V, glorifed the city as the center of Christianity. This was achieved through a design that linked streets, squares, and buildings so that all the major religious buildings of Rome were spatially and visually connected. The design was further enhanced by adding fountains and monuments to the squares. It has been seen that important buildings usually are placed in the most central, convenient, or strategic places. Houses were torn down to make room for the cathedral in the center of the medieval town. Similar decisions have affected the location of castles, palaces, monuments, statehouses, city halls, religious buildings, and even dwellings.

Just as urban design can give meaning and significance to urban life, so too is urban design a product of social influences. The ancient towns of Greece took both their form and size from a pattern based on a lifestyle made possible by a temperate climate. The agora in the center of the city served as a communal meeting place—a place for the exchange of goods and ideas. The size of the Greek city-state was limited to allow a democratic communication. New colonies were established as necessary to relieve the parent city of excess population. The medieval town took its form from the need for protection in a world where danger was ever present outside the walls. In Europe and the United States the eighteenth and nineteenth centuries saw the growth of a middle class and land speculation that satisfied the demands of this class for better housing. Such speculation continues today. Thus, the design of a city is very much a product of social and political forces. If the urban designer is to understand the form of the city, he or she must understand the social and political forces that act upon it.

Technology has played a part in determining urban form. The engineering feats of the ancient Romans had an astonishing effect on their ability to build cities and to govern large areas. Their ability to construct roads made it possible to establish regional communication networks and move armies and materials efficiently. The aqueduct made possible settlement in locations where there were no springs, and the size of a city was no longer determined by the local water supply. The decline of Rome's engineering skills in the Dark Ages meant a radical change in the nature of cities that lasted for many centuries. Many of those technological skills were not regained until the nineteenth century. The industrial revolution not only encouraged the in-migration of people to the city, it also made possible a new form of city. Massive engineering projects, railroads, subways, sewers, new forms of construction, and undreamed-of physical capabilities gave cities seemingly unlimited opportunities for growth. During the nineteenth century, London grew from 1,000,000 to 7,000,000 and Paris from 700,000 to 3,000,000. It was at this same time that the United States and other industrializing nations began to change from predominantly agrarian to predominantly urban nations.

Of all the inventions of the industrial revolution there is nothing to compare with the impact which the internal combustion engine and the introduction of the automobile has had on the very nature of the city. The form of the modern city has been largely shaped in this machine. Other technologies have also had their impacts. Camillo Sitte, as long ago as 1889, saw that new technologies were making profound changes in lifestyle and form of the modern city. People no longer needed to go to the public fountain to draw their water; they simply had to turn on a faucet. The news of the day was delivered to the door in a newspaper, rather than spread through the streets by word of mouth.[2] The cities of today are still feeling the impact of the industrial revolution.

The technological development that is most likely to next have an enormous impact on urban development is our high energy use, a byproduct of the industrial revolution. Will the city of the future shrink in size in response to dwindling energy supplies? Will it become more dense, or be dispersed into smaller, more efficient centers? Will other forms of transit replace the automobile or will new forms of energy transform the automobile into a new type of vehicle? Will the height of buildings be controlled to afford everyone equal access to the sun's energy? While we cannot answer each of these questions directly, knowing something about our past makes it easy to predict that the city of the future will be different from the city of the present.

The Ideology of Urban Design
Since the form of the city has been so closely associated with symbolic elements and has reflected the very nature of society, it should be expected that concern with the form of the city has been a preoccupation of individuals who see the city as a manifestation of certain ideological principles. The ideology of urban design usually takes one of three forms: (1) a concern with the aesthetic order of the city; (2) a concern with an idealized social environment; or, most frequently, (3) an idealized social environment which is expressed through a physical ideal. The rapid technological and social changes of the 1960s and 1970s, which have suggested radically different futures, have recently touched off renewed interest in the conceptualization of ideal environments, especially in Europe and Great Britain.

Proposals for ideal cities based on aesthetic principles can be found around the world.[3] Of those cities designed on the basis of aesthetic principles, few surpass the proposals made during the Renaissance. These ranged from geometric fortified towns to urban environments designed using the aesthetic discipline of perspective.

In contrast to the ideal city based on pragmatic design principles, most of the cities proposed to support an idealized social environment were uto-

An ideal city plan, 1615, by Vincenzo Scamozzi.

pian; i.e., they most frequently sought a social ideal that was impracticable. An interesting exception to this rule was Ebenezer Howard's proposal for a *garden city*. Howard's proposal was in response to the rapidly deteriorating urban environments of the late nineteenth century which, he felt, had grown to a monstrous size. He proposed the creation of new cities with a population limited to 32,000 people, where the social life of the city could be reduced to more human dimensions. The new cities would be grouped around a major central city, whose growth could be controlled by the development of the satellite garden cities.[4] That concept was to become the basis for the construction of many new towns in England and other parts of the world during the first half of the twentieth century. Various proposals for ideal cities have been made since, postulating different forms of social organization. Even the famous proposals of Le Corbusier for an idealized urban environment, the *Radiant City,* and those of Frank Lloyd Wright for an idealized suburban or agrarian city, *Broadacre City,* were based on significant social concepts of urban life.[5]

Le Corbusier envisioned a cosmopolitan environment of urbanites who would sublimate personal desires for the pleasure of the city, and Wright saw a city which would impinge as little as possible on individual freedom and land ownership.

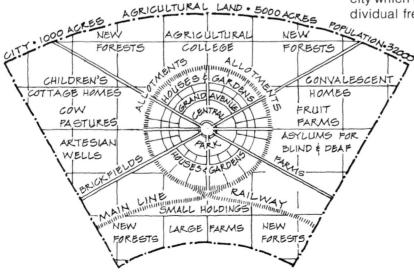

Garden City, 1902, by Ebenezer Howard.

The Corbusier and Wright proposals fall into the third category of ideal cities, those that combine a social and physical ideal. Unlike Howard, who was careful to only draw diagrams of his idealized concept of a city, Corbusier and Wright were quick to draw pictorial illustrations of the appearance of their concepts for a new city based on their interpretation of social issues of the time.

There is a traditional belief that the physical environment can have a positive impact on the social environment of the city—that the way to an ideal social environment in the city is through the creation of an appropriate physical environment. Rapoport has identified three attitudes (borrowed from geographers) towards the effect of the physical environment on people. They are: (a) *environmental determinism*—the view that the physical environment does determine human behavior; (b) *environmental possibilism*—the notion that the psysical environment may provide opportunities for and constraints on human behavior, which is determined by other, mostly cultural, factors; and (c) *environmental probabilism*—the notion that the physical environment provides different choices for human behavior and some choices are more likely to occur than others. Presently, the third notion seems to be the most popular. There is a growing body of empirical research demonstrating that certain kinds of behavior are more likely to occur in some settings than in others, but that a particular design will not guarantee that a specific behavior will occur.

This information on the relationship between the physical environment and human behavior is very important to urban design. This knowledge will not tell architects, urban designers, and planners what to do. However, it will help identify design situations that should be avoided because of certain probable effects on human behavior. It helps predict what designers can expect their designs to encourage or discourage.

If we imagine the design of a courtyard adjacent to a residence, we can illustrate the different kinds of roles design might play in affecting behavior. If our courtyard were surrounded by an 8-foot-high fence, people in the courtyard could not see out, and people outside could not see in. If we reduced the height of the wall to 4 feet, then people could easily look in or out. This is *determinism*. The designer has affected the visual contact between people inside and outside through a decision about the height of the wall. We might further imagine that the courtyard has been built in a neighborhood where there are no other courtyards, where the traditional house simply has a yard around it. Since the courtyard of this house is there it is possible that the resident will use it. The existence of the courtyard, however, is no

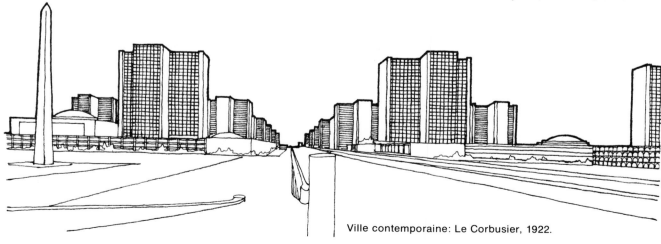

Ville contemporaine: Le Corbusier, 1922.

URBAN DESIGN

guarantee that it will be used. This is *possibilism*. The courtyard simply provides an opportunity for use. Some might use it for a garden, some for children's play, some to hang clothes to dry, some to store junk, and some might not use it at all. If we were to locate the kitchen as the only room immediately adjacent to the courtyard we might predict that if the courtyard were used at all it would most probably be for activities associated with the kitchen. Even though there is nothing that would dictate an associated use of the space with the kitchen, the relationship might suggest a use that would not have been apparent if the adjacent room were a bedroom. This is *probabilism*.

It is important to remember that each culture has its own sense of space and time, of what is appropriate and what is not appropriate. As an example, we can look at peoples in warmer climates who have adopted the concept of a mid-afternoon break as a way of avoiding the heat. As a result, the evening is used much more intensely for socializing—and the temperate evening climate is supportive of sitting outside or strolling. Christopher Alexander has shown that these types of patterns can have a strong influence on urban form. He has examined traditional South American villages to discover how he might design a new environment to support this traditional community pattern.[6] For the designer, determinism, possibilism, and probabilism are all potential responses to a design. Some are more likely than others. The designer must be careful to match his or her design ideology with the realities of human behavior.

Recent Concerns of Urban Design

At the beginning of the twentieth century there was a growing interest in the Western world with the possible impacts of the industrial revolution and other changes in society on architecture and urban design. Numerous proposals for restructuring cities grew out of this interest. A number of these proposals were extremely influential in shaping the thoughts of architects and planners concerned with urban design.

The urban design proposals of Le Corbusier and Frank Lloyd Wright represent the polar attitudes toward urbanization and urban design. Le Corbusier made many highly urbanized proposals. The most famous are his scheme for a city of 3 million inhabitants and a plan for rebuilding Paris (the *Plan Voisin*). The urban design principles he forwarded through these plans were an increase in density of the city, enlargement of the means of circulation, large parks in the city, and decongestion of the center of the city—by building larger buildings raised off the ground by *pilotis*. Frank Lloyd Wright expressed his ideas of a city with the Broadacre City proposal. As its name implies, the proposal was for a low-density development of detached buildings. He envisioned a city of small farms or garden homesteads. His scheme eliminated roads as much as possible and attempted to bring the country into the city rather than create parks.

Both of these men have had a great deal of influence on the architectural profession and the general public. In a sense, they both anticipated and influenced the two major kinds of urban form existing today in the United States: the high-density urban core and the low-density suburb. Ironically, each man excluded the opposite extreme from his proposal. While we might abhor some of the versions of these concepts which have been built, we must admire their brilliance in forecasting future urban development.

The modern movement in architecture during the early part of this century has had a strong influence on contemporary architects, planners, and urban designers. Architects and planners in the early decades of the twentieth century were confronted with assimilating the massive technological and societal changes that so affected life at this time. People associated with the modern movement felt the need to give expression to the new opportunities they saw. Like most radical visionaries, they felt it necessary to discard the past. The planners of

A residential community based on the agrarian model: Reston, Virginia.

The agrarian model with compromise: a typical suburban development.

Le Corbusier's concept of high-density development in a park-like environment: Roehampton Housing Estate, London.

this era proposed sweeping changes in the urban landscape. In hastily pursuing a new structure for urban areas, based upon the oppurtunities afforded by the automobile, new construction technologies, and an unprecedented need for new buildings, they forgot many of the virtues of older forms of urban development. The street was abandoned for the freeway, and the mixture of activities found in older neighborhoods was abandoned for the segregation of activities of the suburbs. During the forties, fifties, and sixties these ideas moved from theory to reality. It was not long, however, before critics called attention to the destructive nature of some of the new concepts.

Beginning at midcentury, there developed an interest in more closely evaluating the character and merits of a newly developing urban scene. Kevin Lynch's *Image of the City* and *The View from the Road* were influential in altering designers' perceptions of urban form. Lynch's early research explored the concept of *image*, the interaction between physical form and people's perception of that form.[7] He was interested in those aspects of the visual character of a city that influence mental perception of the environment. He identified the major image-creating elements of the city as *paths, edges, nodes, districts,* and *landmarks*. That research led him and others to explore how cities might be restructured based upon the idea that people should have a better visual understanding of their environment.[8] He proposed using the expressway as a device for organizing visual elements in a way reminiscent of the technique employed by Pope Sixtus V in baroque Rome, that is, visually connecting major important elements of the city. While Lynch was not reacting directly to the work of the modernists, he firmly established the concept that the elements of the city that already existed should be accepted, and he saw the designer as being responsible for relating all elements of the city in a coherent manner.

Other influential design research was conducted by Robert Venturi and a group of associates. They analyzed the *Strip* in Las Vegas—the highway with widely separated buildings, parking lots, and blinking signs. Their major object was to study the form of strip development and the symbolism its developers used to create an evocative environment.[9] This research became controversial, because strip development was not generally recognized as having any positive aesthetic qualities. Venturi and his associates concluded that the strip environment has many of the design qualities so often admired in historic architecture and urban design—changes in scale, symbolism, ambiguity, and decorative embellishments that have meaning. At the same time the strip accommodates functional relationships in a very direct way. As a result of this and other recent explorations, designers have been reconsidering the preconceptions about architectural form and symbolism taught by the followers of the modern movement. This newer research is proving that much can be learned from existing environments in our own society, even those environments that appear to be un-self-conscious.

Another current point of view is represented by those who see urban design as an integral part of the economic and social process. They have suggested that the way to positively affect the form of the urban environment is through the political process itself. People espousing this point of view fall into two camps: those who accept the existing economic and social process but want to make it work better, and those who feel improvement in urban design will be achieved only through economic and social change.

Those accepting the current condition, in North America, Western Europe, and other industrialized areas, propose the use of local government as a means of shaping urban development through regulation; the careful use of public funds for urban improvements; and the establishment of a working relationship with private interests to assure an environment that will benefit everyone.[10] Others feel that the urban designer lacks the power to effect change in a way that will benefit the majority of people.

Judging from past experience, they suggest that those who are likely to be most affected by change in urban structure are those who can least afford change, the poor and the disenfranchised. These planners feel more attention must be given to the needs of the indigenous population and that the ills of society stem from design that is carried out from the top down.[11]

In summary it might be said that current issues in urban design tend to focus on the relation between self-conscious and un-self-conscious design. What role is the urban designer to play in society? What can be learned from indigenous urban design? What part do the nondesigner and the user of the city have in determining urban form? The opportunities for shaping urban development in the future are great. As the world's population continues to become less agrarian, new urban development is occurring throughout the world. Old cities are trying desperately to survive in a new age. There is a great deal of dissatisfaction with the design of cities today. There will obviously be roles for both self-conscious design and un-self-conscious design, and there will be a number of diverse ways in which the person trained to be sensitive to issues of urban design can assist in making the urban environment a more humane place. The urban designer's role might be as an architect carefully shaping buildings to the urban context. The designer's role might be as a planner, being concerned with the design implications of the municipal budget, or attempting to regulate private development in such a way as to provide benefits to a larger public. Or, the urban designer might be a person working with a neighborhood group, helping to preserve and enhance a unique lifestyle.

THE ELEMENTS OF URBAN DESIGN

The urban environment is made up of a number of elements. The process of manipulating those various elements constitutes a major part of the designer's concern. To a large extent the designer's success will depend upon how well he or she is able to handle all these separate but related elements.

The Space between and around Buildings

While a skilled designer considers the design of interior and exterior space to be related, urban design is usually thought of in terms of the design of space outside a building. The urban designer's responsibility is to give that space a positive relationship to the adjacent buildings and to relate that space to the larger urban pattern. Exterior space can be manipulated in much the same way as interior space.

Positive and Negative Form. The placement of a building in the environment immediately sets up a relationship with the space around it. The addition of other buildings makes the spatial relations more complex. One of the most complex environments thus made was Rome. The sense of that environment was captured by Nolli in a map that shows both the major interior spaces and the exterior spaces between buildings. His map clearly indicates the relationship between interior and exterior spaces; between the negative space, which has not been filled, and the positive space, which has been filled. Venturi, in a similar analysis of Las Vegas, has demonstrated that this concept can also be applied to environments that are less built-up than Rome. It is a useful device that ties together all space, exterior and interior, positive and negative, into one related whole. It suggests architecture's potential for creating exterior as well as interior space.

Townscape and Human Awareness. The term *townscape* was used by Gordon Cullen in his book of the same name.[12] Cullen's major concern was describing the physical appearance of urban space. He was interested in identifying those elements and combinations of elements that give particular aes-

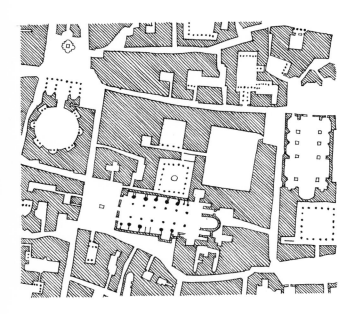

Drawing of Rome, based on the Nolli technique.

thetic satisfaction. Much of that which gives aesthetic satisfaction is closely tied to the context of the environment. Aesthetic satisfaction today is often ruled by fashion and, therefore, it is difficult to define any rules of thumb that might be broadly used for any culture at any time.

Cullen's analysis of urban quality was made with the educated eye of a painter. His analysis, however, supports research that indicates there are several factors that remain fairly constant, regardless of context or cultural variations, in aesthetic concern. Those factors are human *perception, anthropometrics* (measurements), and *stimuli.*

Visual perception is a function of the eye, which receives messages, and the brain, which translates those messages into an image. There are different cultural meanings given to different images. Nevertheless, the perception of space is physically experienced in much the same way by everyone having the gift of sight. For example, there is a useful set of ratios based on the eye's cone of vision that can be used to determine the amount of visual enclosure that might be achieved given different ratios of height of wall to width of floor plane. At a ratio of 1:4 (height:width), enclosure is barely perceived. At a ratio of 1:3, the feeling of enclosure is stronger, but a sense of an outdoor room has not yet been created. A ratio of 1:2 produces a definite visual enclosure, and a 1:1 ratio produces a very strong visual enclosure. These ratios describe what a person actually sees, but a person's sense of enclosure may vary depending upon his or her cultural background. Color and hue are also elements that affect visual sensation. Light surfaces and bright colors tend to advance, to appear closer to the viewer, while dark surfaces and muted colors tend to recede. As Cullen has also suggested, texture contributes to a sense of depth. Obviously, just by using these simple visual phenomena, one can do much to manipulate the quality of a space.

Anthropometrics play an obvious role in our sense of the city. The height of stairs, walls, benches, and so on all directly affect our relationship to the environment. Some useful dimensions to remember are the height of walls. A wall between 12 inches and 24 inches is easy to sit upon; one lower or higher makes sitting awkward. A wall 36 inches high is comfortable to lean upon, and a person of average height can look over it. Each of these height relationships, whether used in conjunction with a staircase, wall, ledge, fence, railing, table, or other element, establishes a very clear response from a user.

Our senses also give us stimuli, or responsive clues. The type of materials used within a space can amplify or absorb sound. Concrete reflects sound, while grass and plantings absorb sound. Smooth surfaces are easier to walk upon than rough surfaces. Thus, rough textures are often used in lieu of "keep-out" signs to discourage or direct people away from a particular area. Concrete and stone reach ambient temperatures very quickly, and thus are cold or warm depending upon the surrounding temperature, whereas wood maintains a more even temperature. The list of considerations goes on, but the point

A strong sense of enclosure: Piazza dei Signori, Verona, Italy.

should be clear. Our response to the environment can be quite predictable if we consider the basic capabilities and limitations of human beings. These factors should be kept in mind for effective urban design.

Physical Determinants of Urban Form

Orthogonal and Organic Form. As mentioned in Chapter 1, the introduction of orthogonal, or right-angled, planning is most often attributed to the Greek architect Hippodamus, who in the fifth century B.C. proposed that Greek cities be laid out in a grid system so that they might grow in an orderly fashion. The Romans institutionalized the grid system in their *castras,* or fortified towns, planted throughout the Roman Empire. Many European cities with grid systems today can trace their origins back to the Roman Empire. The grid system can be found in nearly all cultures. It is a fairly universal mechanism for ordering space. Some would say it is a very boring way of ordering space if overdone. The United States is an extreme example of orthogonal planning, for in 1785

Congress passed a land ordinance decreeing that all the land in the country be divided into townships of 6 square miles. The United States is thus divided into a giant grid, which is echoed by our system of roads.

Organic form is a large category used to try to describe everything not orthogonal. Just as orthogonal planning is a very apparently self-conscious means of dividing space, organic planning is most often thought of as less planned or less self-conscious. A better description of organic planning might be that it responds to other than geometrically preconceived notions of form. Thus, un-self-conscious designs tend not to be orthogonal, because the designer is responding to other forces. Usually, organic plans have developed over time without any grand plan or notion of reaching a completed state.[13]

The difference between orthogonal and non-orthogonal planning is clearly illustrated by the development of Manhattan Island. The southernmost tip of the island was originally called New Amsterdam—settled by the Dutch, it took its form from the paths already laid out by the Indians and from the peculiarities of the landscape. The rest of the island,

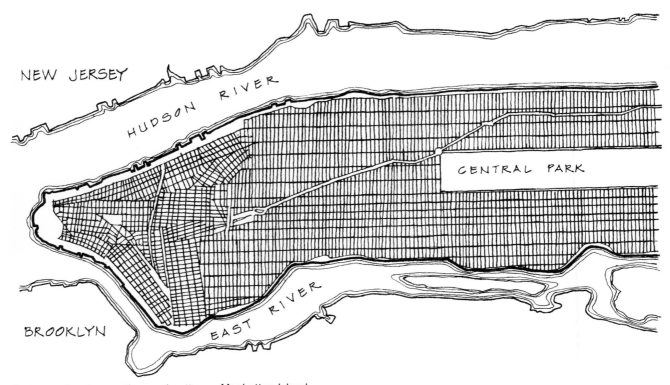

Orthogonal and nonorthogonal patterns: Manhattan Island.

laid out in a grid, is the result of a decision in 1811 to subdivide the land into easily marketed pieces of real estate.

Geometric and Axial Organizing Devices.
Another ordering device traditionally used to organize the relationships of building to each other and the space around them is the principle of *axiality* and *symmetry*. This is frequently used when new buildings are added to an existing complex. Axiality, the relationship of the center lines of buildings' masses to each other, was used by the Romans in developing the Roman Forum over several hundred years. The axial relationships between the disparate buildings of the Forum give it order. Michelangelo used axiality in the construction of the Campidoglio. This area contained various buildings

with no real relationship to each other. Michelangelo was able to bring order to the space through the establishment of a strong line that served as the organizing axis. Bernini used these same organizing concepts in his plan for St. Peter's Square.

Kinetic and Sequential Organizing Devices.
The procession was an important consideration in early urban design. The movement through space, the *kinetic* or active involvement of a viewer in a progression of visual experiences, was used expertly by the Greeks in organizing the approach to the Acropolis. A similar sensitivity was shown by the Kevin Lynch team, which considered the kinetic experience possible in the design of a highway. There are certain visual elements essential for giving a sense of moving through space. The most important

Geometric and axial organization: St. Peter's Square, Rome.

elements are *change* and *modulation*. If we were to imagine an environment composed only of two parallel walls between which one would walk, we would realize the walls give no sense of movement. If the walls move in and out, i.e., if the dimensions between the walls change, we gain a sense of progression through space. If we add a series of regular divisions along the space, we find that these help us measure our movement, much as the dotted stripe along the highway gives us a sense of movement. For the urban designer, a pictorial device that helps organize space kinetically is a technique that views the environment as a series of zones: foreground, middleground, and background. A person experiencing this environment kinetically moves from the foreground into the middleground, and the middleground becomes the foreground, the background becomes the middleground, and a new background comes into view.

Transport Networks. Movement systems have always been a primary factor in determining urban form. Since movement systems, or rights-of-way, are usually public, they not only create the channels along which different kinds of traffic flow, but they also serve to distinguish between that space which is *public* and that which is *private*. Urban transportation systems, whether for vehicles or people, usually fall into one of two geometric forms: a *net* or a *tree*. The distinctions between these two are significant. A network may be cut along any one line, yet the system is not bisected. If a tree geometry is cut along any one line, the system is broken into two unconnected fragments.

The tree system of organization became especially popular with urban designers after Clarence Stein and Henry Wright, two pioneers of urban design in the United States at the beginning of the century, developed a *cul de sac* plan for Radburn, N.J. This plan organized automobile traffic and pedestrian paths as separate systems, the dwelling units linking the two. This form of layout has become quite popular and can be very appropriate for small-scale development. It has been argued, however, that when such a hierarchical tree system is used to plan a very large area, such as a new town, it creates a static environment in which growth and connections are fixed rather than fluid.

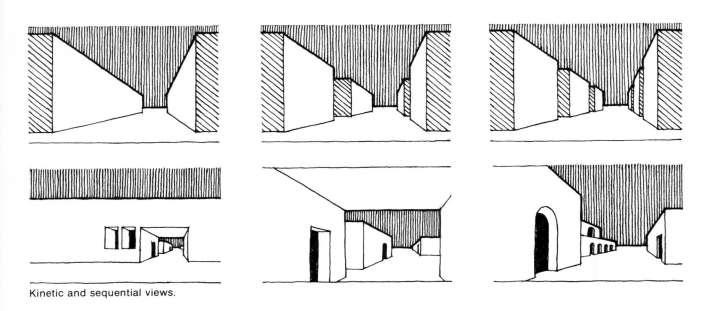

Kinetic and sequential views.

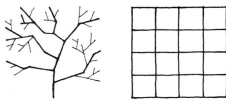

Tree and network pattern transportation systems.

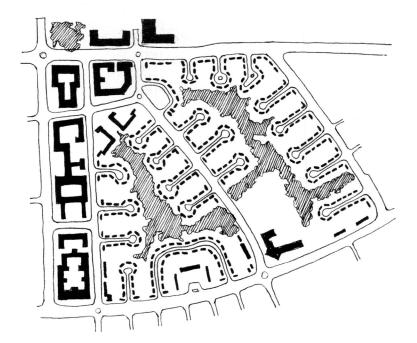

Separation of pedestrians and vehicles: Radburn, New Jersey.

INTRODUCTION TO URBAN PLANNING

Many of the early twentieth-century new towns were organized around a tree geometry. More recent planning has tended to consider the interactive and behavioral attributes of movement systems. Jane Jacobs, an outspoken critic of contemporary planning, has pointed out that streets are much more than transportation systems; they are active areas that support a diverse array of activities including play, lounging, visiting, and so on, activities she feels are just as important to a city as moving from one spot to another.[14]

Communication and Service Networks. Modern technology has introduced other forms of communication besides physical contact. The electronic network—telephone, radio, television, etc.—has become an important and accepted method of linkage between people in urban areas. While many predicted that electronic media would reduce the need for transportation, there seems to be no evidence that it has. One might argue that it has increased the opportunities for personal contact, since meetings between individuals can now be more easily arranged. Also, communication is having a profound effect on tying parts of the globe together and creating new cultural norms. The creation of huge megalopolitan areas has been abetted by communication and this is likely to have an effect on new forms of urban development.

Our expectations have been raised to the point that we now associate cities with a certain level of convenience. Much of this convenience is provided by modern engineering techniques, which service the city through technological systems providing water, sewerage, gas, electricity, telephone, cable TV, and sometimes heat. These networks are increasingly important to urbanization and their presence greatly affects the density of development. Their costs also represent a major consideration in designing the geometry of new settlements. Once a certain service system is established, it is extremely expensive to change it. Most service systems are buried under the street or public rights-of-way to allow easy access to the utilities for periodic maintenance or new connections. The rising costs of these services and the increasing difficulties in finding adequate water and energy supplies and nonpolluting sewerage treatment may have a dramatic effect on future development.

Macro Urban Form. The overall form of the city is shaped by many factors, but chief among them is still transportation. The location of most major cities is determined by access to transportation. Historically the best location has been on a lake, river, ocean, or sea, which give access to other regions. Many of the early urban settlements in the United States were founded upon sites that had been established by the Indians as part of a regional transportation system. The railroad extended urbanization out, away from these first urban centers, and new centers grew up around the depots needed to service the railroad. Until the turn of this century, major cities remained compact and dense, because most people needed to live close to work. The development of the subway and the streetcar opened up vast new areas for development adjacent to the central city, and the growth of the suburbs began. This suburban pattern of growth in the United States has been reinforced by increasing reliance on the automobile and improved highways, which make possible commuting distances to work many times what they were less than a century ago. The pattern is being repeated in other countries that have gained or surpassed the economic affluence of the United States and where automobile ownership has become commonplace. It remains to be seen how much the energy crisis will affect this pattern. To illustrate how important the automobile is to our way of life, U.S. Department of Agriculture figures show that in 1977 the average family began to pay more for the ownership and operation of automobiles than for food.

Public Space and Private Development

The urban designer frequently works with the interface between private space and public space. The importance of that interface is pointed out in Oscar Newman's research on crime and vandalism. His

Vestiges of a medieval square in Florence, Italy.

research has indicated that the clarity of distinction between private and public space can contribute to the security of urban spaces.[15] To a certain extent, the task of urban designers is to be concerned with those areas greater than the scope of a single building complex, yet smaller than an entire metropolitan complex—wedding that which is public and that which is private.

Purpose of Public Space. Each culture has produced its own version of a primary public space. The Greek agora and the Roman fora served both commercial and public interests and were the centers of business and politics. The square of the medieval period served as the marketplace, and the church square (parvis) was used for religious gatherings and the exchange of goods. In some cities the square was little more than a wider part of the street, while in others the square was developed as a separate, lateral extension of the street. Often a square developed at the town gate where the roads out of the city came together. In planned towns, the square frequently was placed at the center of the town, where roads converged. The Renaissance basically refined the medieval square. Monuments and foun-

tains were added, and in some instances (e.g., the Campidoglio in Rome), buildings around the square were actually altered to create a more pleasing exterior space. During the baroque period the civic square became very important and was used as a device to commemorate people and events, through statues, arches, columns, and such. The opportunity to link squares and roadways into larger regional networks was taken. The baroque period also saw the creation of a new kind of square. The residential square was carved out of the existing fabric of the city to bring light, fresh air, and solitude to certain areas and make them more attractive places to live.

Many of these traditional concepts of the use of open space were transferred to the United States. There are few towns that do not have some kind of civic square. More recent commercial ventures have even admitted the value of such squares. Rockefeller Center in New York City boasts a magnificent public space, which is used for different activities at different times of the year. In the 1950s plazas sprang up in front of every new high-rise office building to accentuate the building's importance—with mixed results.

Form and Location of Public Space. History has shown us that the most successful public spaces are those that are an intrinsic part of the life of the city. Many European squares go through a daily metamorphosis, starting in the early morning as a market, being transformed later in the day to a parking lot, and ending at night as an outside dining room. Unfortunately, contemporary urban designers often lose sight of the fact that a public square must be an integral part of the urban fabric in order to succeed. The square also should be linked to the street system, for its success further depends on its accessibility. Finally, the square must develop the qualities of a space—it must be three-dimensional, with a sense of enclosure.

Public Building and Urban Space. It is impossible to deny the symbolic function of open space. This function has been realized from ancient times. To be effective, open space within an urban context must maintain its uniqueness. The importance of open space in a built-up environment is that it is the exception rather than the rule. If every designer puts a plaza in front of an office building, plazas soon lose their significance as special places. The relationship of open space to significant buildings is symbolic as well as functional.

There are two primary ways of relating open space to significant buildings. The first is to design a public space in front of the building, allowing a view of the structure and showing it off. The second treatment is to actually set the building in the middle of an open space. Boston City Hall and the many county courthouses that sit in public squares are good examples.

Influence of Public Space on Urban Form. An astonishing amount of the urban fabric is made up of public space. Rights-of-way—that is, land devoted to streets and other forms of public movement, such as sidewalks—constitute from 30 to 50 percent of the total land area in most cities. Even on Manhattan Island, one of the most densely built areas in the world, streets and sidewalks account for

44 percent of the total land area. The geometry of public space is a major determinant of urban form. It is not surprising, then, that the manipulation of the public space network is a major concern of urban designers. The conscious effort to manipulate streets to affect urban form took hold in the baroque period. More recently, urban designers have made the street a major focus of design inquiry.

Most of North America, as well as other parts of the world, is confronted with an established pattern of right-of-way, usually a grid. Within the grid, however, it usually is possible to achieve many variations in form. Various experiments have been carried out to change the basic configuration of the grid to achieve better circulation patterns and break the larger urban fabric into manageable areas. One such experiment is to close certain streets at mid-block to eliminate through traffic and create new open space for play areas, sitting, and parking. Other experimenters have narrowed the street area at ends of blocks to create a strong feeling of separation between one block and another and to shorten the distance for a pedestrian crossing the street. Still others are investigating the placement of diverters at the intersection of a grid to change the basic geometry. Many of the innovations likely to occur in urban design in the future will be concerned with new uses for existing open space within urban areas.

Architectural Relationships to the Public Right-of-Way. A major design issue in both architecture and urban design is the relationship of the building to the street. This relationship determines not only the character of the building but also the character of the urban fabric. The medieval town with its irregular streets and buildings jutting out into or even spanning the street serves as an example of the nearly complete integration of building and right-of-way. At times in these environments it is impossible to tell whether one is inside or outside a building, as street and building merge. Many cultures clearly define the street by using a wall backed by a courtyard, a private open space that must be traversed before arriving at the door. In nearly every

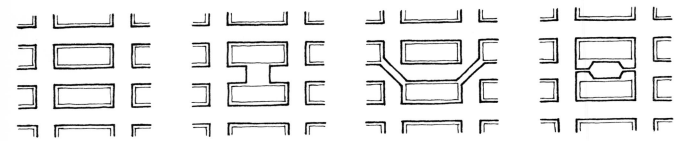

Possible modifications of a grid street system.

culture, there is some attempt to achieve a transition between the street and private realm of the building, either through a space, an articulated doorway, a sidewalk, or some other design device that ties building and street together. The extreme opposite of the medieval town is the U.S. suburb, with each house discreetly set back from the street by a front yard. In this case the front yard serves as the transitional device. In either instance, both the architecture and the urban setting are affected by that relationship.

More recent architectural responses to urban design issues are generating some interesting new patterns in central areas of the city. The more traditional break between street and building is being dissolved. Examples of such breaks might be traced back to ancient times and the Greek and Roman *stoa,* which acted like a covered street. The covered arcade, such as the Galeria in Milan, Italy, brought the street inside a building. The more contemporary versions of this phenomenon include buildings such as John Portman's atrium hotels and Philip Johnson's IDS Building in Minneapolis, a direct extension of a pedestrian street called Nicollet Mall.

The IDS Building serves as a link to another urban design device—the overhead walkway system. There are few major cities in the United States that do not have at least one example of buildings connected by a bridge across a street. In Minneapolis a whole array of buildings is connected at the second story with enclosed walkways. This pedestrian street system combines both private circulation spaces within buildings and public circulation spaces between buildings, a true wedding of architecture and new forms of rights-of-way. Proposals for midtown Manhattan have suggested that such a network might be constructed 40 or 50 stories above the street, alleviating the congestion of the street and making it possible for people to move horizontally within a highly developed area of the city without having to move to ground level.

Recent concern with *megastructures,* very large buildings that incorporate urban infrastructure, hark back to the desire to integrate totally the street and building. Le Corbusier proposed such a megastructure in his Marseilles Block, which contained a street with shops halfway up the height of the building. His idea was picked up by others and used extensively, but not always successfully, in Europe. Rockefeller Center in New York City, a megastructure that is perceived as a group of separate buildings, has perhaps one of the most elaborate and successful underground pedestrian street systems ever constructed as part of a building. Other cities are emulating the concept of the underground pedestrian street network. Montreal contains one of the more successful examples, where not only buildings but also the subway transit system are connected by a completely sheltered system of walks.

Contribution of Private Development to Urban Design. The previous examples are illustrative of an interactive relationship between private development and urban design and between pri-

The inside street: the Galeria in Milan, Italy (courtesy of Kingsbury Marzolf).

vate building and public rights-of-way. After we subtract the 30 to 50 percent of the land that is public and makes up the infrastructure of the city, we have left 70 to 50 percent of the land where individual decisions will largely determine the form of the urban environment. There are generally three constraints on the use of that land. The first consists

of any controls that might be legislated to limit its usage. The second is the social, economic, and cultural context, which affects the use of that space through the complex systems adopted by society. The third comes from the particular desires and needs of the person owning the property. Trade-offs frequently must be made between public and

Hyatt Regency Hotel, San Francisco, by John Portman.

private interests. Such trade-offs are most easily made when everyone is in agreement about a common good.

During the building of the great cathedrals of Europe, as we have noted, private land and dwellings were acquired to make space for the construction of the cathedral in the center of the city. Everyone appreciated the fact that the most symbolically appropriate place for the cathedral was the center of the city, and the building of the cathedral was a community endeavor. Today there is less agreement on common public goals, and the acquisition of private land for public purpose has become an extremely sensitive activity, as has the regulation of private development. A disadvantage, perhaps, of contemporary society is that we have few cultural traditions. Distinctions between major urbanized areas developed today have more to do with climate, economics, and building capability than with local cultural phenomena.

Symptomatic of the problem is the corporate office building, which some have called "the cathedral of the twentieth century," because of its striking appearance in the urban landscape. The office tower is a phenomenon now found around the world,

even in developing countries. In many areas it is still a symbol of progress or change. Office towers and other high-rise structures have literally changed the landscape of the city. Areas such as San Francisco's business district have been transformed. In the case of San Francisco, the change in the skyline has totally obliterated the city's natural topography. The skyline no longer gives one a reading of where the hills and valleys of San Francisco lay. Old landmarks, such as Coite Tower, which marked a prominent hill, have been replaced by new corporate landmarks, not necessarily appropriate to the total city pattern. Consequently, a preoccupation of urban design today is the creation of mechanisms that can encourage or force private development to build in a manner that will complement rather than destroy the existing urban fabric.

URBAN DESIGN AND PHYSICAL PLANNING CONCERNS

Urban design, like any other applied design, is primarily concerned with solving problems. Urban

The San Francisco skyline.

design brings into focus problems of aesthetics in an urban context. Urban design is also concerned directly with problems of the quality of urban life and the way the city functions.

Urban Amenity

The functional problems of the city, the way the city works, and the form of the city are all related. The design of these relationships can bring greater satisfaction to the users of the city and make the city a nicer place to be. Certainly parts of many cities today are wretched places to live, yet the city still seems to function and support the residents in their grim existence. We know, however, that cities can be pleasant places and provide unique opportunities, sights, smells, sounds, and delights.

Definition of Urban Amenity.

Every culture has its own definition of urban amenity, because the concept is tied to the culture's ideas on the nature and function of the city. As a result, we can find no simple definition of urban amenity. The city is the product of society, and, as each society differs, so will the nature of its cities. Ideally, one might say that a city with a great deal of amenity illustrates the concept of synergism—i.e., the whole is greater than the sum of its parts.

First is the setting of the city itself. Each setting and climate has attributes that can be used to advantage. Then there are the activities of the city: business, production, government, education, and entertainment. There are also the physical elements of the city: buildings, roads, and landscape, and their arrangement and quality. These are the ingredients that can create amenity. Design, either self-conscious or un-self-conscious, is what ties these ingredients together. The public park that commands a view of the water, or a hill, valley, or plain, is itself an amenity. The business district that brings people of like interests together, conveniently with access to shopping, restaurants, services, and places to rest, is an amenity. Buildings that provide

protection from the wind and reflect sunlight into open spaces on cold days are amenities. Perhaps the reason the countemporary city is often so barren and lacking in amenity is that, as Hans Blumenfeld has suggested, people today come to the city not to live, but to make a living.[16]

Robert Venturi suggests that we live in a society where people feel uncomfortable sitting in a public square, because they feel they should be working at the office or home with the family. It is possible to design a public space that is an amenity but does respond to these quirks of self-consciousness. Venturi's design for Copley Square in Boston offered such a solution. Rather than a large public space where people would go to see and be seen, as in many European squares, the proposed solution was a series of walkways cutting through the site, with benches for people to use while "just passing through." The solution was positive and responded to the specific needs of its users.[17]

While contemporary society may have lost a sense of "publicness," it is not short of public space. As we have already pointed out, close to one-half of the city is made up of streets and sidewalks that are publicly owned. We also know that the major activities of society—business, government, education, and entertainment—and the buildings in which they are housed—offices, museums, theatres, and restaurants—are located in urbanized areas. By definition, then, the potential ingredients of urban amenity are available in every city.

Identifying Urban Amenity.

It may be easier to identify a *lack* of amenity than the existence of amenity. When things work, they feel natural—there is a good "fit" between our *expectations* and our environment. We expect to be able to see the hills of San Francisco or the bay. We expect to be able to find the shopping area, or the entertainment district, without having to ask directions. We expect the city to have a museum or library. We expect to be able to find a place to eat or drink when we come out of the theatre without having to drive or walk several miles.

We expect to be able to stand out of the wind, sun, or rain while waiting for a bus, taxi, or car. We expect to have a place to go to celebrate when our team wins. We expect to have a place to take friends where we can sit comfortably and visit informally. In short, we all, individually and collectively, have a list of expectations that we hope will be satisfied in the environment. Urban amenity can be measured by how well these expectations are met.

Some people would argue that our expectations are too low, that we do not expect enough from our environment. It can be argued that designers have done too little to raise people's expectations of themselves and their environments. The problem too often is that designers would like people to behave one way and the people themselves would like to behave another. Urban amenity will only be achieved when urban design and individual and collective desires and potential are brought together to make a good fit.

Preserving Urban Amenity. Older settlements have the advantage that the "good fit" between the urban environment and people's aspirations and needs has been worked out incrementally over time. This is not to say that aspirations and needs do not change, but to try to create a brand-new environment that fits the many aspirations and needs of a large number of people is most difficult (as the efforts to create new towns have demonstrated). An emphasis on preservation would not be necessary if it were not for the fact that today there is often pressure to change otherwise suitable urban environments. The push for change is usually caused by economic considerations. Land, urban land in particular, unless protected by public or philanthropic interests, is treated as an economic, nonmovable commodity. Typically, the pressure is to produce more and more income from urban land, which usually means increasing development. If development is not economically feasible, the land and its buildings are often neglected. It has been said that change is the only thing that can be counted on in contemporary urban society. Change can be positive if it contributes to a better fit between existing needs and the urban form of the city, but, too often, changes generated only for economic reasons play havoc with urban amenities.

The impact of the automobile on urban development is a good example of this negative tendency. The automobile is an important mode of transportation for the majority of people in most cities, and people, given a choice, will most frequently use this form of transportation. The emphasis in urban areas, therefore, is on providing easy access and storage for automobiles. The scale of the automobile and its requirements for space are not the same as those of pedestrians.

Most older cities grew up around pedestrian transportation as the primary movement system. Distances between activities and the scale of the city were established as those convenient for pedestrians. But the pressure in "modernizing" the city has been to better accommodate the automobile. As a result, parking structures and broader streets and freeways have been carved out of the existing urban environment. The new scale imposed by the automobile inhibits pedestrian movement. It has been difficult for many to see that an environment for the pedestrian must coexist with the environment for the automobile. As a result many cities have been redesigned only for the automobile. The pedestrian, who frequently is also an automobile user, finds walking inconvenient, if not impossible.

The modern shopping center or shopping mall is an example of an urban design that meshes the two forms of movement systems. To do this in a built environment, however, is much more difficult. As a result, the amenity of comfortable pedestrian movement, which many cities once had, has been sacrificed to the automobile.

At least some people are now aware of the necessity of preserving a pedestrian movement system. In some cases urban amenities are lost forever, simply because people are unaware that an amenity exists until it is gone. Such an amenity might be a view, a building with unique features, or even a whole district of activities. Fortunately we have become more aware of the threat to many parts of the urban landscape that do create amenity, but that awareness has most often occurred because significant parts of the urban environment have been destroyed.

Creating Urban Amenity. The creation of urban amenity, knowing what the constituent parts are, would not seem that difficult. But, generally, no one is really in charge of creating urban amenity, just as no single individual is ever in complete charge of creating an urban design. As a result the creation of urban amenity is rarely accomplished. Urban design is usually an act of public or private good will. It is something given over to the public by representatives. In un-self-conscious societies, such acts of giving may come quite naturally, as in the dedication of space for religious ceremonies, marketing, the keeping of animals, and so forth. In contemporary society the act of giving concerns the street, park, front yard, or public plaza.

Thus much of what might be considered urban amenity is created quite by accident. In some cities valuable open space has been preserved because it simply was unsuitable for building: for example, valleys, steep hills, and flood plains. Modern technology now threatens these amenities as it becomes possible to build almost anywhere if cost is no object. Many urban amenities result from natural forces of economy as much as insight.

There are, however, striking examples of public belief in urban amenity. The *park movement* in the United States during the mid-1800s is one such example. Besides the perseverance of designers like Frederick Law Olmsted and his followers, there was popular support for creating public parks. There are at least twenty American cities with major central parks that can trace their origins back to the enlightened period of the 1800s. Of course, the fact that these public parks raised surrounding land values played no small part in making the development of parks popular among public officials interested in increasing the tax base of the city.

Perhaps each age has its own reservoir of amenities deemed important. A form of open space that has emerged recently is the *vest-pocket park,* usually a small parcel of land in a densely built-up area, which is dedicated to public use. These modest spaces seem to suit very nicely the informal needs of the urban public for a place of relaxation. A more heroic model for public space has been developed by the architect John Portman. Inside large hotel facilities he has created huge atrium spaces that act as a combination indoor street and plaza. Like the central park 100 years earlier, the atrium is being repeated in cities throughout the United States, usually with attendant economic rewards because of the people drawn to these dramatic spaces.

Another movement towards the creation of urban amenity is the effort to make parts of the city into pedestrian spaces. Again this is a concept that has been treated with varying degrees of success. The areas most commonly involved in such treatment are older retail areas, which are attempting to create a more pleasant environment for shoppers, thereby attracting new customers.

Each of these examples has one thing in common: something private has been given up and something public has been gained. The creation of urban amenity must be such a give-and-take process.

Aesthetic Quality

The question of what is beauty has occupied philosophers for centuries. It is a question inherent in a discussion of design.

Definition of Aesthetic Quality. There are two human drives that affect individual reaction to experiences that are either pleasant or unpleasant. One drive is towards order and logic, the other towards complexity and surprise. Individual responses to these two elements vary, as do the collective cultural

Urban amenity: Paley Park, New York—with a waterfall to air-condition and screen noise.

responses of a group. At the same time, responses to these factors can be affected or changed. There is no simple definition of what is aesthetically correct. What is correct depends upon a culture, individual needs, and previous conditioning.

Three important works that challenge accepted aesthetic urban design norms have already been mentioned, and they illustrate this observation about aesthetics. In 1889 Camillo Sitte challenged the very ordered and formal planning of the period and tried to point out the intrinsic artistic qualities of the more complex and less formal urban landscape of the medieval period.[18] Le Corbusier argued for the replacement of the fussy eclectic designs of the beginning of the century with designs that were simple and straightforward.[19] Since the 1960s Robert Venturi has argued for the creation of environments that are more complex and full of surprises.[20] Each argument is buttressed with references to another design context: Sitte cited the medieval; Le Corbusier the products of industrialized society; and Venturi the aesthetic qualities of artifacts produced by popular culture. Each raises important aesthetic issues, many of them still current, and all related to fundamental human aesthetic drives.

Identifying Aesthetic Quality. There are differences between the design of small objects and of large objects. If we think of the city as a large object we are struck by the fact that it has many parts. It is experienced in many ways over relatively long periods of time, and it is a setting for many different kinds of activities by many different kinds of people. While we might be quite satisfied with a small object that is either simple or complex, with an object the size of a city we need both order and complexity. This is where the arguments of Sitte, Le Corbusier, and Venturi have failed.

Whether or not simplicity or diversity is most important in any single instance of the design of the city can only be determined by the context of the design decision. For instance, driving along an expressway can be a very pleasant experience if the curves and grades of the expressway are designed to accommodate appropriate speeds for an automobile and the capabilities of a person operating it. Walking along an expressway, however, is not an aesthetic experience. What is an appropriate mix of order and complexity for a person traveling in an automobile at expressway speeds is not appropriate for a person who is walking. Thus, identification of an urban aesthetic experience has to be seen in context.

Expanding this argument a step further we might ask about the person who must look at the expressway but who does not use it. For the elderly shut-in, for example, the expressway might fill an aesthetic need for contact with the rest of the world, and the movement of automobiles may serve as a visual diversion in an otherwise static environment. For the schoolteacher trying to keep the attention of a class, the expressway becomes an unwanted intrusion. The needs of the users of the environment also become a factor in identifying the aesthetics of urban design.

Sitte, Le Corbusier, and Venturi were all looking for a formal language, a vocabulary of forms, which might be used to solve the particular aesthetic goals they identified. Designers typically need such a vocabulary to help them make aesthetic decisions. The problem for the designer is to make the correct choice for a given situation. That choice is likely to vary with the context. It is most likely to be found in the immediate context in which the urban designer is working. Certainly aesthetic lessons can be learned from other periods and cultures, but the formal language of those other contexts must be translated into a language appropriate to the aesthetic problem (order and/or complexity) at hand.

Creating Aesthetic Quality. Having dismissed the notion that there is one correct aesthetic, we are then confronted with the problem of identifying the appropriate aesthetics for a given context. It is important to remember that aesthetic pleasures involve the senses. Steen Eiler Rasmussen showed that architecture (and by extension urban design) affects the senses, not only of sight, but of touch and hearing as well.[21] Urban design also has the opportunity to affect the sense of smell, if not taste.

There are ordered relationships found in nature that may illicit positive responses from people. The *golden mean,* the ratio of 5:8, is found in many natural forms and has been used by both ancient and contemporary architects to design buildings. The city, however, cannot be perceived all at once, like a simple object or even some buildings, so often such ordering devices applied to urban design are lost at the drawing-board stage. The aesthetic studies most useful for the urban designer are those that link aesthetic satisfaction with the process of perception. It is the interaction among what we sense, how we sense it, and our response to it that makes a complete model of aesthetic awareness. The proper aesthetic experience then is based on expectations and on the environment's ability to deliver a set of expectations through our sensual awareness. Thus when we go to the theatre we expect to be stimulated, and if the environment outside the theatre is stimulating, it both helps to prepare us for the events inside and sustains our excitement as we leave. The use of blinking lights, which has become synonymous with theatres, acts on the retina of the eye, stimulating it and setting us up for a visually exciting experience. On the other hand, a park with a fountain is a nice place to go to "get away from it all." The noise of the fountain serves to mask out other noises, thus isolating us—the rhythm of water in motion is relaxing, and it even conditions the air around it. Neither blinking lights nor fountains can be called aesthetic in themselves; it is the context in which they are used, the response they illicit from our senses, and our expectations that make them a part of an aesthetic experience.

Another important aspect of the aesthetics of urban design relates directly to the principle that the urban design is rarely seen as a whole. Our experience of the environment comes in bits and pieces. Our perception of the environment is based not only on what we experience presently, but what we know about other parts of the environment. Cities considered aesthetic most frequently are able to produce a strong cognitive map; i.e., people are able to mentally map the city and to perceive it as a whole. The satisfaction this gives is psychic. The sense of place, well-being, and security with the familiar are all reinforced by the ability to have a strong mental map of the environment. Lynch has called this mental map *image.* Much research since Lynch's early studies has supported the fact that image is important to individual satisfaction within an environment. Creation of a stronger image, for a city, therefore, can help to create an aesthetically pleasing experience.

Architectural Determinants of Urban Design

Buildings are to cities what bricks and stones are to architecture. Like a building, the city is made of bits and pieces, and whether or not it is artful depends upon the arrangement of the pieces as much as the quality of the pieces themselves. Again like a building, the quality of the city is dependent upon the details, the quality of individual elements within the whole.

Often we see buildings presented as isolated monuments, or cities presented simply as a series of lines on paper, representing the streets. In fact, the city is formed of many buildings, and urban design is concerned with the contribution each one makes to the others. Representation of such relationships often seems to have been lost in present-day cartography, and we must again look at Nolli's map to present this ideal.

Buildings as Activity Generators.

The purpose of buildings is to house activity. The activity may be passive, such as storing goods, or quite lively, such as sheltering people moving from one form of transportation to another. The dynamics of the city are thus set in motion through buildings that are the containers for certain activities.

Each building has its own life and adds its own dynamic to the city. The 20-story office building accepts streams of people every weekday at 8 A.M. and disgorges them at 4 P.M. The 20-story apartment building accepts and disgorges people continuously, even on weekends. The size, form, and even appearance of the two buildings might be the same, but their dynamics are quite different. The school is alive during the day and quiet at night. The theatre is quiet during the day and comes alive at night.

Added to this dimension is the interaction between buildings, the ebb and flow of people and goods from one container to another.

Buildings as Space-Defining Elements.

Besides being containers for activities, buildings are important as objects that occupy space. Like a stone tossed into a pond, a building in the urban landscape generates a force field stretching out into the space around it, or to other objects related to the space it occupies. The impact of that force depends very much upon the building itself.

Peter Smith has described several different kinds of interactions between buildings and their environments.[22] One such relationship he describes as *ambiguous*, in which a building or space is there and yet is not there. It has the ability to move in and out of one's consciousness. Many important buildings are ambiguous. St. Mark's Church in Venice, which is both an object and an edge of a magnificent space, has an exterior wall that becomes an interior wall. Many skyscrapers do the same thing as they appear very dominant within the urban landscape but disappear as one approaches them. Another kind of relationship is *teleological.* That is a building/space relationship where the whole is implied, but can never be seen as a whole. The separate parts can be seen, but the whole object or space is seen only by the mind's eye. An example is the Cathedral at Florence, Italy. An *inductive* relationship is established when buildings and space join together to form a sequential experience, and one is literally pulled through a space by the tension created between the solid mass of a building and the changing void of space. A walk through the colleges of Oxford or Cambridge creates such a dynamic. *Complexity* is another dynamic that can tie building and urban space together. Usually such a building is read in bits and pieces, like a rich tapestry. The sculptured wall of a cathedral or the clutter of signs found in Times Square in New York or Piccadilly Circus in London serve as examples of such a spatial dynamic. Finally there is the *ceremo-*

nial or *heroic* relationship. Building and space come together to be bigger than life, as in the relationship between St. Peter's Church and Square in Rome.

Buildings as Nodes and Landmarks. Within the framework of Lynch's image of the city, buildings have important roles as nodes and landmarks.[23] Their primary role as nodes derives from their role as containers of activity. Most frequently, intense activity contained or generated by a building spills into the surrounding area. Activity tends to generate more activity. A building can serve either as the real node for such activity or as a symbolic focus for the activity. An intersection marked by four gasoline stations becomes a stronger space than a crossroads without buildings simply because the corners are marked and the intensity of the location is clearly implied.

For a building to be a landmark it must be in a significant location, and it must take a significant form. Implied is the notion that other, insignificant buildings must be present for one to stand out in the urban landscape. The contemporary urban landscape often lacks landmarks, not because there are no significant buildings, but because there are too many buildings fighting to be significant. The anonymous is required to make the unique stand out.

Buildings as Edges and Facades. Within the city, buildings serve as walls as well as pieces of furniture. It is the anonymous buildings, the background buildings, that give form to cities and, in the long run, make one city significantly different from others. New York's brownstones, Baltimore's row houses, the Victorian dwellings of San Francisco, and the adobe court houses of the Southwest each serve as the basic cloth of the community. A quality of urbaneness is lost when this cloth has too many holes in it.

Some of the most significant urban spaces have been created by individual designers who were able to sublimate their design to create a space more important than the individual buildings. The subtly articulated facades of the buildings surrounding the Piazza del Campo in Siena allow the Palazzo Pubblico and its campanile to stand out in the space. The buildings that form the background facade for Government Center in Boston were deliberately designed as a background by The Architects Collaborative. Too few contemporary designers have the confidence needed to design a modest building when the occasion demands.

Supporting Urban Activity Patterns

As we have seen, urban design has served various purposes throughout history. In a pluralistic, democratic society, the purpose of urban design should be to make the urbanized environment a better place to live for everyone.

Role of Design in Supporting Activities. Decisions concerning the location of activities are loosely controlled by the government in a democratic society to prevent harmful impacts of particular land uses, such as industry, on other land uses or activities, such as residences. The decision as to where various activities are to be located is answered in the real estate market. The various users of the urban environment locate where it is most convenient and economical for their particular purposes.

An overall characteristic of life in the United States is that there is a great deal of freedom in individual location. The general affluence of the country has allowed people and industries to be quite mobile. Increased access to good transportation almost anywhere in the country has created regional mobility, which has had a major impact on the economic fortunes of many cities. Many older cities have seen their industry and commerce move to what were considered to be better locations outside of the city or even to another region.

Besides creating a pleasant environment there is little that urban design can do to affect these shifts, which are caused by a combination of rational

Nicollet Mall, Minneapolis.

and subjective decisions. Design can play a role when combined with other support. Certainly the attraction of many new areas of development is not just their newness, but the increased amenities they provide as well. The industrial park that provides a more pleasant environment for industry and the covered shopping mall that is a more pleasant place to shop, are examples. Design, however, cannot contribute to the success of the industrial park and shopping mall if they are in the wrong location. The same is true of urban revitalization efforts.

There are, however, numerous cases of successful urban revitalization that have been supported by urban design. Perhaps one of the most successful in a major urban area is Nicollet Mall in the center of downtown Minneapolis. The Mall is a striking example of sensitive urban design, combined with a commonsense approach to solving problems of bus access and automobile parking, along with a commitment by local business to make continued investments in this part of the city rather than elsewhere. The design of the mall helped to influence local business to make those investments; the design scheme was a catalyst. But, without the financial commitment of business to revitalization, this mall would simply be window dressing in an area of continued decline, as many such projects have become.

Influence of Urban Design on Activities.
There are two major impacts urban design can have on activity; one is *climatic* and the other is *generative*. Many of the attributes that we find so gracious in un-self-consciously designed environments derive from common sense, in that the activity and form complement each other. In a temperate climate an open space that is protected from the wind and opened to the sun will support activity many more months than a space continually in shade and exposed to the wind. Yet many playgrounds and public plazas are built that are virtually uninhabitable except for a few days during the year. Designing according to the climate is essential to creating habitable urban environments.

The influence of design on generating activities is most pronounced at a microscale. An environment designed for pedestrians, for example, is likely to generate activities supported by pedestrians. Shops built for high densities of shoppers need similar shops around them. On the other hand, automobile-oriented environments tend to attract activities that service the person in an automobile: activities oriented to convenience, speed, and easy access. Each environment tends to generate similar supportive activities, if there is a market or need for them.

Influence of Activities on Physical Form.
We cannot lose sight of the basic function of the city. That function traditionally has been to provide a place for people to come together, whether for protection, religion, trade, and commerce.
The causes are many and varied and have changed over time. It is apparent that the rationale for the modern city is quite different from that of ancient cities, and serious attention has been given to the question of the necessity of the modern city. With increased mobility, centralization of activity is not as necessary as it once was. As a result the contemporary city is more spread out, more decentralized, than any of the cities of the past.

Jean Gottman described the new form of city developing along the East Coast of the United States at midcentury as a *megalopolis*.[24] There now are megalopolises growing throughout the world. While much of the surface of the globe is still not urbanized, the proportion of the earth's surface that has been developed has increased more than a thousand-fold in the last century. This pattern continues even though population growth in industrialized nations has begun to stabilize. One consequence of this pattern is that urban pollution is becoming a problem of major proportions, threatening not only larger cities, but smaller cities and rural areas as well.

The by-products of urbanization of the globe have become a serious threat to the future habitability of the earth. The pattern of urbanization in the future will undoubtedly have a significant impact on the quality of life on our planet.

MECHANISMS FOR IMPLEMENTING URBAN DESIGN

The implementation of urban design should be linked to its cultural, political, social, and economic context. If an urban design is to be carried out, rather than stand as a theoretical comment, the distinction between the solution and means of implementation will be slight. Rarely is a successful urban design conceived without thought to implementation.

The Process of Creating Urban Design Plans
The single thing that distinguishes urban design from other forms of planning is that the end result is specifically concerned with the physical form and quality of the city. The way the form of the city is affected varies with the context. At one extreme an urban design plan may be as specific as an architectural plan, complete with construction specifications, procedures, financing techniques, and budgets. That is the type of plan needed to implement a project such as Nicollet Mall. At the other extreme, an urban design might simply be a set of guidelines or rules. Such guidelines are used to formulate a policy that affects the decisions of others. The plan of Pope Sixtus V for Rome, which established rules for connecting major churches with streets and for marking the churches with squares and obelisks, was made up of simply conceived guidelines that could be followed by others long after the Pope's retirement. The decision of the city of San Francisco to limit the height of buildings in order to protect the views of surrounding hills is another example of an urban design guideline. That guideline is enforceable through the regulatory powers of the city.

A factor that affects the nature of an urban design plan and the methods of implementation is the *scale* of concern. It is possible to identify four general scales of urban design concern. The largest scale tends to be regional, that is, of the central city and its surrounding hinterland. Above this scale

Large-scale urban design: Chicago 21, by Skidmore, Owings & Merrill (photo by Hedrich-Blessing).

there are few opportunities to directly affect the form of urban areas, except remotely through very broad policy and budgetary decisions. Moving down in scale of concern we come to the city itself; further breakdowns are neighborhoods and blocks. These distinctions are obviously arbitrary, and it is apparent that urban design can be concerned with a scale that might fit between any of these categories. Most frequently the distinction made in development of urban design proposals for these various scales is in the degree of specificity of the proposal. Larger-scale urban design proposals tend to sketch out broad concepts and guidelines that can serve as a basis for more detailed decisions at the smaller

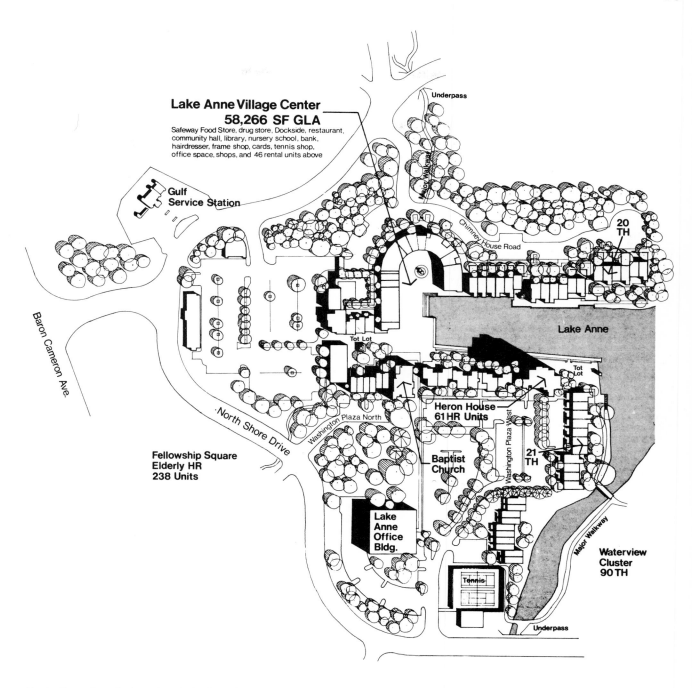

**Lake Anne Village Center
58,266 SF GLA**
Safeway Food Store, drug store, Dockside, restaurant,
community hall, library, nursery school, bank,
hairdresser, frame shop, cards, tennis shop,
office space, shops, and 46 rental units above

**Gulf
Service Station**

Underpass

Major Walkway

Chimney House Road

**20
TH**

Lake Anne

Baron Cameron Ave.

Tot Lot

Tot
Lot

North Shore Drive

Washington Plaza North

**Heron House
61 HR Units**

Washington Plaza West

**21
TH**

**Fellowship Square
Elderly HR
238 Units**

**Baptist
Church**

**Lake
Anne
Office
Bldg.**

Major Walkway

**Waterview
Cluster
90 TH**

Tennis

Underpass

Illustrative urban design plan: Lake Anne Village, Reston, Virginia—New Town by Gulf Reston, Inc.

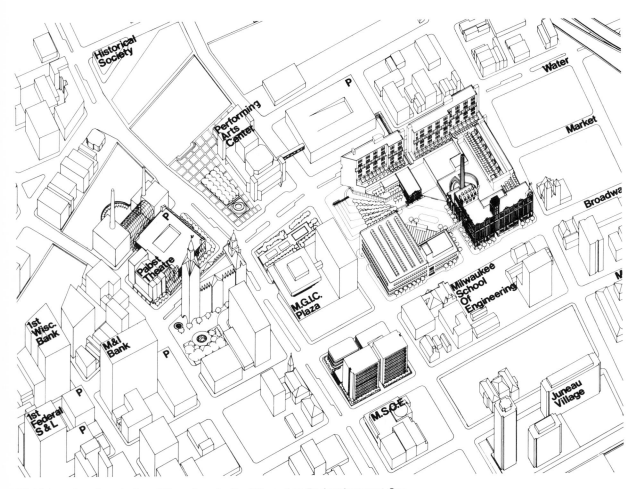

District-scale urban design: Milwaukee, by the Milwaukee Redevelopment Corporation; ELS Design Group; Kahler, Slater, Fitzhugh Scott; and Sasaki Associates. (Courtesy of Steve Dragos, The Milwaukee Redevelopment Corporation).

project level. Often, however, even broad regional design proposals are developed in enough detail to suggest what the probable outcome of certain policy decisions or guidelines might be. It is not infrequent, also, for an urban design proposal to start at a large scale of analysis before coming down to quite specific designs for smaller-scale areas.

Problem Identification and Goal and Objective Setting. As in any other problem-solving activi-

ty, the most important first step is to clearly describe the problem and identify goals. In a culture where the conditions of life are fairly stable and change occurs only incrementally, problem identification and goal setting come quite naturally, and common problems and goals are easily understood by a community. In contemporary society, however, change is the norm, and the goals of individuals and groups are frequently at odds, especially as they affect problems associated with urban design. By definition, goals are fairly loose statements of principle that establish a direction. Rarely do they provide measures by which success can be gauged. A statement of objectives is more programmatic and measureable. An objective is a translation of a goal into something that can be achieved.

Urban design goals and objectives can occur at any scale of urban design concern. Some examples at different scales are shown in the table on page 96. Without a clearly stated set of urban design goals and objectives, urban design proposals can be easily dismissed.

Developing Urban Design Plans and Guidelines. The specific elements of an urban design plan must be determined by the scale and goals of the particular design context. In attempting to formulate an urban design, it is useful to go through the usual procedures associated with solving design problems:

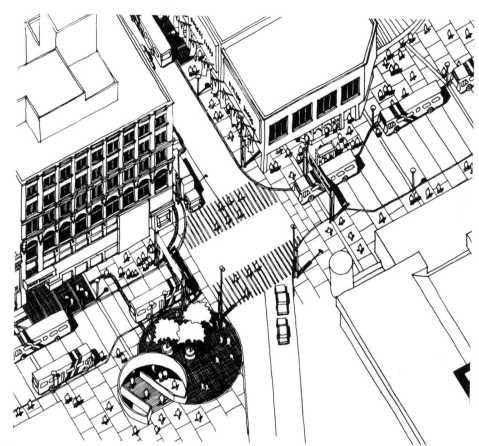

Street-scale urban design: heart of Atlanta shopping district, by Toombs, Amisano, and Wells; and Richard Rothman.

URBAN DESIGN

do not add up to more than the whole. When this occurs there is usually a need for public intervention or controls.

Such controls were common in ancient urban development. The citizens of medieval Siena had to make any new building conform to a law passed in 1262. The height of buildings around Siena's Piazza del Campo was controlled by law so that the town hall would retain its visual prominence. The residences were even required to have windows shaped in accordance with those of the Palazzo Pubblico (the major building on the square).

tions. Restrictive zoning usually applies to three aspects of building—building and land use, building height, and building bulk.

This kind of zoning has been severely criticized because of its many weaknesses. Foremost amongst these is the fact that the best economic use of land is not always anticipated by a zoning plan. Consequently, there is often tremendous political pressure on the public officials who administer the zoning law to change the law. As a result, zoning regulations do not necessarily protect the public from harmful effects. Other critics argue that zoning regulations arbitrarily regulate the establishment of ac-

URBAN DESIGN

98

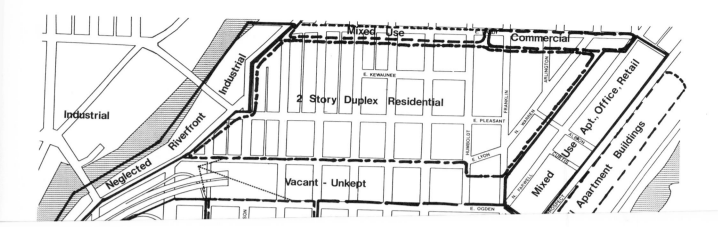

100

tivities that would be better located by the economic process. Nevertheless this form of zoning and urban design control is the one most frequently used by cities in the United States.

Indicative Zoning. At one time indicative zoning was the most popular form of urban development control with urban designers. Quite the opposite of restrictive zoning, this type of land use regulation does instruct people on the form urban development should take. The process has two steps. First a development is proposed for an urban area, usually through the device of a master plan adopted by the community. Then, to help implement the project zoning controls are established to conform with the plan. This approach also has its problems. The major one is that it is quite difficult to predict the future unless you have absolute control over it. Most master plans have attempted to forecast what might happen to an urban area in twenty or thirty years, and time has proven most of these predictions to be wrong. The city does not have absolute control over its future, and few large-scale institutions can exercise such power. As a result, an indicative plan usually quickly becomes obsolete because economic pressures cause someone to build something not in conformance with the master plan. The city cannot force individuals to build something they do not want to. It can prohibit them, but it cannot deny a reasonable proposal that does not endanger the health, safety, or welfare of the community.

Most communities, while they may have long-range plans, have abandoned the notion of a master plan or an indicative planning approach. There have been a few examples where indicative planning has been eminently successful. Edmund N. Bacon in Philadelphia was able to set forth a series of very strong images to help guide development. His indicative plans for Philadelphia became, in a sense, self-fulfilling prophecies. Part of his success came from his insights about the future development of the city, but another part came from the sheer force of his personality and powers of persuasion. Even his

plans, however, went through many changes over the course of time.

Incentive Zoning. The incentive zoning approach provides benefits for developers if they will give the public certain benefits in return. The incentives usually come in the form of a bonus to the developer, such as allowing the project additional space. The bonus is granted if the developer promises to build a public amenity, such as a public plaza or building arcade, which is incorporated into the development. There are two requirements necessary to make this formula work. First, the existing zoning must be rigid enough to inhibit development of the amount of area of space the developer thinks would be profitable. Secondly, the market for space has to be strong enough that the developer will be interested in providing benefits to the community in return for the additional space. Both New York and San Francisco, which have very competitive markets for office space, have tried this technique with some success. A great deal of consideration has to be given ahead of time to what kinds of bonuses will return the most benefits to the community. There is also a danger that such bonuses can lead to the very kind of development monotony this zoning mechanism is usually used to avoid.

Performance Zoning. Performance zoning gives public officials the most latitude in controlling urban form. Instead of a rigid list of requirements describing what cannot be done, a set of urban design criteria that must be met by a developer is established. The developer's proposed scheme is then evaluated in terms of how well it meets the performance criteria. The obvious advantage to this approach is that it gives both the developer and the city a great deal of latitude in evaluating a proposal, and the evaluation involves objective, measurable criteria. Performance zoning is a more direct approach to protecting such things as views or assuring that the sun will penetrate to a public open space. The major disadvantage is that the interpretation of the guidelines is left to a planning staff rather than elected officials. Elected officials are generally reluctant to relinquish their authority, even to a well-trained staff.

Private and Public Responsibilities

We have seen that urban design is formed by the interaction of private and public decisions. It is important to understand this if one hopes to accomplish urban design within the context of contemporary urban society. The successful urban designer should be sensitive to both private and public interests and decisions if he or she has any hope of seeing proposals for improving the urban environment implemented.

Institutional Framework. Important to urban design are the institutions involved. Obviously local government plays a primary role. The power of local government is twofold: it not only controls much of the land and infrastructure, but it also has the legal authority to control private development. Each local government is different, in its structure as well as in its political persuasion. Many of the responsibilities of local government that affect urban design are fragmented or spread out over several jurisdictions. For example, several different authorities may control the acquisition and development of public parks and open space. The transit authority, highway commission, planning commission, zoning commission, and sewer, lighting, and water departments are often separate entities. Most cities have poor mechanisms for coordinating the work of these various groups .

The federal government and state governments usually have roles in urban development. The federal government's primary role is to make funds available to cities for specific urban development activities. Obviously this financial support often affects what and how much gets done. As the percentage of urbanized population has grown, the involvement of the states has increased. Their assistance to urban development has ranged from technical aid for smaller urban communities to major involvement in regional and metropolitan transportation systems.

Nongovernmental institutions also are important. Hospitals, universities and other educational institutions, chambers of commerce, and tourist boards all have a major stake in urban development. Major institutions may have a very direct participatory role as their development plans affect the form of the city directly—not only within their confines but in surrounding neighborhoods as well. Many major institutions now hire their own planning staffs for institutional development both inside and outside the institution. Interest groups, such as chambers of commerce and other business and social groups, also have important roles, in setting goals and objectives. In many cities the impetus behind urban revitalization has been the leadership provided by such public-spirited groups. Behind every major urban design plan there is usually an ad hoc group of citizens and elected officials playing an important part in both promoting and shaping urban development policy.

Private Responsibilities. There is growing awareness that the private sector has not only a great influence on the shape of urban development, but also has a responsibility to affect the quality of urban development. Many people place the blame for the poor quality of our urban environment on business interests and the profit motive. Again we are dealing with a complex set of issues.

Many of the private sector's incentives for seeking profits through means that are harmful or wasteful to the urban environment stem from obsolete laws. One such law is the tax law governing the depreciation of property, which encourages owners to sell property frequently and to put off maintenance of property.

On the other hand, business interests represent a potential for making contributions to the urban environment which neither government nor individuals could offer. The IDS Building in Minneapolis and Rockefeller Center are two examples of such urban developments, which have added much to the enjoyment of the city. There are even examples of business participation in urban revitalization efforts that have had positive effects on residential neighborhoods. It is in the nature of private enterprise to be responsive to public demands. Achieving corporate responsibility for urban development, however, often takes a special effort on the part of citizens and public officials.

The individual citizen has a unique part to play. The city neighborhoods that most impress us with the quality of their environment also impress us because of the care each resident has taken with the maintenance and enhancement of the environment. Such traditions are well-established in some areas. In many countries sweeping the sidewalk in front of one's residence or business is a morning ritual. Each community has its own rituals. The neighborhoods that have no such rituals and where individual concern has disappeared seem to suffer most from urban blight.

The Urban Designer's Role in Merging Public and Private Responsibilities and Interests.
Public and private interests are often seen as divergent. In the area of urban design they must be convergent. Some of the most interesting recent explorations in urban design have attempted to identify ways in which the public and private interest might be merged.

In New York City experiments tried to establish an urban design group within city government to better coordinate the plans of local government and private enterprise. This group used an array of urban design tools, including legal restrictions, such as zoning; indicative planning to aid developers in exploring potential solutions to development problems; and assistance in cutting the red tape that often thwarts the developer. In addition the members exercised astute powers of persuasion. In Dallas, Texas, there has been set in motion a long-term program to encourage active public participation in setting goals for the nature and form of future urban development, redevelopment, and conservation efforts. The attempt has been to bring together public and private interests to work out an articulated set of goals that will guide both public and private development in a way acceptable to the citizens of Dallas.

Community participation is now a byword in most urban design activities. Various experiments have involved the community in design. Some of these have even resulted in successful involvement of citizens in the creation of actual design proposals.

In summation, it is clear that urban design is a broad and complex subject related to the interests of both planners and designers. The urban designers' task is to guide new and changing urban development so that society will be provided with appropriate physical forms. To achieve this end the urban designer must be familiar with the history of society, the elements of design which can be used to manipulate urban form, and the mechanisms for implementing proposals.

NOTES

1. Amos Rapoport, *Human Aspects of Urban Form* (Oxford: Pergamon, 1977).
2. Camillo Sitte, *City Planning According to Artistic Principles* (New York: Random House, 1965), chap. 10, "Artistic Limitations of Modern City Planning."
3. Thomas A. Reiner, *The Place of the Ideal Community in Urban Planning* (Philadelphia: University of Pennsylvania Press, 1963).
4. Ebenezer Howard, *To-morrow: A Peaceful Path to Reform* (London: S. Sonnenschein, 1898); and *Garden Cities of Tomorrow,* ed. F. J. Osborn, new ed. (London: Faber & Faber, 1946).
5. Le Corbusier, *The Radiant City* (New York: Orion Press, 1967): Frank Lloyd Wright, *The Living City* (New York; Horizon Press, 1958).
6. Christopher Alexander, *A Pattern Language: Towns, Building, Construction* (Oxford: Oxford University Press, 1976).
7. Kevin Lynch, *The Image of the City* (Cambridge, Mass.: M.I.T., 1960).
8. Donald Appleyard, Kevin Lynch, and John R. Meyer, *The View from the Road* (Cambridge, Mass.: M.I.T., 1964).
9. Robert Venturi, Denise Scott Brown, and Steven Izenour, *Learning from Las Vegas* (Cambridge, Mass.: M.I.T., 1977).
10. Jonathan Barnett, *Urban Design as Public Policy* (New York: McGraw Hill, 1974).
11. Robert Goodman, *After the Planners* (New York: Simon and Schuster, 1973).
12. Gordon Cullen, *Townscape* (London: Architectural Press, 1961).
13. Sibyl Moholy-Nagy, *Matrix of Man* (New York: Praeger, 1968).
14. Jane Jacobs, *The Death and Life of Great American Cities* (New York: Random House, 1961).
15. Oscar Newman, *Defensible Space: Crime Prevention through Urban Design* (New York: Macmillan, 1972).
16. Hans Blumenfeld, "Criteria for Judging the Quality of the Urban Environment," in *Urban Affairs Annual Reviews,* vol. 3, ed. H. J. Schmandt and W. Bloomberg, Jr. (Beverly Hills, Calif.: Sage, 1969), pp. 137–64.
17. Robert Venturi, *Complexity and Contradiction in Architecture,* 2d ed. (New York: Museum of Modern Art, 1977), pp. 129–31.
18. Sitte, *City Planning.*
19. Le Corbusier, *Radiant City.*
20. Venturi, *Complexity and Contradiction.*
21. Steen Eiler Rasmussen, *Experiencing Architecture* (New York: Wiley, 1959).
22. Peter F. Smith, *The Dynamics of Urbanism* (London: Hutchinson, 1974), pp. 126–71.
23. Lynch, *Image of the City.*
24. Jean Gottman, *Megalopolis* (Cambridge, Mass.: M.I.T., 1961).
25. Doris B. Holleb, *Social and Economic Information for Urban Planning,* vols. 1 and 2 (Chicago: University of Chicago Press, 1970).

FOR FURTHER READING

Alexander, Christopher. *A Pattern Language: Towns, Building, Construction.* Oxford: Oxford University Press, 1976.

Appleyard, Donald; Lynch, Kevin; and Meyer, John R. *The View from the Road.* Cambridge, Mass.: M.I.T., 1964.

Bacon, Edmund N. *Design of Cities.* New York: Penguin, 1974.

Barnett, Jonathan. *Urban Design as Public Policy.* New York: McGraw-Hill, 1974.

Goodman, Robert. *After the Planners.* New York: McGraw-Hill, 1973.

Hall, Edward T. *The Hidden Dimension.* Garden City, N.Y.: Doubleday, 1966.

Halprin, Lawrence. *Cities.* New York: Reinhold, 1963.

Lynch, Kevin. *The Image of the City.* Cambridge, Mass.: M.I.T., 1960.

———. *Site Planning.* Cambridge, Mass.: M.I.T., 1971.

Morris, A. E. J. *History of Urban Form.* New York: Halsted, 1972.

Newman, Oscar. *Defensible Space: Crime Prevention through Urban Design.* New York: Macmillan, 1972.

Sitte, Camillo. *City Planning According to Artistic Principles.* New York: Random House, 1965.

Venturi, Robert; Brown, Denise Scott; and Izenour, Steven. *Learning from Las Vegas: The Forgotten Symbolism of Architectural form.* Cambridge, Mass.: M.I.T., 1977.

Part Two

Theory and Method

R. Hedman

The second part of this volume includes four chapters on the theory and method of urban planning. These are important considerations in the study of urban planning, because the field has evolved from other disciplines and professions. As a result, the theory and method of urban planning are an amalgam of thought, concepts, and techniques that may have been developed originally for such fields as economics, management science, political science, systems analysis, applied mathematics, and others.

The chapters on planning theory reflect the broad basis of planning. Urban planning is inherently concerned with improvement of the public good; hence, we may eliminate from our consideration certain kinds of planning, such as personal, corporate, and military. These chapters also examine the rather complicated set of definitions, roles, and contexts of urban planning, from which a reasonably acceptable synthesis of theory can be made.

The "method of urban planning" refers to policy analysis and quantitative analysis. These two forms of method are the most generic and can be applied to various kinds of urban planning for special functions. They are more general than certain techniques that are used only, for example, in transportation or fiscal planning. Policy analysis and quantitative analysis are the basic tools in the urban planner's kit.

CHAPTER 4

Planning Theory

Ernest R. Alexander

The theory of urban planning has to do with defining and understanding the contexts, practices, and processes of planning, and how they have evolved from their respective historical and cultural bases. This chapter concentrates on the various definitions and models of the urban planning process in order to establish a linkage with practice. As with many other fields and disciplines, it is difficult to perceive this linkage without a broad perspective. Such a view, however, reveals the importance of planning theory to practice; indeed, changes in theory usually precede changes in the way planners work.

PRACTICE AND DEFINITION

The Case for Planning Theory

"Nothing is as practical as theory," said physicist J. Robert Oppenheimer, one of the developers of the atom bomb. It is a paradoxical statement, but it begins to make sense when we realize that theory is actually a way of understanding the world, a framework for our interpretations of facts and experience.

Science is built of facts the way a house is built of bricks: but an accumulation of facts is no more science than a pile of bricks is a house.[1]

Theory, then, is the framework by which bricks can be built into a coherent structure. At the same time as it explains facts, theory has to be applied:

If we have a correct theory, but merely prate about it, pigeonhole it and do not put it into practice, then that theory, however good, has no significance.[2]

Conversely, practice should be informed by theory, not only to structure and explain the world and the environment that is the object of actions, but also to explain the actions to the actors themselves. This kind of action has been called *praxis:* it distinguishes itself from practice as a self-critical activity that recognizes that the external world, including the practitioner, is the product of previous human interactions.

For planners the relationship between theory and practice as expressed in the concept of *praxis* is especially important, because planning, unlike the sciences, is ultimately a prescriptive, not a descriptive, activity. The planner's aim is not to describe the world as it is, but rather to propose ways in which things can be changed.

Both planners and the consumers of planning should be able to judge the success or failure of planning efforts. Their evaluations require a standard of reference, an explanation or model of the planning process: in short, a theory. Planning itself requires a rationale and social legitimation; it "must be justified as the institutionalized application of rational decision-making to social affairs."[3] Because planning *is* an activity that affects society and involves human values, planning theory cannot ignore ideology. In the words of John Dyckman, "the theory of planning must include some theory of the society in which planning is institutionalized."[4]

The Scope of Planning Theory

There is little consensus on a definition of planning theory. Just as the planning profession has drawn its members from a variety of backgrounds, so planning theory has developed by an eclectic accretion of concepts from a wide range of disciplines. The content of theory today reflects a sequence of dominant images, which have succeeded one another since planning was recognized as a distinct area of endeavor.[5]

The first planners emerged from the ranks of the design professions, architecture, and engineering.

They brought with them the concepts of utopianism and comprehensiveness, the rationale for making a better environment, and tools for building it. Economists contributed ideas about equity and the public interest (from welfare economics), decision analysis, and public aggregation of values. Psychologists, sociologists, and political scientists have studied the ways choices are made and implemented by individuals, groups, organizations, governments, and whole societies. From them planning theory has adopted ideas about small group relations, organizational design and behavior, bureaucracy, community power and decision making, government, and intergovernmental relations.

With this background, planning theory is capable of addressing a whole range of issues, which can be grouped as follows: *definitional:*—what is planning?; *substantive*—what do we know about what we are planning, and whom we are planning for?; and *normative*—how to plan, and what is the rationale for planning?

Some of these will be explored in more detail below. Planning theory can involve any or all of these areas, so the definition adopted must be to some extent arbitrary. Here we will not deal with the substantive aspects of planning theory, because such an approach could take us into areas as widely divergent as housing, health, and transportation, a range too broad for the scope of this text.[6]

The core of planning theory is the *planning process*. How do people plan? This question is equally relevant for individuals, groups, firms, and governments. A planning process is evident in an individual's career decisions, a household budget, a club's roster of events, a company's production schedule, a city's capital improvement program, a state water resources plan, and national policies in energy, environment, defense, and human services.

Planning theory examines the components of the planning process: their nature, sequence, and relationship to the context of the process and its output. These matters affect the question of how planning should be done. Planning prescriptions that are divorced from reality are likely to be utopian and impossible to implement.

It is important to separate the *descriptive* aspect of the theoretical examination ("This is how it is") from the *evaluative* ("I think it's fine"/"I think it's terrible") and the *normative* ("This is how it ought to be"). Failure to do so results in either confusion, implicit support of status quo, or wishful thinking.[7]

Another set of questions deals with planning models, contexts, and planners' roles. How are these related to planners' effectiveness in different contexts and to the results of the planning process? How can we discover and analyze the important characteristics of the contexts in which planning takes place? How can we use our understanding to enhance planners' effectiveness?

Planning theory also involves the rationale for planning, which in turn raises some questions about planner's ethics and values. Why do we plan? This question, of course, is meaningless without first identifying the context. Then there can be some answers. Or, we can ask: When is it better to plan and to intervene in an ongoing process, and when is it better not to plan, to leave well enough alone? Are there (or should there be) any rules guiding planners in their professional capacities? Such an ethical stance could be analogous to medicine's traditional bottom line: "Avoid harm." A formal code of professional ethics does exist, but does it really make a difference in planners' behavior? Are planners' norms and values similar to prevailing societal norms, or do they reflect other principles and values?

Finally, there is a place in planning theory for the question of legitimacy. What entitles the planner to plan for others and, by implication, to make decisions and choices for others? This raises the issue of public and client participation in the planning process. It also raises the question of accountability. To whom will the planners answer for their planning decisions. As the public has asked since Roman times, *Quis custodiet ipsos custodes?*—who will guard the guardians?

What Is Planning?

We defined theory in terms that could apply to any field of professional practice. An account of planning theory must therefore, relate it specifically to planning and will subsume the question, "What is planning?" Nearly 20 years ago John Dyckman referred to the discussion of this last question as "a literature of controversy."[8]; recently, Henry Hightower said, "The 'square one' question is: 'What is planning?'"[9] Clearly, not much has changed. Over the years, however, many attempts have been made to find an answer. The various definitions of planning proposed cover a wide range but do not indicate a consensus. Nevertheless, it is worthwhile to explore the main streams of thought, from which have emerged the current alternative, but not necessarily mutually exclusive, definitions of planning.

Planning as a Basic Human Activity. Some view planning as a basic activity that pervades human behavior at every level of society. In this view,

> planning is a process . . . of human thought and action based upon that thought—in point of fact, forethought . . . which is a very general human activity.[10]

The carpenter is planning as he raises his hammer to hit the nail. The business person is planning as he or she listens to the morning weather report in order to decide whether or not to carry an umbrella. Carpool drivers are planning as they decide in what order to pick up passengers. Obviously, many more complex forms of planning go on in households, firms, and organizations.

George Miller and others, in the now-classic *Plans and the Structure of Behavior*, expounded on the pervasiveness of planning. They analyzed the planning components of basic individual behavior and concluded that each action is the result of a complex preliminary process, which they called a *TOTE* unit. TOTE stands for "Test-Operate-Test-Exit," meaning that each action is preceded by an assessment of the situation and a visualization of the action to be undertaken (test); then the action is carried out (operate), its results are evaluated (test), the sequence is concluded (exit), and a new one begins. According to Miller and his associates, plans consist of hierarchies of TOTEs, and "a plan is any hierarchial process in the organism that can control the order in which a sequence of operations is to be performed."[11]

This approach gives planning a universality that may help disabuse planners of the notion that they are engaged in some esoteric activity. At the same time, it does not preclude the notion of expertise. We all walk, run, jump, but this does not prevent us from recognizing a difference between ourselves and Olympic athletes. Similarly, we are quite prepared to handle a disagreement with our spouse or with a colleague, but in a dispute where the stakes are high, we would be well advised to hire a lawyer.

Planning as Rational Choice. A second approach confines planning to matters of deliberate choice and emphasizes the link between planning and rationality. The concept of rationality will be explored later in more detail, but it is sufficient here to define a rational choice as a choice that meets certain standards of logic. Planning then becomes "a process for determining appropriate future actions through a sequence of choices."[12]

Little distinguishes this idea of planning from the rational decision-making process. Planning resembles the process in its attempt to achieve preferred ends, exercise of deliberate choice, comprehensive approach, and link to action—though this last remains unspecified and rather weak. Future orientation is the only characteristic of planning that cannot also be ascribed to the rational decision process.

The problem with this view of planning is its almost exclusive focus on choice. Where is the link with action? If a group makes plans but fails to carry them out because of lack of commitment, is this still planning? The experience of city governments with master plans, which often amounted to little more than colored maps and grandiose objectives, suggests that this is not just an academic question.

Planning as Control of Future Action. This definition embodies what may be an overreaction to the narrowness of the previous one. It implies that planning does not exist when the process does not include implementation. In Wildavsky's definition,

> Planning may be seen as the ability to control the future consequences of present actions. The more consequences one controls, the more one has succeeded in planning. [Planning's] purpose is to make the future different from what it would have been without this intervention.[13]

Critics like Wildavsky believe that planning is limited by our capacity to control future actions and outcomes. Advocates of planning as control also reject the rational-choice model's divorce of planning from implementation, but they characterize the fault as a failure of nerve. John Friedmann proposes a model of planning that "fuses action and planning," saying

> it is possible to assert that any action that is deliberate is also to a certain degree planned. The problem is no longer how to make decision more "rational," but how to improve the quality of the action.[14]

The definition that links planning with action has the same flaws of generality as the rational-choice model. Is one planning when one pays the telephone bill, a decision that influences the future actions of the phone company and that commits resources toward maintaining one's link with the outside world? If so, the definition of planning becomes so diluted as to be devoid of real meaning. Furthermore, it may set standards so high that they are impossible to meet.

Planning as a Special Kind of Problem Solving. We now move from process-oriented definitions of planning to more situational definitions: from what it is that planning does, and how it does it, to the specific realm where planning activity happens. One opinion is that planning is problem solving that is aimed at very particular kinds of problems. Rittel and Webber have called the kinds of problems with which planning must deal "wicked" problems.[15] A "wicked" problem has no definitive formulation, no clear rules, no "true-or-false" answers (they can only be "better" or "worse"), and no clear test for the solution. Each wicked problem is unique, but at the same time each is a symptom of another deeper, more extensive malady. Unlike the scientific experimenter, the problem-solving planner cannot afford mistakes.

In his attempt to define planning, Henry Hightower extends planning beyond "wicked" problems. His definition accounts for planners' tendency to question values, institutions, and given decision rules; their use of rough, imprecise data, in contrast to the exact data used in science and engineering, and their action orientation. But this approach, as begins to seem inevitable, is too inclusive. Planners are indeed familiar with wicked problems, messy data, and desire to see their proposals implemented, but the same could be said of politicians, entrepreneurs, or administrators.

Planning Is What Planners Do. The most pragmatic definition of planning is that of Sir Geoffrey Vickers, a British administrator who began theorizing from his practical experience of running the National Coal Board. For Vickers, planning is what planners do. Describing the contribution of technical experts to public policymaking, Vickers said:

> None of this, perhaps, is planning, but it is work which planners are best fitted to do . . . . This help comes in all the three main areas of the policy-maker's task in designing his problem; in conceiving the terms in which it is soluble; and in comparing the importance of the always conflicting values inherent in any solution.[16]

Unquestionably, this approach has the merits of being simple and intuitively obvious. But if planners are merely people who plan, we are back where we started—without a definition. Others have so far failed to distinguish a set of people with recognizable attributes who are clearly planners, as distinct from those without these qualities who are not.

Defining Planning: An Attempted Synthesis. It must now be clear that a comprehensive definition of planning is not easily found. Nonetheless, we join the long line of definers with hope that being able to draw on their experience will protect us from further errors. Previous definitions were perhaps too careful not to exclude any aspect of planning. Such definitions then end up being almost all-inclusive. Wildavsky puts it succinctly: "If planning is everything, maybe it's nothing."[17]

For those of us who believe that there is something in planning after all, it will be most useful to begin by examining what planning is not. We are considering planning as a process or activity that is the framework for a profession, a discipline, and for social decisions and public policy.

From this perspective we can readily identify some of the things planning is not. Planning is not a purely individual activity. It is done by individuals —to be sure, usually individuals working in groups—in order to affect groups, organizations, or governments. Planning for personal reasons exists too, but it should be distinguished from planning in the societal sense.

Nor is planning present-oriented. How far into the future planning can reasonably be projected is a subject worthy of discussion.[18] Even so, professional planning is primarily concerned with future actions involving a significant element of uncertainty; consequently there is a need for prediction. One may choose between items on a menu using all the tools of rational decision making, but rare is the diner who does not regard it as certain that the dish he or she chose will be brought or that the restaurant will still exist when dessert is served.

Planning cannot be routinized. Many problems are not unique, and these can be attacked with existing solutions or problem-solving algorithms, such as standard operating procedures, rules, or programs.[18a] These, however, are the extreme opposites of the wicked problems Rittel and Webber regarded as the object of planning efforts. This distinction is useful when we try to separate the apparent from the real planning activity in a professional setting. Zoning administrators, for example, may do their jobs in a planning agency, but they will actually be doing very little planning if they are only applying existing zoning rules and ordinances.

Planning has little or nothing in common with trial-and-error approaches to problem solving. This is not to say that a planning process cannot incorporate the experimental method in a limited way, but it will be done in the context of a deliberately conceived strategy. Decision-making methods, which are based upon incremental trials and comparison, are not planning. In fact, Lindblom's *disjointed incrementalism,* which is a formalization of such methods, has been described as "nonplanning."[19]

Finally, planning is not just the imagining of desirable futures. While the articulation of goals or norms and the creation of alternatives are essential parts of the planning process, they are not by themselves planning. Here the distinction between planning and utopian thinking is just as important as a sense of their relationship:

> **Planning, like utopia, depicts a desirable future state of affairs, but, unlike utopia, specifies the means for achieving it.[20]**

Thinking about strategies for social change without intending to implement them, or without having the power to carry them out, may be productive, but it is not planning. Philosophers such as Rousseau, political historians such as Karl Marx, or recent economists such as John Kenneth Galbraith and Milton Friedman, have had profound effects on societies and have clearly influenced the policies of governments. Once again we must say that their theories were not plans, because they could use only persuasion to try to achieve implementation.

If planning is not an individual activity, not present-oriented, not routinized, not trial-and-error, and not academic or utopian, what is it? It must be *societal, future-oriented, nonroutinized, deliberate,* and *action-oriented.* To translate these concepts into a definition, we will propose that *planning is the deliberate social or organizational activity of developing an optimal strategy for achieving a desired set of goals.* Such planning aims to apply the methods of rational choice to determining a best set of future actions addressed to novel problems in complex contexts; it is attended by the power and intention to commit resources and to act as necessary to implement the chosen strategy.

THE PLANNING PROCESS

Rationality

We have seen that rationality is a central feature of planning. Rationality usually has positive associations: to be rational is good. Irrationality is equated at best with social deviance; at worst, with madness. When planning lays claim to rationality, then, it adopts popular values.

But often rationality is value neutral. It is a tool, and whether it is good or bad depends on the uses to which it is put. In its simplest form, rationality is a way of choosing the best means to attain a given end. In a more comprehensive view, rationality includes evaluation and choice of goals as well; this is particularly important in planning, which involves multiple and often conflicting objectives.[21]

Axioms of Rationality. Rationality is a tool that enables us to make choices according to certain standards of logic. These standards, or *axioms,* simplify the complexities of situations and values.[22]

The use of rationality is not intrinsically related to either success or failure; i.e., there is no guarantee that choices arrived at rationally will be *good* choices. In fact, many if not most such choices would be the same if they had been arrived at intuitively. The axioms of rationality simply ensure internal logical consistency, and rational analysis provides a framework to display the decision maker's values and assessments.

The first axiom deals with the expression of values: preferences must be transitive. This means that they can be ranked in order from best to worst. For example, if you prefer steak to fish, and fish to corn, and steak to corn, your preferences are transitive, and you can use rational analysis to choose between these items on a menu. But if you happen to prefer corn to steak and steak to fish, while still liking fish better than corn, your preferences are not transitive. This does not mean you are abnormal, but only that you cannot use rational analysis to make your choice.[23]

The next axiom is that probabilities and utilities must be independent of each other. That is, one's assessment of the likelihood that some event or outcome will happen—its probability—should not be affected by the value one would assign to that event or outcome—its utility. We ignore this axiom when we indulge in "wishful thinking," expecting an unlikely event to occur because we would like it to happen.

A third axiom states that unaffected outcomes are irrelevant to the choice under consideration. This axiom, while intuitively obvious, is often ignored, resulting in the pursuit of unneeded data. If you are choosing between a number of options, there is no need to take into account anything that will not affect or be affected by those options. For example, if the choice on a given day is between walking to work or riding a bicycle, relevant factors may be the weather, time, traffic conditions, and so on. The state of the economy, though crucial for many other decisions, is irrelevant to this particular choice and may safely be ignored. This axiom is invaluable as a simple criterion for setting bounds to any decision analysis, bounds without which most problems of choice would be insoluble.

The last axiom concerns the inadmissibility of dominated choices. Without this, the whole exercise of rational analysis would be pointless. This axiom dictates that if rational analysis shows a particular option to be superior to all the others being evaluated, the superior option must be chosen. It should be obvious that formal logic demands that every requirement be clearly spelled out.

Decision Analysis and Rational Choice. Decision making takes place under three different conditions: *certainty, risk,* and *uncertainty.* Certainty covers those situations when we are sure about our preferences, available options, and their effects. Under conditions of risk, we know too little to be certain about events and outcomes, but we have enough information to allow us to estimate probabilities. With uncertainty, even probabilities of events cannot be assessed. The amount of information needed to transform a state of uncertainty into a situation of risk has been the subject of a good deal of argument; the case has been made that even estimates based on "hunches" or intuitive experience are usable.[24]

An example of choice under certainty is the choice from a menu in a familiar restaurant, where the element of uncertainty about the quality of the food can be eliminated. The only relevant factor is our preference, which is expressed as utility. Utility (the value we assign to the outcome of an action or event) may be an unquantifiable value, which we can only compare qualitatively—i.e., as better or worse—with other values. It may be quantifiable, so that we can estimate how much better one thing is than another scale (we will call these units of measurement *utils*). Or utility can be equated with a concrete output that adequately expresses the satisfaction derived from the different possible outcomes.

Decision analysis multiplies the value we place on an outcome by the probability of its occurrence to determine the *expected utility* of an action. The likelihood of an outcome occurring is also connected to the relevant factors in the environment, which affect the impact of our actions, but over which we have no control. The range is from simple to complex.

A simple example will show how all these elements work in decision analysis to allow a rational choice between alternative actions. Suppose we have to choose between taking an umbrella to work (UMB) or leaving it at home (NONE). The relevant environmental factor is whether it will rain or stay clear. We will call these two alternative states of nature RAIN and DRY. The weather forecaster predicts a 70 percent likelihood of showers; we can therefore assign the probability of 0.7 to RAIN and 0.3 to DRY.

We also have to express our preference for each of four possible outcomes. This may be done in a variety of ways, but here we will simply assign scores in utils to symbolize the value of each outcome. The outcome UMB/RAIN means that we take an umbrella and it rains. This would give us a good deal of satisfaction, and it gets a score of 3. UMB/DRY involves the nuisance of carrying a useless umbrella to work; it is a cost but not a heavy one, so it gets a −1. NONE/RAIN is clearly the worst outcome: a thorough soaking, valued at −5. NONE/DRY also has a positive impact, and gets a score of 3.

All these elements are combined into a matrix as shown in the table below. We are now able to aggregate our values with our estimates of the likelihood of events, apply one or more decision criteria, and choose our preferred option. The decision criteria we use will depend on subjective factors: optimism, aversion to risk, and so on.

One criterion would be to choose the action with the largest total expected value, i.e., the largest sum of expected utilities of all alternative outcomes for an option. In the example, the highest total expected utility is for UMB (1.8), so the umbrella is clearly the preferred option. Another common (and pessimistic) criterion is called the minimax. It means choosing the option with the highest minimum expected value. Which action, in other words, will yield the highest benefits if the worst case for that option should occur? For UMB, the worst is DRY (−0.3); for NONE, it is RAIN (−3.5). The higher minimum expected value is associated with UMB, so that is the action we should choose.[25]

We used two different decision criteria and each time came to the same conclusion. Our choice of an action, in other words, was not "sensitive" to our choice of a decision criterion. Given the weather report in this case, anyone with any common sense would have taken the umbrella. Most real decision problems are much more complex, however, and analysis can then be of real value in arriving at a rational choice and communicating its rationale.

Rational decision analysis is the theoretical basis for most planning analysis. Sophisticated methodological tools used in planning, policy analysis, and program evaluation are based upon these concepts. Such methods usually include the following: benefit-cost analysis, cost-effectiveness analysis, private and public investment analysis, and impact analysis.

Decision Analysis Matrix

State of nature: (Probability)		RAIN (0.7)		DRY (0.3)		
Action		Utilities	Expected utils	Utilities	Expected utils	Total expected utils
	UMB	3	2.1	−1	−0.3	1.8
	NONE	−5	−3.5	3	0.9	−2.6

Aggregation of Choices. Until now we have been discussing rational choices made by individuals or by social units treated as homogeneous undifferentiated wholes. But this is not at all what social units are; even the smallest group is made up of different individuals with different traits, interests, and goals.

The rational choice exercised by one person is still a step away from rational choice by any societal unit. The group's choice has to be arrived at by aggregating individual choices, and the decision must meet certain conditions beyond the aforementioned axioms to qualify as rational. The final decision should reflect the individual preferences, and the same process should produce this outcome, whatever the distribution of individual choices. The process should be democratic; that is, the preferences of people with power and prestige cannot be dominant, nor can a decision be imposed by dictatorial fiat.

It is difficult to determine a choice by aggregating individual preferences, let alone find a fair way of doing so. In most groups the decision is strongly affected by the relative status or power of participants, and the final issue is often effectively decided by the person with the most "clout." Policy for governments or corporations is usually decided by the apparently fair process of voting, but voting systems have their anomalies, too—e.g., it is possible for a U.S. President to be elected by a minority of the popular vote.

Kenneth Arrow confirmed the idea that it is difficult to devise a fair system of social choice. Indeed, he proved in his *Impossibility Theorem* that no system that meets the requirements of rational aggregation of individual preferences can exist.[26]

Social choices, then, should be made by a political process. The political process does not incorporate a logically necessary and obvious aggregation of individual or subunit preferences. In that sense, it is not rational. It blends the values of individual and group participants through organization, commitment, and power, as well as bargaining, cooperation, and conflict resolution. The political process—not rational choice—is the vehicle by which most planning proposals are implemented, a fact that planners forget at their peril.[27]

Models of the Planning Process

Doubts about the possibility of generalizing about planning are reflected in the multiplicity of planning models that have been developed. At some level of abstraction, more removed from the complexities of real-world contexts, generalization may be possible. Such generalization takes the form of models, which have been developed by many students of the planning process, such as Banfield, Friend and Jessop, and Lichfield.[28]

While differing in some specifics and terminology, all these models have one thing in common. They see planning as a sequential, multi-staged process in which many of the phases are linked to their predecessors by *feedback loops*. In other words, the conclusions reached at a later stage may lead to a review of an earlier stage or a reiteration of the whole process. For example, an agency may find that all the alternatives that have been developed to meet certain objectives are too expensive. It may discover in its evaluation (later stage) that none of them is feasible. This is bound to cause a reappraisal of the goals and objectives decided upon at an earlier stage of planning. Or the monitoring and evaluation of the impacts of plans or programs may reveal new problems, which become the stimulus for a new round of planning.

The following major components of the planning process tend to be found in most models of the planning process.

Problem Diagnosis. Planning begins, like the decision process, with some sense of a dissatisfaction with the status quo; if there were no problem, there would be no need for action. The diagnosis of the problem depends on an image of the desired state, which acts as the point of reference. The

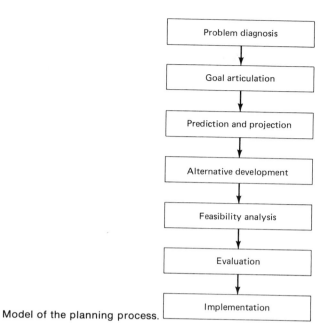

Problem diagnosis

↓

Goal articulation

↓

Prediction and projection

↓

Alternative development

↓

Feasibility analysis

↓

Evaluation

↓

Implementation

Model of the planning process.

image gives form to specific goals, general norms, standards, ideologies, even utopian visions.

The definition of the problem aims the thrust of the solution. Definitions, however, depend on the analytical orientation of the individuals involved:

> The academic expert says to the client: "If the shoe fits, wear it."; the strategic expert says: "The shoe you're wearing doesn't fit, and you should try one like this instead."; and the clinical expert says: "If the shoe doesn't fit, then there's something wrong with your foot."[29]

The planner's role and ideological paradigms will also color definitions of problems. For example, viewing the poor as primarily responsible for their condition is bound up with a preference for a social services strategy against poverty. When social forces are viewed as the main cause of poverty, suggestions for structural change are not far behind.[30]

Goal Articulation.   Goals, as we have seen, relate to problem definitions. Planning was traditionally much more goal-oriented than it is now. City planning often meant little more than the development of a "master plan," which showed a desired end-state, in future year X, with the attainment of certain goals.

One of the most difficult challenges in planning is the translation of vague, incoherent goals into operational objectives; when this is not done, serious dysfunctions may result.[31] While there have been many attempts to develop technical means for goal articulation, the undertaking remains more of an art than a science.[32]

Prediction and Projection.   Future orientation was emphasized in the definition of planning. This means that current data are not enough. The development of alternative solutions to problems always requires projection into the future in order to estimate the conditions, needs, and constraints.

Public works are an extreme case. The California Water Plan required over 20 years lead time. Utility companies commonly allow over a year before implementation can begin, and they usually estimate a project or program life of several years.

Prediction is essential for evaluating and selecting alternatives. Evaluation cannot be done without projecting the impacts of alternative proposals under possible future conditions. Can we predict the future? Yes, to a certain extent, but our success will depend upon the amount of information available and the continuity of the phenomenon being analyzed. Numerous population projections have been made, with an enviable record of success. Yet the U.S. Census Bureau erred in its estimates of 1970 population. The estimates were based on projections of previous trends, and changes in lifestyles that affected marriage and fertility between 1960 and 1970 were not anticipated.

A repertoire of predictive and projective techniques has been developed for different situations of information and uncertainty. There are quantitative projective methods, such as curve-fitting and shift-and-share analysis; more qualitative approaches, such as latent-factors analysis and scenario writing; and information-generating tools, such as the Delphi consultation technique.[33]

Alternative Development. Accounts of the planning process often neglect the development of alternative proposals. This stage has a profound effect on the quality of the final decision, because it is from the range of options that the plan will be chosen. As Lichfield has noted:

> The ability of an evaluation exercise to demonstrate the comparative merits of possible courses of action is limited, ultimately, by the quality of the plans put forward for assessment. A ''good'' plan cannot be chosen from a ''poor'' set of alternatives.[34]

Sometimes, usually in less complex situations, the alternatives are limited, discrete, and obvious (as with the choice of an umbrella on a cloudy day). More often, even when a range of options is apparent, each alternative has to be detailed, and its actions, resources, and timing specified, before formal evaluation can be done. Such detailing is usually carried out in close interaction with other professionals, such as architects, engineers, and/or specialists in the relevant program area.

When a problem is well defined and substantial quantifiable information is available, an optimization approach will combine alternative development with the evaluation stage. Optimization involves modeling or simulating solutions that can attain certain goals within a set of constraints and according to certain parameters.

Yet there are many complex situations in which the problem is ill-defined and possible options are not at all obvious. Then alternatives have to be generated by some combination of existing information and creative invention. Information is found by looking for it. One may use a common heuristic search—one according to a few simple, almost arbitrary, ''rules of thumb''[35]—or one of the more systematic search methods developed for design analysis.[36] Creativity and innovation are required when the problem defies known solutions. Although a good deal of study has been devoted to piercing the mysteries of invention and creation, and some facilitating techniques like ''brainstorming'' have been suggested, nothing approaching a dependable formula has emerged.[37]

Feasibility Analysis. Feasibility analysis asks a question about each option that has been developed or designed: Can it be done, given known constraints and available or projected resources? If the alternatives were well-designed, the answer will be affirmative. But negative answers may reduce the range of options to a short list, to only one alternative or to none. In the last case, the planners will have to redesign some options to make them feasible, or possibly even reassess their original objectives and goals.

Constraints on implementation are easy to identify when they are considered, but too often this area is ignored in planning. The obvious constraints are economic or physical: the size of a budget or an allocation, access to supply sources or markets, ceiling on travel time, minimum site areas, or dimensions to accommodate given needs at acceptable standards. Less tangible constraints may be political or organizational, and these too have to be taken into account for a realistic plan.[38]

Evaluation. The evaluation stage begins when the planners have a number of alternatives they know can be implemented. Which of them shall they implement? If there is only one alternative, there must be a ''go/no-go'' decision, either to carry out the proposed set of actions or to do nothing. This approach puts a strain on the analytic capacities of those involved, because the absolute magnitude of effects becomes important. In other contexts, they know that something is going to be done, and they just have to choose the preferred alternative. With options to compare, the decision makers have some freedom to estimate the relative impact of each.

Which alternative do they like most? What does each of these options do for them? The answer to these questions depends on the evaluation criteria adopted. A commonly used criterion is efficiency: which alternative gives the "biggest bang for the buck"? Benefit-cost analysis, an evaluation method used extensively since it was developed in the 1950s, explicitly addresses this criterion. This method is used when both the costs and the benefits or outputs can be quantified in monetary terms. When outputs cannot easily be expressed in dollar values, as in human services such as day care or mental health, cost-effectiveness analysis is used. With this method, one develops an index that reflects program outputs. Depending on the program, the effectiveness indices might be improvement on standard test scores, reduction in arrest rates, or increase in health indicators.

The criterion of efficiency can be used for cases with one inclusive goal or with a single and homogeneous interest group as the client. Many planning issues, however, involve conflicting goals and multiple interests. The parties in conflict will quickly raise the issue of equity if the planning group forgets it. They will be concerned with incidence and distribution as well as—if not more than—the total of costs and benefits. The equity criterion asks of each option, "Who gets hurt?" There are evaluation methods, developed specifically for planning problems, that attempt to combine efficiency and equity assessments.[39]

Implementation. A few generalizations are possible about implementation experiences. A strong political commitment appears to be a necessary, but not always sufficient, condition for the adoption and successful realization of proposals. Clearly defined goals, which are translatable into objectives that can be monitored, are important. Last, simple projects that can be executed within a framework of relative organizational autonomy are more likely to succeed than complex plans that require the cooperation of numerous interdependent units.

This process would probably be agreed upon by most urban planners. It is essential to note that this process differs from other problem-solving processes, such as systems analysis, operations research, and decision analysis. One difference lies in the difficulty of making explicit or quantifying many of the factors needed for problem solving in urban planning, such as, goals objectives, feasibility, and other measures. With only less clear-cut measures available, urban planners must rely upon compromises between strict rationality and qualitative or informed judgments. This means that the planning process is a hybrid of other problem-solving approaches. It is *systemic* rather than rigidly *systematic*.[40]

Final Questions

Reservations and disagreements have been expressed by scholars, practitioners, and other serious observers about almost every facet of the planning process. Do we carry problems in search of answers? Are solutions just as often looking for problems? Can goals be identified? Is it easier to plan without goals? Should we develop and evaluate options as prescribed by the rational decision process?

Alternative models have been proposed, and there is considerable evidence that they are better descriptions of the way decision making actually takes place in many situations.[41] Nevertheless, the planning process as set out above is still the prevailing paradigm. Planning practices change, but this model of what should be done has yet to be improved upon.

NOTES

1. Henri Poincaré, *Science and Hypothesis* (London: Walter Scott, 1905; paperbound student's edition, New York: Dover, 1952).

2. Mao Tse-tung, "On Practice," 1937.

3. John W. Dyckman, "Introduction to Readings in the Theory of Planning: The State of Planning Theory in America" (mimeo draft, n.d.), p.9.

4. John W. Dyckman, "The Practical Uses of Planning Theory," *Journal of the American Institute of Planners* (JAIP) 35 (September 1969): 300.

5. Thomas D. Galloway and Riad G. Mahayni, "Planning Theory in Retrospect: The Process of Paradigm Change," *JAIP* 43 (January 1977):62–71.

6. Some planning theory texts do cover substantive areas: see Melville C. Branch, *Planning Urban Environment* (Stroudsburg, Pa.: Dowden, Hutchinson & Ross, 1974). Dyckman's "State of Planning Theory" concentrates on the procedural and normative aspects. Faludi suggests that the procedural aspects of planning are theory's proper area of concern: see Andreas Faludi, *Planning Theory* (Oxford: Pergamon, 1973).

7. An example of planning "taking over" the world is provided in Hasan Ozebekhan, "Toward a General Theory of Planning," in *Perspectives of Planning*, ed. Erich Jantsch (Paris: Organization for Economic Cooperation & Development, 1968), pp. 47–158.

8. Dyckman, "State of Planning Theory," p. 6.

9. Henry C. Hightower, "Toward a Definition of Square One: The ACSP School Review Committee and Procedural Planning Theory" (Paper presented at the Western Regional Meeting of the Association of Collegiate Schools of Planning, Port Ludlow, Wash., 18 October 1976).

10. George Chadwick, *A Systems View of Planning* (Oxford: Pergamon, 1971), p. 24.

11. George A. Miller, Eugene Galanter, and Karl H. Pribram, *Plans and the Structure of Behavior* (New York: Holt, 1960), pp. 26–38 and p. 16.

12. Paul Davidoff and Thomas A. Reiner, "A Choice Theory of Planning," *JAIP* 28 (May 1962):103.

13. Aaron Wildavsky, "Does Planning Work?" *The Public Interest* 24 (Summer 1971):101.

14. John Friedman, "Notes on Societal Action," *JAIP* 35 (September 1969):312

15. Horst Rittel and Melvin Webber, "Dilemmas in a General Theory of Planning," *Policy Sciences* 4 (1972):155–69.

16. Sir Geoffrey Vickers, *Value Systems and Social Process* (New York: Basic Books, 1968), pp. 97–98.

17. Aaron Wildavsky, "If Planning is Everything, Maybe It's Nothing," *Policy Sciences* 4 (1973):127–53.

18. See, e.g., Faludi, *Planning Theory*, pp. 184–85; and Martin Meyerson, "Building the Middle-Range Bridge for Comprehensive Planning," *JAIP* 22 (Spring 1956):58–64.

18a. Herbert A. Simon, *The New Science of Management Decision* (New York: Harper, 1960), p. 7.

19. Susan S. Fainstein and Norman I. Fainstein, "City Planning and Political Values," *Urban Affairs Quarterly* 6 (March 1971):348.

20. Martin Meyerson, "Utopian Tradition and the Planning of Cities," *Daedalus* 90 (Winter 1961):180–93.

21. These two types of rationality in the planning context were distinguished by Max Weber, when he was discussing about bureaucracy, and by Karl Mannheim. Weber called the first "formal, or purposive," rationality," and Mannheim called it "functional" rationality. This is defined as the rational choice of means, when ends or goals are given. It contrasts with "value" rationality (Weber) or "substantive" rationality (Mannheim), which is concerned with choice between objectives in the light of considerations of purpose; see Max Weber, *The Theory of Social and Economic Organization* (Edinburgh: William Hodge, 1947); Karl Mannheim, *Man and Society in an Age of Reconstruction* (London: Kegan Paul, 1940).

22. For a formal statement of the axioms of rationality, see *International Encyclopedia of the Social Sciences*, 1968 ed., s.v. "Decision Making: Economic Aspects," by Jacob Marschak.

23. An extensive literature in experimental psychology attests to the prevalence of intransitive preferences; see, for example, C. H. Coombs, *A Theory of Data* (New York: Wiley, 1964), pp. 106–18.

24. This is reviewed in Ward Edwards, "Behavioral Decision Theory," *Annual Review of Psychology* 12 (1961):473–98.

25. An extended, but still simple, explanation of decision analysis is offered in Irwin D. J. Bross, *Design for Decision: An Introduction to Statistical Decision Making* (New York: Free Press, 1961), pp. 6–144.

26. Kenneth J. Arrow, *Social Choice and Individual Values* (New York: Wiley, 1963).

27. Decision making in the political arena and its relation to planning is the subject of numerous studies, some of which are cited in other contexts below. For a useful concise review of this work, see Don T. Allensworth, *The Political Realities of Urban Planning* (New York: Praeger, 1975).

28. Edward C. Banfield, "Notes on a Conceptual Scheme," in *Politics, Planning, and the Public Interest*, by Martin Meyerson and Edward C. Banfield (Glencoe, Ill.: Free Press, 1955), pp. 303–29; J. K. Friend and W. N. Jessop, *Local Government and Strategic Choice* (London: Tavistock, 1969); and Nathaniel Lichfield, Peter Kettle, and Michael Whitbread, *Evaluation in the Planning Process* (Oxford: Pergamon, 1973).

29. Katherine A. Archibald, "Three Views of the Expert's Role in Policy-Making: Systems Analysis Incrementalism, and the Clinical Approach," *Policy Sciences* 1 (Spring 1970):73–86. A more extended example of different analytical approaches eliciting different solutions is given in Graham T. Allison, *Essence of Decision: Explaining the Cuban Missile Crisis* (Boston: Little, Brown, 1971).

30. Roland L. Warren, "The Sociology of Knowledge and the Problems of the Inner Cities," *Social Science Quarterly* 52

(December 1971):469–91.

31. W. Keith Warner and A. Eugene Havens, "Goal Displacement and the Intangibility of Organizational Goals," *Administrative Science Quarterly* 12 (March 1968):539–55.

32. For a review of the experience with one method, PPBS, see *Public Administration Review* 33 (March-April 1973):146–56.

33. Reviews of these techniques and others appear in Erich Jantsch, *Technological Forecasting in Perspective* (Paris: Organisation for Economic Co-operation & Development 1967); and Stephen C. Wheelwright and Spyros Makridakis, *Forecasting Methods for Management*, 2d ed. (New York: Wiley 1977).

34. Lichfield, Kettle, and Whitbread, *Evaluation in the Planning Process*, p. 13.

35. Alan Newell and Herbert A. Simon, *Human Problem Solving* (Englewood Cliffs, N.J.: Prentice-Hall, 1972).

36. Christopher J. Jones, *Design Methods: Seeds of Human Features* (New York: Wiley, 1970).

37. Some of this work is reviewed in Gerald Zaltman, Robert Duncan, and Jonny Holbeck, *Innovations and Organizations* (New York: Wiley, 1973).

38. An example of the analysis of these factors is provided in Anthony J. Mumphrey, Jr., John R. Seley, and Julian Wolpert, "A Decision Model for Locating Controversial Facilities," *JAIP* 37 (November 1971):397–402.

39. A comprehensive review and discussion of these methods is offered in Lichfield, Kettle, and Whitbread, *Evaluation in the Planning Process.*

40. See, A. J. Catanese and A. W. Steiss, *Systemic Planning: Theory and Application* (Lexington, Mass: Heath, 1970).

41. Some of these reservations are expressed in Herbert A. Simon, *Models* of Man (New York: Wiley, 1957): Charles E. Lindblom, "The Science of Muddling Through," *Public Administration Review* 19 (Spring 1959):79–88; Michael D. Cohen, James G. March, and Johann P. Olsen, "A Garbage Cart Model of Organizational Choice," *Administrative Science Quarterly* 17 (March 1972):1–25; Michael D. Cohen and James G. March, *Leadership and Ambiguity* (New York: McGraw-Hill, 1974), pp. 216–29; Michael B. McCaskey, "A Contingency Approach to Planning with Goals and Planning without Goals," *American Academy of Management Journal* 17 (June 1974):281–91; and John D. Steinbruner, *The Cybernetic Theory of Decision* (Princeton, N.J.: Princeton University Press, 1974).

FOR FURTHER READING

Banfield, Edward C. "Notes on a Conceptual Scheme." In *Politics, Planning, and the Public Interest,* by Martin Meyerson and Edward C. Banfield. Glencoe, Ill.: Free Press, 1955. Pp. 303–29.

Branch, Melville C. *Planning Urban Environment.* Stroudsburg, Pa.: Dowden, Hutchinson & Ross, 1974..

Bross, Irwin D. J. *Design for Decision: An Introduction to Statistical Decision Making.* New York: Free Press, 1961.

Chadwick, George. *A Systems View of Planning.* Oxford: Pergamon, 1971.

Davidoff, Paul, and Reiner, Thomas A. "A Choice Theory of Planning." *Journal of the American Institute of Planners (JAIP)* 28 (May 1962):103–15.

Dyckman, John W. "The Practical Uses of Planning Theory." *JAIP* 35 (September 1969):298–300.

Faludi, Andreas. *Planning Theory.* Oxford: Pergamon, 1973.

Fainstein, Susan S. and Norman I., "City Planning and Political Values," *Urban Affairs Quarterly* 6 (March 1971):341–362.

Friedman, John. "Notes on Societal Action." *JAIP* 35 (September 1969):311–18.

Friend, J. K., and Jessop, W. N. *Local Government and Strategic Choice.* London: Tavistock, 1969.

Jones, Christopher J. *Design Methods: Seeds of Human Futures.* New York: Wiley-Interscience, 1970.

Lichfield, Nathaniel; Kettle, Peter; and Whitbread, Michael. *Evaluation in the Planning Process.* Oxford: Pergamon, 1973.

Meyerson, Martin. "Building the Middle-Range Bridge for Comprehensive Planning." *JAIP* 22 (Spring 1956):58–64.

Miller, George A.; Galanter, Eugene; and Pribram, Karl H. *Plans and the Structure of Behavior.* New York: Holt, 1960.

Newell, Alan, and Simon, Herbert A. *Human Problem Solving.* Englewood Cliffs, N.J.: Prentice-Hall, 1972.

Rittel, Horst, and Webber, Melvin. "Dilemmas in a General Theory of Planning." *Policy Sciences* 4 (1973):155–69.

Simon, Herbert A., *Models of Man:* New York: Wiley, 1957.

Wildavsky, Aaron. "If Planning is Everything, Maybe It's Nothing." *Policy Sciences* 4 (1973):127–53.

CHAPTER 5

Planning Roles and Context

Ernest R. Alexander

Urban planning takes place in certain contexts that tend to delimit the process itself as well as constrain implementation. Many of these contexts are beyond the scope of influence of urban planners—indeed their characteristics are inherently societal. This means that urban planners must adopt certain roles if they are to be useful and successful in effecting plans. Such roles may be defined either by planners themselves or by society at large and may change along with changes in societal values and standards. It is within these recognized and emerging roles that planners must work to define how most effectively to carry out their perceived missions. These contexts, too, provide the rationale of societal processes and problems which establishes the legitimacy of urban planning.

MODELS AND ROLES

Planning Models

The large number of planning models reflects the pluralist nature of American practice. American planners work in contexts as diverse as the Department of Housing and Urban Development; state and regional governments; local communities; and neighborhood redevelopment agencies. Planning models have emerged throughout the history of professional thought and practice. Here we will review a few contemporary models for illustrative purposes.

Comprehensive Planning. The comprehensive planning model evolved from the physical planning model that prevailed in the 1920s and 1930s. It recognizes the complexity of factors affecting and affected by what were previously perceived as purely physical or land use decisions. These factors include social and demographic characteristics of population; economic variables, such as income and local or regional economic base; and transportation factors, like travel patterns, modal split, and transportation networks. Comprehensive planning aims to take all these factors into account in a rational, analytic planning process.[1]

During the 1950s and into the early 1960s this model was the dominant one in planning practice. It is still widely applied in land use planning by local government. Comprehensive planning was institutionalized in the 701 program of the *Housing Act of 1954* (which required local governments to prepare comprehensive plans to be eligible for federal grants and programs).

The comprehensive planning model is based on a technocratic ideology that accepts the scientific legitimacy of the planner's expertise. It assumes that the planner knows or can discover other people's needs, and that a central planning agency has the authority and autonomy to develop planning proposals through rational analysis, as well as the power to implement them.[2] Comprehensive planning has been criticized for these assumptions, and for what some have seen as its acceptance of the *status quo*, support of the political establishment, and perpetuation of middle class values.[3]

Social Planning. Social planning evolved in the 1960s, when comprehensive planning concepts were brought into the arena of social and human services. It allows for consideration of the wants of particular groups and involves the extensive use of social science techniques for identification of these needs. This planning approach is oriented to social needs more than to the physical environment. In contrast to the environmental determinism of earlier design-based planning—i.e., its assumption that human behavior can be changed by the physical environment—social planning aims to intervene directly in social interactions. Social planning has had its greatest impact on the planning of government-supported programs, such as those dealing with welfare, health, education, and labor.[4]

Social planning has certain ideological shortcomings. Its assumptions of a central authority and benevolent therapist-planners raise questions about legitimacy and participation in decision making.[5] While its political implications are democratic, and less authoritarian than the comprehensive approach, its client orientation is a concession to the multiplicity of conflicting interests in a plural society.

Advocacy Planning. Reacting to the centralist and technocratic values of the prevailing planning modes in the mid-1960s, some planners created a model of planning which was analogous to the U.S. legal system, which they called *advocacy planning.* The role proposed for planners was to be similar to that of lawyers in the adversary legal system. Advocacy planning was based on the realization that society is not homogeneous but consists of many groups with different interests and values. In this plural society, power is unequally distributed, and access to resources is not the same for the rich and the poor or the educated and the ignorant.[6]

The advocate-planner would be a spokesperson for the poor, neighborhoods, or other groups with inadequate access to government. He or she would provide them with the expertise they need to make their voices heard in public decision making. This role was institutionalized in many of the War on Poverty Programs of the 1960s, such as the Community Action and Model Cities Programs. It continues to be played out today in some community planning efforts and consumer and environmental activism.[7]

Although it corrected some of the biases of other planning models, advocacy planning has limitations. The appropriateness of its legal model in the political context is questionable. Where there is no law, no judge, and no jury, the distribution of power

will resolve conflicting interests through political arbitration. The advocate-planner's best case may not be good enough in that arbitration if compromise does not occur. Some doubt that advocacy planning can go as far as necessary in correcting the unequal distribution of resources.[8] Finally, some question whether any planner can really represent the poor or other excluded groups. Once such a group is identified as a client, it develops its own spokespersons who become its liaison with the planners.[9]

Bureaucratic Planning. Under bureaucratic planning, the planner is the servant of government and its elected officials. The planner takes on the role of a value-neutral administrator.[10] Since bureaucratic planning is more role than process oriented, it is not associated with any one style, although it appears often in planning descriptions of more centralized countries such as Great Britain and France.[11] An emphasis on rationality and systematic analysis leads to the comprehensive planning approach. On the other hand, the bureaucrat planner focusing on feasibility and implementation in a pluralistic environment like American local government may adopt the incremental model described below.

Radical or Anti-Planning. The late 1960s and early 1970s have also seen a number of proposals for the involvement of planners in social change outside the governmental establishment or in active opposition to it. These schemes range from ideological reorientation through community self-regulation and self-help to communitarian planning philosophies.[12]

The trouble with these proposals, as some of their initiators have recognized, is that they can never be more than interstitial in society as we know it. The radical planner, once he or she has won the battle against the *status quo,* cannot avoid becoming part of the very institutions he or she has sworn to alter. Furthermore, many of these models depend on the trust and intimacy of small-group interactions, which have to be replaced by the hierarchy, rules, and accountability of a formal organization when the group's activities grow.

Nonplanning. Several versions of what we call nonplanning have been proposed. They are all based on laissez-faire premises; i.e., that people's behavior and interactions will eventually produce socially optimal outcomes with a minimum of regulation.

The incremental decision model, which was developed in reaction to the limitations of rational analysis, is an example of such an approach. It suggests that policies should be developed by trial and error instead of deliberate planning.[13] The value of the model is illustrated by the unregulated but orderly growth of Houston, Texas, and by a proposal for the experimental deregulation of southeastern England.[14]

Ultimately, the ideal mix between planning and nonplanning is a product of the planner's ideology, view of society, and values. To the extent that one agrees with the moderates that the *status quo* is good and needs only minor changes, with the anarchists that human nature is intrinsically good and is only perverted by rules and controls, or with the cynics that it will do more harm than good to attempt to stretch the narrow limits of our perfectibility, rationality, and ability to control our own futures, he or she will accept nonplanning to some degree. But if one believes that change is both necessary and possible, and that the outcome of many individually sensible decisions is often a state of affairs nobody wants, or that some beneficial control of our own futures is possible, then he or she will be more sensitive to the limits of the nonplanning approach.

Planners' Roles

The evolution of the planning profession has been accompanied by a proliferation of roles for the planners. Common sense supports the conclusion reached in several studies that some roles are more effective in certain contexts than in others. Some of these roles are discussed below.

Technician-Administrator. This is the traditional role of the planner in governmental contexts: the technical expert at the service of elected officials. The role can be effective when political leaders delegate authority to planners. The planner can apply professional expertise to effect objectives that have been well-defined by the policymakers, with confidence that government can muster the support and resources necessary for their realization.

Frequently, however, this situation is the ideal rather than the reality, and the expected relationship between administrative planner and politician breaks down or never even develops. This may happen when the government represents a diversity of interests that are rarely reconciled in the consensus necessary for effective action. Then the neutral administrator role must be supplemented or superseded by one of the other roles before the planner's proposals can have an impact on policy.[15]

Political Roles. Often the planner must actively develop support for plan implementation. He or she may assume the role of a mobilizer, making allies of government agencies or appealing to the public at large, directly or through the media. Since these actions can put the planner at odds with elected officials who are against the policies he or she advocates, the planner is assuming a political role. Political roles put the planner at risk. Failure, or even lack of success in mobilizing a constituency, can cost the planner his or her job.

There are other political roles besides that of the mobilizer. One is the *mediator:* the planner applies professional expertise to the analysis of issues in order to identify salient problems; develops proposals to minimize, reconcile, or eliminate these problems; and wins acceptance for solutions from conflicting groups through skillful manipulation of personal and institutional relationships.

Another role, less overtly public but political nonetheless, is that of *entrepreneur.* The entrepreneur wins support for plans by gathering the resources needed to carry them out. He or she puts together the funds, as well as the necessary administrative approval and political support, to implement plans. The planner often develops entrepreneurial proposals specifically to generate resources for the organization. The success of such efforts gives the entrepreneur planner the necessary base for implementing other plans which may have fewer obvious and short-term benefits.[16]

Advocate and Guerrilla. The advocate role means the representation of special interest groups. These range from neighborhood residents to poor people to organizations, such as churches, consumer agencies, or corporations.

As discussed earlier, the citizen participation required by federal programs in the 1960s meant that the role of the advocate planner became institutionalized. Though most of these programs no longer exist, the advocate planning role lives on in issue-oriented groups such as the Suburban Action Institute, the Sierra Club, and consumer organizations.

The development of neighborhood planning programs has led to the institutionalization of the advocate role in city government. The neighborhood planners, although employed and paid by city hall, are expected to be advocates for the special interests of their communities, sometimes in opposition to the more general public interest represented by the city planning agency.

The advocate role does bring planning a step closer to the people, but often results in an ambivalent situation. Sometimes it creates community planners who are "guerrillas" in the bureaucracy, and the role conflicts have not yet been satisfactorily resolved.[17]

The Social Context of Planning

Our discussion of planning definitions suggested that planning, in any significant sense, is a societal activity. Consequently, an important factor affecting the planning process will be the social context in which it takes place. Planning theory includes hypotheses and findings from the social sciences—sociology, psychology, political science, and others—that give some insight into behavior in these contexts. For the purposes of this broad review they may be clustered as follows into four general categories.

Groups and Organizations. Groups and organizations form the context of almost all social activities. Both groups and organizations are purposeful; that is, they have goals, although these are not necessarily explicit. Groups may be, and generally are, transitory. Usually, when they become permanent (like the Friday night bridge group, which grows into the neighborhood bridge club) they acquire the attributes of organizations.

Organizations are more permanent than groups. Members of an organization share the organization's goals, or at least pretend to do so as long as the benefits of membership command their loyalty. Such benefits often are material: money in the form of salaries or commissions, or other such perquisites.

The member may also enjoy psychological benefits: status and prestige, satisfaction from performing a task well, friendships, or identification with norms or an ideology. Organizations are in a constant exchange relationship with their members, receiving the benefits of these individuals' efforts and skills as long as the members are satisfied with the sum of the benefits the organization supplies in return. These, in a nutshell, are the elements of organizational motivation.

An organization is a social system and is susceptible to analysis like any other social system. The complexity of an organization depends on several factors, including its size, its task and technology, and its environment. The structure of an organization may be envisaged as an interacting assembly of subsystems. Each subsystem is merely a subsidiary organizational unit when seen from the perspective of the organization as a whole, but at its own level, the subsystem is an organization in itself, with its own membership and goals. Alternatively, an organization can be analyzed as an interdependent network of roles, each of which is filled by an individual or a suborganizational unit. The organization chart, with its neat hierarchy of positions and job descriptions, illustrates this concept of structure. But the formal structure and network, important as they are, do not tell the whole story. Equally important to an explanation of organizational effectiveness or failure are the informal networks and group relationships.

Finally, since they are social units, organizations are open systems. That is, they affect and are affected by their environment. Organizational environments have been studied in order to identify their salient dimensions. These include complexity and uncertainty, which have important effects on organizational structure and behavior, organizational change and innovation, and the interactions of organizations with each other.[18]

Organizations include governmental institutions, semi-public agencies, and private firms and corporations. Although planning in the organizational context is usually identified with the public sector, there is also a good deal of planning in business and industry. Here planning may lead to long-range corporate policy. However, it is more often associated with a particular functional area such as marketing, finance, investment, research, or product development.[19]

Bureaucracy. A bureaucracy is a special kind of organization. It is usually thought of as a part of government, but there are also bureaucracies in large private organizations, such as industrial firms. A bureaucratic organization is characterized by task differentiation (specialized jobs); a hierarchical structure (a formal chain of command); expectation that decisions will be made according to rational criteria; and recruitment and promotion based on achievement rather than ascription, on competence and skill rather than kinship. These characteristics are expressed in government by civil service rules, ranks, and standard operating procedures.

In the modern period of industrialization and technological change, bureaucracy has developed as the most effective organizational form for the achievement of given ends. It combines the advantages of rationality, due process for members and clients, and predictable actions and relationships. Nevertheless, the bureaucratic organization is dysfunctional in some situations.

Because of its hierarchical structure and tendency to centralize decision making, bureaucracy has proven to be rigid and slow to adapt to change. The proliferation of rules leads to *goal displacement,* a phenomenon observed in other organizations but which is most typical of bureaucracies. Goal displacement means the substitution of some instrumental objective for the real goal. Filling out a form correctly and completely becomes more important to an official than helping the client, or fulfilling a numerical quota become a manager's objective rather than making a quality product.

Bureaucracies in the public sector encounter the additional problem of accountability. Their ef-

forts ought to be evaluated, but evaluation is difficult because they rarely produce a concrete output. Another flaw in public bureaucracies is that they often concern themselves with growth rather than efficiency. This is because the public official, unlike the private entrepreneur, gets rewards—higher salary, status, and more power—from factors associated with growth, such as additional subordinates, a wider domain of activity, and higher budget allocations.[20] When bureaucracies in the public sector are compared with large corporations, however, they are revealed to be more similar than different; corporate executives, too, get their rewards more from growth or stability than from profit maximization.

Communities. A community is another kind of organization, one that is linked by geography. People belong to a community because they are neighbors, and these links are affirmed in a variety of community organizations and special units of government. Organizational interaction and local politics form the context of many planning efforts at the community level. The organizational actors may be general governments, local interest groups such as the Chamber of Commerce and real estate developers, or special units of government such as school boards, highway commissions, and sewer and water districts.[21] Three schools of thought have emerged to explain how these interactions are structured to produce decisions.

The first view, often called *elitist,* is based on social stratification theory. It sees community decisions as the product of a small group of powerful individuals, often representing upper-class, corporate, and financial interests. The second view sees community decision making as the *pluralist* interplay of numerous interest groups, with different interests or individuals being more powerful in different decision arenas. These two perspectives are not mutually exclusive. A third perspective sees the community as an arena for the interaction of institutionalized or organized interests and groups, with policy the outcome of their respective strategies and games.[22]

These different perceptions provide conceptual frameworks for the analysis of planning and its impacts in the community context. The literature of analysis consists mostly of an increasing number of case studies, with a few attempts at conceptualizing the case findings at a more abstract level.[23] Although we have developed some useful insights, we are still a long way from anything like a normative theory.

Governments. Governments and government agencies are the most common context of formal planning in this country and abroad. Studies of planning in government relate the organization, purpose, and effectiveness of planning activity to the level, functions, and organizational structure of government. One of the first analyses—that of Robert Walker—dealt with the planning agency's position in the organizational structure of local government, comparing the agency's effectiveness as a line agency to its effectiveness in a more direct staff relationship to the chief executive—the mayor or city manager. Its conclusion, favoring the staff position, had a profound impact on the organization of planning in local government.[24]

The metropolitan and regional levels of planning, which for a long time were not institutionalized within any formal governmental body, have been given a great deal of attention. Studies based on the limited but varied experience with these forms have considered the optimal organization and functions of metropolitan and regional governments in general and their planning activities in particular.[25]

The advent of the *New Federalism* brought prominence to planning at the state level. State planning agencies, their orientations , and their locations in state government have been analyzed to determine factors that might affect their operations. This field of analysis is in its infancy and has spawned few concrete propositions as yet. One study, however, concludes that a policy-coordinative orientation is more effective than alternatives such as development or service delivery.[26]

National planning is conspicuous by its absence in the United States. Most studies of planning in the federal government are related to specific sectors such as housing, education, social welfare, and land use and environmental protection.[27] A few exceptions have attempted a generic review of governmental planning and policy development. These studies agree that highly centralized programs have not been very successful here. The effective programs—Social Security and Internal Revenue are examples—are usually either self-administered and only centrally regulated or delivered through market incentives.[28]

Planning contexts differ from culture to culture and nation to nation. Comparative studies, therefore, offer another opportunity for new insights. Some of these try to draw conclusions that can be transferred from one environment to another. Others look more analytically at different countries to see how planning approaches and outcomes vary within their national contexts.[29]

Planning in developing countries, mainly at the national level, precipitated a flood of planning literature in the early 1960s. Much of the data was normative, often based on a review of experience. Hirschman, for example, focused on planning at the project level and presented valuable insights on the positive role of uncertainty and optimism in the planning context. Richard Meier's work, based on his Puerto Rican experience, draws important conclusions about the functions of entrepreneurship and organizational development in less-developed countries.[30] One of the few analyses of development planning in a purely descriptive format was done by Naomi Caiden and Aaron Wildavsky. They draw normative conclusions, however, which are very pessimistic about the potential for comprehensive national planning in the uncertain environment of the Third World.[31]

PLANNING: WHY AND WHAT FOR?

Legitimacy and Authority

"Why plan?" is a moot question in most of the conditions under which planning takes place. We have seen that planning can be viewed as a part of any activity that is more than an instinctive reflex. But more particularly, planning is an essential component of every social decision. Each societal unit, whether it is a family, group, organization, or government, is engaged in planning whenever it makes decisions or develops policies to change something in its own makeup or its environment. We seldom ask whether we should plan; planning takes place all the time.

Naturally, not all planning is carried out by planners, nor should it be. However, when planning is undertaken by public planners rather than private individuals, what are the reasons for delegating this function to them as specialists? Legitimacy is a precursor of authority, authority for planners being that which enables them to evaluate and recommend choices between courses of action that will affect many others.

Planners have traditionally been accepted as design-oriented professionals. Their expertise has expanded to include the ability to aggregate diverse needs into a common public interest and the ability to apply the tools of rationality to the development of public policy.[32] Professional expertise is a widely recognized source of authority. Unfortunately, it is not always enough to win acceptance for planners' proposals in the political arena. The independence of the expert can be a forecaster of impotence, for the power to propose is rarely followed by the authority to implement.

Another source of authority for the planner is bureaucratic position. In the bureaucratic role, planners get their authority from the elected officials of the government they serve. This legitimacy, however, is limited by several factors. Political officials may not be as broadly representative as they should be, so that they respond to the interest groups that elected them rather than to "the public interest." Furthermore, the theoretical distinction between the policymaking master and the administrative servant is blurred in practice, where many policy decisions are in fact made at the administrative level rather than by the legislative body.

A third base for planning authority is user preferences. In a kind of market model, the planner is seen as purveying planning services to diverse interests to meet different expressed needs. The social planning model demands that clients' needs be discovered scientifically, by surveys and other research or by user participation. The advocacy planning model holds that interests will be expressed through a political market.

Lastly, planners' professional values can be a source of authority. In this view, planning is a value-laden profession, and the planner's internalization of values gives him or her the sanction to plan for others. The difficulty with this legitimation is that it holds good only as long as value consensus exists, or values are shared in a homogeneous community of planners and planned-for.

Reviewing this issue, Martin Rein suggests that

> There are multiple sources of legitimacy, (which) cannot all be pursued under the auspices of one planning organization and hence choice is required . . . . Each . . . has its characteristic weaknesses and strengths which present to the planner a set of intractable problems that are moral in character.[33]

Planning's Rationale and Limits

Free Markets and Social Values. We view planning here as an integral part of any deliberate societal activity; therefore the rationale for planning is linked to social action. "Why plan?" is transformed into a question about the times and conditions when society should undertake deliberate action. Most social processes occur without such intervention. Family formation and population change, migration and resettlement, industrialization and technological development have seldom been the result of any conscious decisions. These are powerful social movements, but they are in one sense simply the combination of an infinite number of decisions made by individuals and larger societal units.

The individual decisions and actions that constitute major social trends are of course planned. But they are planned and undertaken in the interests of the specific individual, household, or firm involved. Together they may be beneficent, as when millions of individual purchasing decisions are made with confidence that consumers will have more money to spend, and a market boom is generated. On the other hand, the aggregate self-interest can be unwittingly and systematically destructive.

Garret Hardin called this phenomenon "the tragedy of the commons." He drew an analogy with the destruction of common grazing enclosures in the medieval English village. Without regard for his neighbor's actions or the cumulative effect over time, each householder made the reasonable decision to graze as many cattle on the commons as possible, since the land cost him nothing. As a result, the commons were destroyed by overgrazing, and all the users were left poorer than before. A simple rationing system might have preserved this public resource for the general benefit.[34]

The "tragedy of the commons" was brought about by the effect of externalities, that is, by the external or spillover effects of one individual's or unit's actions on others. Environmental pollution is another classic example of external effects.

The free market may founder on other obstacles. An example is the emergence of monopolies. The local telephone company is a monopoly; once one company has set up its network in a community, the cost of installing a parallel system prevents other firms from competing in the same area. To prevent such monopolies from setting outrageously high prices in the absence of competition, governments have regulated them as public utilities. A different set of legal tools applies to oligopoly—the tendency for a few large firms to dominate production and/or pricing of a class of goods.

Some goods, however, are produced by governments and public organizations. They are distributed by means not recognized by the free market model. Public goods, such as defense or public safety, benefit everyone; like rain, they descend upon the just and the unjust alike. Merit goods, of which education is an example, confer a greater benefit on the individual than he or she may be willing or able to pay for; because of the long-term benefit to society, a merit good may have to be provided below cost, with the deficit made up indirectly, through taxes. In all of these situations social intervention may be justifiable to remedy the dysfunctions of the free market, and every social intervention of this kind involves planning.[35]

Market Rationality and Plan Rationality. An alternative response to perceived failures in free market societies is to institute a planned economy. This is what socialism advocates, and it has been accomplished in Eastern Europe, China, and several countries of the Third World. Directed economies such as these could be seen as victories for planning were it not for their limitations, which include the sacrifice of some of the advantages of free markets.

The advantages and limitations of the free market and planned social intervention are summarized by Ralf Dahrendorff. Both market and plan, he agrees, are rational types of social organization. The market is efficient as a mechanism for transmitting individual wants and needs and is highly adaptable to conditions of uncertainty and change. But if society does not accept the existing distributions of power, resources, and participation, then the market must be supplemented by planned decisions that reflect societal values. These decisions are made through the political system.

Planned rationality is a mechanism for making

deliberate social decisions, guided by purposeful social norms. Unlike the market, where individual, firm, and household decisions are created from the bottom up, the planned economy requires that planning proceed from the top down. Consequently, it depends heavily on predictions and projections and has to assume a large measure of certainty and stability. This makes centrally planned societies unstable and inefficient, as witnessed in Russia's agricultural production or China's "Great Leap Forward."[36]

Planning requires a good deal of stability in order to be effective. The accelerating changes in every sector of modern society have made planning more and more difficult. Some observers even view the rapidity of change as a general threat to the decision-making capability of social organizations; deliberate social action requires a degree of continuity, shared values, and consensus on appropriate decision-making processes, all of which are more and more frequently absent.[37] The challenge of developing processes that will be adaptable to these circumstances has begun to stimulate some planners, but it is a challenge planning practice has yet to meet.[38]

Goals and Values. One response to the question "What is planning for?" holds that planning must be undertaken in situations where the forces of supply and demand, as expressed through the market, fail to meet social needs. These needs will be different, of course, in every particular case. However, is there a common goal or set of human needs at a higher level of abstraction that should be the objective of any planning efforts?

Discussion of the goals and values implicit in planning has been surprisingly limited, in spite of their special relevance to planners. One might assume that the most concrete articulation of goals would be the professional planners' code of ethics, but it is quite vague:

A planner primarily serves the public interest and shall accept or continue employment only when the planner can insure accommodation of the client's or employer's interest with the public interest.[39]

A suggestion of the values that constitute this public interest was offered by a group called Concerned Architects and Planners:

The proper role of professional planners on issues of public policy does, we believe, require a commitment to certain basic common values, and we would hope that our profession would be united in its commitment to those values: humaneness, democracy, rationality.[40]

Professional ethics in planning, then, as in other professions, offer relatively little help in articulating the profession's values. Even when those values are humaneness, democracy, and rationality, the planning code of ethics is too oriented toward the "client-serving, guild-related roles of planners to examine their real effect on the social, economic, and political system in which the planners' activities take place."[41]

The term *public interest* is too vague, and *humaneness, democracy, rationality* perhaps too culture-specific, to serve as planning's ultimate goal. Striving to synthesize a range of planning objectives, Faludi proposed that the goal of planning is the encouragement of human growth.[42] In doing so he recognized Maslow's hierarchy of human needs, ranging from basic material and psychological needs—food, shelter, love, and security—to a desire for personal fulfillment. This form of human growth ensures that needs will be fulfilled at each level of this hierarchy.

As an end for planning, the enhancement of human growth is laudable; it subsumes all other objectives. Human growth should be the ultimate goal not only of planning but of all social activity. On the other hand, this vastness of purpose makes this end less than satisfactory as a practical goal for a profession. No distinction is possible between planning and any other type of thought or action. There is no yardstick by which to evaluate planners' professional contributions and behavior. Human growth is too abstract; and, in concrete terms and contexts, one person's growth may be another's destruction.

The development of a policy plan for Cleveland included an instructive attempt to identify a single goal for planning efforts. Cleveland's planners tried to identify a target and a clientele for public policy. They concluded:

> Equity requires that government institutions give priority attention to the goal of promoting a wider range of choices for those Cleveland residents who have few, if any, choices.[43]

Maximizing choices for all and focusing on those whose choices are most limited may be as near to an operational objective for planning as is possible. The requirements for equity are tangible enough to serve as a yardstick for the evaluation of planning efforts and as a guide for identifying the public interest in comparing the impacts of policy options.

John Friedmann has identified a set of planning goals appropriate to the changing postindustrial society of the United States and the developed West. In this context, says Friedmann, the emerging style of planning will have

to regard the future as open to choice and experimental action

to place the person as a source of moral values in the center of any action

to search for participant forms of social organization

to enlarge the scope for autonomous group action by . . . linking the new communitarian forms of social relations into larger participatory structures capable of sharing effectively in the processes of societal guidance.[44]

These goals can be viewed as complementary to those of the Cleveland group. Those would optimize society as it is, while Friedmann's goals are based on a changed society, or aim to change the present one. In Cleveland, a planning process is taken as given, and a criterion is developed for use in that context. Friedmann suggests that planning ought to aim at changing the planning process itself, and he proposes some objectives for a kind of planning that has yet to exist.

It is not surprising that there is no consensus yet on planning's values and goals; after all, no consensus exists on what planning is. As we begin to detect a convergence among definitions of planning, however, there is a chance for a synthesis of different goals. We agree that planning is a force for change. Whether planners accomplish a change in society by maximizing choice, or whether a change of society forces them to consider Friedmann's proposed planning process, may in the end be a matter of circumstances rather than debate.

NOTES

1. The best exposition of the comprehensive planning approach is found in Melvin C. Branch, ed., *Urban Planning Theory* (Stroudsburg, Pa.: Dowden, Hutchinson & Ross, 1975).
2. For a more detailed comparison of comprehensive planning with other planning models, see Susan S. Fainstein and Norman I. Fainstein, "City Planning and Political Values," *Urban Affairs Quarterly* 6 (March 1971):341–62.
3. John Friedmann, "The Future of Comprehensive Urban Planning: A Critique," *Public Administration Review* 31 (May–June 1971):315–26; and Herbert J. Gans, *People and*

Plans: Essays on Urban Problems and Solutions (New York: Basic Books, 1968).

4. One exposition of social planning is that of Alfred J. Kahn, *Theory and Practice of Social Planning* (New York: Russell Sage, 1969).

5. John W. Dyckman, "Social Planning, Social Planners, and Planned Societies," *Journal of the American Institute of Planners (JAIP)* 26 (March 1960):66–76.

6. Paul Davidoff, "Advocacy and Pluralism in Planning," *JAIP* 31 (November 1965):331–38.

7. Accounts of these efforts include: Earl M. Blecher, *Advocacy Planning for Urban Development* (New York: Praeger, 1970); and Marshall Kaplan, "Advocacy and Urban Planning," *Social Welfare Forum* (New York: Columbia University Press, 1968), pp. 58–77.

8. Donald F. Maziotti, "The Underlying Assumptions of Advocacy Planning: Pluralism and Reform," *JAIP* 40 (January 1974): 38–48.

9. See, e.g., Frances Fox Piven et al., "Symposium: Whom Does the Advocacy Planner Serve?" *Social Policy* (May–June 1970):32–37.

10. Donald A. Barr, "The Professional Urban Planners," *JAIP* 38 (May 1972):155–59.

11. John K. Friend and W. N. Jessop, *Local Government and Strategic Choice* (London: Tavistock, 1969); and Stephen S. Cohen, *Modern Capitalist Planning: The French Model* (Cambridge, Mass.: Harvard University Press, 1969).

12. Robert Goodman, *After the Planners* (New York: Simon & Schuster, 1971); Richard Sennet, *The Uses of Disorder* (New York: Random House, 1970); Stephen Grabow and Allan Heskin, "Foundations for a Radical Concept of Planning," *JAIP* 39 (March 1973):106–14; and John Friedmann, *The Good Society: A Primer of Its Social Practice* (Los Angeles: University of California–Los Angeles, School of Architecture and Urban Planning, 1976).

13. David Braybrooke and Carles E. Lindblom, *A Strategy of Decision: Policy Evaluation as a Social Process* (Glencoe, Ill.: Free Press, 1963).

14. Bernard H. Siegan, *Land Use without Zoning* (Lexington, Mass.: Heath, 1973); and Reyner Banham et al., "Non–Plan: An Experiment in Freedom," *New Society* 388 (March 1969).

15. The technician–administrator role is analyzed and compared with other roles in other contexts by Alan A. Altshuler, *The City Planning Process* (Ithaca, N.Y.: Cornell University Press, 1965); and Francine F. Rabinovitz, *City Politics and Planning* (New York: Atherton, 1969).

16. For a detailed discussion of political roles in planning, see Anthony J. Catanese, *Planners and Local Politics: Impossible Dreams* (Beverly Hills, Calif.: Sage, 1974).

17. Martin L. Needleman and Carolyn E. Needleman, *Guerillas in the Bureaucracy: The Community Planning Experiment in the U.S.* (New York: Wiley, 1974).

18. A classic in the vast literature of organizations is James G. March and Herbert A. Simon, *Organizations* (New York: Wiley, 1958). For a later and more abbreviated review see Amitai Etzioni, *Modern Organizations* (Englewood Cliffs, N.J.: Prentice-Hall, 1964).

19. Russell L. Ackoff, *A Concept of Corporate Planning* (New York: Wiley, 1970); Melville C. Branch, *The Corporate Planning Process* (New York: American Management Association, 1962).

20. Anthony Downs, *Inside Bureaucracy* (Boston: Little, Brown, 1967); William A. Niskanen, Jr., *Bureaucracy and Representative Government* (Chicago: Aldine, 1971).

21. Terry N. Clark, *Community Power and Policy Outputs: A Review of Urban Research* (Beverly Hills, Calif.: Sage, 1973).

22. Roland L. Warren et al., *The Structure of Urban Reform: Community Decision Organizations in Stability and Change* (Lexington, Mass.: Heath, 1974).

23. See, e.g., Richard S. Bolan, "Community Decision Behavior: The Culture of Planning," *JAIP* 35 (September 1969):233–45.

24. Robert A. Walker, *The Planning Function in Urban Government*, 2d ed. (Chicago: University of Chicago Press, 1950).

25. An example at the regional level is Martha Derthick, *Between State and Nation: Regional Organizations in the U.S.* (Washington, D.C.: Brookings, 1974). Cases of metropolitan government are presented in:James F. Blumstein and Walter Benjamin, *Growing Metropolis: Aspects of Development in Nashville* (Nashville, Tenn.: Vanderbilt University Press, 1975); Albert Rose, *Governing Metropolitan Toronto: A Social and Political Analysis 1953–1971* (Berkeley: University of California Press, 1972); and Edward E. Smith and Durward S. Riggs, *Land Use, Open Space, and the Governnment Process: The San Francisco Bay Area Experience* (New York: Praeger, 1974).

26. Donald A. Krueckeberg, "State Environmental Planning: Requirements versus Behavior," *JAIP* 38 (November 1972): 392–96; and David L. Rosebaugh, "State Planning as a Policy Coordinative Process," *JAIP* 42 (January 1976):52–63.

27. Examples are Arthur Solomon, *Housing the Urban Poor: A Critical Evaluation of Federal Policy* (Cambridge, Mass.: M.I.T., 1974); and Walter Williams, *Social Policy Research and Analysis: The Experience in the Federal Social Agencies* (New York: Elsevier, 1971).

28. Robert A. Levine, *Public Planning: Failure and Redirection* (New York: Basic Books, 1972).

29. An example of the first kind of study is Lloyd Rodwin, *Nations and Cities: A Comparison of Strategies for Urban Growth* (Boston: Houghton Mifflin, 1970); one of the second is Marion Clawson and Peter Hall, *Planning and Urban Growth: An Anglo-American Comparison* (Baltimore: Johns Hopkins for Resources for the Future, 1973), which concluded that the differences in context between its two cases made surprisingly little difference in the results.

30. Albert O. Hirschmann, *Development Projects Observed* (Washington, D.C.: Brookings, 1967); Richard L. Meier, *Developmental Planning* (New York: McGraw-Hill, 1965).

31. Naomi Caiden and Aaron Wildavsky, *Planning and Budgeting in Poor Countries* (New York: Wiley, 1974).

32. John W. Dyckman, "The Practical Uses of Planning Theory," *JAIP* 35 (September 1969):299.

33. Martin Rein, "Social Planning: The Search for Legitimacy," *JAIP* 35 (July 1969):243.

34. Garrett Hardin, "The Tragedy of the Commons," *Science* 162 (December 1968):1243–48.

35. An extensive body of literature in welfare economics deals with these issues; for a concise review see Terry Moore, "Why Allow Planners to Do What They Do? A Justification from Economic Theory," *JAIP* 44, 4 (October 1978):387–398.

36. Ralf Dahrendorff, "Market and Plan: Two Types of Rationality," in his *Essays in the Theory of Society* (Stanford,

132

Calif.:Stanford University Press, 1968), pp. 217–27.

37. Geoffrey Vickers, *Freedom in a Rocking Boat: Changing Values in an Unstable Society* (London: Allan Lane, 1970).

38. Such theoretical work as has been done is still very normative, and the ideas are far from being operational; see, e.g., John Friedmann, *Retracking America: A Theory of Transactive Planning* (New York: Doubleday, Anchor Books, 1973).

39. American Institute of Planners, *Code of Professional Responsibility,* Section 1.1 (a) (Washington, D.C.: American Institute of Planners, 1976).

40. Concerned Architects and Planners, "Ecological Effects of the Vietnam War," *JAIP* 38 (September 1972):297.

41. Peter Marcuse, "Professional Ethics and Beyond: Values in Planning," *JAIP* 42 (July 1976):272.

42. Andreas Faludi, *Planning Theory* (Oxford: Pergamon Press, 1973).

43. Norman Krumholz, Janice M. Cogger, and John H. Linner, "The Cleveland Policy Planning Report," *JAIP* 41 (September 1975):299.

44. Friedmann, *Retracking America,* p. 112.

FOR FURTHER READING

Altshuler, Alan A. *The City Planning Process.* Ithaca, N.Y.: Cornell University Press, 1965.

Blecher, Earl M. *Advocacy Planning for Urban Development.* New York: Praeger, 1970.

Branch, Melvin C., ed. *Urban Planning Theory.* Stroudsburg, Pa.: Dowden, Hutchinson & Ross, 1975.

Catanese, Anthony J. *Planners and Local Politics: Impossible Dreams.* Beverly Hills, Calif.: Sage, 1974.

Friedmann, John. *Retracking America: A Theory of Transactive Planning.* New York: Doubleday, Anchor Books, 1973.

Gans, Herbert J. *People and Plans: Essays on Urban Problems and Solutions.* New York: Basic Books, 1968.

Goodman, Robert. *After the Planners.* New York: Simon & Schuster, 1971.

Kahn, Alfred J. *Theory and Practice of Social Planning.* New York: Russell Sage, 1969.

Levine, Robert A. *Public Planning: Failure and Redirection.* New York: Basic Books, 1972.

Needleman, Martin L., and Needleman, Carolyn . *Guerillas in the Bureaucracy: The Community Planning Experiment in the U.S.* New York: Wiley, 1974.

Rabinovitz, Francine F. *City Politics and Planning.* New York: Atherton, 1969.

CHAPTER 6

Policy Analysis

Ernest R. Alexander

Much of urban planning theory and practice deals with the nonphysical aspects of urban systems. For example, urban planning is concerned with health, welfare, jobs, and justice.

While many would argue that these systems eventually lead to some physical presence within the built environment, a distinct planning approach has evolved that focuses on the efficient management and implementation of nonphysical urban systems. This type of planning practice is best seen in methods of policy analysis. This chapter examines the definitions, tools, and applications of policy analysis.

POLICY ANALYSIS: WHAT AND WHY

Planners and Policy Analysis

Policy is concerned with defining the broad goals and strategies of action, whether public or private. The need for expert assistance for doing that is well established:

What the cities want is advice on how to choose the right goals and the most effective policies for every function of government. Similar advice is being sought by all institutions and groups who seek to frame their goals and policies in a deliberate manner.[1]

Policy analysis is becoming an increasingly important function of planners in government and an integral part of many academic urban planning curricula:

A consensus is developing that planners can perform an increasingly important role as urban policy analysts. With the increasing complexity of urban decision-making, political leaders and urban administrators are demanding from planners pragmatic assistance with policy formation and implementation. . . [2]

One should not get the impression, however, that policy analysis has become the monopoly of planners. This is far from the case. While policy analysis has become an important planning tool, policy analysts include people from a wide variety of backgrounds. In fact, the majority are probably individuals with experience in the substantive areas concerned: hospital administrators or physicians for questions involving health resources allocation; police officers for public safety issues; earth scientists for environmental protection issues: and so on. Others doing policy analysis in government may be legislative analysts, administrators, systems analysts, and managers with backgrounds in fields as diverse as political science, public administration, management sciences, urban studies, or law.

There are two basic approaches to defining policy analysis. They are quite different but, in a sense, complementary. The first approach is exclusively descriptive and originates from the field of political science:

Policy analysis is finding out what governments do, why they do it, and what difference it makes.[3]

This definition, while important, is secondary for our purposes.

The second approach is normative. That is, rather than describing policy and its results, policy analysis aims to assist in making and evaluating public policy:

Policy analysis is a means of synthesizing information including research results to produce a format for policy decisions (the laying out of alternative choices), and of determining future needs for policy-relevant information.[4]

This approach to policy analysis is based on a view of problems and problem solving in government that has been called the *steersman metaphor:*

Implicit in this basic characterization of problems and solutions is the image of some person or mechanism that is actively involved in steering, in making the policy decisions that guide the ship of state.[5]

This metaphor shares common roots with the cybernetic view of physical and social systems, which was pioneered by theorists like Norbert Wiener and Von Bertalanffy, and culminated in what is known today as *systems analysis.*

Another source for policy analysis is the view grounded in political science. This approach sees policy as transforming political input into public policy output. Policy analysis combines this perspective with tools of economic analysis, which were often developed for quite different applications.

History

Systems analysis was first used for problem solving during World War II, where it was successfully employed in solving optimization problems such as developing a submarine reconnaissance strategy. By the late 1950s, systems analysts dominated U.S. strategic thinking. This period had been initiated by a systems study of strategic air power, which revolutionized military doctrine in the Pentagon. The study was carried out by the Rand Institute, a think tank that became a pioneer in systems analysis and public policy—first in the military, later in civilian matters. The apex of the influence of systems analysis came when Robert McNamara was Secretary of Defense. His "whiz kids" (many of whom came from Rand and Ford Motors) used these tools to consolidate and centralize civilian control in the Secretary's office over the various armed services.

At the same time that McNamara's Pentagon seemed to be winning the Vietnam War by the application of systems concepts, advocates of systems analysis were proposing its extension into the civilian branches of government. This was realized when the Planning-Programming-Budgeting System was extended to all agencies of the federal government by a 1968 executive order. The results of this effort were mixed, and its limitations were recognized before its eventual abandonment.

Policy analysis superseded the systems-oriented PPBS as a conceptual approach to evaluation and choice of public strategies. It differs from its predecessor in its use of realistic distributional, value, and political considerations. In other words, problems were recognized as more complex: they cannot be addressed in terms of efficiency alone. Besides identifying the best means for achieving given objectives, those objectives themselves may be the objects of scrutiny in relation to higher goals. Different sets of values held by various participants or interest groups may have to be taken into account, and no analysis can be complete without examining "who pays and who gets what."

PRACTICE AND TOOLS

Policy Analysis and Policymaking

One needs a clear understanding of policy analysis in order to understand the applicable methods and techniques. Thus far, we have identified policy analysis as a normative activity—but how does it relate to the various aspects of institutional action: policy, plan, program, implementation, and evaluation?

Policy is part of the stream of deliberation linking goals and values with action. Attempts have been made at a more specific definition of policy, but these also are generally rather vague: the output of policy making, a pattern of responses, a cluster of decision making, and a structure or confluence of values and behavior. A more useful definition of policy was developed by examining the conditions that must be met if something is to be a policy. Thus, a policy was defined as an intention to act in a certain way under given conditions, which are expected to recur. Public policy, in addition, must have a relevant constituency and be openly declared by its representative.[5a]

To distinguish policy from the related concepts of plan and program (which are also statements of intention), we can go back to the idea of the continuum that links values with action. Different stages on this continuum are given different labels, depending on their scope and the extent of their implications:

> If they are trivial and repetitive and demand little cogitation, they may be called routine actions. If they are somewhat more complex, have wider ramifications, and demand more thought, we may refer to them as tactical decisions. For those which have the widest ramifications and the longest time perspective, and which generally require the most information and contemplation, we tend to reserve the term *policy*.[6]

These distinctions are not absolute, but are relative to the level of organization: one's policy may be another's tactics. For example, a college's requirements for admission may be part of its student recruitment policy, but they are only tactical decisions in the context of the affirmative action policy of the federal government.

Besides scope, time horizon, and complexity, other dimensions distinguish the stages of the deliberative process. One of these is commitment: the closer to action you are, the greater the sunk investment in prestige, labor force, and funds, and the smaller the possibility of reversing the process without serious costs. For example, in the San Francisco Bay Area, a metropolitan transportation policy was developed. One of its central features was the construction of a second bridge across San Francisco Bay, south of the existing Bay Bridge. Local interests, however, strenuously opposed the proposal. By the time they succeeded in stopping it, over 6 million dollars had been spent on development and design. In fact, this became one of the proponents' strongest arguments for the bridge's construction.

Another important difference is level of detail and specificity; policies are generally broad, focus on goals and objectives, and leave the details of implementation to be developed later. Plans are more detailed and require specificity about projected resources and impacts to enable evaluation of their feasibility. Programs are usually limited to a single issue, client group, or organizational unit and are specific in terms of resources and phasing. A policy may involve multiple plans and programs, and a plan also may include several different programs or project proposals. By the final stage the commitment to implementation is sufficiently high to warrant the investment of resources of time, labor, and money. The policy analysis process can cover any or all of the deliberative phases linking values and goals to action. Monitoring during implementation and evaluation of program or project impacts is also an essential part of policy analysis.

The accompanying figure illustrates the relationships among different components of policy analysis and various phases of policymaking, planning, program development, and implementation. Some of the important features of policy analysis are the feedback from implementation and the effects of actions taken. In order to learn from experience and avoid repeating past mistakes, monitoring of program implementation and systematic evaluation of program impacts and outcomes are essential.

Walter Williams, from extensive experience in analyzing federal social policy, suggests that

> Outcome data are important to the central analysts to the extent that the results facilitate policy analysis in support of *future, large-scale* agency level decisions. . . . Outcome evaluations ask . . . future oriented questions. Do major programs or components of programs show positive results indicating the feasibility of continuing a program at present

Policy analysis and the deliberative process.

levels or expanding it, and . . . . do smaller segments of programs . . . give evidence of supporting expansion of these ideas to a large number of projects?[7]

What Williams calls "outcome evaluations" (i.e., the identification and assessment of the impacts of a particular program or program package) is often referred to as program evaluation. This must be distinguished from another kind of evaluation related to programs (the *a priori* evaluation of program feasibility and desirability, which is part of policy analysis.). When alternative options are considered, their impacts must be projected and evaluated. Obviously, this kind of evaluation is much more speculative, and its accuracy will depend on many factors. An important factor is the availability of prior experience from which predictions can be generalized. The outcome or program evaluation of previous similar efforts is the best documentation of such experience.

The Policy Analysis Process

Policy analysis is closely related to decision making. Like those in the planning process, the stages of policy analysis are basically identical with the components of the rational decision process. The policy analyst begins by identifying or articulating the goals that the policy options under review are intended to meet. This may be a complex process in itself. Policy is often developed in situations of great political and organizational complexity, and what stimulated the policy analysis may be only indirectly related to goals.

Often policy is focused upon an issue or problem at varying levels of government. We talk about public health insurance policy, the welfare mess, or national security policy at the federal level. State policy may be concerned with higher education, transportation, or air quality. Local government may deal with the distribution of public works, desegregation of schools, or public transit effectiveness. Other policies may address issues such

as recruitment, personnel and career development, product development, or marketing.

Sometimes a crisis stimulates a policy review. A prolonged drought in California in the late 1970s prompted a hard look at the state's water supply and allocation policy. The Soviet Union's success with its Sputnik satellite in the late 1950s led to a reassessment of U.S. education and research policy, with a massive infusion of federal support.

Translating slogans into operational goals and objectives is a difficult and complex task. The analyst in a given situation and context can exert a powerful influence. Bauer and Gergen illustrate this with an example from urban transportation policy. A corporation in a suburban location was concerned with easy access for its staff and with minimizing the effects of public transportation costs on the tax rate. A council member from a core-city ward had quite different problems: how to avoid disruption of his constituency and minimize relocation of residents. The city comptroller's office was most interested in keeping the city's indebtedness as low as possible. Thus, policy analysts in the corporation's headquarters viewed the problem and goals differently from the council member's legislative assistant. Both identified other objectives than the analyst on the staff of the city comptroller.

Strictly rational resolution at this stage of policy analysis is not really possible in any but the simplest cases of unitary actors in a relatively closed system. Usually, ". . .the diversity of interests and values precludes. . . the sort of determinate identification of a single best policy that is implied in the conception of decision making."[8] The best that the analyst can do in this kind of situation (which is the case in most analyses of public or governmental policy) is to try to identify the relevant actors and interests. Because policy arenas are open systems, it is almost impossible to do this completely. The analyst is obliged to simplify the complexity of the real world with a considerable degree of abstraction.

The next stage of policy analysis is the identification of alternative policy options. This may be no more than developing a more systematic and detailed specification of a few well-known, clearly defined, and limited options. However, the analyst adopting this approach runs the risk of missing opportunities for innovation and creativity, which may offer just the solution for the problem. A review based on existing options and precedents may be just another case of "generals fighting the last war." The practice of limiting options because of an accepted institutional image is widespread.

Where previous policies are themselves part of the problem, as is often the case, or offer an inadequate range of options, the analyst has to generate some policy alternatives. This process can range from a systematic search for ideas, from such sources as available literature, members of the organization, professional peers and correspondents, consultants, and the use or recombination of available components, to attempts at the design of novel solutions.

The development of alternatives is followed by the projection and prediction of outcomes and impacts. This is where the lessons of experience, from previous project or program evaluations, are especially useful. Unfortunately, they are still all too rare. Much, if not most, analysis has to make do with very speculative projections of outcomes.

Most of the tools applied in policy analysis are used in the next stage: *evaluation*. Evaluation often involves *testing* as well as evaluation.[9] Testing consists of ensuring the internal consistency of a proposal and, more important and more difficult, assessing its feasibility in the light of known and projected constraints. Feasibility analysis may well be the most important component of policy analysis, for if an option is not feasible, its desirability is irrelevant.

Evaluation consists of assessing the impact of each of the feasible options in terms of previously determined criteria. These criteria differ according to the evaluation methods used. They relate to the interests of the various actors in the policy process and their respective goals and objectives. This final stage of the policy analysis involves synthesizing the evaluations, if that is possible, drawing the appropriate inferences, and making recommendations of preferred policies.

In presenting their conclusions, policy analysts may be tempted to play down the tenuousness of many of the assumptions upon which their projections are based, or the arbitrary nature of most of the methods of aggregation commonly employed. They can thus give their recommendations an air of scientific objectivity that is rarely deserved. The reverse situation is one in which the analyst, often an academic social scientist, presents conclusions so loaded with qualifications that one cannot tell what the analysis actually means. Sometimes this type of analyst refrains from expressing any conclusions or recommendations at all, in dedication to the search for pure scientific truth.

Policy analyses are usually requested by decision makers who need guidance. They do not want obfuscation by pseudoscience, nor do they need pure research, which they could find in the libraries. A good policy analysis will display its conclusions for the decision maker to consider or refute. The analyst's own values will be clearly expressed for the decision maker to weigh. When arbitrary aggregation methods have been employed, their use should be openly admitted, and the sensitivity of conclusions to these limits should be tested and criticized.

Even the most competent analysis, which may follow all these precepts, may be ignored. A number of other factors, many of them quite divorced from the quality of the analysis itself, are necessary for its eventual acceptance.

Analytic Tools

Policy analysis is usually carried out using tools that range from conceptual approaches to operational algorithms. This review will identify some of the major ones.

Systems Approach. The conceptual common denominator underlying much if not all policy analysis is the systems approach. It is usually first applied at the stage of problem definition. The systems approach means that any situation or process can be analyzed as a system.

A system is defined as a set of components whose interdependencies with one another are stronger than their relationship with other elements outside the system—that is, with their environment. Anything affecting one component of a system will affect all the other components, and a change in one component will result in changes in the others.

Systems theory makes much of the organic nature of a system; indeed, it was developed in the context of a mathematician's appreciation of biology. But mechanical combinations can also be systems: a steam engine is a system, and the most popular example of one of the major characteristics of many systems—*homeostasis,* or stabilization by self-regulation—is the thermostat. These are relatively closed systems; that is, they interact with their environments at only a few, clearly controlled points. Most organic and social systems are much more open. Ultimately, the distinction between the system and its environment, for most open systems, is a matter of analytic convenience.

A certain analysis addressed a city health care problem: the long response time between a call for medical help and eventual treatment. The system was defined as ambulance dispatching and response and patient delivery to a hospital emergency room. The variables were the locations of ambulance stations in relation to the distribution of emergency calls and the organization of the dispatching unit. An elegant analysis was carried out, quantifying all the variables, and resulting in concrete recommendations for making better use of the locations of ambulance stations.[10]

We do not know whether the location was the cause of the problem or whether this analysis solved it. If this system was like some health care systems, the problem might not have been solved

with the delivery of the patient at the door of the nearest hospital. Not all hospitals are always open for all emergencies. Some are specialized, and, for some, it makes a difference whether the case is indigent, or has the means or insurance to pay for his or her medical care. Many hospitals have widely varying processing times between admission and treatment for different types of emergencies—times which, in some cases, may mean the difference between life and death. Thus the analyst's decision to include the hospitals as part of the system or to accept them as a given element in the system's environment becomes important.[10a]

Modeling. Once the system to be analyzed is defined and delimited, it will be modeled. Modeling is one of the basic tools of the systems approach. A model is simply an abstracted image of a system. Obviously, to be useful, a model must focus only on those characteristics of the system that are relevant for the analysis.

For example, a landscape is modeled in a map. If the problem is to develop an order of battle, the map should show contours and topographical features such as hills and valleys and other items of strategic importance (settlements, rivers, roads and railways). If the problem is to select the best potential crops, the map should show soils, grades, and water sources. The model should replicate the system as accurately as possible. A contour map that shows a fall where there is actually a rise, or that indicates a gentle grade where there is really a steep cliff, is worse than useless.

A map is a static model of a changing system. It is descriptive; it shows the system as it is at some point in time. Models may also be dynamic; that is, they can simulate processes. They may be normative. A dynamic descriptive model may be simply a moving scale model, like a miniature locomotive. It may be an abstraction of a process, such as a graph showing population increase. The graph may be even further abstracted, if the system is simple enough, in a mathematical formula. A descriptive dynamic model of a complex system will itself be complex; for example, the economy of the United States has been replicated by a model consisting of 81 linked equations.[11]

Normative models do not simply describe; they tell *how* to make or change a system. They also may either be static or dynamic. Architects' plans of a building or engineers' diagrams of a bridge are static normative models. When a system is designed in process terms, a dynamic normative model is used. A recipe is such a model; it describes the process of cooking, in terms of the ingredients and actions, such as, mixing, heating, and cooling, that have to be combined to produce a desired dish.

Laws, regulations, and programs are other examples of dynamic models; they replicate or control the process that will eventually be executed. Computer programs are also dynamic models; they define the sequence of operations the computer will carry out. Because of its demand for full and explicit specification and its capacity to handle extremely complex computations, the computer is a favorite means for modeling and simulation. The components of the system are identified in terms the computer can assimilate and their relationships defined in mathematical or programming terms.

A repertoire of standard models has been developed in this field which has been called systems analysis, operations research, or management science to cover routine or recurring processes and situations. One set of formulas, for example, constitutes a *queuing model*. It abstracts the process that takes place when there is a greater demand for a facility or service than can be satisfied at a given time. This model has been applied to situations as varied as overloaded banking services, traffic jams, and airport landing delays. Another model simulates the flow of elements (such as auto parts, supermarket wares, or military personnel) through a central location, in response to certain laws of demand and supply. This is called an *inventory model,* and it can be used to minimize the inventory

given certain parameters of supply and demand and goals of service.[12]

Obviously the policy analyst finds such models helpful. The temptation is strong, however, to adapt the abstraction of the system to the models conveniently at hand. And the analyst should be aware of this possibility.

Simulations. Models are used in simulations of systems being analyzed. A simulation is a replication, usually considerably abstracted, of a process. Simulations are important predictive tools. Like models, simulations have an air of sophistication that is sometimes fallacious. Some simulations are enormously complex, like the systems they try to replicate. But other effective simulations may be quite simple. A Monopoly game, for example, simulates the workings of the speculative real estate and capital investment market. War games simulate strategic encounters or battlefield conditions and range from the simplicity of a child's toy to the complexity of NATO exercises.

War games illustrate the rationale for the use of simulation; it can help one to predict the impacts of changes in variables and the outcomes of processes with some known and some unknown parameters without having to undergo the real experience. Using a scale model of an airplane, its designers can simulate its behavior under various aerodynamic conditions in a wind tunnel, without having to undertake hazardous flight tests. Simulation of relationships can be expressed in mathematical or logical terms, so that simulations can be done by computer. Then astronauts, for example, could experience computerized simulations of their prospective landings on the moon.

NATO war games, wind tunnels, and moon landings seem quite removed from policy analysis, but the same techniques of simulation are applied. Once a policy, project, or program is modeled, with its essential variables, impacts and outcomes are projected by simulating operations over time under various conditions. The simplest forms of such simulations are linear projections extrapolating future performance from past behavior and experience. There are more complex forms of extrapolations where simulations take into account the interaction of a number of variables and states of action.[13]

To illustrate the application of these conceptual techniques and some of the evaluative methods, let us look at an analysis of a typical policy issue at the state level. The problem was to determine what kind of subsidy would be best for the failing public transit systems in Connecticut. The analysis was stimulated by a crisis precipitated by a drivers' strike for higher pay, which had left three of the state's major cities without bus service for 121 days. R. W. Schmenner, an economist at Yale University, undertook to analyze the problem and advance an alternative to the subsidy design which had been patched together in the aftermath of the strike. He began by developing what he called a "demand model" for bus routes. This related the demand for bus service along a given route to characteristics of the population (density, income, age, and racial makeup), characteristics of the bus service, and relative difficulty of automobile travel in the area. First he used available Connecticut data to specify the relationships and estimate them. Next he simulated the operation of the bus services through time, using historic data, to check the reliability of his estimates. Once this simulation showed the model to be a reasonable approximation of real-world bus-route profit or loss under different conditions, it was projected into the future to predict which routes would be money-makers, which would be money losers, and why. This projection indicated the possible effects of service and fare adjustments and revealed that they would have some, but not much, impact on demand. At the same time, it showed that some routes always had a profit potential.

The analysis revealed that rider characteristics were the major factor affecting potential route profitability. It further showed that, if the public interest required continuing services in areas where the population was poorer, had a greater percentage of

whites, or was less densely distributed, subsidies would be needed. Schmenner then proceeded to specify and evaluate alternative subsidy schemes, using his model to project their possible impact on route profitability. The options he reviewed were: reimbursement of operating losses; subsidy by formulas related to area characteristics or to operating characteristics or to a mixture of the two; and subsidies for which the operators bid in a contracting process with the public agency.

Identifying a number of criteria, Schmenner evaluated the different options. The criteria were related to different goals and included consistency of the scheme with the theoretical basis for a subsidy, economic efficiency, impact on innovation, and administrative costs. He concluded that a "bid-for" subsidy approach would best meet these criteria and he developed a detailed specification of such a policy, which he recommended for implementation.[14]

In this case, apparently simple but actually quite complex, we see all the elements of policy analysis: diagnosis of a problem and identification of a set of variables that make up a system; development of a model of the system and the projection of its operation by simulation; specification of policy options; and evaluation of their impacts by a number of criteria related to relevant goals. The evaluation here was relatively simple and based upon empirical analysis.

Evaluation Tools
No phase of the decision making process has received more attention than the evaluation stage. A group of evaluation methods has been developed for use in decision contexts ranging from comprehensive planning to project selection. They also have been applied in policy analysis. The brief review here will focus on the policy analysis related aspects of these methods.

Benefit-Cost Analysis. Benefit-cost analysis is based upon the theory that the selection of a project or program should be determined by its net contribution to the economy or to some clearly specified economic unit. Based on the economic concept of marginality, this contribution is expressed in a benefit-to-cost ratio. The benefit-cost ratio expresses total benefits generated by a given option, in money, over its total costs.[15]

One of the advantages of benefit-cost analysis is that all the outputs must be quantified in money:

> Because in the public sector one is dealing with a budget constraint, comparisons are ideally made in dollar terms. Program alternatives that each have different measures of effectiveness essentially are impossible to compare. For example, how does one compare a reduction in the incidence of mortality from cancer with better education achieved by minorities through preschool head-start programs?[16]

However, this is also one of its greatest drawbacks, especially in policy analysis. The problems in the example above can easily be imagined: how do you put a value on lives saved, or on the benefits that education bestows apart from an improved earning capacity? When amounts are estimated for outputs like these, they often are based on tenuous and quite subjective assumptions; if, these assumptions change, they may radically alter the conclusions of the analysis.

Nevertheless, benefit-cost analysis is a frequently used evaluation tool in policy analysis, but its use is generally conceptual. Items are often quantified in less detail than they would be for project evaluations, where the options are already much further advanced in their design and specificity. The great value of benefit-cost analysis is as a framework for aggregating a wide range of different costs and benefits for a number of different options into a series of single indicators that decision makers can intuitively understand.

Cost-Effectiveness Analysis. Cost-benefit analysis evolved in the context of project evaluation,

where benefits could be assessed relatively easily in terms of increased revenues to the investor or incomes to the users and beneficiaries. However, in many programs, it is difficult, if not impossible, to quantify the outputs in monetary terms. Cost-effectiveness analysis was developed as a tool for dealing with this problem.

Cost-effectiveness analysis allows the evaluation and comparison of programs with similar outputs without converting those outputs into money. The programs are evaluated in terms of an output or effectiveness indicator, which is expressed as units of output per dollar cost.[16a]

The utility of cost-effectiveness analysis in program evaluation is limited to comparing programs or services with similar outputs. It offers no way to aggregate the outputs of different types of programs (for example, a driver education program to promote the use of safety belts and a day care program for handicapped children) into a common, comparable denominator. It also is difficult to interpret the findings in any absolute sense. For example, it will be clear that a tutorial program delivering a 20 percent improvement in reading scores over a year per $1,000 spent is better than one delivering only a 10 percent improvement per $1,000, but it still is not obvious that either of these programs is a good investment of public money.

Impact Analysis. The assessment and evaluation of the impacts of alternative policy options has always been an integral part of policy analysis. In impact analysis this process is formalized using a matrix and some type of scoring system. The factors to be taken into account in such analyses will vary according to the issue involved: the social impact of relocating a village from a plain that will be flooded by a proposed dam requires quite different analytic dimensions from the fiscal impact of a proposed municipal policy to abate property taxes on certain kinds of home improvements.

Several types of policy issues have become sufficiently commonplace for specific types of impact analyses to have evolved for these areas. The best-known of these is probably the *environmental impact assessment* or *statement*. These analyses were mandated by the National Environmental Policy Act of 1969 for a wide variety of proposals, ranging from power stations to parking lots. Today, in fact, any undertaking that may have a significant effect on the surrounding environment, which is in any way supported by federal money or subject to federal regulation, must be preceded by an environmental impact analysis.[17]

Environmental impact assessment was originally stimulated by concern for our built and natural environment. Traditional environmental impact statements concerned the effects of policies or projects on air and water quality, plant life, and on animals, birds, and fish. Later, people began to realize that human beings are just as much part of the environment as all these others, so that the effect of technology on people deserves equal concern. This led to social impact assessment, now a standard element in environmental impact statements.[17a]

Another type of impact assessment that has become widespread is *fiscal impact analysis.* This evaluation tool has much in common with benefit-cost analysis. Like benefit-cost analysis, it deals with outputs quantified in money terms. Instead of itemizing all costs and benefits to all parties affected, however, fiscal impact analysis concentrates on the costs and benefits to the governmental unit concerned: municipal, special-purpose, state, or federal governments. Fiscal impact analysis compares the governmental costs involved in a project with the revenues or savings it is likely to generate. Taxation policies are obviously prime candidates for fiscal impact analysis, but policies much more removed from the fiscal arena, such as land use control and zoning, have also been the subject of this type of analysis.

Program Evaluation. The importance of program evaluation as a component of policy analysis has been stressed. Besides using analytic methods as a conceptual framework, or as evaluative tools, program evaluation also relies upon a set of methods developed for implementation. These relate to the experimental design of the evaluation and relationships between evaluation design, analytic methods, institutional context, and the eventual acceptance and diffusion of findings.

In developing evaluation designs, practitioners of program evaluation have always been caught in the bind between scientific rigor and practical feasibility. One of the best designs from the strictly scientific point of view involves a minimum of four sample groups: one consisting of participants in the program before its inception; a second of nonparticipants, as a control; and third and fourth groups as similar samples of participants and controls after the program's impacts will be felt. Practical difficulties often stand in the way of implementing a design. The evaluation may be commissioned after the program is underway, eliminating the possibility of any systematic sampling. The client group may be so unique or specialized that a control group is difficult to find. Political or ethical considerations may preclude withholding program benefits from someone who would otherwise be identified as a control. For example, in health-related programs it is difficult to tell sick people that they will not get the treatment they see their counterparts receiving, because they are controls in a social experiment. Numerous experimental designs have been developed to answer this problem. Some approaches (called quasi-experimental) may sacrifice rigor in favor of feasibility, but retain the essential qualities that ensure their ultimate reliability.[17b]

The relationship between program evaluation methods, institutional context, and acceptance has also engaged the attention of theorists and practitioners. Both have learned that sound methods alone are not enough to ensure acceptance of an evaluation's findings by the general public or decision makers. In this respect, however, program evaluation and policy analysis are similar.

HOW DOES IT WORK?

Contexts of Policy Analysis

Policy analysis is inseparable from the issues and contexts involved. Contexts range through all levels of government, from local municipalities to federal agencies and the White House. As the unit of government grows larger and more complex, its analytic needs and resources increase. As a result more policy analysis is done at the higher levels of government than at the lower. Substantial effort by federal agencies, executive commissions, and congressional committees is devoted to analyzing the impacts of existing programs and the probable effects of proposed legislation. A local zoning ordinance, on the other hand, may be passed on the basis of a hunch, special interest pressures, or experience in similar localities.

At the federal government level, policy analysis has been institutionalized in most agencies. Often the policy analyst is closely linked to the agency's top staff and directorate; but sometimes an agency's analysts are buried deep in its bureaucracy. The central analytical office of an agency is charged with the preparation of decision-oriented position papers, with carrying out various forms of ongoing information-gathering activities, and with advising the agency head and other key officials on policy choices. The location of this office in the organizational structure may be a key element in the adoption of its recommendations.

In many cases analysis of public policy issues may be performed outside of government agencies. This is the case for a number of controversies that relate legislation and policy to technology assessment. The dispute on safety requirements for nuclear power plants, the issue of legislation to control recombinant DNA experiments, and the question of landing rights for the Concorde supersonic aircraft are only a few examples. In these areas policy analysis is carried out by the respective interest groups on all sides of the issues: the Concerned American Scientists, the Sierra Club, aircraft manufacturers, and so forth.

The distinction between governmental policy analysis and that of outside interest groups is also blurred by the use of consultants and lobbyists. Think tanks like the Rand Institute or the Brookings Institution are often retained by government agencies as consultants to analyze policy issues (usually, but not always, from a long-range perspective). Such analyses may be extremely influential in forming legislation. Revisions of revenue sharing, for example, have been heavily shaped by the analysis of the program done by the Brookings Institution for the Department of Housing and Urban Development.

Federal Policy Analysis and Research: Some Cases

The realities of policy analysis and implementation in the bureaucratic context can be shown in brief descriptions of a few cases. These lean toward the macro-scale end of the policy spectrum, because there is more interest in recording the birth and death of major federal programs than in the evolution of an obscure city ordinance.

New Federal Policy: The Model Cities Program. In May 1964, President Johnson assembled a task force to review federal policy and find the answer to the problems that plagued American cities. The Metropolitan and Urban Affairs Task Force was chaired by Robert C. Wood, a professor of political science at M.I.T. Other members were academics, administrators, and businessmen. The most active members were the "thinkers" rather than the "doers." The group had less than 3 months to complete its assignment.

Its report was critical of existing programs, especially their narrow focus and lack of coordination.[18] It proposed some radical changes, particularly the idea of block grants to cities and communities. Criticisms of interagency coordination were confirmed by a Bureau of the Budget report that appeared about the same time. A related proposal that would later be adopted also surfaced as a separate memorandum from some members of the task force. They suggested a coordinated interagency effort by two or three large cities to develop and implement a concentrated attack on their social problems. This proposal may have been based on the recent experiences of New Haven; it was reinforced by a brochure ("Detroit: A Demonstration City") submitted to Robert Weaver, then head of the Federal Housing and Home Finance Agency, and to President Johnson by the Mayor of Detroit and Walter Reuther, president of the United Auto Workers Union. A second task force was put together under Wood to develop legislative proposals based on this idea after the need for action was underlined by the Watts riots of 1965.

This group also had about two months for its task. The professional staff analyzed a wide selection of policy alternatives in about twenty-four background papers. None of them was pursued because the policies examined did not appear feasible. The range of options was limited to ideas that would produce tangible results during the current administration's term of office. The "Demonstration Cities" idea, which originated elsewhere, seemed to be the only promising approach. It was developed into a program proposal embodying three principles: concentration of resources, coordination of activities, and mobilization of local initiative and leadership.

These principles were incorporated into proposals for the legislation of a program that would involve a national competition between cities, which would submit ideas for the improvement of living conditions. The most promising proposals would be selected for elaboration and further review. Sixty-six demonstration cities would be chosen to receive two types of federal assistance: the delivery and coordination of the complete array of existing categorical grants, and a generous allocation of supplemental funds to make up the cost of the demonstration program.

The legislation introduced in Congress in January 1966 was closely modeled on the task force report. Some of its most significant aspects were modified in its passage through Congress. In its final version, the act authorized only a fraction of the funding originally proposed, and it diluted the application of the program to selected neighborhoods in a far larger number of cities.

A Potential New Program: Educational Performance Contracting. Educational performance contracting is an arrangement whereby educators, usually affiliated to a contracting organization, are paid by results. Interest in this system was evoked by publicity in the winter of 1970 about a project in Texarkana, where the approach had resulted in a large improvement in student learning. The publicity appeared just as President Nixon delivered a congressional message stressing the need for performance accountability in public programs.

In spite of opposition from teachers' unions, which prevailed in the Office of Education, the Office of Economic Opportunity (OEO) decided to embark upon an analysis of this method. Because of cost and political considerations, their experiment would have to be limited to one year.

Six private firms were hired at three sites, where they taught children in grades 1 through 3 and 7 through 9. Later, two more sites, which were run by local teacher's organizations, were added to compare the relative effectiveness of this type of service with the private market. At each site, the student subjects were carefully matched with control students to isolate the effects of the experiment.

At the end of the year, evaluation of the trial tests showed no significant difference in student performance under the new system compared to the controls. The results had to be qualified by limitations in the experiment, which included the time limitation; many operational breakdowns in applying the system; and the need for "debugging" the programs over this early adjustment period. The small sample size at each of the sites limited the validity of the results on a site-by-site basis.[19] Nevertheless, the results of this experiment contributed to the negative assessments that were accumulating about the performance contracting approach. Only a few years after performance contracting was touted as the salvation of public education, the concept is dead.

Program Evaluation: Headstart. The Headstart Program was launched in 1964 at the height of the War on Poverty. It represented what was accepted as the best current thinking on problems of child development. This thinking stressed the rich developmental potential that could be tapped by early childhood and preschool training. Headstart was a showcase OEO program designed to make such training available to minority and disadvantaged children. In its first summer, Headstart set up a number of six-to-eight-week projects in selected areas all over the country, serving over half a million children. Later it expanded into several full-year projects.

The Office of Research, Plans, Programs, and Evaluation (RPP&E) of OEO wanted an overall assessment of Headstart in order to resolve an ongoing controversy that had arisen in the agency about the program's effectiveness. Early assessment studies had proved inconclusive, a symptom of a problem pervading OEO as a whole. Internal pressures for more rigorous evaluation led to the opening of an Evaluation Division in RRP&E. The design of a thorough national evaluation of Headstart was the project on which this division was to establish its reputation.

However, conflict soon arose between the new division and OEO's program offices on the division of responsibilities. The problem was exacerbated by the vagueness about assignment of functions in OEO instructions. There was also disagreement from Headstart supporters over the proposed methodology and RPP&E's identification of program goals. RPP&E did succeed in defusing this enough to get out a Request for Proposal (RFP) to potential contractors. Responses to the RFP led to a contract

with the Westinghouse Learning Corporation and Ohio University in June 1968. Their evaluation proceeded without incident until negative findings they had communicated in a preliminary report were discovered by the White House. These were mentioned (whether inadvertently or by design is not clear) by President Nixon in his Economic Opportunity Message to Congress in February 1969. The result was a storm of controversy over the evaluation of the program, and mounting public pressures forced release of the Preliminary Draft Report.

The supporters of Headstart vigorously attacked the methodological and conceptual validity of the evaluation in an effort to refute its implied conclusion. Though the final report was reinforced with additional tests of the rigor of the study, it was not any more acceptable. The Headstart Program had succeeded in enlisting in its cause a diverse and articulate constituency. The question of the program's survival was eventually resolved politically.[20]

Conditions for Success

The cases described above give some idea of the diversity of contexts and results of policy analysis. They make clear how difficult it is to generalize across a wide range of different experiences about the development and acceptance of conclusions, the adoption of an analyst's recommendations, and their incorporation into policy. Success of a policy depends on many factors besides the quality of the analysis.

In the urban context, R. Lehne and D. Fisk attempted a systematic study of policy analysis efforts to evaluate the factors that lead to the adoption of conclusions or to rejection. The University of Michigan carried out an extensive survey of executive policymakers to discover why there is so little use made of social research. Williams has also devoted attention to the question of adoption and implementation of policy analysis at the federal level.[21]

The conclusions of these studies indicate that

three types of factors affect the success of a policy analysis: *situational, bureaucratic,* and *technical.* Situational factors are those variables over which nobody has much control. Political changes, such as a switch in administration, interest group pressures, or feasibility constraints imposed from above, may make the conclusions of a perfectly sound analysis quite irrelevant. There may also be an irresolvable gap between the viewpoints of the analyst and the policymaker. Bureaucratic variables are those factors in the organizational context that affect the acceptance of the analyst's conclusions. These may include the status of the analyst, office powers, and institutional relationships with the head of the agency. These can either impede or facilitate adoption of the analysis and its survival through the mazes of bureaucratic politics. It is important that the agency and its head recognize the importance of analysis. Obviously, a good track record in improving institutional success and performance is a great

help in achieving this recognition. Technical factors relate to the policy analysis itself. Some of these may be beyond the analyst's control when the timing and goals of the study are set.

Timing is very important. The analyst should make every effort to have conclusions available in time for them to effect the decisions. The most elegant and rigorous analysis is a failure if its recommendations appear only long after the issues have become moot.

Other relevant factors are more general. A narrowly focused analysis will have higher chances of acceptance and implementation than a broadly conceived study. It is better for an analysis to be limited to a single agency than to raise complex issues of interdependencies. Finally, policymakers are acutely aware of the limits of feasibility in implementation, and an analysis has a better chance of adoption if it gives evidence of having taken these into account.

NOTES

1. Herbert J. Gans, "From Urbanism to Policy Planning," *Journal of the American Institute of Planners (JAIP)* 36 (July 1970):224.

2. Dennis A. Rondinelli, "Urban Planning as Policy Analysis: Management of Urban Change," *JAIP* 39 (January 1973):13.

3. Thomas R. Dye, *Policy Analysis* (University, Ala.: University of Alabama Press, 1976), p. 1.

4. Walter Williams, *Social Policy Research and Analysis: The Experience in the Federal Social Agencies* (New York: Elsevier, 1971), p. xi.

5. Richard R. Nelson, *The Moon and the Ghetto: An Essay on Public Policy Analysis* (New York: Norton, 1977).

5a. Donna H. Kerr, "The Logic of Policy and Successful Policies," *Policy Sciences* 7 (September 1976):351–63.

6. Raymond E. Bauer and Kenneth J. Gergen, *The Study of Policy Formation* (New York: Free Press, 1968), p. 2.

7. Williams, *Social Policy Research and Analysis*, pp. 84–85.

8. Bauer and Gergen, *The Study of Policy Formation*.

9. Nathaniel Lichfield, Peter Kettle, and Michael Whitbread, *Evaluation in the Planning Process* (Oxford: Pergamon, 1973), pp. 4, 5, 15, 20.

10. Jack W. La Patra, *Applying the Systems Approach to Urban Development* (Stroudsburg, Pa.: Dowden, Hutchinson & Ross, 1973), pp. 202–4.

10a. For a more complete review of the limitations of the systems approach in policy analysis see Ida R. Hoos, "Systems Techniques for Managing Society: A Critique," *Public Administration Review* 33 (March–April 1973):157–64.

11. Michael K. Evans, *Macroeconomic Activity: Theory, Forecasting and Control* (New York: Harper & Row, 1969), pp. 429–42.

12. For a review of these models, see C. West Churchman, Russell Ackolt, and E. L. Sonoff, *An Introduction to Operations Research* (New York: Wiley, 1959).

13. Useful introductions to simulation and games are presented in Richard D. Duke, *Gaming: The Future's Language* (New York: Halsted, 1974); and Cathy S. Greenblat and Richard D. Duke, *Gaming Simulation: Rationale, Design and Application* (New York: Halsted, 1975).

14. Roger W. Schmenner, "Bus Subsidies: The Case for

Route-by-Route Bidding in Connecticut," *Policy Analysis* 2 (summer 1976):409–30.

15. E. J. Mishan, *Cost Benefit Analysis,* 2d ed. (London: G. Allen, 1971).

16. Ronald W. Johnson and John M. Pierce, "The Economic Evaluation of Policy Impacts: Cost-Benefit and Cost Effectiveness Analysis," in *Methodologies for Analyzing Public Policies,* ed. Frank P. Scioli, Jr., and Thomas J. Cook (Lexington, Mass.: Heath, 1975), p. 132.

16a. Michael B. Teitz, "Cost-Effectiveness: A Systems Approach to Analysis of Urban Services," *JAIP* 34 (November 1968):303–11.

17. For more detail, see Patric Heffernan and Ruthann Corwin, eds., *Environmental Impact Assessment* (San Francisco: Freeman, Cooper, 1975).

17a. C. P. Woolf, "Social Impact Assessment: The State of the Art," in Dan Carson (ed.) *Man Environment Interactions: Evaluations and Applications,* pt. 1 (Stroudsburg, Pa.: Dowden, Hutchinson & Ross, 1974), pp. 1–44.

17b. Donald Campbell and J. C. Stanley, *Experimental and Quasi-Experimental Designs for Research* (Chicago: Rand-McNally, 1963).

18. Edward C. Banfield, "Making a New Federal Program: Model Cities," in Alan P. Sindler (ed.), *Policy and Politics in America: Six Case Studies* (Boston: Little, Brown, 1973), pp. 125–58.

19. Edward M. Gramlich and Patricia P. Koshel, "Is Real World Experimentation Possible? The Case of Educational Performance Contracting," in *Social Program Implementation,* ed. Walter Williams and Richard F. Elmore (New York: Academic, 1976), pp. 149–66.

20. Williams, *Social Policy Research and Analysis,* pp. 103–30.

21. Richard Lehne and Donald M. Fisk, "The Impact of Urban Policy Analysis," *Urban Affairs Quarterly* 10 (December 1974):115–38; Andrea Morrison, "Policy Makers' Views on Three Categories of Non-Utilization Theories" (Paper presented at the International Sociological Association Congress, Toronto, August 1974), and Williams, *Social Policy Research and Analysis,* Ibid.

FOR FURTHER READING

Bauer, Raymond E., and Gergen, Kenneth J. *The Study of Policy Formation.* New York: Free Press, 1968.

Heffernan, Patric, and Corwin, Ruthann, eds. *Environmental Impact Assessment.* San Francisco: Freeman, Cooper, 1975.

Hinrichs, H. H., and Taylor, G. M. *Systematic Analysis: A Primer on Benefit-Cost Analysis and Program Evaluation.* Pacific Palisades, Ca.: Goodyear, 1972.

Lichfield, Nathaniel; Kettle, Peter; and Whitbread, Michael. *Evaluation in the Planning Process.* Oxford: Pergamon, 1973.

Mishan, E. J. *Cost Benefit Analysis,* 2d ed. London: G. Allen, Editor, 1971.

Quade, E. S., *Analysis for Public Decisions,* New York: Elsevier, 1975.

Rivlin, Alice M., *Systematic Thinking for Social Action,* Washington, D.C.: Brookings Institution, 1971.

Rondinelli, Dennis A. "Urban Planning as Policy Analysis: Management of Urban Change." *Journal of the American Institute of Planners* (January 1973):13–22.

Scioli, Frank P., Jr., and Cook, Thomas J., eds. *Methodologies for Analyzing Public Policies.* Lexington, Mass.: Heath, 1975.

Williams, Walter. *Social Policy Research and Analysis: The Experience in the Federal Social Agencies,* New York: Elsevier, 1971.

CHAPTER 7

Quantitative Methods in Urban Planning

David S. Sawicki

This chapter presents the *generic* tools of urban planning and policy analysis—usually called quantitative methods. Methods are often thought of in terms of orderliness, appropriateness, efficiency, and reiteration—implying that the problems to which such methods are addressed have similar attributes. This is not the case with urban planning. Thus, the subject of urban planning methods must be undertaken with a broad perspective. In this way, the applicability, limitations, and usefulness of each method can be recognized.

BACKGROUND AND ORGANIZATION

There has not yet been a perfect correlation, even taking time lag into account, between the methods being taught in academic programs in planning and those being used in the field. In academe, there is often an uncritical inclusion of various social science methods in planning curricula, while in the field, there has been a reluctance to experiment with new methodologies.

An important aspect of the development and use of method in planning is the relationship between the method and the political system within which it is used. Richard Bolan discussed the varia-tions and relationships among four factors in planning: planning strategy, content, organization, and method.[1] Since we are focusing on method, we can use the other three to help explain which method should be employed. Variations in strategy refer, in part, to the particular style adopted by the practitioner; whether, for example, he or she chooses to act as a facilitator and coordinator within a political system or as an advocate for a particular client group with a specific point of view. Variation in content can refer not only to the area of planning (e.g., housing as distinct from social services), but also to different variations in time, horizon, and scope. Of obvious importance in selecting an appropriate methodology is the position of the planner in or outside of the governmental structure. All of these factors (and others as well) form the context within which a methodology is employed. Within that context, there are a number of options, which vary with the type of problem.

The case has been made for planners to develop an identifiable methodology in order to be able both to address problems systematically and to define more clearly their own professional activity. Unfortunately, the desire for professional definition as well as political power has some negative effects on the methodologies planners employ. It seems to favor sophistication, elaboration, and obfuscation, for the more elaborate the method, the more it resides exclusively in the planners' professional domain, with a language only they understand—and the more power they can expect to have.

The tenets of the profession demand a methodology that addresses each problem directly and is easy for other professionals, politicians, and citizens to understand. Methods should be transparent; the prepared citizen should be able to understand the problem, the data and how it is used, and the results and policy implications of the analysis.

The tension between methodological sophistication and responsiveness may recently have been partly resolved by the movement toward citizen involvement in the planning process. Rather than choosing methods, performing analyses, and then attempting to communicate results, planners can define the problems and select the analytical methods using citizen involvement as one constraint in the choice of a method. Many would regard this not as a constraint, but as a very positive force.

A presentation of methods and techniques can be organized in a number of ways (e.g., according to chronology, disciplinary origin, problem area, or stage in the planning process). Each has advantages and disadvantages. The age of a method does not necessarily relate to its usefulness; some older methods are still the best. Disciplinary origin (economics, sociology, etc.) is not always relevant because one method may be used in a number of

disciplines. The same is true with substantive areas (housing, transportation, etc.).

This chapter therefore is organized by stage of the planning process. This approach supports the stereotype of a single planning process that is sequential, mutually exclusive by step, noninteractive, and nonrepetitive in nature; this is unfortunate, as most planners agree that the planning process is to some degree nonsequential, with steps often overlapping. However, this type of organization can promote a sense of the entirety of the process. The planning process used below to organize the discussion of the various methods is a variant of the rational planning process (problem, definition, systems analysis, evaluation of alternatives, implementation, and ex post evaluation).[1a]

PROBLEM DEFINITION

The first step in most rational models of the planning process involves the identification and delineation of the problem and the attempt to define goals and some measures for achieving them. By defining a problem, we are asserting that we are seeking a state different from the existing one: if we can measure the difference between these two states, we can assess the potential for change. The most common, and probably most useful, quantitative methods associated with this phase use statistical analysis, which involves *descriptive statistics, survey research methods, inductive statistics,* and *information systems and social indicators.*

Descriptive Statistics
Methods should be clear and as transparent as possible; not overly demanding of data; realistic; and relevant to the problem in terms of policy. Simple descriptive statistics and basic arithmetic and algebraic operations are the major tools necessary for problem description. Including statistics in the discussion of some public issue can raise the quality and rationality of the debate immeasurably.

The planning professional, therefore, should have a good grasp of simple descriptive statistics and their measurement: means, medians, ranges, ratios, percentages, and proportions.[2] He or she should also be thoroughly knowledgeable about the range of descriptive statistics that have been applied by planners to problems. These measures are best learned in a substantive problem context; e.g., it would be best to learn about the location quotient in the context of development planning and economic base analysis. Further, there is no one text that summarizes these measures.[3]

Simple statistical measures are often used in measuring a gap—with the status quo being compared to some possible standard that has been established as the goal. Such standards may emanate from governmental requirements or from commonly accepted professional standards. An example might be a given number of beds available per capita for a certain kind of health care delivery. Some agencies of the federal government have recently established routine procedures for identifying community need.[4]

The planner's most common source of data for the problem identification process is the U.S. Census. The Census of Population and Housing, which is now scheduled for every five years rather than ten, gathers data from both an enumeration of all households in the nation and a variety of samples of the households.[5] The information is summarized for a number of reporting units, including, among others: census blocks, census tracts, cities, counties, standard metropolitan statistical areas, states, and the United States as a whole. The data is available through printed reports, microfiche, and computer tapes.[6] Also of interest is a public-use file, available on tape, which is a sample of the complete files of some randomly selected households. Whereas other data are aggregated into areal reporting units before publication, this file gives access to a wide variety of information on individual households, thus all allowing research questions about this unit of analysis.

Though the census is the greatest source of information, there are some problems. First, in areas of high population mobility, such as in some poor communities, there can be difficulties in administering a census. Because of this, the Census Bureau had to correct a number of its 1970 counts several years later. Second, even when the original work is accurate, vast changes can take place in an area in the time between data gathering and publication. Some data are now available on computer tape, thus lessening the delays.

A more serious problem is that census information is a secondary data source. What is available may or may not fit one's needs, and planners may resort to adapting their data needs to what is available. This practice can lead to errors in the process of problem definition, such as the complete misidentification of the client population. A solution to this is to develop a primary data source of information gathered expressly for the purpose at hand. However, in most instances this is not an option, because it is very expensive.

TABLE 7-1

A Descriptive Statistical Profile for a Small Area

Total population	1250
White	750
Black	400
Other races	100
Median age	
Male	28.4
Female	27.6
Median school years	12.2
Median family income	14,800
Number of households	420
Number of housing units	410
Owner occupied	350
Renter occupied	60
Median value of units	36,000
Median contract rent	175

Survey Research Methods

Among the various methods of primary data generation are *field inspection* and the use of *survey research methods*. In the last few years, field inspection has lost favor as a data-gathering technique, partly because of the wealth of data available through secondary data sources. Thus, a planner may never visit the area in question, instead creating a descriptive profile from the available data. There is no substitute, however, for a firsthand look. Though a field inspection may not yield any systematic information or data, it can provide the planner with a base of experience upon which to build a description. Returning to an area at different times of the day, week, and year is important in getting a complete picture of the place. Typically, for small subareas within an urban area, field inspections would be put together with secondary data, and the product would be called a *neighborhood profile*. Many city planning agencies have such profiles for each neighborhood. A physical look at an area is an important first step of this profiling operation.

Survey research methods are probably the most frequently used tools of the planning profession. There are several reasons for this. First, there is no more legitimate activity for planners than speaking with the people. Therefore, criticizing the use of surveys is criticizing the heart of planning; who could object to such a fundamental step? Second, this method can provide the rationale for budget, personnel, and, unfortunately, become an effective substitute for creative thinking, if not for the planning process itself.

Before any survey is undertaken, the objectives of the process must be fully explored in order to determine whether or not some other method might be more appropriate. A scientific survey sample is more expensive than almost any other data-gathering technique, but it can yield high quality data of an invaluable type.

The survey research process has a number of steps:[7]

1 Define the objectives of the survey and consider the use of other possible data-gathering techniques

2 Identify the key questions

3 Design the survey instrument and method of observation

4 Choose a sample type and size

5 Choose the units to be sampled

6 Pretest the instrument itself and the anticipated analytical procedures

7 Redesign the instrument if necessary

8 Administer the survey

9 Code and edit the responses

10 Analyze the results

11 Interpret the results in a policy planning framework

Step one is extremely important. Not until the planner has determined that the necessary resources are available and that the survey is the best technique to achieve the applicable goals should he or she begin.

Following that come decisions about the key questions to be answered by the data-gathering exercise. For example, a federal government program might be sharing the expense of the survey and specify certain requirements that would affect the type of sample, questions asked, sample size, and coding of the results.

Designing the instrument and settling on the method of observation are interdependent steps. Whether the instrument is administered by telephone, mail, or in person determines what questions can be asked and what types of responses can be expected. Establishing the length and difficulty of the instrument is of first priority. This relates both to the budget allocated for the project and to the presumed ability of the interviewers and cooperation of the respondents. The types of questions used and their specific wording are also important. In addition, the planner must anticipate the type of analysis required and the kinds of data categories needed to perform that analysis.

These issues relate to the sample size necessary to achieve statistically significant results. Another important factor in choosing the sample size is the type of sample to be run. Some of the most common are: the *simple random sample, systematic sampling, stratified sampling,* and *cluster sampling.* To choose, one must first define the population to be sampled. It might be, for example, all adults over 18 years old in the city, or all heads of households in that city. Exact terminology is especially important here. For example, *head of household* must be specified for all interviewers, with rules for decisions in unclear situations. Once the sample population has been defined, the type of sample and the specific interviewees can be chosen.

Simple random sampling is the basic technique involved in all kinds of sampling and statistical testing. In a simple random sample, each interviewing unit must have an equal chance of being chosen. The other types of sampling are primarily used to reduce costs. There is a trade-off in every sampling design between the cost involved and the accuracy and significance of the results. For example, if the area to be surveyed is spread out geographically, a cluster sampling technique might allow minimization of transportation time and cost. However, some statistical techniques used in analyzing data can be greatly complicated and occasionally rendered worthless when alternative sample designs are used.

The planner should make sure the questionnaire allows the basic flow of information before it goes out for pretesting. Through pretesting, the planner can establish the length of time needed to complete the survey instrument, the clarity of its language and definitions, and individuals' responses to it. Then it is rewritten and even retested if necessary.

Finally, the survey is administered and the results coded and put on computer cards in order to facilitate analysis. An initial analysis may be done with prewritten programs that can be easily used for certain statistical tests. Descriptive and inferential statistics are created. Finally, these statistical results must be translated into meaningful insights for planning and public policy.

Inductive Statistics
Statistical tools are not substitutes for basic planning methodologies; they are part of them. In the planning process, both descriptive and *inductive statistics* are used. Both types of statistical procedures apply to various steps in the planning process. Descriptive statistical techniques are used to summarize information and make it more useful. *Inductive statistics* have two basic functions. First, they are used in generalizing about the characteristics of an entire population from a sample of that population. (Here the term *population* is used to refer to a total aggregation of some type of unit of analysis, e.g., a population of households or a population of male secondary school teachers.) As an example, suppose we have drawn a sample of 400 households from a neighborhood that has a population of households numbering 1,500, and we find that the mean age of the households' dwelling units is 22.5 years. Inductive statistics allow us to say what this implies about the mean age of the population's units, and how sure we can be of our conclusions. Second, inductive statistics can be used to derive generalizations (about a whole population) based on a number of repeated sample observations.

Information Systems and Social Indicators
Two methodologies associated with descriptive statistics are *information systems* and *social indicators.* In planning, the term *information system* implies the gathering of large quantities of data, its storage in a computer, and organizing and analyzing that data towards some end. One such tool is the *regional land use inventory.* Recently methods have been developed for supplanting the on-site or aerial photo inventory with a remote sensing inventory from a satellite. Though not all necessary regional

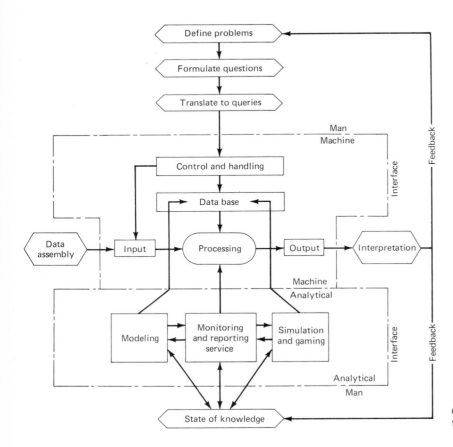

Configuration for an urban information system.

planning information can be gathered this way, a substantial amount of specific small area data can be accumulated. Such data can then be used to provide maps of certain types of areas, develop land-use plans, and suggest the likely effects of alternate development proposals.

The planning department is usually one of many departments participating in an urban information system. Within an *urban data bank* might be found information on general administrative matters, such as personnel accounts and budgetary analysis; parcel-specific land-use data on ownership, land use type, assessed value, zoning, and building permits; public safety and street and highway information; utility information; and school and library ad-

ministration data. Much of this type of information often was not collected for planning purposes, but it does have possible planning uses. Such a data bank makes retrieving data much easier than would be possible through a hand check of the files. Statistical analyses of particular areas are made possible. If, for example, a certain area of the city were applying for renewal funds, a profile of that area could easily be drawn up, with such information as the mean value of the household units in the area; total number of households; and general condition of housing. This information also could be used to develop a model to assess the possible impacts of the building of a new freeway through an area, or some other physical development proposal.

Enthusiasm in the mid-1960s about the use of information systems in planning was followed by a round of criticism, largely directed at the unfocused nature of the data collection efforts.[8] Large banks of data were amassed without any organizing concepts or analytical ideas behind them. Today, the efforts at data collection are on a smaller scale and are more focused on objectives relevant to some overall planning context.

Another group of statistical concepts is classified as *social indicators*. Such indicators relate closely to the problem definition phase of planning. In the late 1960s and early 1970s, social indicators were proposed to supplement the economic indicators available for the United States. This idea became popular because of the social unrest at the time and the resulting feeling that some measures of performance of the social system were necessary. It was believed that a set of social indicators would facilitate the identification of societal, and especially urban, problems. The central notion was that a number of statistical indicators would be designed to monitor facets of society (e.g., health, education, housing, welfare) over an extended period of time, permitting the analyst to spot both long-and short-term trends.

From the start, this approach had problems, the most severe being a lack of consensus about what aspects of societal performance should be monitored. For example, academicians often were uncomfortable with the measures espoused by the more pragmatic and activist groups. Despite the inevitable statistical difficulties, a number of studies measuring social change for a group of metropolitan areas were completed. In one of these, 15 dimensions of quality with representative statistical indicators were compared for 18 major cities.[9] At the present time, however, very few cities have an organized set of social indicators that can be updated each year to gauge trends and uncover problems. Progress at the national level has been equally slow.

SYSTEMS ANALYSIS

The second step in the planning process, which we will call *systems analysis,* involves the design of alternatives for attacking the problems defined in the first step. Systems analysis is identified with a number of techniques and some specific analytic tools, especially those involving simulation and modelling.[10]

This second step includes these substeps: assessment of the environment of the system; identification and design of alternatives; design of models for estimating the impact of these alternatives, and the gathering of data and estimation of the parameters of the models. In these areas systems analysis has done much to improve the planning process.

Once again, no clean lines can be drawn between this step in the planning process and steps one or three, but the emphasis in step two is on learning—about the problem, its causes, and the factors associated with these causes. In assessing the environment of the system, we want to know the context within which the problem has been defined. For example, one can view housing problems in terms of housing supply and demand or as a general welfare problem. If we define the context of a problem

A simple systems model.

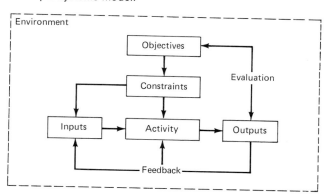

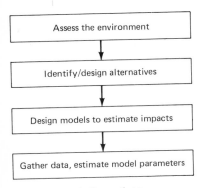

The design of alternatives.

very broadly, we are less likely to decide prematurely on narrow solutions that could cause other problems; for example, supplying housing to a needy group while ignoring their inability to meet maintenance requirements because of lack of funds. The larger context of income and welfare, the percentage of household budgets allocated to housing, and housing supply and demand must all be considered. The danger of a broad approach is that it can be so abstract that no practical solutions result.

To identify and design alternatives that solve a problem, one must first understand the problem. Traditionally, only the techniques of descriptive and inductive statistics were used to clarify the causal relationships among a set of characteristics associated with a problem. For example, in a client population with a need for narcotics addiction treatment, there are variables involved that can be at least partly controlled through public policy, as well as variables that are outside the control of public actions. Examples of the former might be the number of treatment centers, their hours, type of treatment, personnel, follow-up programs, and recruitment programs. Examples of the latter type might be the size of the addicted population, the ages and incomes involved, employable skill levels; and attitudes about participation in such programs. Often, however, it is difficult to distin-

guish between the two types of variables. The tools of systems analysis can be very helpful in eliminating many of the problems associated with traditional methods.

Models

Developing a *model* often can aid in the identification of the key policy variables and the development of precise goal statements. A model can simply be verbal, derived from a review of the literature. Often these simple models are merely analogies with other comparable situations. A model can be slightly more sophisticated, based on exact variables and their relationships to one another. It can be mathematical in nature, with the relationships among variables specified quantitatively. The problem situation and available resources dictate the level of sophistication of the model. In planning the economic development of an area, we can develop highly sophisticated mathematical models to assess the impact of a certain activity on the economy. On the other hand, problems like drug addiction are more complex, and they have not been studied as systematically or extensively. But the value of even simple verbal modelling of such a situation should not be overlooked.

Three types of models are used in planning. *Descriptive models* characterize certain features of the system. They are not necessarily problem-oriented models, but instead can be considered learning devices—test-tube experiments for urban planners. These descriptive models used in systems analysis have resulted in solid contributions to planning, especially in the area of urban spatial theory. *Prescriptive models* are those that arrive at a single solution to a problem, or multiple solutions for a variety of possible circumstances. In the early 1960s the promise of such models was tremendous, but most urban problem situations have proved too complex for solutions achieved strictly through modelling. *Normative models* are ideal descriptions of the system and can serve as goals toward which the actual system can be directed.

Population Analysis

One of the most important subjects for urban planners is population growth and change. Invariably planners are interested in the population size of a place or of a particular client group, as well as in the characteristics of such groups.

There are a variety of simple population forecasting models, which are for the most part descriptive models.[11] The simplest of these techniques use historic trends of population change to extrapolate future trends. These methods include *linear* and *exponential models* and *comparative* and *ratio methods*. The latter two also use historic population data from a reference area other than that requiring the projection. These models, though simple to use, have a number of deficiencies. First, they do not break down population change into its components: births, deaths, and migration. Second, they cannot explain the forces behind the predicted change, and there is no theory underlying their primarily mechanistic results. Third, these models often fall short, because more than simple population totals are usually needed. They do not usually provide any clues to changes in population characteristics such as age, sex, income, or ethnicity. Despite these disadvantages, some simple mechanical models are the best predictors in certain situations.

A more helpful method is the *cohort-survival technique*. It does break up the phenomenon of population change into its three component parts. Change for each component is described and predicted separately. The three components are then combined and applied to cohorts, or groups of people aggregated by one or more characteristics (e.g., males aged 25-30), and projections are made for a future time period.

There are more complex methods of predicting population change. Migration has been the subject of numerous studies and *multiple regression,* a statistical technique that relates a variety of factors (in this case, employment and income factors relating to the origin and destination of migration), has been used to predict migration within the United States. In

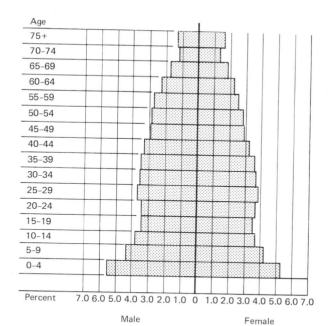

Typical age-sex cohorts.

addition, population submodels have been developed as part of larger, more comprehensive modelling efforts. For example, a comprehensive regional planning model concerned primarily with economic growth might contain a population projection submodel related to the predicted changes in the local economy. The opening of a steel plant with 2,000 workers obviously would affect the size and composition of the population of the surrounding region.

Analysis of Regional and Local Economies

Regional and local income and employment analysis uses techniques we can identify as models. Urban planners are interested in changes in the local economy because of the effect such changes could have on other public activities, including land use, housing, transportation, public facilities, and social service delivery systems. The purpose of such an analysis is usually to predict the quantity and quality of employment opportunities and the location of those opportunities in relation to potential employees. In addition, there is usually concern about how employers' gains and losses will affect the municipality's fiscal position.

The organizing principle of most regional analysis is first to assess what changes will take place in those industries whose goods or services are largely exported out of the region, and then to estimate the effect that those changes will have on the rest of the economy. The entire process is sometimes called a *community economic base study.*

A variety of techniques are used to project changes in the area's exporting economy. Each method usually involves first identifying those local industries (in the broad sense of the term) that are the chief exporters. This can be done by comparing the activity level of the local industry (in employment, dollar sales, or production volume) to the national level. If, for example, an area has four times the percentage of employees in textiles as the nation, the area is probably exporting textiles. Two methods for measuring the activity level are the *location quotient* and the *minimum requirements approach.*

Having identified the exporters, the planner must then predict the future of these activities and any economically and spatially related activities (often called linked industries). Are these activities growing or declining at the national level? Is their concentration around the nation likely to shift, or will they remain where they are?

There are two sets of methods commonly used for projecting what will happen to the exporting activities. The first, the *ratio method,* projects changes in a region's share of a certain economic export activity. This is done by predicting change over time in the activity for the United States as a whole and then deciding either that a specific area will maintain its current share or that its share will change. Changes in share are called *shifts.* Changes in the level of exporting activity in one sector can occur either

because of changes at the national level or because of regional shifts. We can assume a constant share, a constant rate of shift, or a changing shift. This process is called *shift/share analysis.*

Another technique for projecting the future of exporting activity uses *econometric methods.* These multiequation models were initially used to test economic theories, but they have also been applied with some success to descriptions of regional economies. The idea is to relate a large number of theoretical explanatory variables to regional output by using statistical tools. These relationships can be complex, nonlinear, and often time-lagged. The models constructed can be used to predict the impact on the regional economy of various policies aimed at regional development.

Once changes in this basic or export sector have been assessed, it is possible to use certain techniques to estimate the effects these initial changes will have on the rest of the regional economy. Two associated methodologies involve the *multiplier concept* and the *input-output study.* The multiplier measures the effect of changes in the sector based on the premise that increases in export sales from the region will directly increase the regional income. This income will then be used for saving, investment, and consumption. This investment and consumption, depending on where it is spent, can also increase the level of local economic activity. The multiplier is an attempt to measure all of these waves of economic effects.

Input-output studies are more sophisticated versions of multiplier analysis. The exporting sector is not treated as a large undifferentiated mass, but is broken up into a number of subsectors. The number of subsectors is determined largely by the size and budget of the research effort. Having decided on the number and types of subsectors to be included, the analyst runs a survey to estimate the level of inputs and outputs among all subsectors. The results of this survey are displayed in an input-output table, and mathematical analysis of the data enables the planner to judge the impact on other sectors and on the overall regional economy of a change in any one sector. Input-output studies tend to be quite expensive, and these techniques are more often used for learning about regional and local economies than for problem solving.

Modelling

We have discussed population and the urban economy as they might be dealt with in systems analysis. The aim of this step in the planning process is to gather knowledge on the subject at hand, and modelling, in the broadest sense of the term, is a method for doing this. Modelling efforts in urban planning can be split into large-scale comprehensive models that focus on land use or transportation and small-scale models that are problem-oriented and focus on any number of situations. Large-scale modelling was used mostly in the 1960s, and the level of activity has since dropped off considerably. These models were focused on specific metropolitan areas rather than being abstract. In each model the metropolitan area was divided up into geographic subareas, and a principle objective of the model was to allocate activities to these subareas. All these models were large, some containing over 15,000 items of data, and thus required the use of a computer. For example, a city would be broken down into 75 subareas and for each area a variety of economic activities would be reported, including population, employment, and land use. Each characteristic would be subdivided into a number of types (e.g., land uses could be separated into 20 different categories). The model would be calibrated at one point in time and then run forward through future time periods, ostensibly predicting overall changes for the metropolitan area and determining the shift of activities for each subarea.

These modelling efforts often used a number of methodologies in their routines. For example, many models involved a major cohort-survival population projection broken down by subareas, as well as a dozen other techniques. In addition, many of these large-scale models used other sophisticated tools commonly identified with operations research and/or systems analysis, such as linear, nonlinear, and dynamic programming; mathematical gaming techniques; and systems simulations based on calculus and optimization techniques.[12]

Planners advanced two basic goals for these major modelling efforts. First, they thought it should be possible to analyze objectively plans for urban areas. The existing plan development and evaluation practice was regarded as unscientific and subjective, and, therefore, suspect. This goal disappeared quickly, because the model builders were isolated from the decision makers and had little impact on the actual development and implementation of plans. Second, planners thought large-scale models could be used in the development of a more substantial urban and regional theory—that is, a theory of how cities function, where activities are located and why, and how these areas change over time. There has been considerable debate as to whether or not the large-scale modelling movement did cause a knowledge explosion in urban and regional theory proportionate to the expenditure.

The fundamental problem with these large-scale models was that they included everything rather than focusing on a specific problem confronting public officials. They modelled the whole urban fabric, assuming the answers to specific problems could be derived from the masses of data and the computerized relationships assembled. Invariably, this was impossible. The modellers wanted to serve too many purposes at one time. A single model was expected to predict population and economic growth; locate that growth in subareas of a metropolitan area; predict the impact of the construction of a new highway segment or the clearance of a city slum; evaluate the best location for a new library; and measure the overall consequences of a change in a zoning policy.

Douglas B. Lee has offered three suggestions for improving modelling efforts. The first is to obtain a balance between theory, objectivity, and intuition.

This balance would be part of the second objective: to make the models problem-oriented and related to policy by starting with a specific problem and developing a focused model that could lead to relevant insights. The third suggestion is to use small models, not only because they are then more likely to address real policy problems, but also because they will be more "transparent" and comprehensible to a larger group of professionals and lay people.[13]

There has not yet been a great deal of experimentation with smaller-scale problem-oriented models, despite general agreement that this is the preferred direction for future modelling efforts. In discussing small-scale models, it may be useful to distinguish between small-scale management models and small-scale planning or policy models. The former have limited objectives and a single focus, and the problems they deal with are finite. The latter have multiple objectives and foci and are more open-ended and ambiguous.

The work of the Rand Corporation for the New York City Fire Department can illustrate the difference between the two. Rand made contributions in four areas: communications systems; manpower and equipment deployment; management information; and new technology. The last, which was the introduction of a chemical into the water that increased flow volumes by 70 percent, can be categorized neither as a management nor as a policy problem, though this innovation had definite ramifications for both planning and management. It was basically a technical problem. The communications problem involved a study of the receipt and processing of emergency calls and of the dispatching of equipment in response. Partly through the development of a simulation model, a bottleneck in the process was redesigned at minimal cost so that it could handle almost double the prior load. This appears to be a management problem. Rand also studied the deployment of fire-fighting resources to calls. Once again, a simulation model was developed and the traditional policy of sending the closest units to the call analyzed. Not only did the Rand modellers come up with a better dispatching practice, saving the city millions of dollars, but they also participated in a contract dispute between fire fighters and the city. Once again the problem was one of management, though it did involve dispatching policy.

For a planning policy example, let us suppose that, rather than having a minimum base response to any fire emergency call as an objective, certain sections of the city are to be given less effective coverage. This posture could be rationalized by pointing out that different areas of the city have different property values. If the policy were to minimize the amount of property damage loss, richer areas of the city would get priority. If each area of the city could be rated in terms of probability of false alarms, priority would go to areas with the highest probability of a real alarm. Thus, response time would vary widely according to the location of the call. Such a fire department policy could exist, emanating from a broader citywide policy of differential service quality; it would demand evaluation and conscious decision by policymakers and politicians.

Among the suggestions offered for research on small-scale urban policy models are evaluations of:

1 A model that examines various issues surrounding the location of office activity in cities

2 Models of public facility location that focus on that public decision's effect on other aspects of city development

3 Models of the conversion process from agricultural to urban land

4 Models that focus on leisure and recreation activities in cities, especially their location in terms of accessibility[14]

Thus, it is probable that future models for understanding certain urban phenomena will be small-scale and problem-oriented, rather than large-scale and comprehensive.

EVALUATION OF ALTERNATIVE POLICIES AND PLANS

The third step in the planning process is evaluation. By this stage, the problems have been defined, the models built in order to study them in more detail, and some alternative plans or policies have been designed. In the third step, these alternative policies and plans will be tested, using either the models developed earlier or *impact models*. The alternatives will then be weighed against one another within a *goals attainment framework,* and one or more policy or plan choices will be made. These conclusions and proposals are usually presented to some public decision-making body.

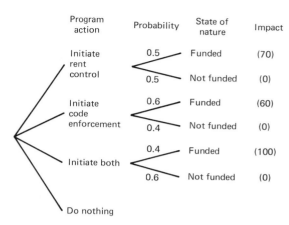

Typical decision analysis tree.

Decision Theory and Analysis

Choice is an integral concept in this step. Several techniques from probability theory are of interest here. At a theoretical level, *decision theory* can be an aid in learning how to attack problems of choice.[15] At a more pragmatic level, the use of *decision trees* to describe alternative policies, evaluate the probability of certain events connected to them, and to make choices is basic.

Decision analysis can be broken down into two stages. The first is to list the principal characteristics of all policies considered. Second is to list the *states of nature,* with the probability of their occurrence. For example, let us assume three housing policies for our possible choices: initiate a rent control program; initiate a code enforcement program; or do nothing. There are four possible alternatives: 1 only, 2 only, 1 and 2, or 3 only. Next we determine characteristics of these programs that are relevant to the types of decisions: budget sizes, conditions of eligibility for the program, and effect on certain population groups. Then we list all possible states of nature relevant to the above characteristics. Once these characteristics and relevant states are fully enumerated, we can describe their possible combinations, called *events.* The likelihood of each such event can be

evaluated and assigned a numerical probability. A value system that ascribes a relative value to each one of the events can be developed from the point of view of the decision maker, general public, or specific subgroups of the population. This is *utility theory.* Finally, once we know the probability of events and the value ascribed to each of them for our system, we can choose the optimal policy.

Planners usually rely on the political system to aggregate individual values and utilities. This does result in some dissatisfaction, since it is not really possible to combine individual utilities into a single optimal value system. However, the decision analysis process has more legitimacy than a planner using his or her own values to make a choice. The greatest value of decision theory is in its ability to aid the planner in structuring problems and decision-making frameworks.

Environmental and Fiscal Impact Methodologies

Two types of evaluation methods are *environmental* and *fiscal impact analysis.* Though neither is strictly a quantitative analytic technique, both use some quantitative techniques.

The environmental impact statement (EIS) is a document that details the potential effects of a major development or project on its environment. These forecasted consequences may include ecological and environmental pollution, changes in land use or socioeconomic factors, and the destruction of historic or otherwise unique sites. As mentioned earlier, these analyses were mandated by the National Environmental Policy Act and must meet a number of procedural requirements of federal, state, and local governments. The most common methodology for assessing environmental impact is the checklist approach, a simple listing of the potential effects of the proposed project with little attempt at assessing the magnitude or interdependencies of the effects.[16] The matrix technique, an elaboration of the checklist, does include the projected magnitude and importance of each effect.[17]

Many of the quantitative techniques used for the EIS try to ascertain the views of the groups to be affected by the proposed development and evaluate their magnitude and importance. These techniques can be viewed as tools to structure a discussion of the possible impacts. Simulation games involve players in a situation designed to derive their reactions to development proposals. A simulation game can structure a discussion of not only the impacts the players foresee but also the causal relationships they perceive and the assumptions behind their own logic. Gaming techniques are often highly successful in environmental impact work because they are so well-suited to interactive group situations.[18]

There are a number of procedures established for organizing group discussions of impacts, but they all follow a basic organization: (1) information is given out on the proposed project; (2) participants are organized into teams and are asked to respond by listing possible impacts; (3) the group looks at all listed impacts and elaborates, eliminates, and recombines them; and (4) the participants vote using secret ballots until they reach a consensual impact assessment. The *Delphi technique* is a particular group process designed to generate expert opinion.[19] Its results tend to be organized and technical in nature, depending, of course, largely on its administration . *Scenarios* and surveys are used in much the same manner as the Delphi technique. The aim is to provide nonexperts with a detailed and uniform description of project impacts and then to survey their opinions on the impacts.

Fiscal impact analyses have been performed for units of government that are considering land-use changes, development proposals, or other new policies.[20] The question addressed by such analyses is whether the governmental unit will be better or worse off financially if the project is built. In fiscal impact studies, cost-revenue analysis is performed to determine on a cash flow basis what the city will pay for each development, and what the city receives in property taxes and other revenues and benefits. There have also been numerous more generalized studies of the fiscal impact of certain land development, such as residential development and housing types.[21]

Methods of Economic Analysis

Cost-benefit, cost-effectiveness, and *planning-programming-budgeting systems* are all used to evaluate the economic rationality of public projects. Cost-effectiveness analysis attempts to evaluate the effectiveness of a number of programs or policies in achieving one specific goal. The programs tend to be short-term, and, at times, the budget is fixed. Cost-benefit analysis, on the other hand, can be used to compare the long-run economic effects of a number of projects, and choose the best one.

Cost-benefit and cost-effectiveness techniques have been in use in government ever since they were used to analyze water resource development projects in the 1930s. The revival of these techniques was sparked in the mid-1960s by an executive order signed by President Lyndon Johnson which required each executive agency of the federal government to develop a planning-programming-budgeting (PPBS) system. This impetus was amplified by a requirement that cities participating in the Model Cities Program use program evaluation techniques in their analytical process. Techniques which had been aimed primarily at water-resource projects at the federal level were quickly adapted to other subject matter areas at the local level.

Instead of organizing budgets on a line item basis (e.g., salaries, equipment, etc.), the PPBS process separates them into *programs*. Each program budget also is grouped with others into a larger goals-achievement framework, so that for any one general goal, one can look at the total programs and expenses directed toward it. Each program's sucess is measured in terms of its stated output objectives. This means that quantifiable objectives must be developed for each program.

Despite an initially positive response to the development of citywide PPBS systems, the record of achievement has been less than impressive.[22] The investment required to change any budgeting system is incredible, and the institutional barriers in the way of such change are usually substantial. In addition, the system itself has conceptual and pragmatic problems. For example, there have been tremendous difficulties in evaluating programs that address multiple goals or affect other goals or program areas. Often, it has been impossible to obtain the data necessary to measure the outputs of the programs. Data are often available, but not in the exact format required for solid measurement. Thus, the real contribution of the PPBS movement has been its two analytic tools, cost-benefit and cost-effectiveness analysis, which are still used.

The evaluation of a Job Corps labor retraining program can provide an interesting example of cost-effectiveness analysis.[23] First the objectives of such a program must be established, and then the costs of alternative programs compared. The chosen measurement objectives can affect the program design. If low dropout rates were the goal, selective screening of admissions would be encouraged. If the differential between incoming and leaving test scores were chosen, short-term gains would be emphasized more than long-run gains. To aim for the highest number of participants in the program would be short-sighted and would probably reduce the program's benefits to any individual. What is needed is a measure of the program's effectiveness at moving participants into the mainstream, both economic and social, of the working force. This example points up the difficulty of designing sophisticated but practical effectiveness measures.

Several other issues arise in the use of cost effectiveness analysis. First is the problem of project indivisibilities. For example, the chosen program may have been analyzed in $500,000 chunks, but it is funded at $1.4 million. The solution to this kind of problem is sometimes to select a mixture of programs (i.e., perhaps two chunks of the first program and $400,000 of another type). Another problem is that many programs address more than one goal. Unless one unit of measurement, usually dollars, is appropriate to all these goals, the usefulness of cost-effectiveness analysis becomes questionable. Lastly, many programs run for longer than one year, and some method must be established to compare the costs and benefits of the first year with those predicted for the future. The procedures of accounting can be helpful here if everything is measured in dollars, for discount tables, can be used. The only issues are the discount (or interest) rate, the time period of the project, and the level of uncertainty surrounding the project's costs and benefits. Cost effectiveness analysis is most often performed on one-year projects or on those that have their costs discounted to the present and expressed as equivalent annual costs.

This brings us to benefit-cost analysis.[24] Cost-effectiveness analysis is usually fixed on one objective in one substantive area and often deals with problems that are not easily translated into dollar costs and benefits. Benefit-cost analysis, since it uses dollar values for all costs and benefits, can have multiple objectives scattered over several substantive areas. Rather than annual calculations or equivalent annual costs, cost-benefit analysis is all present and future costs and benefits discounted to the present year. The benefit-cost ratio then becomes all discounted benefits for the project divided by all discounted costs. Should the budget be unlimited—an unlikely circumstance given today's public fiscal positions—the decision would be to undertake all projects with a benefit-cost ratio greater than one and not to initiate any of those with a ratio less than one. However, with a limited budget, the decision would be to implement the projects with the highest ratios, in descending order, until the budget was expended. Most cost-benefit studies look not only at the benefit-cost ratio, but also at the discounted benefits minus the discounted costs and the rate of return of each project. (The rate of return of a project is defined at that discount rate that makes the discounted benefits equal to the discounted costs—the percentage return needed to break even). Under certain circumstances, the ratio of capital to operating costs for the project and their distribution over time may mean that each of these three indicators determines a different choice.

Benefit-cost analysis suffers some problems in execution as well as in conception. It does not share with cost-effectiveness analysis the difficulty in developing meaningful but practical output measures, because its outputs (benefits) can all be measured in dollar values. However, the challenge is measuring all costs and benefits in dollars; this process is called *shadow pricing*. Consequently, projects that have benefits not easily quantified tend to suffer; less easily measured benefits are excluded from the equation, and the project that involves them does not measure up. This affects especially those projects with important secondary benefits, or *spillover effects,* not directly related to the major program goal, for these secondary benefits usually cannot be measured in dollars.

Because the cost-benefit technique was developed at the national level for water resource projects, when the techniques are used on the local level, care must be taken in defining the population involved. This obviously is not a concern when the analysis is for the entire nation. A simplified analysis of a freeway section can provide a case in point. Let us assume that all discounted benefits to all parties (all governments and all individuals) are $4 million and all discounted costs are $5 million. The benefit-cost ratio would then be 0.8, and the decision would be not to build. This decision is predicated on the notion of economic efficiency for the nation as a whole. However, let us assume now that the decision is to be made by a typical county government, and that its share of the cost is 10 percent and the federal share is 90 percent. From the federal point of view the analysis is sound, but from the county point of view it is not. For a mere 10 percent of $5 million, or $500,000, the county would receive $4 million in benefits. From the county point of view, the benefit-cost ratio is really $4 million/$.5 million, or 8.0, and their decision is to build. To ignore the federal share formula, or to give county decision makers an analysis from the national point of view only, can be politically naïve, yielding an analysis that would likely be ignored.

Since it was originally defined as the difference between national income with the project and without the project, benefit-cost analysis is narrowly conceived of as a tool of economic efficiency. But the types of policies and programs that urban planners work with, especially at the local level, are not always aimed strictly at economic efficiency. Some are attempts to get market forces operating in the public sector, and others are efforts to redistribute income and wealth. However, the economic model underlying the benefit-cost framework assumes that the existing distribution of wealth is acceptable, so that projects that reinforce the *status quo* are reasonable. There have been attempts at introducing distributional (equity) questions into the benefit framework by weighting benefits according to the subgroup of the population that is to receive them. In the final analysis, a number of analysts would argue that the benefit-cost technique is best used as an efficiency tool only where it is really appropriate.

Goals-Achievement and Planning Balance Sheet Approaches

A number of evaluation techniques have been developed to deal more explicitly with objectives other than economic efficiency. Two will be sketched here: the *goals-achievement matrix method* and the *planning balance sheet method*.[25] Neither has received much attention in the United States, but both have been used extensively in England. It is likely that North American planners will become increasingly interested in these types of techniques.

Both techniques generally follow a five-step evaluation process:

1 List the objectives

2 Develop measures of each objective

3 Weight each objective

4 Evaluate the way each alternative meets each objective

5 Select the best alternative

While cost-benefit analysis assumes that objectives are met by individuals purchasing goods and services in the marketplace at existing prices, the goals-achievement method is based on the planner's subjective assessment of objectives and the value of benefits and costs to particular groups. Thus, the benefit-cost analyst relies on the marketplace to reveal individual preferences, while the matrix analyst hopes to be able to assess the subjective preferences of groups for nonmarket goods. Matrix methods are therefore, in effect, more comprehensive than cost-benefit methods. However, the assignment of weights to objectives in the matrix approach is subjective and consequently open to criticism.

The following procedure will provide a description of the formulation of a goals-achievement matrix evaluation. First, a set of goals and objectives is formulated for the plan or policy (in theory, before the plan is designed). The measures of objectives are then defined so that progress toward the objec-

tives can be gauged. Typically a five-point measurement scale is used. Next, the relative importance of objectives is established through either a ranking procedure or a scoring procedure. Then, each plan's level of achievement of each objective is estimated and weighted by the values placed on the objectives themselves. In some instances, the incidence of benefits for particular population subgroups is estimated. Finally, the alternatives are made comparable by summing the weighted achievement levels of all the objectives for each plan to provide an overall index of achievement.

The planning balance sheet method differs from the goals-achievement method in several respects. Using a comparable matrix, the balance sheet approach measures costs and benefits in monetary terms as much as possible. Possible objectives and benefits and costs are listed by the population subgroups for which they are relevant. The costs and benefits are measured in the same terms as the objectives. The terms may be monetary ones, physical units, or even indices of goals achievement. Instead of discussing intangibles in an aside to the cost benefit analysis, the balance sheet method considers such items explicitly.

These two approaches have so far had limited application to the evaluation of social policy, being confined largely to the analysis of physical development proposals. However, they can be usefully applied to all sorts of planning problems.

Sensitivity and Break-Even Analysis

A sensitivity analysis alters some of the values previously assumed to be constant within an evaluation in order to see whether how much such changes would affect the outcome. When changing a variable affects the outcome a great deal, the variable is said to be a sensitive one. Once the sensitive variables in any evaluation are isolated, the analyst should determine the level of uncertainty surrounding the value of the variable (and of the assumptions made in determining the value of the variable). If the assumptions are firm and the level of uncertainty minimal, the analysis can stand as is; otherwise, the analyst would do well to present the conclusions in more conditional terms.[26]

For example, often in cost-benefit studies of transportation proposals, the most sensitive variable is the value of people's time spent in transit. One might start out calculating benefit-cost ratios with an accepted value of $3 per hour. However, when testing sensitivity, one may want to vary that amount from zero up to $10 per hour. One could discuss why time might be worth either almost nothing or a great deal. Additionally, one might wish to determine the break-even point, where the value of people's time makes the benefit-cost ratio go just over unity and ostensibly causes the decision to switch from "don't build" to "build." Communicating such a figure to decision makers might provide them with insights that would improve their decisions. Sensitivity analysis can of course be performed for many of the analytic tools discussed in this and other sections.

IMPLEMENTATION AND EX POST EVALUATION

The last step of the planning process includes implementation and ex post evaluation. There are a few quantitative methods that may be useful to the urban planner for implementation in the planning process. Implementation, however, remains largely an area of nonquantitative techniques such as persuasion, coalition building, and management. We do not want to overstate the use of quantitative techniques for implementation.

Two aspects of implementation will be explored briefly: first, several management techniques of program scheduling for implementation, and second, the inherently political connection between quantitative method and implementation. Following implementation, it is possible, but unfortunately not commonplace, to invest time and resources in ex post evaluation. The discussion of ex post evaluation

can be divided into two parts. First, there can be evaluations of the programs themselves and their actual costs and effectiveness. This can be viewed as a follow-up to step two of the planning process; i.e., we can ask, Were our models accurate? Did we properly understand the problem, especially our causal models of it, and did we properly project the impact of our solutions? This is by far the most popular type of ex post evaluation. Second, we can analyze our ex ante evaluation models themselves as a follow-up to step three of the planning process. That is, were our evaluations themselves accurate? Did the programs or policies attack the intended objectives and affect the intended client groups? Did anything go wrong in implementation?

Program Implementation Methods

At times planners become involved in the actual implementation of a policy or a program. Presuming that the program is made up of a number of interrelated tasks that have distinct beginnings and ends, two techniques especially can be used for scheduling portions of the program, allocating resources to these portions, keeping track of progress toward completion, and rescheduling and reallocating resources as information comes in on the progress toward implementation.

The *program evaluation and review technique* (PERT) has three steps: first, define the various tasks involved in program execution; second, link them in sequences; and third, using probability distributions of time estimates, reallocate time resources among the tasks in order to complete the project most efficiently. The *critical path method* (CPM), on the other hand, is a method for speeding the completion of a project using both time and cost estimates, adjusting schedules to fit some prescribed time constraint.[27]

The connection between the planner's quantitative methodologies and the implementation of his or her plans, policies, or programs is an important topic. Any actor in the political process—and the planner is one such actor—has a number of ways to gather and use political power and influence. The planner may try to develop a reputation for being objective, nonpolitical, and wise; he or she may habitually take into account many more factors than other actors, using a comprehensive approach rather than being tied to a special interest; or he or she may offer specialized knowledge or expertise.

Another method that may endow the planner with political power is the use of scientific rationality and sophisticated, if not mystical, procedures. Of late this particular factor has lost some of its potency, but it is still important. To hold one's own in the political arena, it is necessary at least to be able to understand and criticize the methodologies and arguments of the more specialized disciplines and interest groups. Therefore, a strong case can be made for the planner commanding a methodology as sophisticated as those of the other actors.

Methods of Evaluation after Implementation

Once implementation has occurred, two types of evaluation, with associated quantitative methodologies, can be done. The first is the evaluation of our understanding of the problem itself, i.e., an evaluation of our models. Let us suppose that the problem before us was alcoholic treatment and rehabilitation. After searching the literature, we developed a model for attacking the problem of alcoholism, from which we designed a program. Now, having evaluated and implemented the program, we might wish to see whether or not our models of the alcoholic treatment process were accurate. Did we anticipate correctly the use levels, recidivism and success rates, and costs? Was our model of the behavior of the population of alcohol users accurate? Did our experience sustain the findings of other, similar programs? Much of the social legislation enacted in the 1960s required parallel social research projects, and even at this time, a number of social programs have evaluation at the local level built into the program budget.

The literature of this type of evaluation is dominated by the writings of economists and sociologists, who examine the efficacy of social action programs and related behavioral models. The latest form of these social program evaluations is the *systematic experiment*. The most notable examples are the housing maintenance and income maintenance experiments. Both of these are multimillion-dollar efforts to assess the impact of a major change in the direction of American social policy and the specific programs concerned. The methodologies involved in the various types of evaluation correspond to methods of planning in their popularity, with descriptive and inferential statistics the most common.[28]

The second type of ex post evaluation examines the evaluation techniques themselves. That is, if evaluative models were used to choose the best program, and these models forecast the contributions of the programs to certain goals as well as their impact on certain population subgroups, were these evaluation models accurate, and was the best program chosen as a result? How was the program administered? Was it effective? Again, the methods to be used in such an evaluation would parallel the methods of planning as a whole, but thus far such evaluations are rare.[29]

THE FUTURE OF QUANTITATIVE METHODS IN PLANNING[30]

The future of methodology in planning will be largely determined by social forces and by the federal government's response to those forces, which may include:

1 A possible general move in government to make more decisions public decisions, with even more public control and management

2 A resurgence of interest in (and a thrust toward) reprivitization.

3 A trend toward more decentralized forms of decision making and meaningful citizen participation in public policymaking

4 An increased concern about the issues of the redistribution of wealth in America, with a concentration on the way various public policies affect redistribution

5 A new emphasis on local government control of quality of life through growth controls, some exclusionary in effect, if not in intent

6 Movement toward a service-based economy, resulting in a demand for different types of activities and new spatial implications

7 A continuation of present trends of suburbanization and low urban density and a shift to even more non-metropolitan development

8 A continuation of the present shifts in development from the northeastern and central states to the southern and southwestern regions.

Urban planning is a relatively new profession; its major period of growth occurred very recently, but it has had a bright start. Against the backdrop of the eight social forces mentioned above, four characteristics of planning suggest clues to the future of the profession and its methodology.

First, if there has been one theme central to the work of American planners over the years, it has been the study of urban and regional spatial form. The decisions associated with the location of activities in metropolitan areas, regions, and even nations have been largely made by planners.

Second, the profession of planning is staffed with persons who share an interest in social policy. Most planners are sensitive to the issues of social equity in the United States today, and their methodologies tend to reflect this awareness.

Third, because of the unique position of planners in most government agencies, they have become experts in participatory policymaking, in involving citizens in the public planning and decision-making processes. Planners in all sectors have learned how to use citizen input meaningfully.

Finally, our planning methodologies are admit-tedly eclectic, and planning approaches have been multidisciplinary. Although it is true that the profession has sometimes too quickly adopted or too easily dismissed methodologies from other disciplines, it has been rather successful at combining a technical approach with a political one.

What these trends and characteristics portend for the future of planning methodology is not entirely clear, but they do suggest ways to enhance urban planning's position in the public arena. These suggestions are for the most part prescriptive, though signs of some of them have already surfaced.

Planners need to develop transparent methodologies that demystify the planning and policymaking processes. In other words, any methodology developed or employed must lend itself to understanding by the well-informed citizen. It follows that it is essential that planners continue to develop their analyses with communities. The term *participatory analysis* can be used to identify this notion.

The efforts of planners to develop and use methodologies should continue to take place in the context of public policy. That is, they should maintain a problem focus rather than a disciplinary focus. This focus on problems means that planners' efforts should be small-scale rather than comprehensive. This does not exclude coordinated approaches to problem solving. There are still those who believe that, with proper levels of research funding, all purpose methodologies could be developed for identifying and solving a great variety of problems, but most professionals now feel that this trend would misallocate both funds and professional energy.

Because many of the trends noted above imply that both the sources of problems and their solutions involve equity as well as locational variables, planners must concentrate on methodologies that deal with these two issues.

Most importantly, planners need to return to more normative and prescriptive modes of thought. Planners have gained political knowledge over the last two decades, but some would say they have capitulated to the negative aspects of political life.

Too often, the talk is of short-term, mundane problems and solutions. Some would argue that only by this incrementalist approach can planning maintain any political strength, but it could also be persuasively argued that power would accrue from the reappearance of a more long-range, idealistic, and visionary posture. Few other professions have ever had such a posture, and it could improve the planning field's ability to adapt to emerging societal trends and to develop a truly responsive and politically effective methodology.

NOTES

1. Richard S. Bolan, "Emerging Views of Planning," *Journal of the American Institute of Planners (JAIP)* 33 (July 1967):233–45.

1a. The organization and substance of this chapter owes a profound debt to the writings and thinking of Michael B. Teitz. See his article in David Godschalk ed., *Planning in America* (Washington, D.C.: American Institute of Planners, 1974).

2. Several textbooks can be suggested for this purpose. They include: Hubert M. Blalock, *Social Statistics.* 2d ed. (New York: McGraw-Hill, 1972), and R. J. Wonnacott and T. H. Wonnacott, *Introductory Statistics* (New York: Wiley, 1969).

3. The measures are dispersed in the literatures of planning, economics, geography, demography, human ecology, and regional science, among others. However, several main sources can be suggested. For simple economic descriptors, see Walter Isard et al., *Methods of Regional Analysis* (New York: Technology Press of M.I.T. and Wiley, 1960). For many demographic descriptors, see Henry Shrycock and Jacob Siegel, *The Methods and Materials of Demography*, 2 vols. (Washington, D.C.: GPO, 1973).

4. A classic article on needs assessment methodology is Janel Scheff Reiner et al., "Client Analysis and the Planning of Public Programs," *JAIP* 29 (November 1963):270–82. For a more comprehensive review of needs assessment methodologies, see E. C. Baumherer and G. A. Hellar, *Analysis and Synthesis of Needs Assessment Research in the Field of Human Services* (Denver: University of Colorado Center for Social Research and Development, 1974).

5. The major portion of population and housing statistics appears in two volumes: U.S. Department of Commerce, Bureau of the Census, *1970 Census of Population and Housing.* See the *1970 Census of Population and Housing Publication and Computer Tape Program* for a detailed listing of available published and unpublished data. For a concise compilation see the Bureau's *County and City Data Book, 1972* (Washington, D.C.: GPO, 1973).

6. See U.S. Department of Commerce, Bureau of the Census, *Bureau of the Census Catalog.* It is issued quarterly and describes census materials released during each quarter. Occasional summaries of available materials are also included.

7. There are numerous books available on both the general topic of survey research methods and detailed aspects of the process, like question design. For an excellent introduction, see Carol Weiss and Harry Hatry, *An Introduction to Sample Surveys for Government Managers* (Washington, D.C.: Urban Institute, 1971). For good textbooks on the entire process with detailed references, see: C. A. Moser and G. Kalton, *Survey Research Methods in Social Investigation*, 2d ed. (New York: Basic Books, 1972); and Herbert Hyman, *Survey Design and Analysis: Principles, Cases, and Procedures* (New York: Free Press, 1955).

8. For a comprehensive overview of urban information systems, written early in their development and thus optimistic, see: Systems Development Corporation, *Urban and Regional Information Systems* (Washington, D.C.: GPO, 1968); and Edward Hearle and Raymond Mason, *A Data Processing System for State and Local Governments* (Englewood Cliffs, N.J.: Prentice-Hall, 1963). For excellent criticism of information systems, see two articles by Ida Hoos: "Information Systems and Public Planning," *Management Science* 13 (1967):817–31; and "Systems Techniques for Managing Society: A Critique," *Public Administration Review* 33 (1973):157–64.

9. See Michael J. Flax, *A Study in Comparative Urban Indicators: Conditions in Eighteen Large Metropolitan Areas* (Washington, D.C.: Urban Institute, 1972).

10. There is a large amount of literature on the topic of systems analysis and the tools of operations research in planning, much of it overly optimistic. James Hughes and Lawrence Mann provided an excellent review of the topic in "Review Article: Systems and Planning Theory," *JAIP* 35 (September 1969):330–33. Anthony J. Catanese and Alan W. Steiss provided a good summary of many of the concepts and mathematics underlying the approach in *Systems Planning: Theory and Application* (Lexington, Mass.: Heath, Lexington Books, 1970).

11. For forecasting population change at the local level there are two primary source books. Donald B. Pittenger's *Projecting State and Local Populations* (Cambridge, Mass.: Ballinger, 1976) is an invaluable reference on all local population projection techniques. Henry Shryock and Jacob Siegel's *The Methods and Materials of Demography*, 2 vols. (Washington, D.C.: GPO, 1973),

available from the Bureau of the Census, is a comprehensive demographic sourcebook from which many tools important in doing population projection can be obtained.

12. An introduction to many of these techniques is provided by Anthony J. Catanese, *Scientific Methods of Urban Analysis* (Urbana: University of Illinois Press, 1972).

13. See Douglas B. Lee, Jr., "Requiem for Large Scale Models," *JAIP* 39 (May 1973):163–78. This article caused a considerable reaction when first published. Critics often overlook the numerous positive suggestions Lee made for directing modeling into more policy-oriented and productive areas.

14. Michael A. Goldberg, "Simulating Cities: Process, Product, and Prognosis," *JAIP* 43 (April 1977):148–57.

15. The classic introductory text is Irwin D. Bross, *Design for Decision* (New York: Macmillan, 1953). In a stricter planning context, see Ruth P. Mack, *Planning on Uncertainty: Decision Making in Business and Government Administration* (New York: Wiley-Interscience, 1971). Two other excellent references are : Howard Raiffa, *Decision Analysis: Introductory Lectures on Choices under Uncertainty* (Reading, Mass.: Addison-Wesley, 1968); and Ralph L. Keeney and Howard Raiffa, *Decisions with Multiple Objectives: Preferences and Value Tradeoffs* (New York: Wiley, 1976). The latter includes a number of helpful case studies.

16. There are numerous books available on this topic. Two good ones are: Patrick Heffernan and Ruthann Corwin, eds., *Environmental Impact Assessment* (San Francisco: Freeman, Cooper, 1975); and Sherman J. Rosen, *Manual for Environmental Impact Evaluation* (Englewood Cliffs, N.J.: Prentice-Hall, 1976).

17. For a useful summary of the use of these techniques in the context of impact assessment, see Dean Runyan, "Tools for Community-Managed Impact Assessment," *JAIP* 43 (April 1977):125–34.

18. A good example is Richard D. Duke and Cathy S. Greenblat, *IMPASSE* (Ann Arbor: University of Michigan Environmental Simulation Laboratory, 1973). For a good textbook on games in general (and games of this type in particular), see Cathy S. Greenblat and Richard D. Duke, *Gaming-Simulation: Rationale, Design and Applications*. (New York: Halsted, 1975).

19. H. Linstone and M. Turoff, *The Delphi Method: Technique and Application* (Reading, Mass.: Addison-Wesley, 1975).

20. Robert W. Burchell and David Listokin, *The Fiscal Impact Handbook: Projecting the Local Costs and Revenues Related to Growth* (New Brunswick, N.J.: Center for Urban Policy Research, University, 1978).

21. See, for example, Real Estate Research Corporation, *The Costs of Sprawl*, 3 vols. (Washington, D.C.: GPO, 1975).

22. See Selma J. Muskin, "P.P.B. for the Cities: Problems and the Next Steps," in *Financing the Metropolis*, ed. John P. Crecine, *Urban Affairs Annual Review*, vol. 4 (Beverly Hills, Ca.: Sage, 1970), pp. 247–84. For a broader and more contemporary view of city budgeting, see James C. Snyder, *Fiscal Management and Planning in Local Government* (Lexington, Mass.: Heath, Lexington Books, 1977).

23. Michael B. Teitz provides this example in "Cost Effectiveness: A Systems Approach to Analysis of Urban Services," *JAIP* 34 (September 1968):303–11. For a text on C/E, see J. Morley English, ed. *Cost Effectiveness: The Economic Evaluation of Engineered Systems* (New York: Wiley, 1968).

24. There is an overwhelming body of literature available on both the broad and narrow aspects of C/B. Two high-quality introductions are: Edward J. Mishan, *Cost Benefit Analysis*, 2d ed. (London: G. Allen, 1971); and G. H. Peters, *Cost Benefit Analysis and Public Expenditure*, 3d ed. (London: Institute of Economic Affairs, 1973).

25. Both methods are presented in Nathaniel Lichfield, Peter Kettle, and Michael Whitbread, *Evaluation in the Planning Process* (Elmsford, N.Y.: Pergamon, 1975).

26. An example of the use of sensitivity analysis (in this case in the context of benefit-cost analysis) is provided by David S. Sawicki, "Break-Even Benefit-Cost Analysis of Alternative Express Transit Systems," *Journal of Transport Economics and Policy* 8, no. 3 (1974):1–20.

27. For a good introduction to these techniques, see Richard I. Levin and Charles A. Kirkpatrick, *Planning and Control with PERT/CPM* (New York: McGraw-Hill, 1966).

28. There are a number of excellent introductory tests on social program evaluation. Three classics are: Francis G. Caro, ed., *Readings in Evaluation Research*, 2d ed. (New York: Russell Sage, 1977); Edward A. Suchman, *Evaluative Research: Principles and Practice in Public Service Action Programs* (New York: Russell Sage, 1967); and Carol H. Weiss, *Evaluation Research: Methods of Assessing Program Effectiveness* (Englewood Cliffs, N.J.: Prentice-Hall, 1972).

29. Jeffrey L. Pressman and Aaron B. Wildavsky, *Implementation* (Berkeley: University of California Press, 1973); Eugene Bardack, *The Implementation Game: What Happens after a Bill Becomes a Law* (Cambridge, Mass.: 1977); Walter Williams and Richard F. Elmore, eds. *Social Program Implementation* (New York: Academic, 1976).

30. See Michael B. Teitz in David Godschalk, ed., *Planning in America*.

FOR FURTHER READING

Blalock, Hubert M., Jr. *Social Statistics.* 2d ed. New York: McGraw-Hill, 1972.

Campbell, D. T., and Stanley, J. C. *Experimental and Quasi-Experimental Designs for Research.* Chicago: Rand McNally, 1966.

Catanese, Anthony J. *Scientific Methods of Urban Analysis.* Urbana, Ill.: University of Illinois Press, 1972.

————, and Steiss, Alan W. *Systemic Planning: Theory and Application.* Lexington, Mass.: Heath, Lexington Books, 1970.

Godschalk, David R., ed. *Planning in America: Learning from Turbulence.* Washington D.C.: American Institute of Planners, 1974.

Isard, Walter, et al. *Methods of Regional Analysis.* New York: Technology Press of M.I.T. and Wiley, 1960.

Kaplan, Abraham B. *The Conduct of Inquiry: Methodology for Behavioral Science.* San Francisco: Chandler, 1964.

Krueckeberg, Donald A., and Silvers, Arthur L. *Urban Planning Analysis: Methods and Models.* New York: Wiley, 1974.

Lichfield, Nathaniel; Kettle, Peter; and Whitbread, Michael. *Evaluation in the Planning Process.* Elmsford, N.Y.: Pergamon, 1975.

Mack, Ruth P. *Planning on Uncertainty: Decision Making in Business and Government Administration.* New York: Wiley-Interscience, 1971.

Mishan, E. J. *Cost Benefit Analysis.* 2d ed. London: G. Allen, 1971.

Moser, C. A., and Kalton, G. *Survey Methods in Social Investigation.* 2d ed. New York: Basic Books, 1972.

Perloff, Harvey, and Wingo, Lowdon, eds. *Issues in Urban Economics.* Baltimore: Johns Hopkins for Resources for the Future, 1968.

Pittenger, Donald B. *Projecting State and Local Populations.* Cambridge, Mass.: Ballinger, 1976.

Raiffa, Howard. *Decision Analysis: Introductory Lectures on Choices under Uncertainty.* Reading, Mass.: Addison-Wesley, 1968.

Robinson, Ira. *Decision-Making in Urban Planning: An Introduction to New Methodologies.* Beverly Hills, Calif.: Sage, 1972.

Rogers, Andrei. *Matrix Methods in Urban and Regional Analysis.* San Francisco: Holden-Day, 1971.

Snyder, James C. *Fiscal Management and Planning in Local Government.* Lexington, Mass.: Heath, Lexington Books, 1977.

Thompson, Wilbur R. *A Preface to Urban Economics.* Baltimore: Johns Hopkins for Resources for the Future. 1965.

U.S. Department of Commerce. Bureau of the Census. *The Methods and Materials of Demography,* by Henry S. Shrycock and Jacobs S. Siegel et al., rev. 2 vols. Washington, D.C.: GPO, 1973.

Part Three
Functional Planning Practice

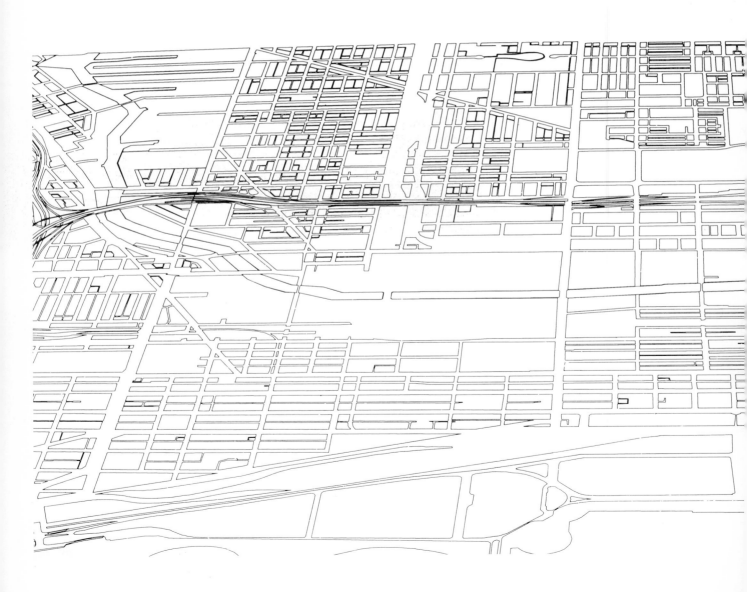

The third part of this volume deals with a number of functional areas of planning practice within the framework of urban planning. In functional planning, attention is focused upon the resolution of problems in a specific area within the more general set of urban conditions.

The examples of functional planning that are discussed are largely physical, but they are viewed from economic, political, social, and environmental vantage points. This part starts with an overview of physical planning. It is followed by a review of environmental concerns and a discussion of planning for specific areas, such as housing, land use, transportation, public works, historical preservation, and fiscal resources.

This physical basis and environmental perspective give these discussions a sense of unity, because urban planning inevitably results in a set of policies and recommendations that deal with the built environment as effected by economic and fiscal constraints.

CHAPTER 8

Physical Planning

Larry Witzling

Physical planning involves the spatial distribution of goals, objects, functions, and activities in urban areas. The content of physical planning continues to change, yet it remains an inherently traditional approach. Physical planning may be regarded as the nuts-and-bolts of the way the built environment is conceived.

INTRODUCTION: THE CHANGING ROLE AND DEFINITION OF PHYSICAL PLANNING

Traditionally professional urban planning has been characterized as physical planning. The image of urban planners laying out streets, houses, parks, and public buildings is still prevalent in the minds of the general public. However, this image is no longer accurate, and, at times, it is misleading. Today physical planning is not the single basic activity with which urban planners implement their recommendations. In contemporary practice and education, the planner is concerned with critical social, economic, environmental, and political problems that affect the well-being of the city. Economic, fiscal, and social plans are as important as the physical plan. The presumption that the physical plan always constrains or directs other modes of planning is no longer valid. However, this shift in emphasis to a variety of planning modes has actually increased the significance of physical planning. That is, as the scope of urban planning has broadened, the opportunities for using physical planning have grown.

The changing role of physical planning has been accompanied by a change in its definition. The traditional meaning of physical planning focused upon the design and regulation of major public and private physical improvements. Now the widened scope of urban planning requires a more general interpretation of the content and purpose of physical planning. For example, when a planner works on a city's economic redevelopment policy, he or she

175

may propose certain residential areas for revitalization. The selection of such revitalization areas is a form of physical planning that does not necessarily include any explicit design decisions (i.e., no new streets, houses, or other physical improvements are proposed). Similarly, a social services program might include both a description of the number and type of services to be provided and a physical plan for the distribution of those services. Other situations involving "new" types of physical planning activities could include: deciding where a new airport should be located; developing the routes and schedules for a mass transit system; and establishing a historic preservation program.

Physical planning must now be defined to include all these diverse examples without excluding the more traditional focus upon the design of the "built environment." One such definition is that physical planning is the determination of the *spatial distribution of human actions and conditions to achieve predetermined goals.* This concept is the key to understanding the expanded role of physical planning.

SPATIAL DISTRIBUTIONS: A FRAMEWORK FOR PHYSICAL PLANNING

All human actions and conditions are distributed in space: groups, cultural beliefs, buildings, vehicles, environmental pollutants, political power, energy consumption, skills, and technology. Any of these variables can be defined, observed, located, and translated into a map to show how they are distributed in space. Almost all urban planning activities sooner or later refer to a map showing the spatial distribution of critical variables that typically include population figures, economic and social conditions, and characteristics of the physical environment. Interest in the spatial distribution of activities and conditions is not limited to urban planning. Many disciplines, including geography, architecture, engineering, economics, agriculture, sociology, anthropology, business, and public health use the concept of spatial distribution for solving problems.

Simply including spatial distributions in the analysis of an urban problem does not imply that physical planning is taking place. Only when a spatial distribution is part of an action recommended to achieve some purpose can we say that a physical plan is being proposed. For example, if a planner analyzes the socioeconomic conditions in areas of the city and recommends a social program which does not differentiate between areas, then there is no physical plan, only a social plan. However, if social programs vary among areas, there is a physical plan.

What kinds of actions and conditions do planners spatially distribute, and for what purposes? There are essentially four types of variables whose spatial distribution is manipulated in physical plans: *objects, functions, activities,* and *goals.*

The Spatial Distribution of Objects

Within the context of physical planning, the spatial distribution of *objects* refers to items such as buildings, parks, trees, roads, highways, sewer lines, and utility plants. Spatially distributed objects may be as small as traffic signs and as large as airports. This aspect of physical plans comes closest to the traditional image of the urban planner. For example, the layout of pathways, residences, and marketplaces was a function of the planners in ancient Greece. Today planners are still actively engaged in planning the layout of suburban subdivisions, the design of new towns, and the location and distribution of parks, recreational facilities, hospitals, schools, museums, libraries, and art centers.

There are other less obvious situations in which planners are concerned with the spatial distribution of objects. The location of a series of firehouses or ambulance stations is a form of physi-

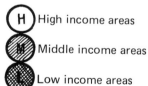

H High income areas

M Middle income areas

L Low income areas

Spatial distribution of income levels.

cal planning in which objects are placed to achieve an effective distribution of critical public services. Larger objects, such as industrial parks, highways, and shopping centers, also must be planned and located in space.

Although the explicit functions of these objects are of paramount importance to the physcial planner, they have many other attributes with which the planner must be concerned. For example, while an urban highway fulfills the function of transportation, because of its properties as a physical object it has a significant impact upon the quality of life within the neighborhoods through which it passes. Determining what impacts will occur and who will be affected is critical in the spatial distribution of such objects. Similarly, in the design of a downtown

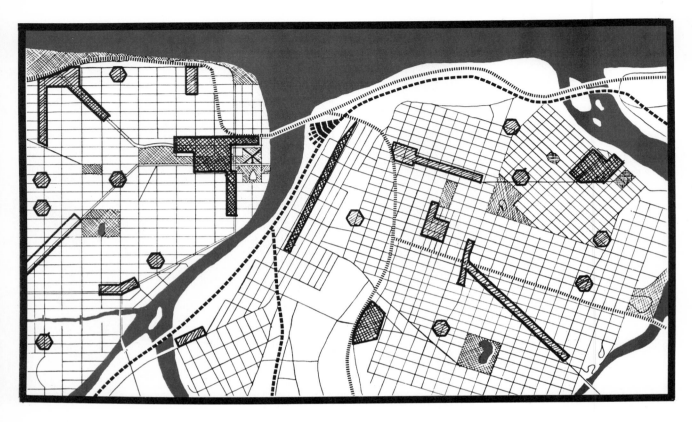

Major commercial centers   Secondary commercial centers

Neighborhood "convenience" shopping areas

Spatial distribution of retail commercial activities.

center the <u>aesthetic qualities of the objects are as</u> <u>significant as the functions of the buildings.</u> Thus <u>the spatial distribution of objects is often an extremely complex problem that relates not only to</u> <u>the proper location of an object from the standpoint</u> <u>of its explicit purpose, but also to its form and visual quality, symbolic import, and its interaction with</u> <u>other objects and human activities.</u>

INTRODUCTION TO URBAN PLANNING

The Spatial Distribution of Functions

<u>In the spatial distribution of *functions*, the planner is</u> concerned with <u>police and fire protection, sanitation</u> services, <u>utilities, transportation, education, and so</u> <u>forth.</u> Essentially, these are service functions provided by local government. The spatial distribution of public service functions is closely related to the distribution of objects described above, and it also

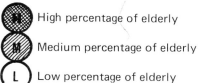 High percentage of elderly

Medium percentage of elderly

Low percentage of elderly

Spatial distribution of elderly population.

is one of the traditional purposes of urban physical planning.

The proper distribution of service functions is fundamental to a city's welfare. For example, the provision and location of sewers, water lines, gas lines, and electric power are related intimately to the patterns of residential and commercial development. The distribution of service functions can es-

sentially control urban growth. Similarly, the disposition of transportation services such as streets, highways, mass transit systems, traffic signalling, and parking regulations can influence significantly the patterns of economic growth and decline. For example, improving access between the central city and a suburban area can promote residential migration to that suburb. Conversely, improving an

PHYSICAL PLANNING

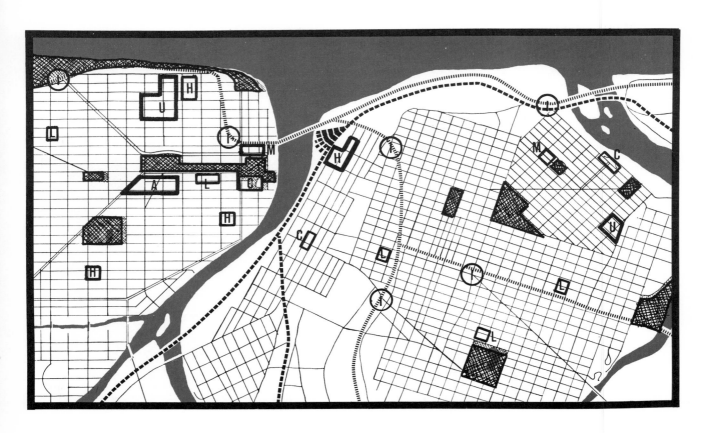

(I) Major highway interchanges	/A/ Arts center
[M] Museums	[H] Hospitals
[L] Libraries	[U] Universities/colleges
▨ Parks	[C] Other cultural institutions and major civic buildings

Spatial distribution of objects.

inner-city mass transit system might increase the probability that residents will remain in their current neighborhoods. Service functions can take the form of lines or linear networks running through the city, or they can be formed as areas, precincts, districts, or catchments. Police, fire protection, and sanitation functions are typically distributed by defining specific service areas within which one police station, firehouse, or sanitation unit assumes major responsibility for service delivery. Schools, post offices, and libraries are typically distributed on a district or areal basis.

Other public service functions are distributed on neither a linear nor district basis but are intended for use by the entire urban area. For example, recreational and cultural functions (occurring in major parks, stadiums, fair grounds, museums, and zoos) provide services to a large area, but they must be distributed in space so that they are accessible to the various groups and communities that make up the city and their negative impacts on the specific adjacent areas are minimized.

Although the spatial distribution of service functions is related directly to the distribution of the objects, or physical components, in which they are embodied, it is still a separate physical planning issue. Determining the boundaries of a police precinct or school district is a different problem from selecting the specific site for the police station or school building. Recommending that major recreational opportunities should be provided to a selected region of a city is an issue separable from the location and design of a specific park.

The spatial distribution of service functions must be viewed as a set of overlapping and interacting networks. In other words, utility lines, transportation systems, sanitation, police and fire protection, and education are not completely independent of each other, but form a mix of interrelated functions. The physical planning of such functions is usually quite complicated and often requires a comprehensive perspective of public service functions within which the distribution of any single function is determined.

The Spatial Distribution of Activities

The spatial distribution of *activity* relates to the regulatory and programming activities of urban government. In this case *regulatory* refers to those governmental activities that restrict or require specific actions, while *programming* refers to activities that encourage or promote specific actions. Both types of governmental activities are usually embodied in legislation or administrative actions that influence the spatial distribution of the behaviors and actions of individuals, private businesses and corporations, and other institutions outside the direct supervision of city government.

The best-known form of urban regulatory behavior is zoning, in which a city is divided into various districts, each of which has an associated set of restrictions governing the way the land may be used. For example, one area may be zoned so that only single-family residences at a density of no more than two per acre may be constructed, while other zones are designated for commercial, manufacturing activity, higher density residential development, or special uses (e.g., recreational, institutional, and so forth). Zoning may also be used to control the aesthetic features of an area.

There are, however, many other regulatory activities. For example, designating an area as a *historic preservation district* restricts the manner in which structures in that area can be remodelled or even prohibits the demolition of certain structures, in order to preserve the character of the area. Similarly, a city government can implement an extensive building code enforcement campaign in selected neighborhoods in order to improve the quality of the buildings and discourage the type of neglect often correlated with absentee landlords. This too is a spatially distributed regulatory activity. In contrast to the restriction of activity, programs can be used to encourage specific activities in different areas. Such programs are usually economic or social in character. For example, the designation of urban renewal areas is intended to encourage specific forms of development within selected urban areas. Unfortunately, urban renewal has had many

182

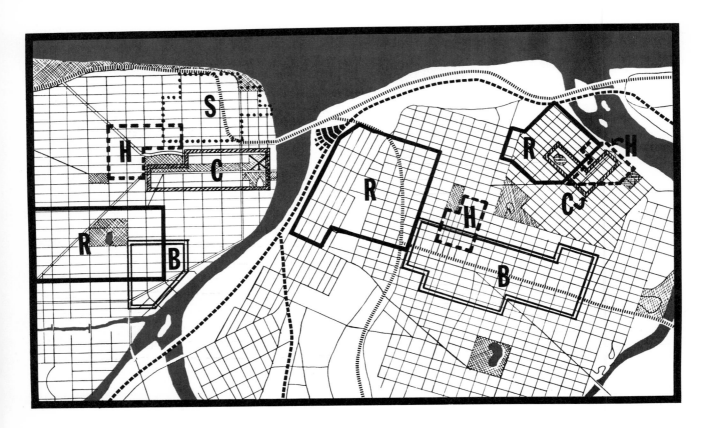

R	Home loan/rehabilitation programs
B	Building code enforcement programs
H	Historic preservation districts

C	Civic beautification projects
S	Health screening program

Spatial distribution of activities.

negative effects on those specially selected areas. A variety of programs have been established (often by the federal government) in which cities focus rent subsidies, housing programs, home improvement loans, and other financial and technical aids in certain target areas. This spatial distribution of programmed activities is also a form of physical planning.

Other spatially distributed programmed activities include the promotion of street festivals and celebrations, summer programs for youth, drug rehabilitation and treatment, and health care for the elderly.

INTRODUCTION TO URBAN PLANNING

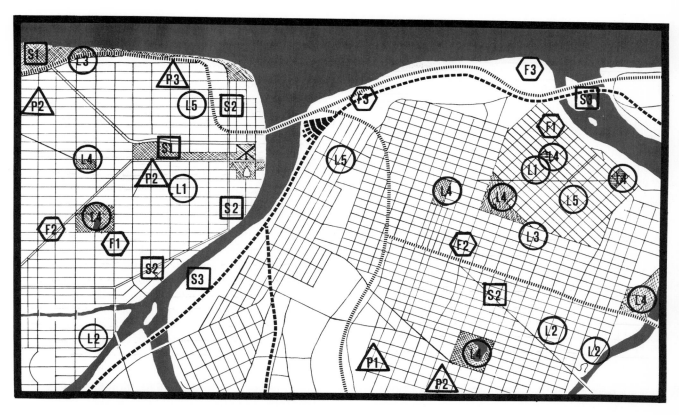

Local ("city") planning activities:

- **L1** Urban redevelopment authority projects
- **L2** Public housing
- **L3** Recreation programs
- **L4** City parks
- **L5** Social services centers

State planning activities:

- **S1** State parks
- **S2** Highway improvements
- **S3** Regulation of natural resources

Federal planning activities:

- **F1** Mortgage subsidies to home owners
- **F2** Small business loans
- **F3** Coast Guard supervision and control

Private sector planning activities:

- **P1** Development of major shopping center
- **P2** "Condominium" housing development
- **P3** Institutional expansion

Spatial distribution of local, state, federal, and private planning activities.

Such activities vary in size and content, and their spatial distribution is often a critical factor in their success.

The spatial distribution of activities is often inclusive of the distribution of objects and functions, but since it involves a greater or perhaps different variety of urban problems and issues, it should be considered as a separate mode of physical planning. Thus, direct consideration of the spatial distribution of regulatory and programmed activities adds one more level of complexity to physical planning.

The Spatial Distribution of Goals

The most general and inclusive form of physical planning is the spatial distribution of goals. It encompasses a distribution of objects, functions, and activities. A physical plan that shows the distribution of urban goals is in fact a physical planning *policy*. Such a policy articulates how the planner intends to accomplish his or her goals in different parts of the city. The distribution of goals and the means to achieve them can be associated with an entire district such as a residential neighborhood or downtown area; with a linear network, such as a commercial strip or a road system; or with a specific point, such as a park or civic center.

The spatial distribution of goals can occur at a variety of levels and involve many different contents. For example, several communities may be designated for neighborhood improvement. This relatively general goal might include the construction of new dwellings, housing rehabilitation, reorganization of the provision of services, special financial programs to encourage commercial growth, new parks, and/or modifications in the zoning regulations. The actual manifestation of the goal of neighborhood improvement will take a different form and content for each neighborhood.

Another general goal that is often part of a physical planning policy is economic development. The manifestation of this goal will also involve a variety of objects, functions, and activities distributed in various spatial patterns. For example, one district may be selected for an industrial park, which would include construction of roads, sewers, and utilities, as well as modifications in the existing linear network of highways and mass transit to improve access to the park. Commercial development, may be part of an economic goal, leading, for example, to both the rezoning of certain areas to promote commercial change and the selection of sites for encouraging the growth of new shopping centers. Part of an economic development goal might include legislated changes in the distribution of property and business taxes in order to attract new investments in appropriate parts of the city.

The spatial distribution of public goals is the most difficult and ambiguous type of physical planning. First, the distribution of goals is an intensely political process. Mayors, members of city councils, state and federal elected officials, local community organizations, and private businesses and corporations all have vested interests in different parts of the city. Consequently, the announcement of a goal that affects specific areas of the city will imply benefits for some persons and costs for others. Although the distribution of objects, functions, and activities have obvious political implications, the distribution of goals and intentions is a more pervasive, more long-run, and more powerful political issue.

Second, the rational determination of goals is exceedingly difficult. For example, should a goal be adopted if it will have a minor positive impact on the entire city and a major negative impact on one small neighborhood? Even without the implicit problem of aggregating the values of all the subsets of the urban population, we are still limited in our knowledge of what goals are appropriate and how to achieve them. Numerous failures in urban renewal programs, public housing, and highway planning stem partially from our lack of knowledge as to how cities really work. Even with the best information, there are still many unpredictable events that affect the selection of a goal and means for achieving it.

Third, a physical planning policy for the spatial distribution of goals is not a single document, with all of the goals laid out on one map. To the contrary, an urban physical planning policy is a collection of various documents, regulations, public statements, and programs that are designated or advocated by many different public agencies, elected officials, and private organizations. Not only city planning departments, but also mayors' offices, school boards, business associations, departments of public works, state and federal agencies, and neighborhood organizations have reports, plans, programs, proposed legislation, and other documents that constitute a city's de facto physical planning policy. Thus, the spatial distribution of goals should be conceived of as a dynamic process in which the content of the goals will change, the intentions of the goals will often conflict, and the representation of the goals will take a variety of forms.

PHYSICAL PLANNERS

Where do we find urban physical planners? The simplest most conventional response is to label as physical planners those persons who work within a department of city planning, whose tasks involve recommending different *spatial distributions*. But there are many other individuals and groups involved directly in such tasks who work for a wide spectrum of public and private organizations. We will consider four categories of urban physical planning contexts: local public agencies, state and regional public organizations, federal agencies, and private groups and individuals.

Physical Planners in Local Public Agencies

Local public agencies include agencies within city, township, and county governments as well as those for special purpose districts (e.g., school districts). In addition to the traditional department of city plan-

ning, there are other governmental subunits that prepare and advocate physical plans: departments of public works; bureaus of traffic engineering; transit authorities; park departments; police, fire, health, and sanitation departments; and so forth. Many other local governmental subunits that usually are not thought of as affecting physical plans, do have a direct impact on spatial distributions. For example, a building inspection agency or tax assessor's office may adopt different operational policies for different parts of the city, which, in effect, constitute a physical plan. There are many local social service programs that either serve only selected neighborhoods or adopt different service policies in different neighborhoods.

In recent decades one of the most important local government units involved in physical planning has been the urban renewal agency or redevelopment authority. This type of agency is given special authority to assemble parcels of land through the power of eminent domain and to organize the development of that land in accordance with an overall physical plan. Initially, urban renewal programs were directed toward slum clearance and residential contruction in central city areas. Over the years, however, the content and purpose of urban renewal programs have grown to encompass central business district (CBD) development, housing rehabilitation, middle-income housing, construction of institutions and community facilities, historic preservation, and commercial revitalization. Urban renewal programs have had mixed success. While cautiously planned and executed projects have had positive impacts, bureaucratic red tape and insensitivity to the needs of residents have often resulted in dismal failures.

With the exception of those in city planning departments and urban renewal agancies, few of the persons within these local government subunits have been trained as urban planners. These individuals usually have received training within other disciplines (e.g., engineering, social welfare, public administration) where physical planning is only one, sometimes minor, factor in the decisions they make. As a result, physical planning policy is often fragmentary and incremental so that the responsibility of coordinating and synthesizing physical plans is given to a planning department where expertise in interagency coordination and political negotiation becomes critical.

Physical Planners in State and Regional Organizations

Government agencies at the state and regional level create physical plans for sets of urban areas. At the state level there are agencies dealing with highways, park systems, and public institutions (such as educational, correctional, and health facilities) and, more recently, departments that deal with environmental protection, natural resources, and energy consumption and distribution. In addition, many states have departments which are focusing directly on physical planning functions.

Although the authority and legitimacy of city government derives from state law, planning at the state level does not necessarily dominate and take precedence over city planning decisions. In practice there are many trade-offs and compromises intended to integrate the physical planning decisions at both governmental levels. For example, the state planners who determine the location and character of a state park or recreation area are usually concerned with how that park will fit in with the objectives of the physical planners at the local level. Similarly, a state university system makes many physical planning decisions that would result in political friction as well as a poor physical plan, if they were not coordinated with local physical planning.

An equally difficult coordination problem concerns the activities of neighboring cities and municipalities. A major metropolitan area is surrounded by many smaller cities and townships, and the interrelationships pose significant physical planning problems. Consequently, many areas have regional planning agencies that recommend and sometimes implement actions to coordinate the developments among a number of urban areas. Physical planning, especially of transportation systems, utility systems, and land use management, is a major function of these regional agencies. At times, the problem of regional coordination spreads beyond the boundaries of one state, and interstate regional advisory commissions are formed (e.g., the TriState Planning Commission serves New York, New Jersey, and Connecticut).

Similar to regional planning agencies are special-purpose public authorities that perform physical planning activities above the city level. For example, the Port Authority of New York and New Jersey plans and coordinates intercity and interstate transit facilities and systems (and constructed the World Trade Center). The Tennessee Valley Authority oversees the development and distribution of hydroelectric power and facilities, water resources, and distribution. More recently, the Bay Area Rapid Transit System (BART) in California planned, constructed, and now operates a mass transit system. All these public organizations have significant impacts upon the physical plans of individual cities.

Physical Planners in Federal Government

The Federal Government exerts significant control over the physical planning of individual municipalities, especially through special legislation and administrative policies that discourage or promote specific spatial patterns of activity. Not only the Department of Housing and Urban Development, but also the Departments of Transportation, the Interior, Agriculture, Commerce, and Health, Education and Welfare are responsible for legislation and policy that directly influences the physical planning of cities.

Physical planning at the federal level usually does not determine the specific spatial distribution of activities for a particular city, but rather establishes overall policies and administrative criteria that place general constraints upon physical planning actions. For example, a housing subsidy program or neighborhood development program may not specify which areas of cities should be affected, but it will state that those areas must meet certain criteria, such as median level of income, number of owner-occupied units, and average assessed valuation. Thus, the selection of urban areas within which programs will be implemented is left to physical planners at the local level, as long as their plans meet federal guidelines.

The impact of the Federal Government on urban planning cannot be overemphasized. In addition to programs aimed directly at local physical planning operations, there are many other federal actions and policies that influence physical planning activity. Federally funded research activities increase our knowledge of urban areas and physical planning. New construction undertaken by all branches of the Federal Government (e.g., office buildings, parks, military installations, and power plants), are obvious examples of physical planning. Federal economic and monetary policies affect the physical patterns of change in urban areas (e.g., the creation of jobs in urban areas influences the economic health of specific neighborhoods). Decisions of the U.S. Supreme Court determine the legitimacy of zoning and other land-use regulations. As in physical planning at the state, regional, and local levels, the persons who actually generate and implement federal physical planning activity represent a wide variety of professional disciplines and values, political roles, and job responsibilities.

Physical Planners in the Private Sector

Many physical planning decisions are made by private individuals and organizations. Physical planning by the private sector may have an impact as significant as public planning. Private and public planning are complements of each other; i.e., physical planning decisions made by public agencies influence the urban conditions to which private persons and groups respond, and vice versa. Six categories are discussed below: consultants; land and building entrepreneurs; community organizations; private corporations; private institutions; and individuals.

First a wide range of consultant professions provide physical planning services to private organizations such as architectural, engineering, planning, and management firms. Such consultants might be employed to locate and lay out a golf course, perform a market feasibility study for the location of a major shopping center; lay out a new industrial production center; design a downtown office complex; or plan a residential subdivision. These consultants usually are professional planners; they are often trained in the same academic programs that produce publicly employed physical planners.

Second, many private entrepreneurs deal with land development and speculation, construction, real estate investment, and similar activities. Land developers, for example, do physical planning when they purchase a tract of land, lay out residential plots and roads, and construct and market the houses. This activity establishes a direct relationship between local city zoning and planning authorities and the developer. Persons actively engaged in real estate investment act as go-betweens for property owners and prospective investors; they match-up parcels of land and structures with individuals and firms seeking to invest, relocate, or expand. Thus, real estate investment firms influence directly what specific land uses will occur.

Third, community organizations play a role in physical planning. For example, neighborhood groups frequently advocate specific planning recommendations, such as where to locate a school or park, what type of housing should be built, etc. Such organizations are a major political force in local affairs, and consequently can exert considerable influence. At times, community groups hire professional advocate planners to prepare and promote physical plans advantageous to the community.

Fourth, private corporations often engage in physical planning as part of their in-house operations. For example, they must decide where to locate a new plant or office building; determine the size of a new facility; or design and construct special facilities for employees. The self-interest of large corporations is tied to the spatial distribution of activities (e.g., market areas, available labor, and transit systems) in the areas where they do business.

Fifth, many private institutions (especially hospitals and universities), which use large amounts of land, employ many people, and construct and operate major building complexes, have a significant impact on the economic and social development of a city. Such institutions not only have to plan their internal physical organization, but also must be concerned with their physical relationship to the immediate neighborhood and within the larger urban context. Thus private institutions become advocates of those urban physical plans most in their interest.

Finally, individuals and families make physical planning decisions, such as what area to live in, what places to shop, which parks to use, what job to take. Individually these decisions do not seem especially significant, but collectively, the impact of these planning decisions is enormous. Such decisions can revitalize whole neighborhoods, turn downtowns into ghost towns, or radically change a city's property tax base. Obviously such decisions are related to the decisions of public and private organizations that concern such matters as zoning regulations, new job opportunities, and transportation systems. However, because such organizations can only influence, rather than control completely, individual behavior, the physical planning decisions of individual citizens are a major force in determining the spatial patterns of cities.

BASIC COMPONENTS OF A FORMAL PHYSICAL PLAN

This section will describe the components of one type of plan: a formal plan prepared by or for a local public agency in which the spatial distribution of objects, functions, activities, and goals is explicitly recognized and mapped. The substance of plans varies among cities and may contain some or all these components. First, there is an analysis of the larger problem to demonstrate the potential benefit of a physical plan. Second, there is a detailed analysis of major physical and spatial patterns. Third, there are specific recommendations for the spatial distribution of goals, activities, functions, and objects. Fourth, there is a strategy for implementing, monitoring, and evaluating the physical plan itself. These four components are interrelated, and they are frequently reiterated in the course of plan development. The planner may bounce back and forth between examining the larger problem, developing the recommended plan, analyzing specific spatial patterns, and preparing an implementation strategy.

Components of a Physical Plan

1. *Analysis of the Problem-Solving Context*
   History of the situation
   Description of the situation
   Problem needs
   Solution resources
   Subsequent activities

2. *Analysis of Major Physical Patterns*
   Land use
   Infrastructure
   Transportation
   Physical conditions
   Social and economic conditions
   Image

3. *Proposed Spatial Distributions*
   Recommended goals
   Recommended activities
   Recommended functions
   Recommended objects

4. *Implementation Strategy*
   Costs and benefits
   Scheduling and staging
   Implementation management
   Monitoring and evaluation

Analysis of the Problem-Solving Context

Most physical plans are not merely the ends of a problem-solving process, but are the means to some larger objective such as economic development, social welfare, or neighborhood improvement. Consequently, the first step in analyzing the problem-solving context of a formal physical plan is to examine the larger issues to see if a physical plan is really part of the answer. The purpose of this examination is to ensure that the physical plan will be relevant. For example, let us assume that the overall objective is *neighborhood improvement,* and the appropriate neighborhoods have already been selected. The question now is: Should more resources be allocated to physical planning than to other activities such as social welfare, political organization, and economic development? The answer frequently is that a formal physical plan will be justified only if it is properly coordinated to these other activities. The plan itself will not be useful unless it is integrated from the outset with social, economic, and political plans.

This first task in delineating the scope of a physical plan is primarily an analytical function. The physical planner typically gathers information from a variety of sources: census surveys and other published reports, politicians, community organizations, and other government agencies. Frequently this activity is interdisciplinary, requiring coordination among physical planners as well as other specialists in relevant fields, such as economics, social welfare, health services, and real estate development.

This initial analysis of the problem situation is formalized in a report or official document. Although there are no hard-and-fast rules about how such a report should be organized, several subjects usually are covered: the history of the situation, the existing situation, problem needs, resources for a solution, and subsequent activities.

History of the Situation.
Except for major catastrophes or crises, urban problems do not appear suddenly out of nowhere. Thus an explanation of the history of the situation usually is necessary. In the area of neighborhood improvement, the history might include major events that have affected the community for the past 20 years; new programs that have been implemented; population changes in the area; and shifts in the surrounding neighborhoods. An accurate history of the problem situation is a valuable technique in identifying the root issues and possibly the solutions.

A Detailed Description of the Existing Situation.
A wide range of existing conditions and activities are critical determinants of the problem situation. Typically these include socioeconomic characteristics, physical conditions, and programmatic activities. For neighborhood improvement, the socioeconomic variables might include age and income distributions, occupational and educational patterns, and residential mobility. Physical conditions in this example would include housing characteristics and patterns, density, overcrowding, existing utilities, vacant land, public improvements, and commercial structures. The programmatic activities might include educational and recreational programs, job training, social welfare, health service, loan programs, and similar government activities.

Problem Needs.
Invariably the basis for analyzing a problem-solving situation is an articulation of the specific needs of the client population or community. These needs should be outlined and differentiated, by priority, into manageable components. The needs might be categorized as social, economic, and physical or according to population subgroups, such as elderly, youth, handicapped, unemployed, and low income. The identification of needs usually provides the first major opportunity for asserting the necessity for physical planning.

Solution Resources.
In conjunction with problem needs, the analysis of the problem-solving

context should identify the resources that potentially could be used to solve the problem. These include the available financial, organizational, social, and political resources. The planner can specify here how physical planning activities can be used to solve the problem. For example, neighborhood improvement may be aided by a new zoning ordinance, preparation of plans by an outside consultant or new governmental agency, or by requesting federal funds for new construction.

Subsequent Activities. Finally, the analysis should include recommendations for subsequent activities. Although problem needs and solution resources have been identified, they may not all be appropriate or feasible. Moreover, they may not be matched properly to each other; i.e., a particular need will not really be met by the available resource. A strategy for taking the next steps must be described. What types of activities should occur? Who should do them? What should be their outcomes?

These five components of an analysis of the problem-solving context provide an example but are not necessarily useful in all situations. However, it is critical that the first step in a physical planning activity include a broad image of the context in which the activity will occur. If the analysis shows that physical planning, is in fact unimportant or even unneccessarily, this is important. The remainder of the physical planning process will be meaningless if its relevance to larger objectives is not established at the outset.

Analysis of Major Physical Patterns

Although an analysis of the problem-solving context frequently involves maps and graphic descriptions of the situation, many other variables must be considered in the development of a physical plan. First, there is usually a *land use* map that denotes, for example, residential and commercial activities, public uses, parks, institutions such as churches and hospitals, factories, and vacant land. Often there is a map showing the *infrastructure*—streets, pedestrian ways, sewers, gas and water lines, and power lines. There may be a related map of the *transportation* system, including traffic volumes and mass transit routes. Depending upon the problem, there may be a set of maps representing important *physical conditions*. For example, in a neighborhood improvement plan, there may be a map locating structures in need of repair, those in good condition, and those to be demolished. In other problems the special conditions that are mapped might be *social or economic* in nature, such as persons who are in need of a social service program or commercial properties with high assessed values. When the planning problem is concerned more directly with objects, there are often maps of the organization of existing physical forms (e.g., showing the linear patterns, exterior spaces, districts, vegetation patterns, three-dimensional qualities of the area, and critical architectural features).

Finally, there is often a map describing the *image* of the physical planning area. This map would show the distinctive features that influence the way people recognize and use the area. One standard classification of image-making physical features includes: (1) *paths*—both major and minor vehicular and pedestrian routes, (2) *districts*—identifiable areas or neighborhoods, such as a shopping district, downtown, or an area with older, smaller homes, (3) *edges*—the boundaries that define districts, including topographical features like rivers and mountains, special land uses such as airports or industrial plants, and major roads and highways; (4) *nodes*—central places with relatively intense concentrations of activity, such as, shopping centers, parks, railway stations, or major street intersections, and (5) *landmarks*—distinctive objects used to identify special places, such as church steeples, unusual buildings, vistas, billboards, or highway or railway overpasses.[1]

Proposed Spatial Distribution of Goals, Activities, Functions, and Objects

Ultimately, the physical plan must make a specific recommendation for what should be done. Generating these recommendations is a function not only of the preceding analytical phases but also of professional expertise, intuition, tradition, and critical judgment. Often several alternative physical plans are prepared, and the analysis recommends one alternative as the best. These recommendations discuss goals, activities, functions, and objects.

Recommended Goals. The recommended goals are usually derived from the analysis of the larger problem-solving context. However, the physical plan should show which goals are to be assigned to different subareas. For example, in a neighborhood improvement plan, several subareas (or targets) might be mapped for residential improvement; other subareas designated for commercial development; and still others for aesthetic improvement. Typically each goal is represented by a specific graphic pattern or outline showing the places where the goal applies.

Recommended Activities. Each goal is related to a specific subset of constituent activities. Determining these activities is equivalent to operationalizing the goals. In the neighborhood improvement problem, a map might be prepared showing how the goal of residential improvement is differentiated into such activities as a new zoning regulation, home repair and maintenance program, and new residential construction. Similarly, the goal of commercial development might be separated into such activities as consolidation of businesses, new investment opportunities, and business improvement loans. Alternative locations for these different activities might also be identified. Each activity is graphically correlated to its goal. The audience for the physical plan can see how each goal translates into alternative subsets of activities.

Recommended Functions. Like the distribution of activities, the designation of functions is an operationalization of the basic goals. Both the activities and functions related to one goal might be represented on the same map. The functions that would achieve a goal of neighborhood aesthetic improvement might include tree planting, increased sanitation service, and street repair, while the activities to accomplish this goal might include reconditioning facades and signage restrictions. Other possible functions in a neighborhood improvement project might include construction of new roads, street closings, provision of new utility lines, and new boundaries for a police, fire, or school district. Again, each function would be given a specific graphic representation on the map correlated to a specific goal.

Recommended Objects. Most physical plans recommend the construction or modification of physical objects. Most people think of this activity as the core of physical planning. The established goals, activities, and functions provide the criteria or constraints for the physical design of objects.

Since physical design problems often require special expertise, this activity is often a job for professional architects, landscape architects, and/or engineers, whose plans go beyond the simple location of an object to the detailed drawings of what the object will look like, how it can be constructed, and what it is likely to cost. These professionals make sophisticated aesthetic and technical judgments that go beyond the normal domain of urban planning. The associated graphic representations of objects include artist's sketches, architectural models, and engineering drawings. It is the physical planner's responsibility to ensure that the professionals' designs of the physical objects fulfill the initial goals. Alternative designs may be developed, and the physical planner uses his or her judgment to decide which design is most appropriate. Although in many situations the physical planning team has the capability to design physical objects, this activity must be recognized as a specialized operation requiring many financial and human resources.

Development of an Implementation Strategy

The feasibility of a recommended physical plan is as critical as its substantive content. Feasibility is not determined after the fact. How a plan is to be implemented must be considered from the outset, along with the goals and specific features of the plan.

There are no established rules for devising the implementation of a physical plan. Usually, however, reference is made to the plan's costs and benefits, the scheduling or phasing of activities to implement the plan, the necessary managerial procedures, and the manner in which the plan will be monitored and evaluated.

Determining the Costs and Benefits of the Physical Plan.

The most important tools of implementation are the capital improvement program and capital budget. Both are discussed later, but for the present, it is important to examine costs and benefits of physical plans. Estimating the costs and benefits of a physical plan is a complex task. The costs, for example, include not only the initial capital expenditures, but also the operational funds needed to maintain the functions, activities, and objects created. Capital and operating budgets include items such as personnel (specialized consultants as well as regular staff), equipment, materials, labor, and others. Since cost estimating is so complex it usually is done in several stages, and the final, detailed estimate is done by specially trained professionals in the city government. When costs include major construction items that will be built by private firms (such as a hospital or a park), the costs may be determined by bidding, in which the private firms who wish to contract for the work submit their own cost estimates to the city.

Estimating the benefits is also difficult. In a public project there are not only direct monetary revenues to be considered (such as increased property taxes), but also many intangible factors, such as improved health, safety, and welfare. Physical plans also have spillover effects that will affect population groups and areas not initially considered part of the physical plan. For example, a new public facility will create new jobs, change daily patterns of transportation, and affect levels of service at other facilities. Typically, a physical plan contains a budget approximation that lists the initial capital costs and short-run operational costs. If the project is sufficiently large, or if there is significant political interest, a cost-benefit or similar analysis may be presented to demonstrate the overall effect of the plan on the urban area.

Scheduling and Staging a Physical Plan.

Time is as significant and complicated a resource as money. If the numerous constituent activities in most planning projects are not properly coordinated, the project will fail. Frequently, for example if the planners of a certain project do not understand fully the logical sequence of activities, they will miss the scheduled deadline. Usually the scheduling of activities is coordinated with the budget, especially since physical plans often take several years to complete. Many physical plans are initially designed to be accomplished in phases or stages, with the implementation of latter stages contingent upon successful completion of earlier stages. For example, in an urban renewal project the construction of a new park might be scheduled to occur only after completion of new residential units. Similarly the widening of streets may be slated to begin upon the completion of a new exit or entrance ramp to a limited-access highway. The staging of a physical planning project may become a major political issue in that one group will not be satisfied unless the part of the plan in which they have a special interest is given a high priority and made part of an earlier implementation stage.

Managing the Implementation of a Physical Plan. Human resources, as well as financial and temporal resources, must be deployed. The implementation of a physical plan depends on a careful managerial structure to carry out the necessary activities. The responsibility and the authority for different decisions must be delegated in an appropriate manner. Frequently, new staff, outside consultants, or private firms are hired to accomplish specialized tasks. The more difficult problem, however, is delegating responsibilities and authority among all the various government agencies and elected officials whose cooperation is essential to the success of a project. Local agencies and officials as well as those at regional, state, and national government levels are involved. Management of a physical planning project also may require structured citizen participation, so that special procedures for eliciting and using citizen opinions must be devised.

Monitoring and Evaluating a Physical Plan. The details of an implementation plan should include provisions for both monitoring the implementation to see that it is done properly and evaluating the final product to see if it matches the original intentions. Typically the monitoring function is built into the managerial structure. At any point during implementation activities can be deleted, modified, or added, either to ensure that the plan unfolds as desired or to change it if the initial objectives have been modified. Most physical plans are not finally completed as first intended. There are always unexpected events that prevent parts of the plan from being affected, create new opportunities for improving the plan, or show why some aspect of the plan is inappropriate and needs to be altered.

Evaluation of a physical plan is carried out after the plan is completed and operational. An evaluation measures the extent to which the plan fulfills its original goals and discovers any unpredicted positive or negative effects of the project. Equally impor-

tant, the evaluation allows the planners to find out which ideas were successful and which were failures. Too often the evaluation function is eliminated from the implementation plan because it seems like an unnecessary expense. Recently, however, urban planners have come to realize that unless they evaluate their projects properly, they will not know whether the thought processes and activities should be repeated, emulated, avoided, or discouraged in the future.

TYPES OF URBAN PHYSICAL PLANS

Traditionally, certain types of physcial plans have been dominant in American city planning. This section will review several types of traditional physical plans and describe their underlying concepts, the processes whereby they are developed, and what the final products look like. Perhaps the most important type of plan to be discussed is the comprehensive plan, the historic mainstay of American urban planning. In addition, there have always been certain parts of cities that have exhibited distinct types of problems, and, subsequently, specifically appropriate physical plans have emerged. The most notable places for which distinct physical plans have evolved are central business districts, or downtowns; inner-city neighborhoods; suburbs, or outer-city neighborhoods; large institutional complexes; and new towns.

The Comprehensive Plan
The *comprehensive plan* (also known as a master plan or *general plan*) represents one of the most significant concepts in twentieth-century American urban planning. The underlying idea is that a long-term plan (for example, over 20 to 30 years) for the overall physical development of an entire city can be used to organize and direct the social, economic, political, and physical forces within an urban area in a rational and productive manner. It is an ambitious

concept, to say the least. The comprehensive plan is an official public document involving not only a set of goals but also a policy to attain those goals. Thousands of cities have used the comprehensive plan as a method to determine long-range goals, and as a legal tool to implement those goals (e.g., the comprehensive plan can be used as a legal basis for altering zoning ordinances and taking property).

The comprehensive plan is a long-term policy for the spatial distribution of objects, functions, activities, and goals. It serves to coordinate government activities at the local level and regulate private development of land. It is based upon an analysis of the overall urban situation as well as a detailed analysis of existing spatial patterns.

There has been considerable debate over the rationality of the comprehensive plan. It is argued, for example, that the knowledge necessary to create a comprehensive plan is far beyond even our collective wisdom. On the other hand, the comprehensive plan does not have to be perfect (i.e., all its recommendations do not have to be the best for the general health and welfare of the public). Rather it only has to be useful as a guide for achieving a better pattern of urban physical development than would otherwise be possible. But even when the overall rationality of the comprehensive plan is accepted, there is still much debate over its content because of the plan's potential power; i.e., it represents a specific distribution and or redistribution of costs and benefits (social, economic, and political) among the various segments of the urban population.

The process of creating such an important document is often lengthy and difficult. Typically a preliminary comprehensive plan is prepared by the staff of the city planning department (possibly with the help of outside consultants). During this phase the staff usually works closely with other government agencies and officials. The preliminary plan is presented to the legislative body that has the authority to amend and adopt it. By this point the preliminary plan has been made public and is open to debate among government officials and private citizens and groups. It is critical that the plan be easily understood in order to allow participation by persons without technical training and to maximize the educational value of the plan. At this stage the comprehensive plan is a significant learning device; it allows the technical staff, public officials, and general public to inform each other of their perceptions and goals. Once the plan has been debated publicly it is amended into final form and officially adopted by the legislative authority and published and distributed to interested parties. Subsequently, the comprehensive plan should be reviewed and amended annually and, completely reconsidered at longer intervals (e.g., every five years). In other words, the comprehensive plan is as much a policy-formation process as it is a recommendation for a specific physical product.

The actual document consists of several sections similar in concept to the components described earlier. An introduction describes who prepared the plan, under what authority, and what general public purpose is being served. Ordinarily this is followed by a summary of the major recommendations (this lets the audience know what to expect from the remainder of the document). Next, the analytic information upon which the plan is based and the general social and economic objectives are described. This is followed by the major substance of the document, the physical development proposals. Such proposals often are categorized as follows: land use recommendations (including residential, commercial, industrial, and institutional uses); recommendations for new and modified community facilities (parks, health centers, libraries, etc.); a transportation and circulation scheme (for mass transit, private and commercial vehicles, and pedestrians); a plan for civic beautification (urban design proposals to improve the image and aesthetic quality of the city); and a utilities plan (sewers, water lines, etc.). Following the physical development proposals are concluding sections describing how the plan will be implemented and used.

See note book

It should come as no surprise that the comprehensive plan appears to be a summary of the issues dealt with in previous sections of this chapter, for such a plan has always been intended as a holistic synthesis of physical planning recommendations. Although many communities (especially cities with fewer than 100,000 people) still prepare and use comprehensive plans productively the recent trend is to prepare the equivalent of a comprehensive plan for a specific urban area or subarea (e.g., a down-town, suburban township, etc.). Thus the comprehensive plan has evolved into a variety of physical plans.

Plans for City Centers

Downtown redevelopment projects have been created within hundreds of cities of all sizes and types (including for example, Atlanta, Baltimore, Binghamton, Calgary, Columbus, Denver, Hartford, Kalamazoo, Kansas City, Louisville, Montreal, Newark, San Antonio, Toronto, and White Plains).[2] The general concept underlying these plans stems from the belief that the central business district (CBD) of an urban area is the key to the city's vitality. The CBD provides the major public image for both residents and visitors. It represents the greatest land value and property investment, provides a concentrated physical framework for social and economic transactions and activities, and is often the only area with which almost all city residents are familiar. The CBD requires tremendous maintenance and renovation in order to function properly. Most cities simply cannot afford to allocate haphazardly major public and private investments to the CBD, and careful physical planning becomes a necessity.

The processes of developing CBD plans are varied. They may be developed by an existing staff department, new governmental unit, privately funded organization, consulting firm, or some combination of these. Whatever group is assigned the responsibility of plan preparation, the process always involves close political cooperation among government, private business, adjacent residential neighborhoods, and, because of the magnitude of the investment, state and regional agencies as well as suburban communities.

As with the comprehensive plan, a proposal is developed, presented for debate and modification, adopted officially, and subjected to subsequent amendment and revision. The implementation of a CBD plan usually requires delegation of legal authority to a government unit or quasi-public group (often a redevelopment authority) for assembly and disposition of land and physical development activities. In some instances a private (sometimes nonprofit) development corporation is established to develop new properties (i.e., it assembles land, razes existing structures, and designs and finances new construction). Although downtown redevelopment is a continual process it usually occurs in waves or spurts. One or two decades may be marked by intensive development efforts, after which the level of activity subsides, until the CBD again becomes dysfunctional.

CBD development typically results in major changes in urban design as well as alterations in public services (especially utilities and transportation). The urban design products of the plan may include new office buildings, commercial structures, hotels, and public institutions, as well as new walkway systems, underground concourses, plazas, parking structures, malls and boulevards, supergraphics, street furnishings, and mass transit facilities. Often CBD development is organized around a public convention center, civic center, performing arts center, or shopping mall.

In most downtown development, especially in large metropolitan centers, careful attention is given to the visual integration of all the elements. The visual coherence and symbolic value of the design is critical in providing the inhabitants with an understanding of their city and its potential. Aesthetic and architectural issues often are exhibited to a greater

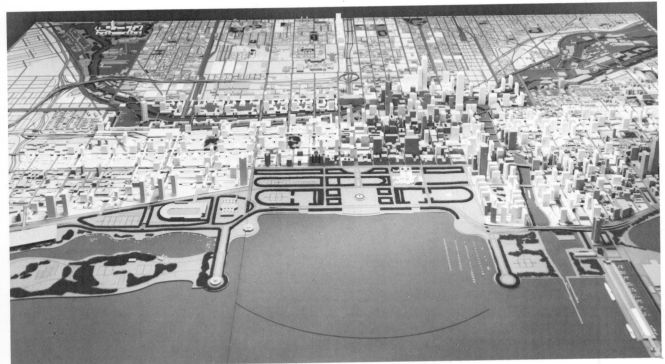

Central area plan: Chicago 21, by Skidmore, Owings, & Merrill (photo by Hedrich-Blessing).

degree in downtown plans than in other physical plans.

Plans for Inner-City Neighborhoods

Most American cities, especially the larger metropolitan areas, have experienced a continuous cycle of growth, decline, and, sometimes, revitalization. Many urban neighborhoods are composed of older residential structures that require increasing maintenance and rehabilitation. Traditionally, the city has been responsible for maintaining the physical infrastructure of its neighborhoods, while the residential property owners have been expected to maintain the housing stock. However, the health and welfare of a residential neighborhood is corre-

lated with the socioeconomic status and behavior of inhabitants. For example, a neighborhood with many owner-occupants with higher than median incomes is likely to be maintained by both residents and public agencies in order to preserve the high property values and property tax revenue. Conversely, communities with many absentee owners and with predominantly poor residents are likely to decline because of a cycle of property neglect by landlords, inability to effect change by the residents, government disinterest, and other political and cultural forces. Physical planning for this type of declining neighborhood is becoming increasingly important.

In addition, many poor inner-city neighborhoods in large metropolitan areas are experiencing a return by middle income families from suburban areas. These families often attempt to re-vitalize these declining neighborhoods. While such returning middle-and upper-income populations bring with them the political support necessary to effect neighborhood plans their return also means potential conflict with the long-term inhabitants.

The process of developing neighborhood plans is quite different from that for comprehensive or CBD plans. It relies much more heavily on community organization and participation by the residents, prop-erty owners, and business persons who service the area. Although there is usually some political support for neighborhood plans, there is also political opposition, or at least conflict, because of the simple fact that neighborhoods are competing with each other. Political competition is a natural part of all planning efforts, but it plays a more central role in inner-city physical planning.

Often neighborhood plans are prepared by advocate planners. The process of developing the

Neighborhood redevelopment: Little Five Points Area, Atlanta, by Toombs, Amisano, and Wells; and Richard Rothman. (Courtesy city of Atlanta)

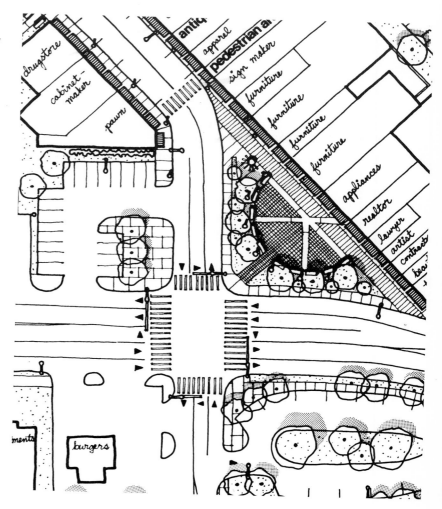

specific plan is similar to that outlined in previous sections in which an analysis of the overall problem situation is developed; a detailed description of the current problem is prepared; specific recommendations are made; and a strategy for implementation is offered. There is, however, a significantly greater emphasis placed on citizen participation in the development of such plans, because of the need to represent accurately the community interests and to provide a vehicle for organizing and strengthening the political force of the community.

The substantive recommendations of a neighborhood plan obviously require fewer resources than a comprehensive or downtown plan. Since the physical, social, and economic characteristics of the neighborhood are usually more homogeneous than those of the entire city, the proposed developments are not only on a smaller physical scale but also less complex. For example, a neighborhood physical plan might focus on the construction of one new public facility and the modification of a few government programs to promote housing rehabilitation. Another plan might focus solely upon the revitalization of a small commercial strip, and possibly on some new privately financed residential construction. The social, economic, and political problems are not necessarily less difficult, but the physical planning proposals can usually focus on a relatively well-defined set of issues.

Plans for Suburbs

The suburban areas surrounding central cities are subject to their own physical planning problems. Some suburbs, especially those on the fringe of metropolitan areas, are so large that they require their own comprehensive plans and CBD redevelopments. There is one type of physical planning problem that occurs most frequently in suburban districts—the subdivision of land for residential development. There are typically within these districts large tracts of land that either have not been developed or contain low-intensity land use (such as agri-

culture or forestry). As suburban areas expand, these undeveloped tracts often are purchased by private individuals or firms; subdivided into individual lots, with necessary roads and utilities supplied; and built up by either developers or individual buyers. Alternatively, clusters of apartment blocks or condominiums are created. Regardless of the pattern of ownership and occupancy, there are many common problems that necessitate a special type of physical plan for subdivision.

The process of creating a residential subdivision is essentially a dialogue among public regulatory agencies (such as the zoning commission or city planning commission), local citizens who have interests in the development of adjacent lands, and the private developers who plan and build the subdivision. A private developer who perceives an opportunity to profit from creating a subdivision first examines the applicable statutes and regulations to make sure that the proposed development is legally feasible. Then the developer purchases the land and submits a subdivision plan to the local authorities for approval. This approval process may be relatively smooth and uneventful, or it may cause intense debate and opposition, leading to major changes in the plan. The plan must conform to density regulations; it must provide adequate means for installation of public utilities; its system of streets and sidewalks must be safe; and so forth. The population increases to be brought about by the new development will be examined by agencies providing public services (police and fire protection, schools, and health services). Often, public hearings are held at which private citizens present their views on the new development. Usually, those who like the existing rural atmosphere, low density, and minimal traffic flow will oppose the development while local merchants and others whose livelihoods would prosper with new population will support it.

An actual subdivision proposal consists of a set of plan drawings (sometimes called *plats*), which designate the proposed property lines; street system (including parking); location of sewers, water

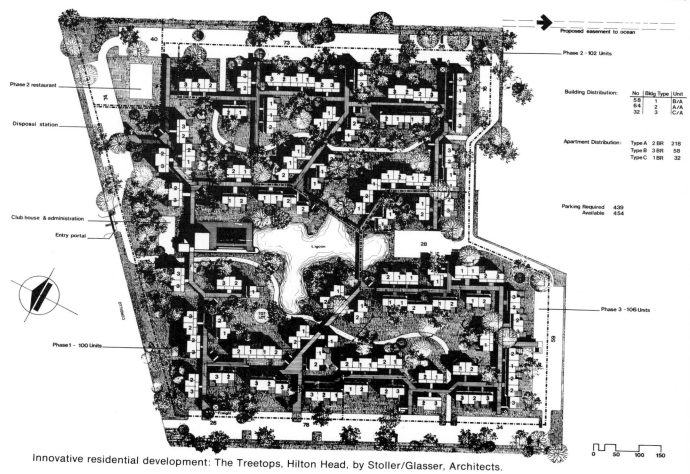

Innovative residential development: The Treetops, Hilton Head, by Stoller/Glasser, Architects.

lines, and power lines; topographical changes that will be made; proposed landscaping; and form, location, size, and occupancy pattern of dwelling units. At times residential subdivisions will be designed to include other amenities and ancillary land uses. For example, the developer may raise the density of one part of the subdivision in order to devote other portions of the acreage to parks and open space. Similarly, part of the land may be devoted to commercial development. The develop-

ment of residential condominium communities often includes special recreational and community facilities, such as tennis courts, clubhouses, swimming pools, golf courses, and artificial lakes.

Plans for Institutions
Most large institutions, such as universities, hospital complexes, prisons, research centers, and large government facilities, require special types of physi-

Residential area plan: Columbia, Maryland, by Howard Research and Development Corporation and the Rouse Company. (Courtesy of Design Department of the Howard Research and Development Corporation; a project of the Rouse Company and the Connecticut General Insurance Company)

cal plans. These institutions consist of many structures, sometimes interconnected, requiring special systems for the distribution of energy and other utilities. Plans are required for the initial development of such building complexes and for their maintenance, redevelopment, and expansion. These plans must be oriented to both the internal workings of the institution and its environment, whether a rural setting or a dense population center.

Such institutional plans often come from the particular institution involved, so that the process whereby the plans are developed and implemented varies with that organizational structure. Most of these plans require special programming. The functions and internal activities of such institutions are so varied and interdependent that special research is necessary to establish the spatial pattern of activities. This research involves interaction with the specific clients or users of the institution as well as projections about the use of facilities. Although many institutions have their own in-house planning staffs to maintain and regulate physical development, the initial designs or major expansions of institutions are frequently prepared by outside consultants. Approval and amendment of an institutional plan are subject not only to the internal organizational structure but also to the legal and political constraints of the surrounding community.

An institutional plan includes the standard components (analysis of the overall problem, specific recommendations for physical development, and strategy for implementation), prepared as an official document for distribution among the institutional offices, local government, and other interested parties. The physical design proposals are quite specific and include building plans and elevations, artist's renderings, and plans for landscaping, parking facilities, and utility distribution systems.

Plans for New Towns

The development of new towns has long been a major physical planning activity, which derives not from the interest of a local urban area, but from the authority of national and regional government. In recent times, new towns have been created by private enterprises as well. Traditionally, new towns are developed to be as self-sufficient as any other city. New towns often serve a special purpose: the establishment of a new seat of government (Brasilia, Chandigarh, Washington, D.C.) ; settlement of new territory (in Israel and Holland); industrial development (especially in developing countries) ; and regional land use organization (Hook and Cumbernauld in the United Kingdom).

In the United States several *greenbelt* communities were built during the New Deal (e.g., Greenbelt, Maryland; Greenhills, Ohio; Greendale, Wisconsin). Also, there have been *company* towns, constructed to serve the labor force of single private corporations such as Pullman, Illinois and Kohler, Wisconsin. More recently, private development and investment organizations have constructed the new towns of Columbia, Maryland and Reston, Virginia.

The concept of the new town has been expanded in recent years. A new town is no longer conceived solely as an isolated or satellite community, but often as an integral part of a metropolitan network or larger urban region. Moreover, the idea of a new town *in town* has emerged as a method for redeveloping portions of central cities. This concept goes beyond the small-scale revitalization of neighborhoods to large-scale rehabilitation and new development of major sections of cities.

The processes whereby new towns are created are significant, but since new towns require abundant financial and managerial resources, complex legislation and political support at many different levels, and many years for completion, there are few general procedural patterns. Once the authority to create such plans has been established, decisions must be made as to the specific location, character, and size of each new town. Preparation of plans for *different features of the town are reiterated several times,* and construction of the physical infrastructure

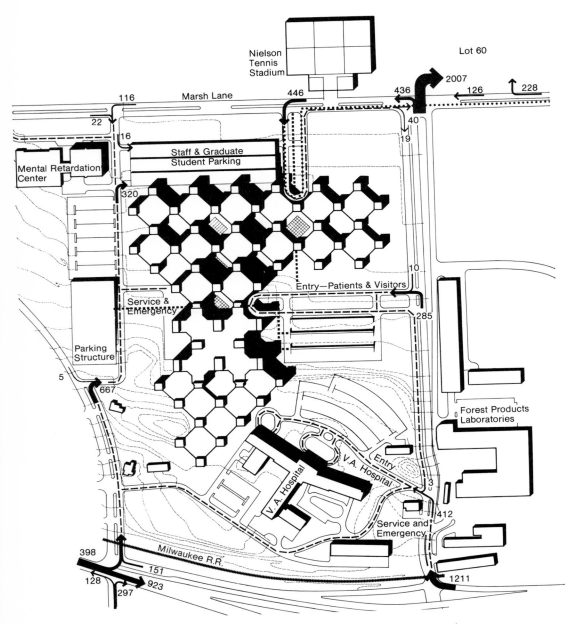

Institutional plan: University of Wisconsin Medical Center, by Hellmuth, Obata & Kassabaum.

A new town plan: Reston, Virginia, by Gulf Reston, Inc.

and major topographic changes is frequently initiated before more detailed plans for all the structures have been established. There is continual feedback between new and revised physical plans and completed construction. The new town is often opened and inhabited before the last stage of development. Once this occurs there is a local population with its own political interests and governmental structure, which will effect future development.

A new town plan is necessarily more inclusive than a comprehensive plan. It covers everything from the ground up: goals, activities, functions, and objects. It is meaningless to conceive a new town plan as a single working document, even though a summary document may be published to inform the general public, potential investors, and other professional planners. In addition to a full range of industrial, commercial, residential, and civic structures, roads, and public utilities, a new town plan includes regional elements. In other words, since a new town is a component of a larger region, some modification of the physical character of that region is necessary. This may involve, for example, new intercity transit facilities, development of energy and water resources, and major changes in the natural environment.

Other Types of Physical Plans

There are many other conventionally developed special-purpose plans. For example, park planning requires consideration of a set of problems involving maintenance of the natural environment, landscaping, controlled access, and programming for special uses. There are special plans for transportation systems, public works, historic preservation, and environmental protection. Finally, housing plans, consider specialized architectural problems of major concern to the physical planner: for example, the creation of private and community outdoor spaces, aesthetics, parking, landscaping, pedestrian paths, recreational facilities, and social interaction.

CONCLUSION

Our concepts of physical planning activity have developed in response to our knowledge about cities and the methods whereby we control urban spatial patterns, but the end product of physical planning goes far beyond the spatial disposition of physical entities to consideration of a variety of cultural, social, economic, and political objectives.

Physical planning activity is an increasingly important and integral part of the other political and social processes used to manipulate urban areas. While the traditional role of the professional physical planner will always remain viable, we should expect the emergence of new physical planning roles within a variety of professions (both public and private) aided by the planned spatial distribution of urban areas.

NOTES

1. Kevin Lynch, *The Image of the City* (Cambridge, Mass.: M.I.T., 1960), pp. 46–90.
2. Louis G. Redstone, *The New Downtowns* (New York: McGraw-Hill, 1976).

FOR FURTHER READING

Altshuler, Alan A. *The City Planning Process.* Ithaca, N.Y.: Cornell University Press, 1965.

Barnett, Jonathan. *Urban Design as Public Policy.* New York: Architectural Record, 1974.

Bellush, Jewel, and Hausknecht, Murray, eds. *Urban Renewal: People, Politics, and Planning.* Garden City, N.Y.: Doubleday, Anchor Books, 1967.

Black, Alan. "The Comprehensive Plan." In *Principles and Practice of Urban Planning.* Edited by William I. Goodman and Eric C. Freund. Washington, D.C.: International City Managers' Association, 1968. pp. 349–78.

Branch, Melville C. *Planning Urban Environment.* Stroudsburg, Pa.: Dowden, Hutchinson & Ross, 1974.

Campbell, Carlos, C. *New Towns: Another Way to Live.* Reston, Va.: Reston, 1976.

Catanese, Anthony J. *Planners and Local Politics: Impossible Dreams.* Beverly Hills, Calif.: Sage, 1974.

Chapin, F. Stuart, Jr. *Urban Land Use Planning.* 2d ed. Urbana: University of Illinois Press, 1965.

Choay, Francoise. *The Modern City: Planning in the 19th Century.* New York: Braziller, 1969.

Cullen, Gordon. *The Concise Townscape.* New York: Van Nostrand, 1971.

Davidoff, Paul. "Advocacy and Pluralism in Planning." *Journal of the American Institute of Planners (JAIP)* 31 (November 1965): 19–26.

DeChiara, Joseph, and Koppelman, Lee. *Manual of Housing: Planning and Design Criteria.* Englewood Cliffs, N.J.: Prentice-Hall, 1975.

———. *Urban Planning and Design Criteria.* 2d ed. New York: Van Nostrand, 1975.

Galantay, Ervin Y. *New Towns: Antiquity to the Present.* New York: Braziller, 1975.

Gale, Stephen, and Moore, Eric G., eds. *The Manipulated City.* Chicago: Maaroufa Press, 1975.

Gallion, Arthur B., and Eisner, Simon. *The Urban Pattern.* 3d ed. New York: Van Nostrand, 1975.

Johnson, James H. *Urban Geography.* 2d ed. Elmsford, N.Y.: Pergamon, 1972.

Kaufman, Jerome L. "Urban Renewal." In *Principles and Practice of Urban Planning.* Edited by William I. Goodman and Eric C. Freund. Washington, D.C.: International City Managers' Association, 1968. pp. 485–519.

Kent, T. J., Jr. *The Urban General Plan.* San Francisco: Chandler, 1964.

Krueckeberg, Donald A., and Silvers, Arthur L. *Urban Planning Analysis: Methods and Models.* New York: Wiley, 1974.

Le Corbusier. *The Radiant City.* New York: Orion, 1933.

Lynch, Kevin. *The Image of the City.* Cambridge, Mass.: M.I.T. 1960.

———. *Site Planning.* 2d ed. Cambridge, Mass: M.I.T., 1971.

Rabinovitz, Francine F. *City Politics and Planning.* Chicago: Aldine, 1974.

Redstone, Louis G. *The New Downtowns.* New York: McGraw-Hill, 1976.

Reiner, Thomas A. *The Place of the Ideal Community in Urban Planning.* Philadelphia: University of Pennsylvania Press, 1963.

Rudofsky, Bernard. *Streets for People.* Garden City, N.Y.: Doubleday, 1969.

Scott, Mel. *American City Planning.* Berkeley: University of California Press, 1971.

Walker, Robert A. *The Planning Function in Urban Government.* Chicago: University of Chicago Press, 1941.

Wiebenson, Dora. *Tony Garnier: The Cité Industrielle.* New York: Braziller, 1969.

Wingo, Lowdon, Jr., ed. *Cities and Space: The Future Use of Urban Land.* Baltimore: Johns Hopkins for Resources for the Future, 1963.

Zucker, Paul. *Town and Square.* Cambridge, Mass.: M.I.T., 1959.

CHAPTER 9

Environmental Planning

David C. Hoeh

In recent times, concern with the natural environment has become part of functional planning of all kinds. This is why it is so important to review the interest in the environment, along with the resulting theories, concepts, and practices that have emerged. This is not to say that urban planning has not been environmental in its outlook; rather it is to note the articulation that has occurred. This articulation has been somewhat polemical as well as factual, and activist in orientation as much as technical. In essence we have seen the so-called environmental movement lead to reinterpretations of physical planning practices as well as new perspectives and dimensions.

INTRODUCTION

In a startling book published in the early 1960s, Rachel Carson was one of the first to point out the disastrous effects of our technological progress.[1] The trash by-products of civilization were traced as the cause of the *Silent Spring*. Yet, people had come to accept as the cost of progress much of the damage that exploitation of land and resources had caused. What was even more frightening than the visible destruction was the invisible attrition of the environment caused by accumulative wastes and chemicals that were slowly building to the point where existence of life was threatened. There seemed to be a particular message in *Silent Spring* for each profession. Instead of being applauded for improving the social conditions and aiding progress, planners were pictured as destroyers.

Since the appearance of *Silent Spring*, those disciplines and professions dealing most closely with the natural environment have detected even more serious problems as the result of the quest of civilization. Carson told the story of our destruction, but she believed that rational humans could change and save themselves before the damage became irreversible. The environmental movement begun in the late 1960s was the first major recognition of the damage that had been done to the living space. This awareness was accompanied by the initial efforts to reduce and eliminate the destruction, as well as to correct the damage of the past.

The inventory of crises is extensive. Obviously the issue of most concern to the planning profession is the environmental impact of contemporary urban settlement. In place of small villages and scattered farmhouses, humankind has produced settlements that spread for miles. The urban crisis is the consequence not only of the changing form of the city, but also of needless land and resources consumption.

As metropolitan regions have grown, the environmental destruction that had been confined to the centers has spread. What is encouraging, however, is that in our evolutionary journey to urbanization we have been learning more about how our environment works. With this imperfect knowledge we can become more sensitive to the consequences of urbanization and to how the earth can be protected so that civilization can survive.

AN ENVIRONMENTAL ERA

The modern planner is a synthesizer and generalist, but is most of all a policy advisor. To be successful the planner must draw upon many disciplines to produce a proper planning analysis. Above all the contemporary planner should be capable of gaining the attention of those who make the decisions that determine how resources are to be used.

To illustrate how important the role of the planner has become, it is useful to recall earlier eras of environmental concern. The first consciousness of the limit of American resources came with the end of the frontier in the late decades of the nineteenth century. President Theodore Roosevelt, himself an outdoorsman and student of natural history, discovered that the vast American resources were not only limited and declining but were even threatened with destruction. He realized that some form of public action was necessary to protect the remaining natural wonders. Against the opposition of formidable private interests and the background of very limited public consciousness Teddy Roosevelt started an environmental movement that established a system of national parks and forests.

Franklin D. Roosevelt, leading a country economically depressed and devastated by drought, dust, and flood, set in motion machinery to correct abuses that had gone on since the earliest settlements. The solution of the 1930s and early 1940s was to engineer the land, to contain and channel the floods, and to replant the protecting cover of the forests and grasslands. It was an era of public works and immense engineering projects.

Facing war in the early 1940s the nation turned away from conservation and reclamation interests. Resources had to be used to make war. Public interest in conservation was lost in the rush to win and, then, in the desire to sustain postwar recovery and world leadership. The fifties decade was an era of economic development, fueled by cheap energy. A massive defense highway program was launched, making possible the automobile-dependent suburb. Farms, forests, lake shores, and streams disappeared under the inexorable pressure of the suburban developer. Not until the late 1950s did the American public again register consciousness of the resources it was destroying.

An awakened public slowly began noticing the ugliness, monotony and lack of character of the environment it had created. Once preoccupied with suburbanization and the quest for economic security, Americans rediscovered the outdoors. In response to these changes, in 1958 President Eisenhower convened the *Outdoor Recreation Resources Review Commission (ORRRC)*. Its work was completed in 1962 during Kennedy's administration, and it sparked a new interest in protecting lands for a wide variety of recreational uses. Stimulating the Kennedy administration's concern was not only a demand for new recreational opportunities but also the realization that unique natural resources were beginning to disappear. Even once-remote spots were within convenient reach of millions of visitors. Lands once safe from the possibility of suburbanization became attractions for the new *exurban* developer. Rural areas were the sites of development made possible by the nation's affluence, the low cost of gasoline, and the interstate highway system.

A wave of seasonal home development burst upon the unprepared and fragile natural environment of the rural areas nearest the great cities. This trend more than any other created the present environmental consciousness. The damage resulting from this unrestrained development was clear to all. What had been seen as a boon for the tax base of poor and sparsely settled rural communities became an unending nightmare. Roads that had been poorly built and located now had to be well-maintained. Potable water sources became polluted and septic tanks backed up, forcing the local governments to build sewers and provide water systems. The costs of fire fighting, police protection, waste disposal, and numerous other services increased so much that most seasonal home developments failed to support with their taxes the public services demanded.

To assist states in protecting valuable natural sites and broadening opportunities for public recreation, President Kennedy sought passage of the first major conservation/recreation land acquisition program since the 1930s. The *Land and Water Conservation Act of 1963* provided matching funds for states and localities to acquire threatened recreation sites and natural resources. President Johnson continued the effort to protect natural resources with federal action and to stimulate comparable actions at the state and local levels. The *Highway Beautification Act,* the *Wilderness Areas Preservation Act,* and numerous other legislative or administrative actions embodied a wider public consciousness of the finite nature of the natural environment.

Much of the Kennedy/Johnson legislation was supported by a public in favor of natural and aesthetic preservation, and such legislation rarely conflicted with major economic interests. Not until later in the decade did the demand increase for environmentally conscious laws. The *Water Quality Act of 1970, Air Quality Act of 1969,* amendments to the *Water Quality Act of 1972,* and above all, the *National Environmental Policy Act of 1970,* were produced by Congress and the Nixon administration in response to public demand. Instead of aiming at narrow environmental targets, this web of legislation covered most environmental issues and concerns of the recent decades. The movement continued with the Carter administration's programs for national heritage areas and its land use and urban growth policies.

This review of natural resource and environmental protection legislation reveals the importance of public policymaking to sound environmental planning. Regardless of the skills of the environmental planners, without the support of public policymakers they can do little.

This lesson has been quickly learned in the 1970s. Amateurish conservation groups have become politically sophisticated and effective public interest organizations. Landmark legislation and court decisions carry the imprint of national, regional, state, and local conservation and environmental protection organizations that until quite recently were able to attract little interest. The Sierra Club, Audubon Society, Nature Conservancy, Appalachian Mountain Club, and many others have become effective advocates for environmentally responsible public policy. In addition, the concerns of these groups have broadened. What was once only an interest in environmental protection and basic conservation has become an appreciation of resource capabilities, management, and planning.

THEORIES AND CONCEPTS

As understanding of the natural system increased and theories of its capabilities were tested, the scientific background for the practice of environmental planning was established. Environmental planners are responsible for interpreting research findings and applying them toward improving aspects of the human settlements.

For example, when constructing new housing it has been common practice to prepare the site by automatically removing all trees, vegetation, and natural habitats and levelling the ground. After construction the site is landscaped into a manicured setting useful only for the human occupant. Any natural system that once supported a variety of life no longer exists.

The environmental planner argues that there is another way to develop land for human uses. That other way draws upon not only the experience of the landscape architect and the civil engineer but also the findings of the biologist, zoologist, botanist, ecologist, hydrologist, organic chemist, and others in the natural sciences. The planner also must be cognizant of sociology, psychology, anthropology, and even archeology in order to understand the patterns of human behavior and settlement. The challenge for the contemporary planner is to create a settlement that is in harmony with its natural surroundings and provides a healthful environment for man.

Two overriding principles have emerged in dealing with this challenge. The first is to recognize that the existing *natural systems* that have evolved are not without their own capacities to serve human settlement. This principle is captured in an important work by Ian McHarg, *Design with Nature*.[2] Instead of viewing the natural systems as hostile or inconsistent with human settlement, to be changed through manipulative engineering, the planner should examine closely the capabilities of natural systems to support human settlement.

The second principle concerns *impact*. Some natural systems are more able than others to sustain the impact of human settlement and use. Some systems suffer little damage and often contribute to healthful environments for human settlements, while others are unable to survive even limited adjustment to human uses. The natural sciences have provided a wider appreciation for the ability of natural systems to sustain the impact of development. From these two principles has developed a series of basic environmental planning concepts and theories.

Essential Theories of Natural Systems

Natural System Balance and Homeostasis. Studies of natural systems have discovered that while natural systems are dynamic, complex natural ecologies do reach states of balance where populations are regulated. For higher animals, the system that keeps internal temperatures even is called *homeostasis*. In natural systems, homeostasis is defined as a tendency toward maintenance of relatively stable social conditions among groups with respect to various factors. When animal populations grow beyond the capacity of their habitats to sustain them with food and adequate social conditions, countervailing factors such as reduction in food intake, increased disease, and even diminished fertility occur to reduce the population to that which the environment can sustain.

When a human settlement destroys a natural system through careless development, the result is much like that which affects animal populations. Disease, starvation, lost fertility, social conflict, and natural disasters have traditionally regulated human populations that have exceeded their environments' capacity to support them. The improper disposal of human wastes led to the plagues that devastated the populations of European cities during the Middle Ages. Careless agricultural practices in the United States led to dust bowls and massive soil erosion during the 1930s that threatened food supplies. Only through public works, such as sewerage disposal systems, water supply systems, food transporting and production systems, and numerous other systems, have we been able to defy the consequences of exceeding the ability of specific environments to support our populations. The question posed by the theory of homeostasis is how long we can defy the natural systems before countervailing forces occur to reduce the human population.

The Laws of Thermodynamics. The *First Law of Thermodynamics* states that energy can neither be created nor destroyed. The *Second Law of Thermodynamics* specifies in which direction physical change occurs. Energy represented by heat always moves from hotter to colder. The implication of these laws is that natural systems depend upon external sources of energy. The source for the energy that sustains life is the sun. Whether its energy is stored, as in coal and petroleum resources, or expended in the production of plants and animals, the sun remains as the primary source of human sustenance. The ability to use the sun as the basic energy source is demonstrated by the accompanying representation of the natural cycle of life.

Concepts Important to Environmental Planning

Carrying Capacity. From the theory of homeostasis, we know that a natural system has the capacity to regulate aberrant behavior on the part of populations. What is also implied in that theory is the ability of a natural system to support populations that are in balance without suffering destruction. We know that some environments are tougher than others and some have greater production capability than others. For instance, tropical forests exhibit a variety of life and productive abilities that far surpasses the fragile ecology of mountains. The capacity of a jungle to repair damage caused by abuse greatly exceeds the ability of an alpine ecology to

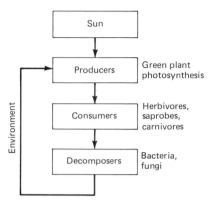

Natural cycle of life.

reconstruct even the impact of a human foot. Certain natural circulation systems have the capacity to absorb and dissipate enormous quantities of pollutants while others become stagnated quickly.

Thus, in order to make sound planning decisions, the planner must know the *carrying capacities* of the natural system in the planning area. Each aspect of the environment should be considered by the planner. He or she must make a careful inventory of relevant characteristics, an assessment of the capacity of the natural systems, and a determination of the limitations of human uses. These can be used to estimate the safe carrying capacity for development in an area to avoid any *overload*.

Critical Areas and Fragile Zone Assessments. An important planning concept that is an extension of the idea of carrying capacity involves the assessment of *critical areas* and *fragile natural zones*. Both include sites that may be incompatible with proposed human use or even with the continued existence of the natural system.

A coastal area exemplifies both the critical area and fragile zone concepts. A coastal area is vulnerable to flooding, violent storms, and continuous erosion. Construction in a coastal area means a high probability of damage to the buildings and injury to the occupants. The coastal area suffers greater damage from human impact than do many other systems. The plant and animal life in a coastal area is vulnerable or fragile and recovers from damage with difficulty. Construction in coastal areas usually means destruction of the fragile natural system that protects the land from the sea. The shoreline erodes and a once-productive environment loses both natural and economic value.

It is useful to separate the concepts of critical areas and fragile zones. Critical areas exhibit physical characteristics that make them more vulnerable. Physical hazard areas such as coastlines, flood plains, marshlands, earthquake or geological fault zones, steep slopes, landslide areas, and others must be carefully evaluated before development. Fragile zones refer to certain areas supporting specific natural systems. Many fragile zones, like the coastal area, are also critical areas. Some fragile zones are wetlands, marshes, wildfowl breeding areas, productive aquatic systems, beach and dune systems, upland tree and plant associations; aquifer recharge areas, special micro-climate areas protecting animal or fish habitats, and desert and dryland areas.

Regeneration and Restoration. As noted above , while some systems are capable of withstanding human impact with relatively little damage, others may be completely altered or destroyed. *Regenerative* and *restorative concepts* can be used to assess the ability of a natural system to exist in harmony with human development. Even systems that sustain tremendous damage can be easily recovered while others require many years to erase the smallest imprint. The planner who is aware of the regenerative and restorative capacities of natural systems can regulate impacts.

For example, flowing rivers and flushing tidal bays have a greater capability to naturally oxygenate and biologically degrade organic wastes than stagnant rivers or bays. Upland development should be avoided entirely or accomplished with great care in order to prevent construction that will cause erosion, pollute upland water systems, increase flood hazards, and destroy plant associations and animal habitats. The flatlands, where plants and trees flourish, usually recover from construction damage more rapidly.

Certain natural systems will sustain human developments if careful site selection, development planning, use programming, and construction management of natural systems can be used. When the regenerative and restorative capacities of the natural systems are exceeded, then the systems tend to die. If human settlement is to survive, the functions of the natural system must be restored or replaced.

For example, while we may be able to extract our wastes from our waters in order to reuse water, we have not been able to accomplish the same for the air. There is no substitute for clean air, and no way to clean it once it has been polluted. This means that we must withold air-polluting wastes, decompose them at the source, or avoid the processes that create exhaust.

Natural System Overrides. The survival of the city serves as an example of our success in *overriding* the limitations of natural systems. Most of the overriding of natural systems has been accomplished with little awareness of the consequences of such actions. For example, marshes were dredged, drained, and filled to support cities without any understanding of the fact that the nutrients of these wetlands can feed and help spawn enormous biological, zoological, and botanic populations. When rivers were dammed for power or to prevent floods, fish migration was stopped and nutrients no longer reached the seas and flood plains. The consequences of years of engineering to accommodate human needs, ideas of settlement, and desire for comfort are just now becoming known.

With our knowledge of how natural systems function and of their capacities and regenerative capabilities, it now is sometimes possible to override the limitations of natural systems without destroying their functions. The planner who overrides the capacity of a natural system must work with care, using the system itself to support the override and using the override to protect the natural system. It is possible to build communities of considerable population density without destroying or having to override all of the natural systems. Air quality can be retained, much plant and animal life may survive, the topographic character of the land may remain, and other natural systems and amenities may continue to flourish in the face of great pressures.

For example, understanding how a natural drainage system functions and its capacity to absorb water helps to determine whether that system can work to support human development. An appreciation of the effectiveness of a natural system to absorb water may mean that it would not be necessary to build massive storm-water sewer systems or pipe in a water supply that might otherwise come from underground. Storm water may simply soak into the ground or run off in the way it did before development. The benefits of such planning are many. Construction costs are reduced, a natural system is protected, and attractive surroundings are preserved.

Recovery. We are slowly learning that it is possible to *recover* at least some of what we have lost. While it is not possible to regain a marsh once it has been dredged and filled or to recover the extinct passenger pigeon, sometimes it is feasible to clean a river, purify a lake, reforest a mountain, restore a population of migratory fish, and recreate lost animal habitats. We can relocate settlements away from critical areas and fragile zones permitting these areas to recover and survive. We can reintroduce natural conditions into urban environments as part of our redevelopment efforts. It is part of the task of the planner to discover the opportunities for recovering lost natural and environmental characteristics in order to recreate a sense of natural harmony.

ENVIRONMENTAL PLANNING PRACTICE

In practice, planning is not a substitute for the work of the natural scientist. The planner should *respond* to the findings of the natural sciences, interpret them as they apply to planning situations, and carefully observe the consequences. The planner is not separate from the natural scientist but is part of the observation and feedback loop essential in research and application. Planning is appealing in the relative certainty of the principles applied and simplicity of most methods. Planning analysis leads to sound conclusions when definitions and characteristics of the environment are clear.

The overall objective of contemporary planning theory is to provide those responsible for creating land use and community development policy with a sound basis for their decisions. The process of planning analysis should be seen as one which clarifies the consequences of decisions rather than one that determines decisions. That is, while an analysis may point to one particular decision, it should also show what could be traded for other benefits and what systems might be overridden with least damage to produce the desired result.

The objective of the environmental planning process is to find ways to do things with the least natural system damage as possible. To this point environmental planning has been defined as being concerned with the interaction of human works with natural systems. In practice the definition has been expanded to include a wide variety of impacts that result from land use decisions. A resources inventory for example, includes development impacts not only on natural systems but also upon built systems, such as water supplies, sewerage disposal facilities, historic/archelogical resources, public facilities, transportation services, financial resources, and visual resources.

The Planning Area
Planning is practiced on both the large and small scales. Environmental planning may apply to the

whole earth as a total resources system, or to continents, nations, regions, states, subregions, localities, or specific sites. Resource systems do not observe political boundaries. It is advisable, however, to select for analysis a planning area that conforms with the boundaries of a policymaking political jurisdiction. If it is necessary to exceed that jurisdiction, then the analysis should be divided to show policymakers which portions of the advice directly involve them and which do not.

For the purpose of illustrating environmental planning methodology, a sample geographic *study area* is shown. The example is limited by the boundaries of one political jurisdiction (a town) but is part of a larger political area (a region) as well as a larger geographic region. The area has been settled for more than 200 years, but it now faces major growth pressures that require careful management in order to preserve existing natural systems and prevailing community amenities.

While not all of the following are always observed in determining the appropriate dimensions of a planning area, most should be accounted for in making the selection. Presumably, as with our example, the planning area is politically determined. Also given is the overall objective for which the planning is being accomplished, for example, to manage expected growth pressures. What the planner should then add are secondary factors such as:

1 Development affecting the plan to be accomplished outside the jurisdiction of the specific planning entity

2 Watersheds, river barriers, aquifers, and related water systems that extend beyond or through the planning area

3 Special geologies and mineral structures that may be desired for exploitation, which could disrupt planning decisions

4 Special habitats, migratory routes, nesting grounds, and wintering areas, the disruption of which would stress specie survival

5 Air sheds and circulation systems that extend beyond the planning area

6 Particular economic systems, such as farming, forestry, agriculture, that if disrupted or diminished by different land uses might fail.

With this assessment should come a summary evaluation of whether the generalized objective of the planning can reasonably be accomplished. If the preliminary assessment shows that the proposed actions are not feasible, then the planner should advise that proceeding with the planning would be a waste of time. For this example, the goals and objectives are to: (1) protect the natural environment and character of the town, and (2) determine where anticipated growth might be best accommodated. Once it has been determined that these goals and objectives are reasonable, a review of the overall planning situation is in order.

A number of characteristics could be recorded to place the planning area in the proper context. Selected for this sample analysis are those that reveal the study area's natural characteristics as part of the larger political region. The first map shows the water basin boundaries and the quality classifications of streams and rivers. Elevation, soils suitability, and precipitation are shown in the following three maps. Together, these show that, compared to other parts of the region, the study area is higher, has less developed land, and experiences greater precipitation. A preliminary finding might be that the study area is not appropriate for major new development; other areas might be more suitable.

Basic Inventories

Inventories of characteristics and conditions are the first step in developing the basis for an *environmental plan*. Each planning area contains a variety of conditions that require inventory. Different climates, topography, and vegetation zones call for an inventory. A common checklist helps the planner to avoid overlooking a minor but perhaps important characteristic. Numerous inventory systems have

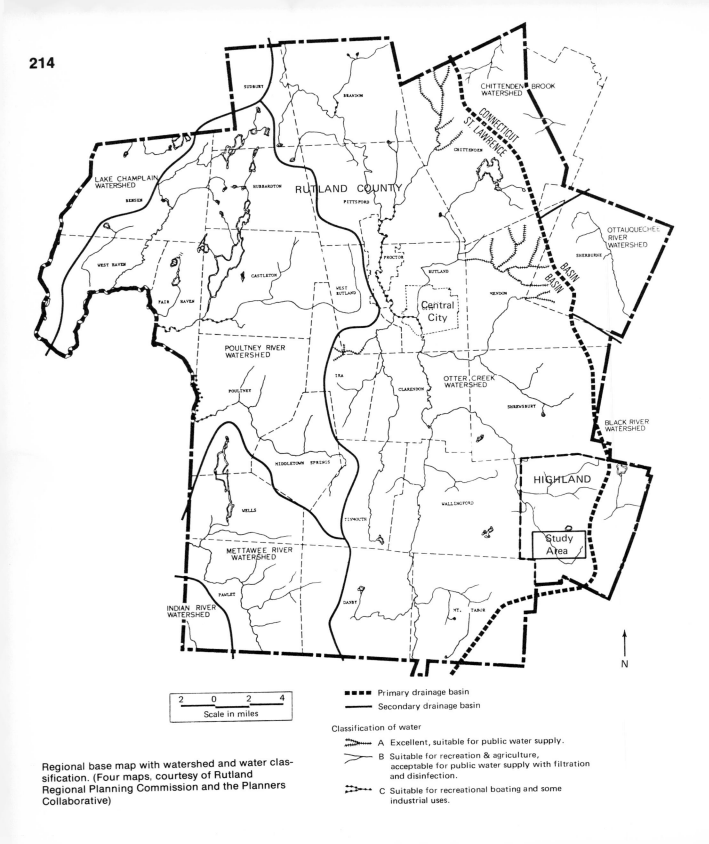

Regional base map with watershed and water classification. (Four maps, courtesy of Rutland Regional Planning Commission and the Planners Collaborative)

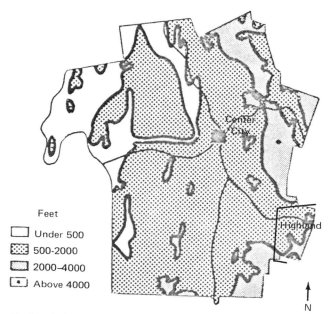

Feet

☐ Under 500
▨ 500–2000
▨ 2000–4000
☐ Above 4000

N

Regional elevations.

(3) Soil drainage and suitability: inventory soil characteristics, noting poorly drained areas, absorption capabilities, foundation suitability, and related characteristics that would aid or prevent certain uses

(4) Ecological systems: inventory plant associations, such as forest types, grasslands, and barren areas, noting especially productive areas of both naturally occurring species and domestic agriculture

(5) Climates: assess the impact of the zonal climate upon existing conditions, noting microclimate conditions that might affect uses

(6) Geology: inventory both bedrock and surface geology to identify characteristics that might support or limit uses. Note especially fault zones, unstable or weak rock structures, and mineral deposits that should remain protected from development

b *Land values in use.* In most situations some human activity has occurred within a planning area, which must be accounted for by the planner. Along with the inventory of natural systems and characteristics there also should be an account of those land uses that have been built. The relationship between composition and use is often close. For example, prime agricultural land is usually land that is of a particular soil character, well drained, flat, and with a suitable geologic foundation.

(1) Agricultural land: inventory prime land and secondary land including also land suitable for agriculture but not currently in use

(2) Woodlands and productive forest areas

(3) Microecological systems: inventory microzones that contain rare or endangered plants or that have unique productive capabilities because of water retention

(4) Scenic vistas and prospects: inventory naturally occurring scenic amenities such as overlooks, views, or perspectives needing protection

(5) Land uses: Inventory existing and planned land uses such as housing, commercial and industrial development, parks, reserves and recreation areas, transportation, public facilities and facility sites, and other existing relevant land commitments

been used in environmental planning; they all share common elements. First there is a general classification, such as land, water, climate, and ecological systems, and social or cultural characteristics. Then inventories tend to account for specific characteristics of the major categories, values that these characteristics offer, and values that are in particular demand.

The following outline is an example of an inventory list that accounts for composition, values in use, and values in demand as they should be considered by planners.

1 *Land Inventory*
  a *Physiographic composition of land*
    (1) Topography: inventory slopes and elevation to determine suitability for uses
    (2) Surface drainage: inventory surface water systems, such as streams, lakes, ponds, floodways, flood plains, and dry washes

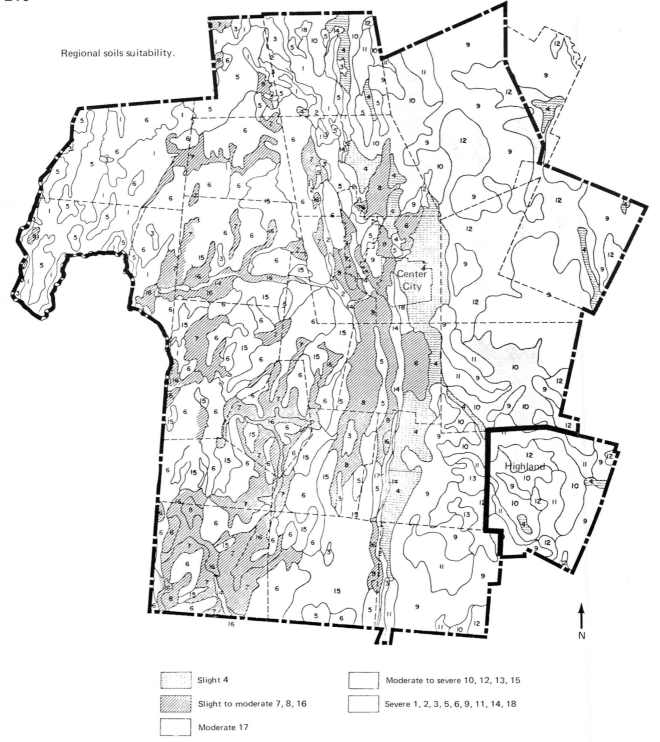

Regional soils suitability.

Slight 4	Moderate to severe 10, 12, 13, 15
Slight to moderate 7, 8, 16	Severe 1, 2, 3, 5, 6, 9, 11, 14, 18
Moderate 17	

N

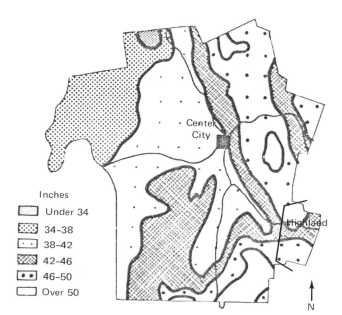

Inches

▨ Under 34
▨ 34–38
▨ 38–42
▨ 42–46
▨ 46–50
▨ Over 50

N

Regional average annual precipitation.

c *Land values in demand.* To relate the inventories to the planning it is important to determine what land values will be in demand, because the planning will have to respond to these pressures. Some of these pressures can be projected from existing uses, while others will have to be determined by hypothesizing future conditions that the planning should anticipate. Typical land values in demand are for:
  (1) Residences
  (2) Commerce
  (3) Agriculture
  (4) Industry
  (5) Transportation
  (6) Recreation
  (7) Conservation
2 *Water Inventory*
  a *Composition of water*
    (1) Aquifer, aquifer-recharge areas, and groundwater systems: inventory to determine locations, extent, and capacities
    (2) Surface water systems: inventory streams and flowing waters; ponds, lakes, estuaries, and bays;

marshes, swamps, and flood storage and absorption areas. Determine water table levels and fluctuation, watersheds, and related natural filtering and purification systems
    (3) Shorelands, coastal areas, and aquatic life support system: inventory and delineate, showing the extent of the protective margins needed to preserve the related water resources
  b *Water values in use*
    (1) Water quality and quantity: evaluate, note sources, calculate volumes, and determine replacement capacities. Salt and mineral infiltration possibilities should be assessed if maintenance supplies are diminished
    (2) Water system drainage and waste absorption capacities: inventory the capability of water systems to drain lands and to absorb excess runoff and wastes
    (3) Water usage: inventory water uses for drinking, processing, cooking, waste disposal, and other needs in order to match supply and demand.
  c *Water values in demand*
    (1) Drinking
    (2) Waste disposal
    (3) Cooking
    (4) Power generation
    (5) Recreation
    (6) Agriculture
    (7) Industrial processes
    (8) Ecosystem maintenance
    (9) Aesthetics
3 *Climatic Conditions Inventory*
  a *Composition of climate systems*
    (1) Climate characteristics: inventory zone conditions (arctic, temperate, tropical, or desert) and characteristics specific to the planning area. Note temperature ranges, sun percentages, seasonal changes, precipitation, and the frequency of particular events such as blizzards, tornadoes, hurricanes, heavy rains, and tidal waves
    (2) Planning area–specific climates: inventory characteristics that may modify the normal area climate, such as proximity to a large lake or the ocean, valleys, areas experiencing temperature inversions, snow belts, or dry areas
    (3) Airsheds: determine the structure of the airshed influencing the air flows of the area

(4) Microclimate: assess the nature of microclimatic conditions that may positively or negatively affect land uses. Some of these might be: areas of poor air circulation or good air circulation, areas of early frost and late thaws or the reverse, and areas of heavy rains or little rain

b *Climate values in demand*
  (1) Waste air absorption and air circulation effectiveness
  (2) Air drainage for certain agricultural crops
  (3) Seasonal characteristics that offer development opportunities for activities such as skiing and water sports, as well as patterns of flows required for agriculture and of importance in other land uses
  (4) Climate conditions that reduce or increase energy costs and consumption

4 *Ecological Systems Inventory*
  a *Composition of ecological systems*
    (1) Wildlife species and habitat: inventory species and habitat to determine characteristics that would be changed or threatened. Include in the inventory aquatic as well as terrestrial species, noting migratory patterns and special interdependencies between plants, animals, and natural conditions
    (2) Ecosystem supports: determine characteristics that play special supporting roles for either a micro or a macro ecosystem
    (3) Indication of stress and survival: establish measures to determine levels of stress and the ability of ecosystems to withstand use conflicts and development pressures
    (4) Ecosystem condition: determine extent to which the ecosystem has either been modified to serve development such as agriculture, recreation, forest production or has remained natural
  b *Ecological values in use.* This list can be short or long depending upon the extent of dependency between uses and the surviving ecosystems of the planning area. The key determinants will be the extent to which the ecosystem contributes to or participates in the production system. For an agricultural area that interaction can be extensive; it may include the extensively modified ecosystem of crop production, animal raising, and tree farming, or it may incorporate the less-managed activities of occasional tree harvesting

and range or pasture stock raising. Recreation uses may extend from carefully designed playfields to trail systems in remote wilderness areas. The underlying basis for this inventory should be a determination of the extent that an ecosystem has been or might be stressed and even destroyed by change.

  c *Ecosystem values in demand*
    (1) Natural system maintenance and specie survival
    (2) Recreation uses
    (3) Food supply
    (4) Fiber, fuel, and building material
    (5) Aesthetics
    (6) Survival and ecological balance
    (7) Natural absorption and waste disposition capacities

5 *Cultural-Social Inventories*
  a *Composition of a cultural-social inventory.* The record of human activity is assessed to note evidence of what should be preserved and protected. Included also should be those aspects of the natural environment that provide a sense of spiritual vitality and location in time.
    (1) Human values: inventory historic buildings, places, and sites that are important records of human accomplishments, social and cultural evolutions, and conflict
    (2) Natural history: inventory significant evidence of national history, geology, habitats, species, unique views, prospects, land forms, and so forth that serve to provide us with both values of time and spiritual awareness
    (3) Prehistory and archeological evidence: inventory sites of significant prehistory and archeological importance as a record of human activity and origins
    (4) Visual and social amenities: inventory those aspects of the visual and social environment that have importance to a community and might otherwise by overlooked
  b *Cultural-social values in use.* The variety of historic sites, buildings, and other evidence as well as the necessity to protect valuable natural historical evidence suggests numerous use and preservation values. In some cases values are derived from the use of a site or building, or even from the activity itself. In other cases the value is in protecting a site from use that would conflict with what the site has to offer. As

with other inventory activities the challenge is to define those aspects necessary to determine the best policy options

c *Cultural-social values in demand.* Each of the characteristics collected within this inventory has its own demand constituencies. Historical societies, conservation and natural history organizations, the archeological and anthropological disciplines, scenic preservation groups, and others have become protectors and users of the values in the cultural/social inventory.

Methods of Analysis

The inventory process usually determines the most appropriate method of analysis. A lengthy and complex inventory for a large region will demand a multifaceted method of analysis, while a less complex inventory of a smaller planning area will require a less complicated approach. Since the policies to be determined from an environmental planning analysis relate primarily to land uses, all analytical methods ultimately require some mapped expression. That mapping may be a simple designation of inventory findings, or it may be a complex composite of characteristics and values.

The analysis to determine the land use and development options usually involves direct mapping or overlay mapping of inventories and/or creation of a matrix that relates inventory variables. Either method can fulfill the analytical demands of complex or simple environmental planning problems. Mapping methods seem to be more deterministic; i.e., the interpretation involves reacting to the mapped lines or symbols of characteristics to be observed by the policymaker. Regardless of variations in mapping technique, the mapped characteristics tend to determine rather specifically the range of policy options. Using a matrix means the planner can represent inventory characteristics as quantitative variables. Thus, a matrix makes it possible to assign values and calculate environmental protection priorities and land use options.

The objective of both mapping or matrix methods is to determine the degree to which a pos-

sible land use is compatible with the environment. It is important to be able to judge which possible uses can be accommodated within a particular environment without damage. The planner should use the method of analysis that will enable him or her to calculate impact and understand possible trade-off opportunities between development benefits and environmental impact in a given evaluation situation.

Mapping and Overlay Analysis. While simple map drawings may often suffice, more complex planning problems require the use of overlays over base maps. The U.S. Geological Survey (USGS) map shown can be used as a base map; it includes topography, surface water systems, roads, and settlements. Planners often use USGS maps because of their high accuracy, extensive coverage, and availability.

The figure on page 221 illustrates the use of the overlay system for our example study area. This overlay identifies areas where the slope (greater than 15 percent) and elevation (above 2000 feet) mean certain land uses may damage a sensitive environment. The next figure identifies water systems, including streams, lakes, marshes and flood-prone areas. A protective buffer zone is mapped along these elements to prevent development in ecologically sensitive areas and/or flood-prone areas.

Soils suitability, in terms of suitability for development, is shown in the figure on page 223. Drained and stable soils are best for development, while unstable, marshy, and poorly drained soils are more appropriate to other uses. Soils best suited for agriculture and forestry should be reserved for those uses. The figure on page 224 illustrates existing land uses, which always must be considered in an environmental analysis.

Each overlay reveals a specific area of environmental planning information alone; together, they produce the basis for the environmental plan. Each overlay should be reviewed to determine whether or not it reveals characteristics that should be given

U. S. Geological Survey topographic base map with study area.

| 1 | 0 | 1 | 2 | 3 | 4 Miles |

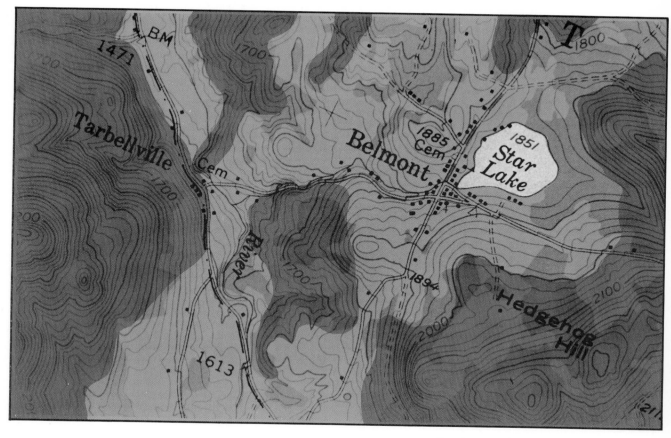

Area slope and elevation map.

Development limitation

Severe: Elev. above
2000;
Slope + 15%

Slight to moderate

N

priority in developing the environmental policy. In this example, the need to protect water systems from pollution and degradation and to protect development from flooding and destruction means that a protective margin of at least 100 feet is a high priority.

By using the overlays it is possible to determine which areas are especially sensitive to development impact and which could bear development without serious damage. The composite of all the overlays reveals the environmentally sensitive areas of the study area as well as those areas currently being used or developed. At this point it is important to return to the statement of goals and objectives that introduced the environmental planning analysis: the

ENVIRONMENTAL PLANNING

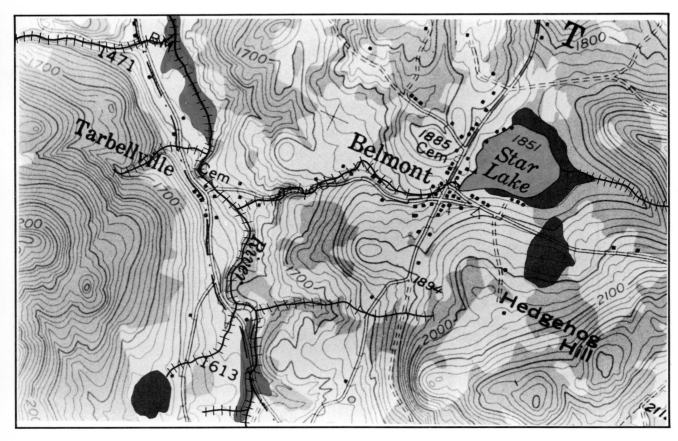

Area water systems.

Lakes	
Rivers, brooks	
Flood prone areas	
Marshes, wet areas	

N

environmental character of the community is to be protected and future development is to be directed to produce the least possible negative impact.

The composite overlay map can be used to create a new map that represents an environmentally responsive land use plan for the study area. This new map articulates those parts of the area that will support development and those that should be reserved as prime agricultural land. Any other part would be damaged environmentally by extensive development. In summary, we now have a map that identifies: (1) those characteristics of the planning area where development would cause serious environmental damage; (2) those areas where it may be

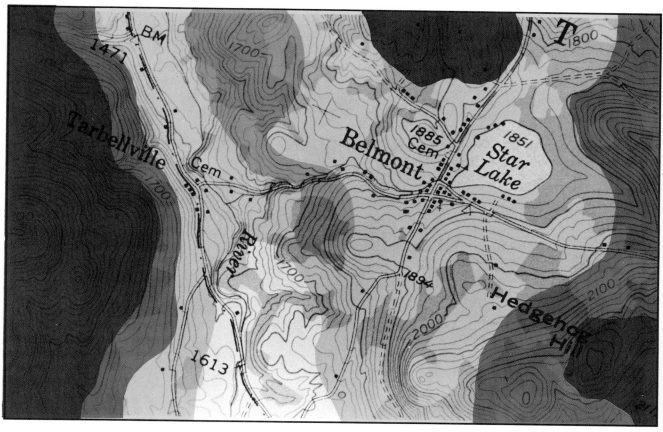

Soil suitability for development.

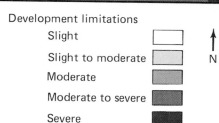

Development limitations

Slight

Slight to moderate

Moderate

Moderate to severe

Severe

N

hazardous to develop; (3) those areas that should be protected because of agricultural value; and (4) those areas where development might safely occur.

It is obvious that the overlay mapping process has limitations in complex environmental planning situations. Too many overlays will result in a map that is unreadable and of no value as a planning tool. Consequently, it may be desirable to combine similar characteristics in one overlay or to synthesize a group of inventory elements into a generalized map category. This is often done with soil mapping, where soil suitability for development is generalized to show soil types appropriate or inappropriate for development. Such a soil suitability analy-

ENVIRONMENTAL PLANNING

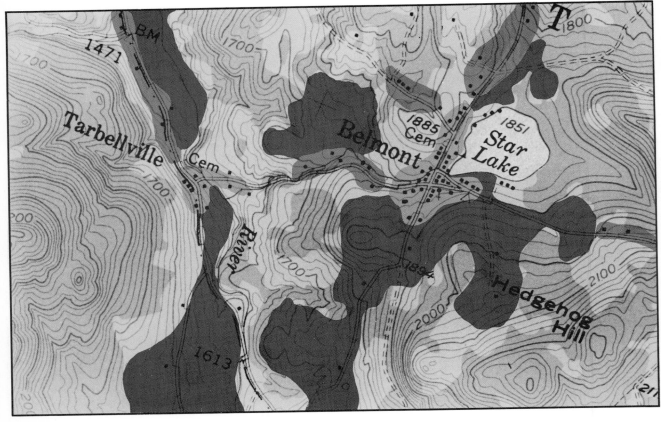

Area land use.

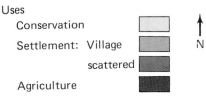

Uses
Conservation
Settlement: Village
scattered
Agriculture

N

sis may also be combined with slope and elevation characteristics, woodland and upland soils, prime agricultural soils, and often, poorly drained marsh area soils.

Overlay mapping of groups of characteristics may also be useful in clarifying planning and development options. For example, bedrock geologies, groundwater, and soil associations might well be combined in one overlay series to advise the planner of the foundation and water-supply limitations in a particular planning area. Likewise, if a planning objective is to protect wildlife habitats, forest resources, and the quality of groundwater systems, a sequence of overlays should make these objectives clear.

There are numerous tools to aid the planner in

INTRODUCTION TO URBAN PLANNING

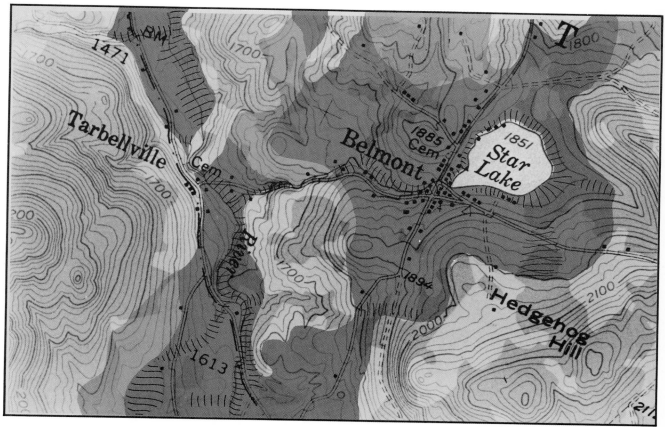

Composite analysis: limitations to development.

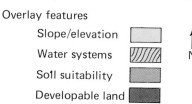

Overlay features

Slope/elevation		
Water systems		N
Soil suitability		
Developable land		

accomplishing effective overlay mapping of inventories. In addition to the USGS topographical maps, bedrock and surficial geology maps, and various soil association and suitability maps provided by the Soil Conservation Service, there are geologic fault maps (for earthquake-prone areas); river basin, drainage area, floodplain, and floodway maps; and various mapped records of forest cover, plant asso-ciations, and climatic conditions. Important new mapping tools have been made possible by aerial photographic and satellite photographic technology. A variety of photographic and remote sensing technologies provide useful analytic tools to the planner faced with a large-scale inventory and analysis problem.

While field checks and specific environmental

ENVIRONMENTAL PLANNING

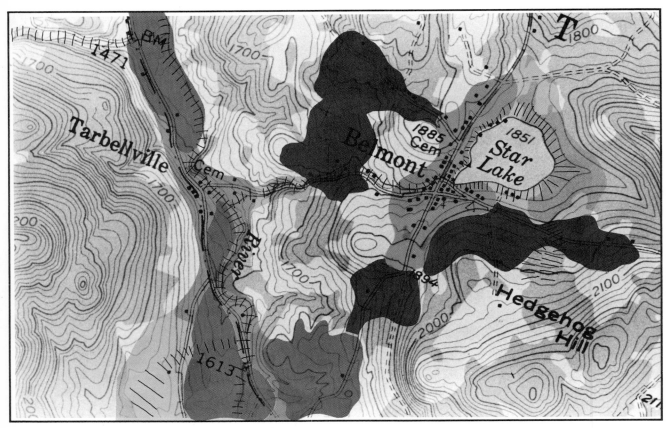

Environmental land use map.

Proposed uses

Upland conservation	☐
Conservation	▨
Village cluster	▨
Prime agricultural land	▨
Water resource protection	▨
Reserve for future development	■

N ↑

studies are necessary to provide detailed descriptions of an area to be developed or protected, it is possible to conduct adequate environmental planning analyses from secondary sources. The scale of the existing inventories and description of characteristics is usually sufficient to allow the environmental planner to describe the appropriate use and policy options.

INTRODUCTION TO URBAN PLANNING

Once the planner has completed this analysis, he or she can devise the environmental protection and development policy. That policy may take the form of a master plan for protection and development or of a series of policy statements to guide land-use and development decisions. The following policy statement suggests actions that are needed in order to implement the environmental planning and development regulation findings for our example.

Recommended Policies

1 Restrict or prevent development on slopes of 15 percent or more and at elevations more than 2,000 feet above sea level.

2 Protect lakeshores, stream banks, wet areas, and flood-prone areas from development by requiring that development be set back no fewer than 100 feet from the edge of such water systems.

3 Encourage the location of future residential and commercial uses in village clusters where soils are suitable and sewer and water services can be provided.

4 Adopt zoning regulations and a zoning map reflecting a desirable land-use pattern for the town's future development.

5 Adopt subdivision regulations. These are especially important if the town's interest in new developments is to be protected and town planning goals attained.

6 Adopt an official map, indicating among other things where future public investments in road construction and other facilities might occur.

7 Amend and periodically review the town plan to reflect the findings of this and subsequent investigations.

Matrix Analysis. A matrix analysis allows the planner to quantify variables in a way that will reveal where impacts would be most or least severe. It also makes a wider inventory of characteristics more manageable than do overlay and direct mapping. It is possible to analyze a multivariate matrix with a computer and to incorporate into the analysis a large number of variables without having to synthe-size individual variables into groups. It is also possible to map the policy options indicated by the analysis and even to vary the analysis in order to emphasize different variables.

In order to create a computer analysis and computer-drawn map it is necessary to cover the study area with a grid. The grid provides spatial coordinates that can be programmed for computer analysis. Each cell in the grid can be given a number that reflects the characteristic of the environment of the cell (see Table 9-1). The cell might be assigned a number reflecting a dominant characteristic (such as steep slope or water), or the number could be produced from a matrix calculation of a number of variables. The method selected depends upon the relative importance of the variables. If one characteristic is dominant and all the others insignificant, a simple numerical assignment is adequate; if the variables interact with or influence one another, a more complex calculation of the grid notation is necessary.

The sample matrix which follows was used to calculate the numbers recorded in the grid. Even from the numerical pattern it is possible to observe the pattern of characteristics that would create the computer-drafted map.

Environmental Plans and Policy Advisories

The environmental inventory and analysis have been devised to guide planning decisions. As we have seen, the analysis usually determines to a considerable extent what uses are compatible with the protection of various ecological systems and environmental characteristics. When these analyses do not clearly determine a use or conservation policy, the environmental planner's task becomes more difficult.

For example, in the illustration above much of the land in the planning area is constrained in some way (e.g., by slope and elevation). Some is flood plains, flood ways (as with stream or pond margins) or wetlands. Some is also constrained as

TABLE 9-1

Example Matrix Analysis: Development Suitability for One Cell

Characteristic	Weight	Low 0	1	2	3	High 5
Elevation	5				20	
Slope	5					25
Soil	6				24	
Wildlife habitat	4			12		
Geology	4				16	
Marsh	8	0				
Flood-prone	10	0				
Unique amenity	7		14			
Historic significance	7	0				

Total score: 111

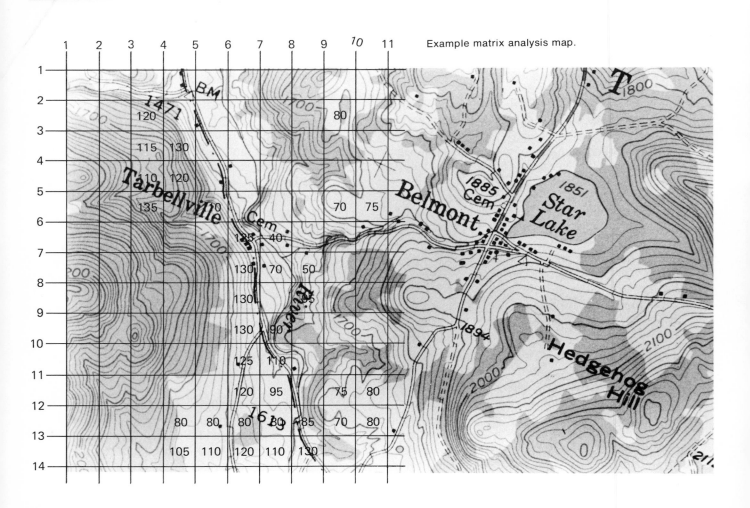

Example matrix analysis map.

being adjacent to arterial highways where access is limited. Other land is best suited for agricultural uses. What remains is land that has been developed for housing and community services or is near such existing development and could serve to support additional development. Furthermore, the land suitable for development is also scattered. One policy might be to allow development to occur at will on any suitable land. The result of such a policy would be scattered development, which would impose added public service costs upon the town. An alternative might be to concentrate development where it could be better served. Areas suitable for development but away from existing settlements would be held until all the land near existing settlements had been used.

The above policy advisory implies that a preexisting situation, the present village, in part determines the planning and development policy. If, on the other hand, an analysis finds that the existing development is poorly located and further development at that site would have great destructive impact, a new site for future development would be advised. This option is reasonable when existing development is limited but not when the area is heavily developed. For example, in spite of the fact that San Francisco is located in an earthquake-prone area, it would not be feasible to curtail future development and transpose it to areas where earthquakes are less likely.

Although existing development and trends tend to determine planning policy, it is possible to define hazard areas and to discover unique environmental resources that might be recovered. Numerous projects and developments have been stopped or even reversed in order to recover natural amenities or prevent additional or permanent damage. Airport construction in the Florida Everglades was stopped after two-thirds of the facility had been completed. The Cross Florida Barge Canal project was stopped even though much of it had been built. The San Francisco Bay Conservation District Commission has the authority to regulate uses on the Bay and seeks to halt uses that are not consistent with the objective of protecting and restoring the natural amenities of the estuary.

As with any planning effort, the environmental planner faces the task of trying to predict and project a future. The implications of the policy statements and planning advisories allow the planner to project alternate futures. The potential results of one set of policies can be compared with those of another set. The planner is challenged with documenting and illustrating the costs and benefits of each alternative so that the decision makers can understand the consequences.

Implementation of Environmental Planning

The implementation and management of any plan require special attention. Because an *environmental plan* involves interaction with various natural systems, careful management of the plan is essential. Since it is not possible to anticipate all of the consequences of the particular land uses in any plan, it is important to monitor the impact as land uses change. This monitoring provides feedback that can be used to modify the environmental plan and guide its management to ensure that its objectives are achieved. Skillful management can allow the expansion of compatible uses, help to eliminate preexisting and/or incompatible uses, and at the same time insure that the natural capacities of the environment are not exceeded. An effective environmental management process depends on well-developed, workable, and clearly stated policies. These policies may form the preamble of a management plan or they may be part of more traditional implementation tools, such as land use controls.

The traditional implementation strategy has been to adopt a system of land use controls similar to zoning ordinances. First the aspects of the natural environment that are to be protected or used are mapped in zones. Each land use zone is described, and the uses allowed within each zone are listed. Both the zone map and the use descriptions are then adopted by the appropriate unit of government. Usually it is necessary to adopt new ordinances and descriptions in order to change the zones, but adjustments for exceptions can be made through an appeals process.

A system of land-use controls is adequate for most situations, but the zoning tends to be inflexible or unable to respond to unanticipated circumstances. The system does have the virtue of being definite; the potential developer or land user can see precisely what may or may not be done within a particular zone. When questions arise, an established body of law exists to help shape judicial decisions, so actions are reasonably predictable. However, the inflexibility of the zoning system for environmental protection means there is no assurance that the environmental protection objective will be accomplished. Achieving environmental objectives through a zoning ordinance often requires complicated descriptions of the aspects to be protected and the uses seen as compatible. Imprecise terms, such as *carrying capacity* and *critical areas,* are not easily incorporated into a zoning ordinance as standards to be used in judging the compatibility of uses.

Consequently, some jurisdictions are now adopting *use permit* processes based upon environmental protection criteria. The system recognizes the difficulty of mapping and predicting all possible compatible and incompatible uses. To determine whether or not a permit should be granted for a particular use, a hearing is held during which the proponent of a use presents evidence as to the probable impact of the desired use. The permit granting authority usually includes a series of criteria which are applied in the review of the use. Some jurisdictions give status in the permit hearing to a wide variety of interested parties, extending from local officials and neighbors to state agencies and interest groups. The criteria serve to guide the proponent of the use as well as those reviewing the proposal. The criteria may be mapped and adopted much as a zoning ordinance. The difference between the two is

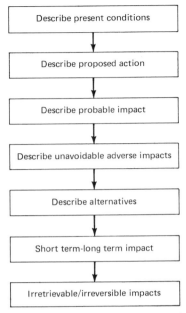

Environmental impact statement framework.

that the mapping serves as a decision guideline rather than as a definite use restriction.

The environmental impact review tends to fit the circumstances rather than to anticipate hypothetical uses. The process is often criticized because it is less certain for the developer than zoning. On the other hand, a proposed use that a permit review finds compatible might have been prohibited by a zoning ordinance. The permit review process does not necessarily anticipate all possible use options, but it does imply that the granting of a permit is contingent upon adherence to certain policies and criteria for use.

The development permit review system has been enacted in Vermont based upon a land capability evaluation. Certain criteria have been adopted as guidelines against which a land use or development proposal must be measured before a permit is granted. The process evaluates impacts, and it has led to improved, environmentally responsive land use decisions. The standards for the district environmental commission decisions are specified in *Section 12* of Vermont's *Act 250: Land Use and Development Law*. The district commissions may refuse to grant a permit if they find that the proposed subdivision or development would be "detrimental to the public health, safety or general welfare," but each commission must give specific reasons for its denial of a permit. To grant a permit, the commission must find that the development:

1 Will not result in undue water or air pollution. In making this determination it shall at least consider: the elevation of the land above sea level; and in relation to the floodplains, the nature of soil and subsoil and their ability to adequately support waste disposal; the slope of the land and its effect on effluents; the availability of streams for disposal of effluents; and the applicable health and water resources department regulations.

2 Does have sufficient water available for the reasonable foreseeable needs of the subdivision or development

3 Will not cause an unreasonable burden on an existing water supply, if one is to be utilized

4 Will not cause unreasonable soil erosion or reduction in the capacity of the land to hold water so that dangerous or unhealthy conditions may result

5 Will not cause unreasonable highway congestion or unsafe conditions with respect to use of the highways existing or proposed

6 Will not cause an unreasonable burden on the ability of a municipality to provide educational services

7 Will not place an unreasonable burden on the ability of the local government to provide municipality or governmental services

8 Will not have an undue adverse effect on the scenic or natural beauty of the area, aesthetics, historic sites, or rare and irreplaceable natural areas

9 Is in conformance with a duly adopted development plan, land use plan, or land capability plan (the statewide plans required by the law)

10 Is in conformance with any duly adopted local or regional plan

The burden of proof is on the applicant for criteria 1 through 4, 9, and 10, and on the opposing parties for critera 5 through 8.

While less definite in what is allowed or prohibited than a conventional zoning ordinance, the development impact review does allow the evaluation of each proposal according to its merits. Instead of prohibiting or regulating classes of uses, the Vermont system regulates classes of impacts. As a result, developers tend to carefully evaluate probable impacts before applying for a permit in order to avoid delay in securing one.

THE ENVIRONMENTAL PLANNER AND ENVIRONMENTAL LAW

During the past decade the U.S. Congress and state legislatures have enacted an important body of laws intended to protect the environment. These laws have resulted from an increased public awareness of the damage has been done to the natural environment.

The most important and all-encompassing of these laws has been the National Environmental Policy Act of 1969 (NEPA). The act requires that the Federal Government prepare a national environmental protection policy and create a Council for Environmental Quality to monitor national progress toward environmental policy goals. Buried deep in the law was Section 102 (2) (c), which required the preparation of an environmental impact statement (EIS) for all federal projects. The statement was to be not just an accounting of natural, physical consequences of a project, but, rather, an evaluation of a proposed action's impact upon the total human environment. However, there was no requirement that the findings of the report had to be taken into consideration.

What Congress saw as an innocuous provision ultimately has become the most powerful aspect of the EPA. In response to a series of public interest group and environmental protection organization suits concerning when and how the EIS requirement was to be applied, the courts held that whenever a federal action affecting the environment is proposed, an EIS must be prepared. The force of this requirement is not that the findings of an EIS must be observed, but that an adequate assessment must be completed before any proposed action may proceed.

The extensive litigation that has swirled around this issue has focused not on whether the findings of the EIS are considered in the final decision on a project, but whether an EIS must be prepared and how to determine that the EIS is adequate. Does the statement record and account for all of the possible impacts, was the methodology used comprehensive and valid, and can the anticipated impacts be ameliorated in some fashion or will they be permanent?

Once an EIS is determined to be adequate and is accepted by the agency required to prepare such a report, the agency decides whether or not to observe the findings. In practice, however, an EIS is ignored by the responsible agency at its own risk. To go forward with an activity that has been found to be potentially damaging to the environment is likely to produce serious public reaction and possible political repercussions.

The importance of the EPA and its EIS provision in the public decision process is explained by two factors. First, the courts have held that any project subject to federal regulations and/or funding (even projects not specifically within the federal domain) must also meet the EIS requirement. State and local projects using federal grants-in-aid fall within this category. Second, the effectiveness of the federal EIS provision in evaluating impacts has prompted many states to adopt their own EPAs and EIS provisions.

The basic framework for an EIS as stated in federal law and in many state statutes is outlined in the figure on page 230.[3] An evaluation sequence that concentrates on alternatives to a proposed action

has been advised. Instead of accepting the proposed action as the only possible course, alternative actions designed to produce the same or a similar result should be given comparable evaluation. The evaluation should also consider a "no action" alternative. The following sequence has been suggested to accomplish an EIS:[4]

1 Describe present conditions

2 Describe alternative actions

3 Describe the probable impact of each alternative by relating the expected future conditions to present conditions

4 Identify the alternative choices and indicate the evaluation that led to them

5 Describe probable impacts of proposed actions in detail; and

6 Describe techniques to be used to minimize harm

Given the wide definition of impacts in federal law, the evaluation of the impacts must be equally broad. As the science and technology of impact assessment grows, the sophistication of the analysis will expand as well.

A concern for the planner today is the relationship between environmental planning and the preparation of environmental impact statements. Are these interchangeable activities? Is one possible without the other, or are they dependent actions? Is the quality of decisions improved by having both processes available? It appears that one process is not a substitute for the other. Carefully prepared environmental inventory, analyses, and plans can contribute significantly to the preparation of concise and definite environmental impact statements. The methodology of the planner is designed to account for conditions and situations that are the basic material of an EIS. The key word for both the planner and the EIS technician is *impact.* All environmental concerns begin and end with a consideration of impact.

CONCLUSION

The mass of environmentally conscious law (enacted by the U.S. Congress and by many state legislatures) embodies the basic principles and theories of environmental planning. The Clean Water Act and amendments require not only that carrying capacity standards be set for water but also that water systems be planned and protected from adverse impacts from insensitive land uses. The Clean Air Act requires similar protection for the quality of the air and land-use policies that will eliminate airborne poisons. The Coastal Zone Management Act identifies the nation's coastal areas, including the Great Lakes, as critical areas that are particularly sensitive to damage as the result of heedless human development. The National Environmental Policy Act and its state and local descendants include impact evaluation requirements that have greatly influenced development proposals. Environmental legislation is concerned with shoreline and floodplain protection; upland and steep slope protection; watershed and river basin protection; wetland, estuary, and tidal marshland protection; agricultural land and forest areas conservation; scenic areas, wild rivers, and wilderness areas protection; and many other aspects of the human and natural environment.

While the environmental movement peaked with massive legislative accomplishments in the late 1960s and early 1970s, there has been no lessening of commitment to environmental protection. Concern about land use policies, energy conservation, natural resources conservation, and related areas have only served to increase the public's environmental consciousness.

NOTES

1. Rachel Carson, *Silent Spring* (Boston: Houghton Mifflin, 1962).
2. Ian L. McHarg, *Design with Nature* (Garden City, N.Y.: Doubleday, Natural History Press for the American Museum of Natural History, 1969; paperback ed., 1971).
3. U.S., National Environmental Policy Act of 1969, sec. 102 (2) (c).
4. Robert W. Burchell and David Listokin, *The New Environmental Impact Handbook* (New Brunswick, N.J.: Center for Urban Policy Research, Rutgers University, 1975).

FOR FURTHER READING

Burchell, Robert W., and Listokin, David. *Future Land Use: Energy, Environmental and Legal Constraints*. New Brunswick, N.J.: Center for Urban Policy Research, Rutgers University, 1975.

————. *The New Environmental Impact Handbook*. New Brunswick, N.J.: Center for Urban Policy Research, Rutgers University, 1975.

Fanning, Odom. *Man and His Environment: Citizen Action*. New York: Harper & Row, 1975.

Handler, Bruce. *Caring for the Land: Environmental Principles for Site Design and Review*. Chicago: American Society of Planning Officials, 1977.

Mandelker, Daniel R. *Environmental and Land Controls Legislation*. Indianapolis: Bobbs-Merrill, 1976.

McHarg, Ian L. *Design with Nature*. Garden City, N.Y.: Doubleday, Natural History Press for the American Museum of Natural History, 1969; paperback ed., 1971.

Moss, Elaine, ed. *Land Use Controls in the United States*. New York: James Wade, Dial Press, 1977.

Reilly, William K., ed. *The Use of Land: A Citizens' Policy Guide to Urban Growth*. New York: Thomas Y. Crowell, 1973.

Stearns, Forrest W., and Montag, Tom, eds. *The Urban Ecosystem: A Holistic Approach*. Stroudsburg, Pa.: Dowden, Hutchinson & Ross, Halsted Press, 1974.

CHAPTER 10

Land Use Planning

W. Paul Farmer and Julie A. Gibb

The commitment to land use planning in the United States tends to rise and fall with the perception of domestic problems. When problems appear to be directly related to land (environmental degradation, sprawl, congestion, fiscal problems, etc.) the support for land use regulation is evident. Conversely, when problems seem only indirectly related (inflation, unemployment, social services, etc.), public support recedes. A high point was reached with Earth Day 1970 and the advent of the environmental movement. This followed a period of low concern in the 1950s and 1960s.

Urban planners, however, have always dealt with the issues of land use—recognizing it as the one resource (land, labor, and capital) which is truly finite. This chapter presents the basic issues of land use and regulation as they relate to urban planning.

CONCERN FOR LAND USE AND DEVELOPMENT REGULATION

Although most citizens would not choose land use as one of the major problems facing the United States today, when they make choices about where to live, the quality of life is usually an important consideration. This interest in the quality of life has supported land-use planning from the City Beautiful era of the nineteenth century to the growth control concerns of the 1970s.

What is land? Is it private property, its ownership and use protected by the Constitution; is it a factor in the production of goods and services; or is it an element of the public trust, to be preserved for future generations? These varied views of the land resource suggest possible conflicts in land use planning and development regulation. Environmentalists push for more and more restrictions on the development of land and checkpoints in the development process. Fair housing advocates argue against regulations which they feel unduly restrict the mobility of the low income and minority populations. Developers argue that public regulations shackle the industry, raising costs and reducing the critical supply of new housing. The energy crisis has brought about a new concern for the livability of central cities, and soaring municipal budgets have brought about demands for no growth or slow growth policies. These crosscurrents have created a number of *myths* identified by William K. Reilly, president of the Conservation Foundation:

1 The increasing reaction against unplanned growth is basically irrational, a kind of mass hysteria fostered by environmentalists. (Actually, an interest in the regulation of growth and development can be traced throughout the history of this country.)

2 No growth—or at least no urban growth—is a reasonable alternative for the country. (Population redistribution among regions or even within metropolitan areas creates a demand for new development, even when there is a zero population growth.)

3 State and local governments cannot substantially restrict the use of land unless they are prepared to buy it. (Government can go to great lengths in regulating the use of land without actual purchase.)

4 There is nothing wrong with the current planning process that enforcement of existing plans would not cure. (Flaws in the planning process itself and in its implementation are at least as severe as problems of enforcement.)

5 The basic task of sound planning is to assess the level of facilities and services people want before the actual need occurs. (Resource-oriented planning is an alternative to traditional demand-oriented planning.)

6 The energy crisis will solve land use problems by forcing a revitalization of older cities and a return to dense patterns of settlement. (This ignores alternatives such as reducing energy consumption, and it dismisses the living habits of a large sector of the population.)[1]

Discussion of these myths indicates that an interdisciplinary approach is required to reduce existing inefficiencies and abuses in the land-use system. For example, land-use planners must learn to work with complex political and legal constraints, and they must become familiar with demography, economics, management, and other disciplines.

A Framework for Land Use Planning

Activities, people, and locations all interact; each can be examined in terms of its relationships with the others. One framework for land use planning is illustrated in the figure below. Among the questions that might be asked are: who lives in a certain location; what activities exist there; which activities relate to groups of people; and what is the spatial distribution of different groups? People have reasons for living where they do. They may wish to be near jobs, relatives, or amenities such as beaches or parks. Businesses and industries also have locational preferences. They may wish to operate near their market, their raw materials, or major transportation links. Locational preference results in patterns of *concentration* or *dispersion*. Land use planners can either reinforce these natural patterns or create new patterns through zoning and other land use controls.

Elements of land use planning.

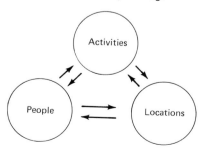

Locational choices are represented schematically in the accompanying figure, in which demand prices for land parcels are shown under two conditions: in a free market and with government regulation. A through F are parcels of land, each owned by an individual who is free to sell to the highest bidder. Numerals I through VI represent activities or people able to purchase parcels of land on the open market. Each land parcel can command a certain price because of its unique characteristics. This results in the matrix of demand prices shown in part (a) of the figure. If the owners of parcels A through F were free to examine the matrix of demand prices, each

would probably sell to the highest bidder, and the locational pattern indicated by the asterisks in part (a) of the figure would result. This free market paradigm, however, would allow the construction of a slaughterhouse adjacent to a single-family residence, with a variety of undesirable results.

In order to prevent this kind of *negative externality*, most communities in the United States have enacted zoning ordinances to regulate the use of land. Through zoning, a municipality divides its land area into zones, specifying certain uses for each. This process is shown in part (b) of the figure. Parcels A and B are zoned solely for industrial use; parcels C and D for commercial use; and parcels E and F for residential use. Activities I through VI are shown as residences, retail activities, and industry. Since people desiring to build residences are restricted to lots E and F, their demand prices for parcels A through D are zero. Similarly, retail operators have positive demand prices only for lots C and D, while industrial operators must choose from lots A and B. This situation results in two locational shifts from the free market conditions shown in part (a). Retail activity IV shifts from lot F to lot C, while residential activity II shifts from lot C to lot F. Actual behavior under zoning controls is variable, but several consequences are suggested by comparing demand prices of parts (a) and (b). For example, residential unit I would bid $11,000 for parcel E in a free market but would pay $12,000 for the same parcel under zoning. This difference could be attributed to greater certainty that parcels surrounding lot E will remain residential. The risk of a slaughterhouse or other noxious use entering the neighborhood is reduced.[2]

In addition to use restrictions, the development pattern of a community is determined by variables of supply and demand. Demand for land, like all resources, depends on population size, income, and preferences, as well as on the distribution of income and the prices of land and other resources. Demand can be broken down into a

Demand prices for land parcels under free market conditions and government regulation.

| | | Locations (land parcels) | | | | |
	A	B	C	D	E	F
I	7	3	5	0	11*	1
II	0	0	17*	4	9	8
III	9	2	2	7*	4	6
IV	2	0	13	3	7	9*
V	11*	2	4	5	9	0
VI	9	4*	13	4	7	7

Activities (or people)

(a)

| | | Zones | | | | |
| | | Industrial | | Commercial | | Residential |
		A	B	C	D	E	F
Residence	I	0	0	0	0	12*	4
Residence	II	0	0	0	0	9	9*
Retail	III	0	0	4	7*	0	0
Retail	IV	0	0	13*	5	0	0
Industry	V	11*	2	0	0	0	0
Industry	VI	9	4*	0	0	0	0

(b)

number of subareas: housing, industrial, commercial, office, and so forth. The supply of land is fixed, but the supply of developed land (or development) is affected by the goals of developers and the state of development technology—and most importantly, by the cost of the factors of production: land, labor, and capital. Other sectors of the economy are all competing for these resources. For example, labor can be used to construct buildings or automobiles; capital can be invested in housing or in oil development; and land can be allocated to houses, offices, agriculture, or other uses. Awareness of these factors is essential to understanding urban land-use planning, as public sector planning directly affects the land use development process and markets.

The Process

At the local level the development process can be examined as one in which virgin land is changed to urban uses and existing urban uses are sometimes continued, terminated, or changed to new uses through conversions or redevelopment. In the initial stage of the development process rural land might have been used for dairy farming for the past one hundred years but, due to the growth of a nearby metropolitan area, has acquired development potential. The second stage occurs when a potential buyer has actually contacted the farmer and they have entered into discussions regarding sale of the land. The critical stage is reached when a developer has made the decision to purchase the land and programming for urban uses occurs. The fourth stage sees actual development of the land. The conversion from rural to urban uses is complete in stage five, when a residential unit or other land use is established.

The development process is thus a series of stages, with different actors involved in the decisions which lead to transitions from one stage to the next. Each of the actors has different concerns,

and a variety of public sector agencies are involved at various stages. Land use planners are employed by private sector development firms as well as public sector regulating agencies. Land use planning is a management process in which development occurs according to overall community goals and objectives, influenced by the personal goals of the individual actors in both the private and public sectors.

The Actors

Different actors make decisions at each stage of the development process. Similarly, different public agencies may exert control at each stage. For example, if the community zones land, the developer must at some point obtain the desired classification; whether residence, office, or industrial. Though rezoning might feasibly occur at any point, the developer's concern for the correct zoning category begins when the parcel is first considered as a possible site.

Marion Clawson describes the relationship among the actors in the development process as a combination of cooperation and competition.[3] The actors must cooperate to some extent so that land can be made available for construction. The various actors are competitive, however, in that they may all desire the same site or need similar rezonings for competitive developments. They are also competitive to the extent that their interests conflict.

It is appropriate to begin with *home buyers* when discussing the actors in the process because housing construction is the largest use of urban land. The decision to purchase a home frequently corresponds with some change in the life of the individual—a job promotion resulting in higher income or a job move resulting in relocation, the family may have grown, or the present neighborhood may be changing in some way undesirable to the homeowner. Home buyers often expect the new neighborhood to be maintained so that their housing, commonly their largest investment, will retain its value or even appreciate.

Another group of actors in the land use process represent the *home-building industry,* characterized by a large number of firms operating at a relatively small scale. The *owner-builder* represents the noncommercial end of the home-building spectrum. Owner-builders are generally not familiar with specialized building techniques or with the government approval process (building permits, zoning approvals, compliance with building codes, etc.). A second type of builder is the *general contractor,* who contracts to build housing on land owned by another. A general contractor has specialized knowledge of the building industry as well as familiarity with the regulatory industry. He or she is generally limited to the techniques of the industry at a given point in time. Additionally, the smaller general contractors seldom realize scale economies in terms of purchasing, advertising or marketing. The large-scale, or *operative, builder* represents the most commercial end of the spectrum in terms of units constructed, knowledge of building techniques and the regulatory process, and ability to realize scale economies. Operative builders are capturing an increasingly larger share of the housing market in the United States, particularly for homes in the middle-and upper-middle price ranges.

Land owners make up another category of actors. They may be farmers, developers, or speculators who have purchased lands specifically for later development or sale.

The public sector affects the land development process through its *elected officials.* This group must make final decisions on zoning ordinances, rezoning, infrastructure needed for development, and public purchase of land for schools, parks, and other uses. These officials frequently rely on the advice of citizens appointed to zoning boards, plan commissions, or boards of zoning appeals. In addition, these officials use information and analysis from *professional urban planners.*

Special interest groups, such as environ-mentalists, are involved in the development process. Sometimes they participate actively, other times they work behind the scenes. Chambers of commerce, neighborhood associations, and political groups also affect the process. The proliferation of such groups in the past decade has complicated and slowed the development procedure, adding to the factors weighed in a development decision, the complexity of public hearings, and the types of permits required. Finally, a critical group of actors is that in control of the source of private funds, the *lenders* and bankers engaged in the money market. These actors have become increasingly significant in recent years. Their role varies somewhat with economic cycles, but the fiscal interests have become a permanent influence on the course of development.

A common characteristic of decision making by all these actors might be uncertainty, due to a lack of information. There are no economic indicators for the typical urban land market, in contrast to the numerous statistics measuring the national economy.

Very little is known about the actual interests and motivations of the individual actors in the land-use process, although research has increased our level of knowledge in the last few years. Shirley Weiss and Edward Kaiser have analyzed three decision factors: (1) *contextual* characteristics; (2) *decision agent* characteristics; and (3) *property* characteristics.[4] Contextual characteristics are basic socioeconomic variables, such as economic structure and growth, as well as basic public policy variables, such as capital improvement programming, zoning and other regulatory powers, and provision of basic public services. The decision agent characteristics vary depending upon the actor. They might include age, income, an individual's investment portfolio, employment, and income expectations. Property characteristics provide information about the land parcels. There are three types of property characteristics: (1) physical characteristics, such as topography; (2) locational characteristics such as, accessibility to employment, schools, or shopping; and (3) institutional site characteristics, such as those imposed by public institutions on the site, including zoning.

Kaiser and Weiss describe a predevelopment landowner whose decision to hold or sell depends on at least two factors: income and satisfaction received from the land and expected future value of the land versus present value. The latter aspect involves factors like the annual holding cost, cost of shifting to another investment, opportunity costs, and time period of investment. The satisfaction received from land might result from farming as a way of life, privacy, or status from ownership. Public policy influences the predevelopment landowner's decision to sell by affecting the land's present and future market value and establishing the owner's expected stream of costs and revenues.

Decision agent characteristics seem to be most influential for the predevelopment landowner. This conclusion is supported by an evaluation by the U.S. Council on Environmental Quality of preferential assessment for the preservation of agricultural land.[5] It concluded that most of the preferential assessment programs were effective only as a means of granting tax relief to farmers. They were not effective in preserving land because of the variety of decision agent characteristics of participating farmers. For the developer, Kaiser and Weiss found that the contextual characteristic of public policy affects expected cost, revenues, and degree of risk. In the developer's decision, expected revenue seems to be far more important than expected cost, since costs are relatively predictable. Ability to predict market demands can determine the developer's success.

Property characteristics are also very important to the developer's decision to purchase and develop land. Appropriate zoning, infrastructure, and public services enhance the social prestige and value of land parcels. Major developers usually have access to choice sites, because they have more capital, greater influence, and more aggressive marketing techniques than smaller firms. Downtown redevelopment and prestigious subdivisions are frequently the preserve of the large developer, while the small developers compete for sites with fewer amenities and for projects smaller in size and impact. The process might be viewed as one in which public policy and large developers jointly determine the location and timing of major urban growth, while small developers and builders fill in the overall scheme. For the individual buying a home, the property characteristics of the actual development, house, and neighborhood, along with the public services available, are most important. Public policy variables affect the journey to work, and decision agent characteristics help determine desirability of residence and neighborhood. Individual preferences are reflected in the manner in which neighborhoods go through life cycles, as families move in, age, and move out. A dramatic illustration is the suburban development in Nassau County, N.Y. It became built up after World War II, and in the 1970s Nassau County had to close a number of educational facilities less than 20 years old. Meanwhile, Suffolk County, the next county out from New York City, was at an earlier stage of the cycle and faced the need for extensive construction of schools.

The End Product

Theories. The land use process described focuses on the conversion of individual parcels of land from rural to urban uses and on the role of public and private sector actors in that conversion. What is the end product of land development? The figure on page 240 depicts three major theories of development that explain the overall structure of cities.[6] The *concentric ring theory* is based on the pioneering work of Ernest Burgess, who identified five zones of land use: (1) a central business district (CBD) representing the center of activity, generally close to the site of the original settlement; (2) a zone of transition, mixing commercial and industrial uses; (3) a low-income housing zone in the metropolitan area, containing older housing units;

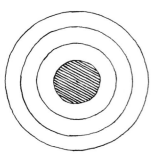

CONCENTRIC
RING

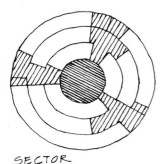

SECTOR

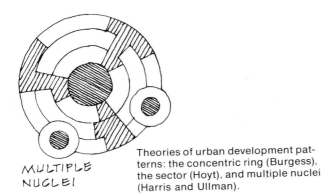

MULTIPLE
NUCLEI

Theories of urban development patterns: the concentric ring (Burgess), the sector (Hoyt), and multiple nuclei (Harris and Ullman).

static while the transition zone enlarges into the central zone. Although this model is very simple, it does have a certain descriptive value.

The *sector theory* was first proposed by Homer Hoyt in 1939. It suggests that cities grow not in strict concentric zones, but rather in sectors of similar types of development. That is, residential areas might expand outward along existing transportation links, topographic features, natural amenities, or the like. Chicago's Gold Coast and north suburbs show this pattern quite clearly.

The *multiple nuclei theory* was developed in 1945 by Chauncy Harris and Edward Ullman, after initial explorations by R. D. McKenzie. It varies from previous views in that the downtown area is not considered to be the only focal point for growth. Land use patterns are seen to develop as a series of nuclei, each with a different function. Each center develops from the spatial interdependence of certain functions. For example, manufacturing and transportation uses may form one nucleus. Likewise, hotels, offices, and transshipment facilities may develop around an airport, such as Chicago's O'Hare Field.

These three theories were developed over the twenty-five-year period from 1920 to 1945, and each added to the knowledge of cities. Over time, however, the concentric zones became sectors as transit and highways elongated land use patterns. Eventually, nuclei developed—or were more formally identified—as transportation and economic development added new dimensions to land uses. Hence, when evaluating the land-use patterns of a large older city, which has undergone such changes, it may be possible to find all three patterns. Rarely do contemporary cities illustrate entirely any one theory of land use.

Urban Sprawl. Urban sprawl is the term frequently applied to describe development patterns in many U.S. cities, but it lacks precise definition. Urban sprawl can refer to at least three different patterns: (1) low-density, continuous development; (2) ribbon development; and (3) leapfrog de-

(4) a middle-income housing zone, frequently including some of the older suburbs; and (5) the outlying zone of newer suburban developments. Given this pattern and a growth situation, each zone is held to invade the outer adjacent zone, with a rippling effect. With decline, the outer zones remain

velopment. Low-density patterns have been described as sprawl for at least 50 years, as housing and related land uses have occupied ever-increasing amounts of land. Ribbon development has also existed for a long time. It describes development that follows streetcar lines, subways, and commuter railroads, leaving the interstices undeveloped. Highways promote ribbon development, although the limited access interstate system also encourages concentration around interchanges. Leapfrog development describes urban growth not as a continuous movement from established cities, but as a skipping over of parcels of land because of property or decision agent characteristics. Low density and leapfrog urban sprawl are more often criticized, since the former supposedly wastes the land resource, while the latter raises the cost of development by requiring a spread of highways and utilities as well as increased travel time and energy consumption.

Until recently it was commonly assumed that urban sprawl was costly and inefficient, although little was actually known about its effects. The Real Estate Research Corporation has prepared a study of the problem for three federal agencies, the Council on Environmental Quality, HUD and the EPA.[7] The study sought to analyze costs of development for a variety of housing types in three hypothetical communities. It covered a wide range of costs, ranging from capital and operating costs for residential development, schools, infrastructure, public facilities and land, to environmental effects and personal costs, such as travel time, traffic accidents, and use of discretionary time. A major conclusion was that costs were almost always relatively higher for low-density development. The overall conclusion, which supports long standing criticisms, was that denser developments cost less than low-density sprawl developments. Most of these costs seem to be related to density of development. Thus, the costs of sprawl can be reduced through land use planning, primarily when planning promotes denser development.

A number of factors account for the three development patterns categorized as urban sprawl. Since each of the public and private sector actors involved responds to different forces, collective decisions are not always possible. Physical features channel development. Public development of infrastructure frequently occurs in such a way that new development, usually at lower densities than existing development, is favored. Freeways have vastly expanded land resources available for development at little cost to the primary beneficiaries: landowners, developers, and subsequent residents. The same is true for additional infrastructure, such as storm and sanitary sewers, often financed with federal government grants. Public regulation, usually at the local level, also contributes to low-density suburban development by encouraging it in rural areas, which have fewer development controls. Recently such rural communities have begun to adopt strict regulations or *growth controls* in response to what is viewed as excessive development. Federal government policies, such as capital gains taxes and FHA mortgages, tend to favor single-family home development at the expense of denser, multifamily construction. Urban sprawl is created by all these factors. Effecting major changes in undesirable development patterns require governmental policy revisions at all levels, as well as new behavior in the private sector.

Exclusionary Practices. Existing land use planning and regulation has been criticized as contributing to the exclusion of racial and economic minorities from large parts of the metropolitan areas, particularly suburban municipalities. Anthony Downs has argued that governmental policies generally lead to a dual environment, with the system serving the majority quite well and the minority quite poorly:

> Urban development in America is frequently described as "chaotic" and "unplanned" because it produces what many critics call "urban sprawl." But economically, politically, and socially, American urban development occurs in a systematic, highly predictable manner. It leads to precisely the

results desired by those who dominate it. As a consequence, most urban households with incomes above the national median or somewhat lower enjoy relatively high quality neighborhood environments.[8]

Downs states that a dual pattern is created first by requiring that every American household live in a decent housing unit and defining decent according to prevailing middle-class standards; then by differentially enforcing regulations so that decent housing conditions are maintained in the suburbs, and ignored in central city areas. To those who would argue that the existence of suburbs and ghettos is simply the result of a natural, free market process, Downs says:

> On the contrary, it is created, sustained, and furthered by public policies and laws that prevent free markets from operating. Those policies and laws are designed to protect the vested interests of the urban majority at a terrible cost to the poor who constitute a relative minority in our society.[9]

One of the reasons for this exclusivity (and one of the reasons for the general acceptance of zoning in the United States) is the problem of externalities in an urban environment. The accompanying figure indicates hypothetical construction costs for four houses in an urban area. Three of the houses are in the same general price range, $75,000 each. The fourth house, however, located on parcel C, is to be constructed at a cost of only $30,000. If these four housing units were constructed at the same time and then offered for sale, their selling prices would not precisely reflect the construction costs. Parcel C's high-cost neighbors would be a positive benefit to the house on lot C and raise its selling price from approximately $35,000 to $40,000 (disregarding lot values). But this house would have the opposite effect on lot houses A, B, and D, which might sell for only $70,000. The nonmarket transfer of value to the house on lot C is called an externality. It would be in the economic self-interest of owners, A, B, and D to encourage the public sector to regulate development so that a house of like or higher value would be guaranteed for parcel C; in other words, to seek to prevent negative externalities from affecting their investments. These regulations can take the form of zoning classifications that prohibit multifamily construction in an area of single-family homes or that prevent the construction of smaller single-family homes. Such minimum house or lot size require-

Externalities among residential uses.

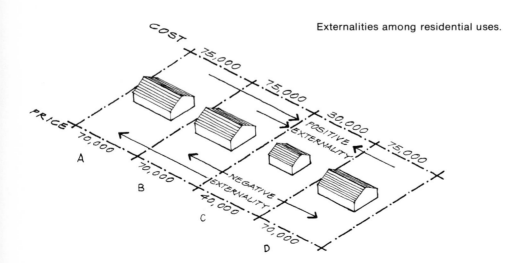

ments have the effect of creating an income floor in terms of those who could afford to move into the area. The result is a strong clustering by income and the typical one-class suburb or development.

Land use planning and land use regulations have become the foci of those seeking to secure equal housing opportunities for minorities. Three approaches have been used. First, efforts are made to protect against direct racial discrimination through acts such as local fair housing legislation. Second, efforts are made to increase the supply of low-and moderate-income housing, often with the aid of federal government subsidies. Third, dispersal of low-and moderate-income housing is attempted from areas of minority and poverty concentrations in central cities to outlying areas.

Increased legal attacks on land use regulations that have exclusionary effects are directly related to federal housing activities in the 1960s. Until then, the public approach to housing lower-income people in the United States was publicly constructed housing. This usually required formation of a local housing authority, generally having powers to operate only within the jurisdiction of the municipality. It is not surprising that most such housing authorities were created by central city governing bodies rather than by suburban municipalities. During the Johnson Administration, however, housing aid was made available to limited profit-making and non-profit sponsors, such as religious organizations, who were free to seek locations for projects anywhere in the metropolitan area. These groups could purchase land on the free market and then seek the necessary density which would allow sales prices or rents affordable by low-and moderate-income persons. Thus developer/sponsors had an economic self-interest in attacking zoning ordinances that blocked their projects. Efforts have now evolved from the litigation over exclusionary land use plans to efforts to include low-income groups and racial minorities through land use plans and regulations, rather than to exclude them. These so-called *inclusionary* land-use programs apply the

government's regulatory power over land to increase the number of low- and moderate-income housing units within the community's boundaries, frequently in consideration of the overall needs of the metropolitan area.

Environmental Concerns. Environmental concerns represent still another attack on traditional land use planning and regulatory approaches. The degradation of the environment is seen as part of the typical land development process, because development has resulted in ecological (especially water runoff and quality) problems. Sprawl has resulted in dependence on the automobile and, consequently, air pollution. Historically, neither developers nor public bodies have given much attention to environment-development relationships. However, the new level of environmental awareness, and tighter federal and state environmental controls, have led to a reevaluation of land use planning and regulation. The capacity of land to support development with a minimum of environmental harm is now a starting place for much land-use planning.

Planning and Reform

It is clear that the traditional land development process has not led to fully satisfactory land use patterns. There is a need for continuing land use planning and regulation, as well as for reform in the process of using land. Traditionally, the urban planner has approached the problem via the physical master land-use and transportation plan or the comprehensive plan. The former attempted to lay out future patterns of land use in response to projected needs and a perceived community consensus as to the ideal urban environment. Some of these plans had, and continue to have, major impacts on subsequent development, while others have had little apparent effect. The land use plan, now usually part of a more comprehensive urban plan, remains as the primary planning vehicle for land use planning. Zoning ordinances, subdivision regulations, and other rules provide the implementation component. However, the emphasis is shifting from the physical plan to more rational regulation of the process.

The reformers seek to rationalize the planning and development process, modify the form of the end product, and/or change the roles of the various actors in the process. It is clear that the urban plan-ner's ability to predict long-range future activity and land use needs and to prescribe appropriate physi-cal patterns is limited, but to a certain point, this is land-use planning. In a practical sense, the question is not how to plan, but rather how to improve the en-tire system of land development and use. Much of the present concern focuses on the public sector's

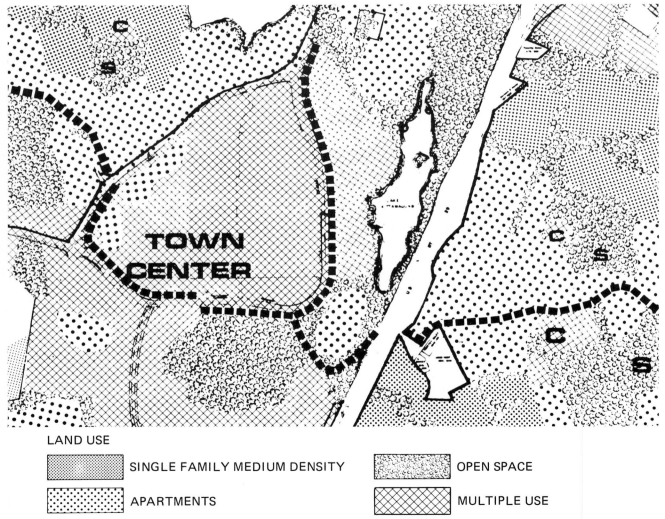

LAND USE

SINGLE FAMILY MEDIUM DENSITY

APARTMENTS

OPEN SPACE

MULTIPLE USE

Land use plan: part of Columbia, Maryland, New Town. (Courtesy of design department of the Howard Research and Development: a project of the Rouse Company and the Connecticut General Insurance Company)

Urban area land use plan: Tenth Street area, Atlanta, by Nichols, Carter, and Seay/Grant, Architects. (Courtesy of Leon Eplan and the city of Atlanta)

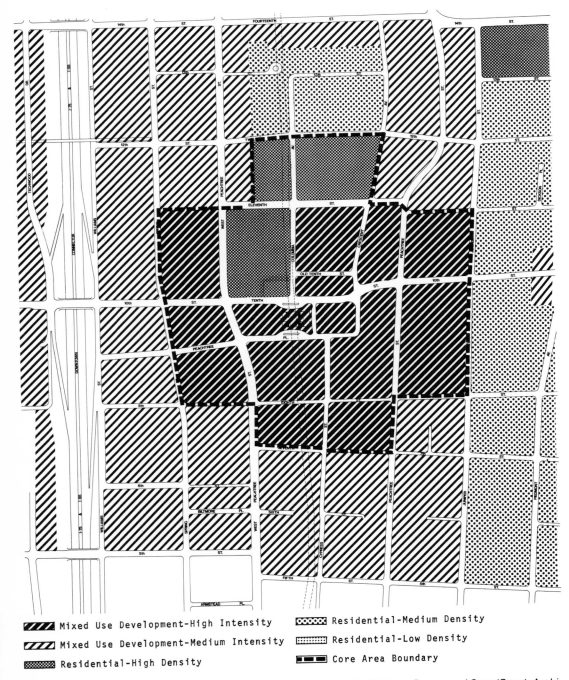

Mixed Use Development-High Intensity   Residential-Medium Density

Mixed Use Development-Medium Intensity   Residential-Low Density

Residential-High Density   Core Area Boundary

Urban area development intensity plan: Tenth Street Area, Atlanta, by Nichols, Carter, and Seay/Grant, Architects. (Courtesy of Leon Eplan and the city of Atlanta)

responsibility for implementing land-use plans and regulating land development and use, which involves zoning, subdivision regulation, and other legal systems. Substantial reform is most likely to come with a reordering of government powers, changes in the methods of regulatory authority, stricter controls under existing authority, and more knowledge about the impacts of land development and use.

PUBLIC REGULATION OF LAND USE: CONTROLS AND LEGAL LIMITS

The primary sources of governmental authority to regulate the use of land are the police power, eminent domain, and the power to tax. The police power regulates actions and activities to protect the health, safety, morals, and general welfare of the community without compensation to individuals. Eminent domain, the power of condemnation, allows government to take property for public benefit with compensation to the affected individuals. Taxation affects land use, but is generally not considered to be a direct method of land-use regulation.

Zoning: History

Zoning is the division of land according to building design and use. Land in most incorporated areas of the United States is zoned by local governments, and it may be developed, built upon, and used only according to the way it is zoned. The author of a leading treatise on zoning describes it in this way:

> Comprehensive zoning consists of the division of the whole territory of the municipality into districts, and the imposition of restrictions upon the use of land in such district. . . . Zoning regulations are drafted and enacted by the legislative authority, and they may be enforced by municipal action. They permit a municipality to apply constant and consistent pressure upon landowners to the end

that land use will be guided by the community plan and the public interest.[10]

Cities have used zoning since the late nineteenth century. The first modern ordinance was enacted in New York City in 1916, but it wasn't until 1926 that the U.S. Supreme Court considered the legality of comprehensive zoning controls. In the landmark decision of *City of Euclid v. Ambler Realty Company,* the Court discussed the need for an imposed pattern of land use and upheld the concept of comprehensive or Euclidean zoning:

> [T]hese . . . reasons [health and security of children, fire and traffic safety, decreased noise, healthier environment with residential zoning] are sufficiently cogent to preclude us from saying, as it must be said before the ordinance can be declared unconstitutional, that such provisions are clearly arbitrary and unreasonable, having no substantial relation to the public health, safety, morals, and general welfare.[11]

The *Euclid* decision gave a legal imprimatur to local controls on land use through zoning. It was to remain virtually unqualified by the Supreme Court for fifty years.

The process of zoning was meant to separate land uses so that each parcel might reach its highest and best use without interference from an adjacent use. An efficient, workable, planned system was the goal. To this end industrial zones were routinely separated from commercial zones; and residential zones set apart from both industrial and commercial districts. Zoning techniques were at first quite simple; zoning separated the community into three basic districts and prohibited uses considered harmful from each area. (Table 10-1 represents a typical zoning hierarchy.) Residential zones were absolutely protected from the more harmful intrusions of commercial and industrial uses. Industry was prohibited in commercial districts, but homes were allowed because their effects on commercial business were not considered negative. Industrial

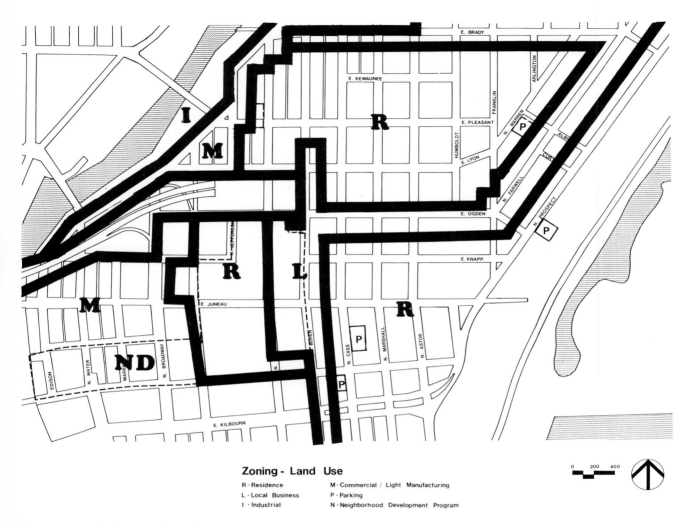

Zoning - Land Use

R - Residence   M - Commercial / Light Manufacturing
L - Local Business   P - Parking
I - Industrial   N - Neighborhood Development Program

Typical zoning land use category map.

TABLE 10-1

A Typical Zoning Hierarchy

A	Agricultural	O	Office
P	Public	I	Institutional
R-1	Residential, low density	C-1	Outlying commercial
R-2	Residential, medium density	C-2	Central commercial
R-3	Residential, high density	Ind.-1	Light industrial
C.U.P.	Community unit plan	Ind.-2	Heavy industrial

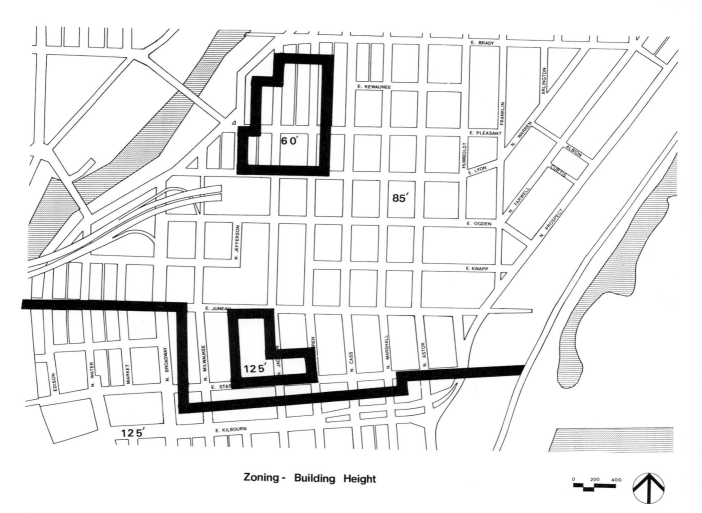

Zoning - Building Height

Typical zoning building height limit map.

zones often contained all three uses, since higher uses there could not negatively affect industry.

The original rationale behind all this regulation was to promote the public's health, safety, moral protection, and welfare. Specifically, zoning prevented overcrowding, maintained property values, encouraged stable and homogeneous neighborhoods, and controlled traffic flow. Regulation of competing businesses, though not generally acknowledged as a goal, was nevertheless a frequent result of zoning. More recently zoning has been upheld as a valid tool for furthering the cultural, historical, and aesthetic objectives of a community. The extent to which zoning and related land use laws may be used to control, direct, or halt growth of business or population has not yet been settled by the courts, but

LAND USE PLANNING

some municipalities now are zoning for growth control and using other local powers, such as control over utility extensions, for a similar purpose.

Historically, local officials in the U.S. have overzoned, particularly high income residential areas. At first, little thought was given to controlling or directing growth. Land use theory only covered simplifying public services, protecting single family life, and promoting efficiency by clustering similar uses. Zoning and public services largely followed rather than guided development. Thus a city established residential zones around both old and developing single-family areas. However, if a few commercial uses began to change the character of a neighborhood, that change might justify a zoning amendment, even though maintaining the neighborhood might have been wiser. On the other hand, strict adherence to the clustering of similar uses could block development in areas where the market would conveniently have taken it. If an area was mostly residential, attempts to justify commercial zoning were usually rejected regardless of suitability of the land for commercial business or of any need for more commercial growth in the community.

Whether or not local officials in the 1920s and 1930s believed zoning would actually determine land development, such government direction of land use did not occur. Though the system on paper was fairly rigid, when market forces met a zoning roadblock, municipal officials under pressure to allow development (actually, they considered any growth positive for the community) cleared the way by fashioning a way around existing zoning or simply by recommending rezoning. In this way, ad hoc changes in the zoning system caused by market conditions became a part of land use regulation in America. Not all requests for change were granted, of course, but enough flexibility was introduced into zoning procedures to render it likely that local government would respond to economic pressure in determining type of land use, location, rate of growth, pattern, and appearance.

Implementing Zoning Controls

In the 1920s a model zoning ordinance, the *Standard State Zoning Enabling Act,* was prepared by the Department of Commerce, and adopted in some form by many states. The Act established a text and map as the two elements of a zoning ordinance, with the text defining zones in terms of permitted and conditional uses and the map locating each zone within the community. The model act set out procedures for changing a zoning designation, established a zoning commission to advise the local legislative body, and creating a board of adjustment to allow variances and conditional uses or exceptions where appropriate. In the standard act the local legislature is empowered to:

> . . . regulate and restrict the height, number of stories, and size of buildings and other structures; the percentage of a lot that may be occupied; the size of yards, courts, and other open spaces; the density of population; and the location and use of buildings, structures, and land for trade, industry, residence, or other purposes.[12]

Most modern zoning ordinances today contain the act's four basic categories of regulation: *use, height, bulk,* and *density.* The text contains a list of permitted, accessory, and conditional uses for each zone. Height regulations vary by district, usually with the highest construction permitted in the downtown district. Bulk limits primarily refer to horizontal regulation, such as building setbacks. Density refers to the number of units or people allowed per parcel, and it is controlled through such techniques as minimum lot sizes, yard sizes, setbacks, and limited floor area ratios. Intensive uses are those with relatively higher densities or a greater variety of uses.

The *timing* and *classification* of land use under traditional zoning presented a rigidity that was quickly modified by municipalities. A variety of techniques and characterizations made the system more adaptable (perhaps too adaptable) than it first appeared. Possibly one of the more disingenuous maneuvers, still prevalent today, was the wholesale granting of variances. Technically a variance from existing design restrictions or uses prescribed in the ordinance is granted only upon a showing of unnecessary hardship caused by unique circumstances relating to the particular parcel. In some jurisdictions variances from use restrictions were at one time rare, but today both use and area variances are more easily granted, with area variances often allowed upon a showing of only practical difficulty. The original requirements of proof for a variance have been relaxed. A zoning board will, for example, weigh any harm to the public from the variance against harm to the owner if existing zoning is strictly applied. It may even base its decision upon a consideration of whether or not there is a lack of reasonable economic return on the property as zoned.

Special exceptions and *conditional uses* are authorized in the zoning ordinance, but these too are sometimes employed so that local officials can look more closely at the use in question. Compromises beyond those set out in the zoning text might precede the grant of an exception or conditional use. *Buffer zones* impose stronger controls on certain properties in order to establish intermediate territory between incompatible *uses. Holding zones* protect existing (usually low-density) uses from pressures for rezoning to more intensive uses. *Spot zoning,* or rezoning of a parcel of land to a use classification different from that of its surrounding area, is unconstitutional if found to be an arbitrary exercise of local authority, which does not conform to comprehensive planning and which is detrimental to adjacent property. However, when a reasonable relation to legitimate zoning purposes can be shown (for example, in a rezoning for historic purposes), spot zoning may be upheld.

Another technique that makes land use regulation more responsive to particular circumstances is *subdivision controls. General plat approval* is delegated to localities by *subdivision enabling acts.* More specific regulations are then developed by the local planning commission or legislative authority to conform with official maps and comprehensive community plans. Street grading, curbing and lighting; density; drainage; and utility extensions are all arranged by way of the subdivision approval process in two steps: *preliminary* and *final plat approval.*

Apart from administrative routes to zoning change, landowners also have recourse to the local legislature and to the courts. The legislative body will grant zoning amendments to the zoning text or map upon a showing of consistency of the proposed change with the comprehensive plan. Consultation with the plan commission always occurs, although its advice is not binding upon the legislative body. A public hearing must be held before the amendment is put to a vote. The orthodox rule is that in order to justify a zoning amendment, it must be shown that a mistake in the original ordinance or a subsequent change in circumstances occurred, but many municipalities have relaxed this general guide. Some simply inquire whether or not the amendment relates directly to public health, safety, morals, or welfare. The importance of the generally stated enabling act requirement that the zoning amendment be made in accordance with the comprehensive plan varies according to the municipality, the status of local planning, and, not infrequently, the land use background of the reviewing court. Inconsistency of an amendment with the plan is always forgivable; inconsistency with the public welfare, as currently defined, is not.

Zoning Today

In the 1970s local governments began to use zoning as a mechanism for continuing overview of development. The ad hoc nature of the system contradicts those enabling statutes mandating consistency with the comprehensive plan, but if zoning is still a case-by-case proposition, at least some types of cases are apt to be more closely scrutinized.

Planned Unit Development (PUD) review is an example. PUDs are large development proposals; when they are brought before zoning officials, they are sent through a series of planning steps until a

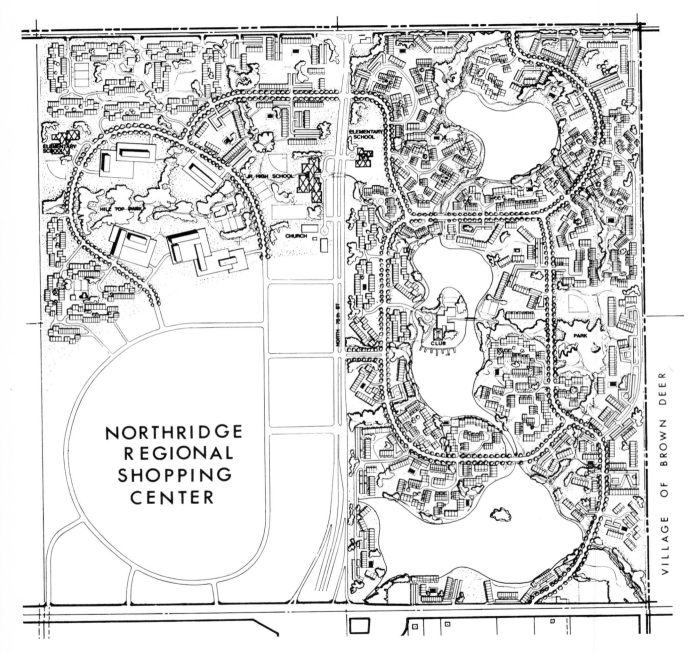

NORTHRIDGE
REGIONAL
SHOPPING
CENTER

VILLAGE OF BROWN DEER

A planned unit development: Northridge Lakes, by Lawrence Halprin (courtesy of William Wenzler and Associates.)

finalized project plan is approved. The legislative body first authorizes a PUD district as a type of *floating zone*. A developer then introduces an initial development plan for approval. Subsequently, developer and plan commission agree on a mix of residential, commercial, and sometimes industrial uses, with most efficient and flexible use of the land the objective. Benefits may be creative land development, better use of open space, and greater environmental protection, but there may be delays in the monitoring process and there is no guarantee of final approval. The procedures and standards of Planned Unit Development allow for planning review of land use at the time the use is proposed and ensure compliance with zoning objectives even while more flexible use of land is arranged.

Incentive zoning creates a trade-off system between landowner and municipality. In return for an amenity (such as a public plaza) a developer may be allowed to build more rentable floor area than normally allowed by the zoning ordinance. Special theater and historic districts are examples of incentive zoning. Its increased popularity reflects the growing sophistication of local land use systems. What may seem sophisticated to the regulator, however, may look intrusive to the regulatee.

With closer control over land use comes less freedom for the landowner and the market, and attacks on stricter land-use regulations accompany each new local control. The complaint, of course, stems from the private landowner's unhappiness with delays in development, restricted use (or in the case of required dedication of land for public use, total loss of a parcel of land), and reduced profits.

The growth not only of single developments but of entire communities can now be directed through zoning and related local controls. Utility extensions and provision of other public facilities; smaller yearly quotas of building permits; the setting of maximum allowable population; creation of moratoria to freeze development for periods of time; and downzoning large areas (that is, reducing allowable density) are all mechanisms used by local government in the 1970s to direct land use. While early twentieth-century zoners may never have dreamed of controlling economic growth, their successors do not question it.

Although conscious control of growth through zoning ordinances is a relatively new governmental objective, for decades many communities encouraged the construction of middle-and upper-income housing and discouraged residences for families with lower incomes through aforementioned exclusionary zoning. One New Jersey state court judge has described exclusionary zoning as:

> . . . the dark side of municipal land use regulation—the use of the zoning power to advance the parochial interests of the municipality at the expense of the surrounding region and to establish and perpetuate social and economic segregation.[13]

Despite legal challenges to growth control and exclusionary zoning, both practices remain popular. One of the major justifications of zoning the Supreme Court relied on in the *Euclid* case was the greater security, health, traffic safety, and peacefulness of residential areas when they are not zoned for apartments. Economic exclusivity in residential zoning has been accepted ever since the *Euclid* decision. The evils attendant on apartment houses have been outlined in hundreds of state court zoning cases; economic discrimination, except when linked to recognized constitutional rights (such as voting), has never been elevated by the courts to the status of an equal protection violation.

Recently perceived land-use problem areas include the natural environment and energy use. One example of adapting zoning to environmental notions is the use of *performance standards* instead of or in addition to regular zoning. Performance standards set upper limits on measurable characteristics of land use, such as noise level and water and air pollution. Rather than focus on permissible uses as the standard zoning code does, performance standards focus on permissible environmental effects of uses. Given existing problems with such programs as housing code and building code enforcement, however, it is obvious that the necessary monitoring and compliance mechanisms for performance standards are not easily achieved. This idea represents another swing away from a theory that simply allocates uses to their proper zones and amends the system to allow reasonable uses and economic returns without controlling environmental effects. Preoccupation with energy sources and use will also make itself felt in land use regulation. The first regulations to encourage the use of solar energy systems have been added to ordinary zoning restrictions.

Other Land Use Controls

By virtue of their *police power,* local municipalities may promote the public health, safety, morals, and welfare in several ways. A city directs traffic, licenses liquor stores, tests grade schoolers' hearing, and requires hot running water in homes. Localities receive other powers from the state as well. The other two primary sources of municipal authority that relate to land are *eminent domain* and *taxation.*

Eminent domain allows the government to take private land for the public benefit after proceedings that fairly notify and offer the property owner a judicial hearing and after just compensation to the owner. Once public need for the land has been established, the owner is limited primarily to challenging the sufficiency of the compensation. Consequently, a landowner has less recourse under eminent domain proceedings than he or she has under zoning regulations.

Eminent domain, however, is not as broad an authority as police power. Only for projects benefiting the public can land be taken away. The distinction is that a government takes land under eminent domain for the public good, while it regulates under police power for the prevention of public harm. Since the Constitution declares public protection from harm to be a necessary responsibility of government, citizens are not compensated when the government restricts uses of land under the police power.

This benefit-harm distinction between eminent domain and police power may be more a convenient characterization than a real difference. However greatly one admires red clay roof tiles, it is somewhat difficult to accept the idea that a town's imposition under a zoning ordinance of Spanish-style architectural design on all homes is preventing harm to the community. One might similarly take issue with a claim that eminent domain appropriations for urban renewal in the mid-twentieth century created overall public benefit. Yet this distinction remains with us, and arguments abound on the precise dividing line between an eminent domain *taking* of land, which requires citizen compensation, and a police power regulation, which does not.

The most obvious example of the third major constitutional source of authority of land use, the taxing power, is the *property tax.* A major generator of local revenue, the property tax causes numerous problems. Because of its regressiveness and subsequent burden on poorer families, properties are unequitably assessed, and delinquency often results. Inner-city housing rehabilitation, often desired by local officials and promoted with low-cost loans, leads to higher assessments and higher taxes. Property owners and landlords are understandably reluctant to upgrade their properties. Differential tax rates contribute to the movement of business and industry from city to suburb, further undermining economic stability within cities. Many suggestions have been made relating to the use of the property tax to improve land development rather than add to deterioration and abandonment. Some cities have lowered property taxes on home improvement for a certain number of years. Tax incentives and abatements may be used to keep industry in a city; conversely, special assessments may be placed on undesirable land uses. Fourteen states authorize tax incremental financing, using increased property taxes resulting from development to pay for redevelopment. Numerous studies have examined the effects of the property tax on urban blight, and most have concluded major revisions of the tax are in order if we wish even to neutralize its present effects on land use and development.

Legal Limitations to Land Use Regulations

State Delegation. Cities have no inherent authority to make or enforce laws. Instead, a local government must be delegated its legal authority, whether through provisions for home rule charters in state constitutions or through various statutes. Yet, because of the history of centering the responsibility for land use regulation on the locality, the fact that only state and federal governments are sovereign is often forgotten. It should be emphasized that the state has preemptive power over its lesser governmental units. When a state decides to legislate in a certain area, when it moves to repeal delegations of authority to cities, or when it passes environmental legislation that conflicts with existing local regulations, it is acting legally. It may repeal authority formerly given to its subunits, and it may preempt local laws through its own. Hawaii and Vermont, for example, have preempted most land use authority from their subordinate units of government. The federal government has certain preemptive power over state law. Consequently, when local officials and other citizens object to moves toward greater regional, state, and federal involvement in land use control, they may not resist these controls by asserting that their rights are being usurped. Currently, states may be establishing historic land use decisions and regulations, but legally their authority is clear.

Zoning and the Police Power. Because a zoning ordinance is legislation, it enjoys a *presumption of validity*. In other words, a reviewing court will presume that the ordinance bears a reasonable relation to police power purposes. Challengers to the or-

dinance must then take the burden of proving that it has no reasonable or substantial relationship to proper zoning purposes. Unless a court is convinced that a locality has zoned in an arbitrary or capricious manner, the challenger will not prevail.

An attack on zoning may take on an entire ordinance, part of the ordinance, or a single application of it. Since the *Euclid* case the overall concept of a comprehensive zoning ordinance has not been challenged. However, if an ordinance were passed under a model zoning enabling act and required conformance with a comprehensive planning effort, if no planning existed in the community, the validity of the entire ordinance might be challenged for failure to conform to statutory requirements. Or, if industrial zoning were placed on land entirely unusable for industry, this part of the city's zoning ordinance could be attacked as arbitrary and capricious.

By far the majority of challenges to zoning regulations occur in relation to a particular piece of property. The zoning application may be defective in a number of ways: it may be unreasonable under police power limits; it may be an abuse of authority because the act was not within the city's delegated powers; or it may be unconstitutional as applied. The standard complaint of a landowner is diminution in value or use. At some point a property's zoning designation may reduce its value to such a degree that a court will hold the land has been effectively *taken* by the government. When this point is reached the court requires governmental compensation for the land's reasonable value according to eminent domain theory. Similarly, if the development of the land is so restricted by zoning or other police power regulations that no reasonable use under applicable zoning remains, a taking can again be found and compensation ordered. In this instance both the police power reasonableness standard and the constitutional protection against takings are involved.

What constitutes unreasonable loss of use or value? The notion of general welfare, upon which courts sustain or strike police power acts, changes as society changes. There exists no formula a landowner can check before going to court. Economic burden to the owner is one measure of reason-ableness, but it is not conclusive. Land use cases re-peatedly balance loss to the landowner with preven-tion of perceived harm to the public, while empha-sizing the latter's flexibility.

An example of changing notions of general wel-fare is provided in the case of *Just v. Marinette County*, in which the landowners were not permitted to fill part of their property in order to build a resi-dence, because the state's wetlands protection act imposed such severe restrictions. The court dis-cussed the scope of police power and the kind of balancing test necessary:

> The real issue is whether the conservancy district provisions and the wetlands filling restrictions are unconstitutional because they amount to a con-structive taking of the Justs' land without compen-sation. Marinette County and the state of Wisconsin argue the restrictions of the conservancy district and wetlands provisions constitute a proper exer-cise of the police power of the state and do not so severely limit the use or depreciate the value of the land as to constitute a taking without compensa-tion.
>
> To state the issue in more meaningful terms, it is a conflict between the public interest in stopping the despoilation of natural resources, which our citizens until recently have taken as inevitable and for granted, and an owner's asserted right to use his property as he wishes. . . . Whether a taking has occurred depends upon whether "the restriction practically or substantially renders the land useless for all reasonable purposes." . . . The loss caused the individual must be weighed to determine if it is more than he should bear.[14]

The *Just* court balanced the landowners' losses against what it termed public rights in existing natu-ral wetlands resources and concluded:

> An owner of land has no absolute and unlimited right to change the essential natural character of his land so as to use it for a purpose for which it was unsuited in its natural state and which injures the rights of others. The exercise of the police

power in zoning must be reasonable and we think it is not an unreasonable exercise of that power to prevent harm to public rights by limiting the use of private property to its natural uses.[15]

The plaintiffs had argued that eminent domain should apply because a public benefit in improved, protected wetlands was the purpose of the regula-tion. The court answered this by reiterating the public's *present* right in preserving wetlands. A reg-ulation maintaining that right would be a protection from harm, falling within the scope of the police power.

Other Issues in Land Use Law

Aside from the police power versus eminent domain problem, constitutional error can be based upon the *equal protection clause* of the *Fourteenth Amend-ment*. In such situations a landowner would claim he or she is similarly situated with other landowners but is being treated differently for no reason relating to the public health, safety, or welfare. The constitu-tional guarantee of due process before a govern-mental taking of an individual's life, liberty or prop-erty is called into question when a police power regulation is applied but a taking is claimed. Due process is interpreted today largely as a notion of fairness in procedure rather than fairness in sub-stance of the law. The court thus will not inquire into the utility or good sense of the legislation, but will strike a police power regulation only upon the arbi-trary and capricious basis. *Due process* assures that the law is applied in a fair way.

First Amendment issues have also been raised in land use litigation. Growth controls and other re-strictive zoning regulations such as limits on the number of unrelated persons living together, lead to claims that a city is violating rights to travel, privacy, and free association. Exclusionary zoning triggers attacks on the basis of racial discrimination and un-reasonable separation of people based on their eco-nomic status. Laws regulating billboards and other advertising, such as residential "For Sale" signs, are challenged as interfering with First Amendment freedoms of speech and petition. Finally, the claim of a taking is always possible. The *Just* case presents an example of the taking argument in the context of recently passed environmental controls.

Trends In Land Use Regulations

Increased interest in the comprehensive plan requirement exists today, in part because of greater state and federal involvement in land use. There is a general recognition in the public sector that government must raise its present level of coordination and reasoned decision making. The ad hoc process of zoning is seen by many as a poor way to ensure the efficient and environmentally safe use of land. The majority view may still support the idea that zoning is planning, but increasing numbers of courts are requiring review of zoning applications in light of existing planning. The plan for the community therefore is used as evidence of the reasonableness of an ordinance. A growing minority of courts requires actual consistency with the adopted comprehensive plan. As a result,

> Developers and citizen groups now recognize that community policy is most effectively influenced by challenging the planning assumptions at the adop-

tion stage rather than waiting for a focused land use controversy.[16]

Though most land use control remains with localities and is still discretionary and parochial, greater regional and state involvement in land use is emerging. Fourteen states have enacted shorelands/wetlands laws; seven identify and regulate environmental areas designated critical areas; twenty-two regulate power plant siting. All levels of government are applying environmental laws, from national air and water pollution control acts, to state wetlands acts, to local performance standards.

The concept of transfer of development rights is gaining in acceptance. This concept holds that the bundle of rights associated with land ownership is severable; hence, development rights may be traded. In order to protect against some loss to the public good, such as a scenic, historic, or other special area, the development rights may be traded or transferred to another land parcel.[17]

There is a need for growth management in many areas of the country today, yet legal and planning issues have yet to be addressed by concerned cities in a fair and rational manner. A critical planning question is the extent to which the types of regulation existing today actually relate to the major problems facing cities and metropolitan areas of the United States.

NOTES

1. William K. Reilly, "Six Myths about Land Use in the United States," in Randall W. Scott, et al. (eds.), *Management and Control of Growth,* vol. 1 (Washington, D.C.: Urban Land Institute, 1974), pp. 100–104.

2. Early in the century it was widely assumed that apartment buildings constituted noxious uses when allowed in single-family areas because of the noise, traffic, and unsightliness they could bring to the neighborhood. See the Supreme Court's 1926 opinion in *Village of Euclid v. Ambler Realty Company,* 272 U.S. 365 (1926).

3. Marion Clawson, *Suburban Land Conversion in the Unit-* ed States (Baltimore: Johns Hopkins for Resources for the Future, 1971), pp. 78–89.

4. Edward J. Kaiser and Shirley F. Weiss, "Public Policy and the Residential Development Process," *Journal of the American Institute of Planners (JAIP)* 36 (January 1970):30–37.

5. John C. Keene et al., *Untaxing Open Space: An Evaluation of the Effectiveness of Differential Assessment of Farms and Open Space* (Washington, D.C.: GPO, 1976).

6. See F. Stuart Chapin, Jr., *Urban Land Use Planning,* 2d ed. (Urbana: University of Illinois Press, 1965) for a more extensive review of these theories.

7. Real Estate Research Corporation, *The Costs of Sprawl* (Washington, D.C.: GPO, 1975).

8. Anthony Downs, *Opening Up the Suburbs* (New Haven: Yale University Press, 1973), p. 1.

9. Ibid., p. 11.

10. Anderson, *American Law of Zoning* (Lawyers Cooperative and Bancroft Witney, 1976), 1.13.

11. 272 U.S. 365, 395 (1926).

12. As cited in Donald G. Hagman, *Urban Planning and Land Development Control Law* (St. Paul: West Publishing Co., 1971), p. 80.

13. J. Pashman, concurring in *Southern Burlington County NAACP v. Township of Mt. Laurel,* 67 N.J. 151 (1975).

14. 56 Wis. 2d 7, 14–15 (1972).

15. Ibid., at 17.

16. Tarlock, "Consistency with Adopted Land Use Plans as a Standard of Judicial Review: The Case Against," *Urban Law Annual* 9 (1975):70, 74.

17. See John Costonis, *Space Adrift* (Urbana: University of Illinois Press, 1974).

FOR FURTHER READING

American Law Institute. *A Model Land Development Code.* Philadelphia: American Law Institute, 1976.

Andrews, Richard B., ed. *Urban Land Use Policy.* New York: Free Press, 1972.

Babcock, Richard F. *The Zoning Game.* Madison: University of Wisconsin Press, 1966.

Bosselman, Fred, and Callies, David. *The Quiet Revolution in Land Use Control.* Washington, D.C.: GPO for the U.S. Council on Environmental Quality, 1971.

Bosselman, Fred: Callies, David; and Banta, John. *The Taking Issue: An Analysis of the Constitutional Limits of Land Use Control.* Washington, D.C.: GPO, 1973.

Clawson, Marion, ed. *Modernizing Urban Land Policy.* Baltimore: Johns Hopkins for Resources for the Future, 1973.

Gleeson, Michael E., et al. *Urban Growth Management Systems: An Evaluation of Policy-Related Research.* Chicago: American Society of Planning Officials, 1975.

Hagman, Donald G., and Misczynski, Dean. *Windfalls for Wipeouts.* Chicago: American Society of Planning Officials, 1977.

Healy, Robert G. *Land Use and the States.* Baltimore: Johns Hopkins for Resources for the Future, 1976.

Mandelker, Daniel R. *Environmental and Land Controls Legislation.* Indianapolis: Bobbs-Merrill, 1976.

National Committee against Discrimination in Housing (NCDH) and Urban Land Institute (ULI). *Fair Housing and Exclusionary Land Use.* Washington, D.C.: Urban Land Institute, 1974.

Parsons, Kermit C., et al. *Public Land Acquisition for New Communities and the Control of Urban Growth.* Ithaca, N.Y.: Center for Urban Development Research, Cornell University Press, 1973.

Reps, John W. "Requiem for Zoning." In *Planning, 1964.* Chicago: American Society of Planning Officials, 1964. Pp. 56–67.

———. "The Future of American Planning—Requiem or Renaissance?" *Land Use Controls* 1, no. 2 (1967):1–16.

Scott, Randall W., et al. *Management and Control of Growth.* 3 vols. Washington, D.C.: Urban Land Institute, 1975.

Sullivan, Edward, and Kressel, Laurence. "Twenty Years After—Renewed Significance of the Comprehensive Plan Requirement." *Urban Law Annual* 9 (1975):33ff.

CHAPTER 11

Transportation and Public Facilities Planning

Edward Beimborn

This chapter deals with functional planning for transportation and public works. These two functions are often organized in the same department at the local level, and the practice is similar for both areas. These are the best examples of what is meant by infrastructure when used to describe urban structure. Transportation facilities, water supply, drainage, and sewerage systems are those physical aspects that provide the basic physical framework for urban growth or decline. These public facilities can guide growth or decline, or they can merely accommodate changes in development. With such potential for controlling the direction and extent of development, transportation and public facilities occupy a special place in urban planning.

TRANSPORTATION PLANNING

One of the most vital elements of an urban community is its transportation system. Streets, highways, public transit, airports, and railroads are essential to the orderly functioning of an urban area by providing mobility for people and goods as well as access to land. Planning for these facilities involves a comprehensive analysis of the ability of the transportation systems to accommodate future changes in demand with minimal cost and negative impacts for the community.

Levels of Transportation Planning

Transportation planning activities can be directed at a number of different geographic levels and time horizons. Geographic levels can include: (1) *regional planning*—aimed at the development of an overall transportation system for a large urban region; (2) *subregional planning*—aimed at the needs of a smaller area, such as a downtown region, individual community, or neighborhood; (3) *corridor level planning*—aimed at improvements along a particular corridor, such as a freeway corridor or a subway line: and (4) *spot improvements planning*

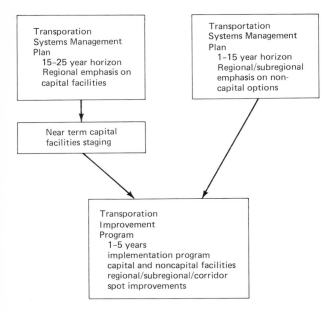

Levels of transportation planning.

—aimed at the needs of particular intersections and highway segments. Planning can also differ in terms of time involved, from short-range to long-range projects.

Planning regulations issued by the U.S. Department of Transportation recognize the diverse levels at which planning can take place and require three separate but interrelated activities for transportation planning: a *Long-Range Transportation Plan; Transportation Systems Management (TSM) Plan,* and *Transportation Improvement Program (TIP).* The relationship among these activities is shown in the accompanying figure. Long-Range Planning looks at regional transportation needs over a 15- to 25-year period. Primary emphasis in the long-range plan is on determining the needs for developing fixed, high-capital facilities, such as freeways or major transit links, which require substantial lead time and planning in order to minimize adverse effects. The long-range plan also provides the basic

framework for regional transportation development and land use growth and development. As part of the long-range plan a staging of the proposed improvements is prepared. The staging indicates when the different improvements should be implemented. This is important, because it provides the linkage between the long-range plan and the transportation improvement program.

The Transportation Systems Management Plan differs from the long-range plan in that it emphasizes managerial improvements, low-capital improvements, and nonfixed facilities. The TSM involves a detailed look at how the transportation system is operated and managed, and it may cover such things as freeway control systems, better traffic signals, improved transit management, car-pool programs, and improved traffic flow on local streets. These types of improvements can be implemented in a relatively short time and their planning horizon is 5 to 15 years.

The Transportation Improvement Program (TIP) is a detailed schedule of specific projects that can be implemented over a five-year period. It is developed out of both the long-range plan and TSM, and it normally includes both the construction of fixed facilities, such as new highways and transit links, and improvements in the operation and management of existing facilities. Each of the three plans are updated annually, with major revisions occurring less frequently.

Basis for Transportation Planning

Legislative and Organizational Basis. Transportation planning in an urban area is based upon the 1962 Federal Aid Highway Act, which states that, "after July 1, 1965, the secretary shall not approve... any programs for projects in any urban area of more than 50,000 population unless he finds such projects are based on a continuing, comprehensive planning process carried out cooperatively by states and local communities." This act in effect required that urban communities establish urban transportation planning agencies in order to continue to receive federal money for the construction of highway (and later transit) facilities. In order to implement the law, actions were necessary by the federal, state, and local governments to define what was meant by a *continuing, comprehensive, and cooperative planning process* and to develop procedures for the preparation of urban transportation plans. Because most of the procedures for plan preparation were developed for computer use, a fairly standardized process for urban transportation planning has developed. Thus most urban areas in the United States (and certain other countries as well) follow the same series of procedures in the development of their transportation plans.

The Federal Highway Act of 1962 also created a need for new organizational structures to carry out planning activities. Most urban areas responded with the creation of regional planning agencies for the preparation of both transportation plans and for other planning functions (such as land-use planning and environmental planning). These regional agencies have transportation planning jurisdiction over not only the central city, but also its suburbs and surrounding counties.

Theoretical Basis. The development of transportation plans is based upon a number of theoretical concepts about the way cities function and the role of transportation. The first of these is an understanding of the relationship between transportation and land use. This relationship is called the *land use–transportation cycle*. When transportation access to a parcel of land is improved, the land becomes more attractive and is often developed for urban use. As land is developed, the greater amount of activity leads to an increase in travel demands. This increased demand in turn causes an overloading of the transportation facilities, responded to with a corresponding increase in supply. The cycle is repeated again as increased accessibility affects the pattern of land uses.

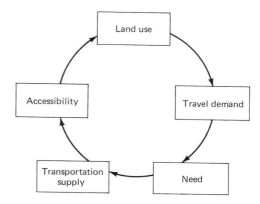

The land use–transportation cycle.

A common example of this pattern can be seen in the bypass or beltway highways that have been constructed around large cities. These roads, originally built to relieve congestion in the city by diverting some of the traffic around it, have attracted major developments, such as shopping centers, residential areas, and industrial plants. These developments themselves generate large amounts of traffic, which may lead to congestion in the beltway as well as the streets that it was supposed to relieve.

Because of the close relationship between land use and transportation, the urban transportation planning process involves the planning of land uses as well as transportation. As future land use patterns are planned, transportation plans are developed to properly serve them. In some cases, transportation facilities are not expanded, in order to limit urban development of an area better suited to other uses (such as prime agricultural areas, areas with poor soils, or unique environmental areas).

The second theoretical concept underlying transportation planning is that of *derived demand*. This theory, which is related to the land use–transportation cycle, states that the demand for travel derives from the demand to do other things. Thus, most people do not travel just for the sake of traveling, but rather for specific purposes, such as to work, shop, or visit. Through this concept, it is possible to

TRANSPORTATION AND PUBLIC FACILITIES PLANNING

relate the amount of trip making that takes place to the level of land use activities. For example, the number of trips into a shopping center can be related to the size of the center and to the employment there. Therefore, it is possible to predict future travel patterns as a function of land use characteristics.

The concept of *impedance minimization* refers to the attempt to reduce the negative aspects of trip making, such as cost, time, discomfort, and inconvenience. Travelers behave in such a way as to minimize the impedance of travel as they perceive it. This concept is used to explain the choice of a route of travel between points (use of a minimum time path); the choice of a mode of travel (combination of mimimum cost, travel time, and inconvenience); and choice of a destination (minimization of travel time to a place that serves the travel need).

With these three basic concepts, a procedure has evolved for the planning of urban transportation facilities and services. This complex process involves the application of a series of mathematical models to large volumes of data, as well as extensive interaction with elected officials, technical personnel, and the community.

The Urban Transportation Planning Process

The urban transportation planning process involves a series of interconnected steps. The process begins with the organization of the study and major tasks of inventories and problem definition. Inventory information is used to calibrate models for forecasting and travel simulation. Problem definition leads to formulation of goals, criteria, and design standards, which in turn are used to develop alternate land use and transportation plans. Plan testing and evaluation is done by comparing the alternate plans and by forecasting their performance against the criteria. When suitable plans emerge, they are subjected to public review and comment and after formal adoption, move toward implementation. At a number of stages in the process, the alternate plans may be revised as new information and feedback are obtained.

Study Organization The first major step in the planning process is the organization of the study and detailed planning of the subsequent steps. Activities at this stage include formation of advisory committees made up of citizens and technicians; scheduling of tasks; defining the study area; and development of a traffic analysis zone system and network structure. The *traffic analysis zone system* is an essential part of the modeling system. The study area is divided into a set of small geographic areas, and all activities are assumed to take place at the *centroids* of these zones. Forecasts of population, land-use activity, automobile ownership, and other characteristics are made for each zone.

Problem Definition. In the problem definition phase, regional goals are formulated for both land use and transportation. Transportation goals generally fall in three major categories: (1) those concerned with mobility: (2) those concerned with the costs of transportation; and (3) those concerned with the impacts of transportation on the community and environment. From the set of goals, more specific objectives and criteria by which to measure them are developed. These objectives are used to help to quantify what is meant by the goals. For example, the general goal of improving mobility can be stated more specifically by the objectives of reducing the miles of highway that become congested (and measured against the criteria of miles of highway that operate with a forecast traffic level greater than their capacity); to provide better transit service on existing routes (measured by average waiting times); to provide better access to jobs (measured by number of jobs within 30 minutes travel time); and so forth.

It is also possible to develop *design standards* from the objectives and goals. Design standards specify minimum or maximum values of particular parameters used to develop alternative plans. For

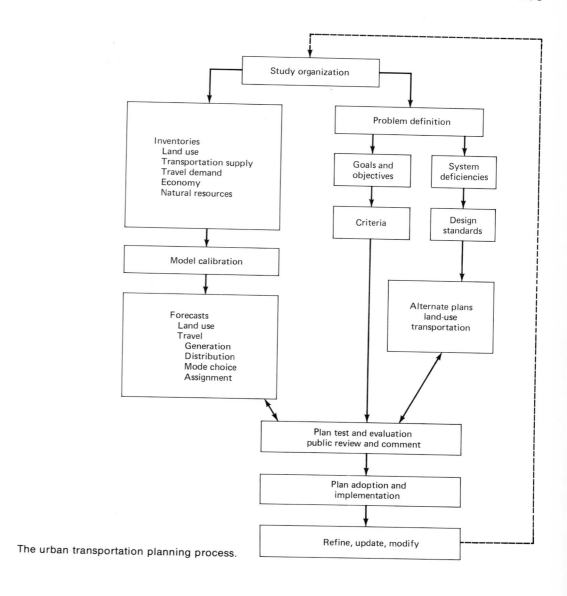

The urban transportation planning process.

example, for a goal of providing mobility, design standards can be developed which specify characteristics of the transit system such as maximum headway, distance between stops, and parking requirements at transit stations. With a given set of design standards and a specification of the defi-

ciencies in the current system, alternatives can be formulated.

Data Collection. Basic data are needed on the characteristics of the existing system, including information about land-use patterns, transportation supply, travel demand, economic conditions, and natural resources. Land use data would include information on how every parcel of land in the region is being used, and how it is zoned for future use. These kinds of data are obtained periodically in order to give an accurate picture on how the use of land changes over time.

Two basic types of transportation data are collected: data on the *supply* and *demand*. Transportation supply data include a comprehensive inventory of the major highway and transit facilities in the area. Highway data include capacities, operating speeds, traffic volumes, accidents, signalization, parking regulations, and other characteristics. Transit data include route locations, schedules, equipment, and fare structure. Travel demand data are usually obtained through an *origin destination survey* or through special small area surveys. In such surveys a random sample is taken from the appropriate group, and these people are asked about their travel patterns. Data are collected about origin and destination of trips, purpose, mode of transit, time of arrival, major routes, and land use at the destination. Other special surveys may be conducted of truck and taxi use, trips passing through the region, weekend travel, and transit use.

In addition to land use and transportation data, data on economic and natural resources are collected. Economic data include employment information, nature of the labor force, and information on the interchange of goods and services between segments of the economy. Natural resource data might cover the suitability of soils for urban development, air pollution, water quality, and inventories of recreational facilities.

Model Calibration. The data collected in the inventory phase are then used to calibrate a series of mathematical models used to forecast future conditions and patterns. Each model that is used has a series of *parameters* that are set by comparing patterns that can be observed from the data collection activities with those that are simulated by the model.

By adjusting the parameters, the best fit between the model and actual conditions can be obtained. For example, *travel demand models* are adjusted so that simulated traffic volumes on certain links are nearly the same as actual traffic volumes measured in the field. Once such calibration is completed, the models can be used with some confidence to predict future conditions. The models can be modified over time as more data on actual patterns become available.

Land-Use Forecasts. The next major step is to develop forecasts. Forecasts are made of future land-use demand and travel patterns in order to test the alternate plans against the criteria. This process is fairly complex and requires the use of a series of mathematical models.

The amount of land that will be needed in the future is forecast by looking at population and employment projections and their associated land needs. Rates of land use for different categories are developed from present land development patterns and discussions with advisory committees. These rates might specify different types of residential density, commercial land use, parks, and institutional uses for every additional 1,000 persons. These rates of land use can then be applied to the forecasted growth to determine the types of land that will be needed in the future. It is sometimes desirable to prepare more than one forecast to reflect different policies of urban growth. For example, one forecast may be based upon high-density urban development and another upon a low-density pattern.

The forecast of land-use demand does not include a forecast where the development will take place. To allocate land use demand, there must be a determination of the available unused land. This would include lands that are outside flood plains, contain soils suitable for urban development, and are not designated for other use. Then an *allocation* can be determined by considering previous land use plans and zoning regulations. The prediction may be based upon past development trends or upon modified trends. Another method of allocation of land use demand uses mathematical modeling. Growth indices are developed for each parcel of land to relate it to location, utilities, public services, and nearby development. Future growth is then allocated to each analysis zone based upon its growth relative to other analysis zones. Other mathematical procedures that simulate land development decisions, competitive aspects of land use, or optimization procedures may be used.

Travel Demand Simulation. Simulation of travel demand is done by using a sequence of four major mathematical models—*trip generation, trip distribution, mode choice,* and *traffic assignment.* These models take as input the forecast level of land use at each traffic analysis zone and produce an output of expected traffic volume on each link of the transportation network in the future year. The function of each of these four models is shown schematically in the accompanying figure.

Trip generation. Trip generation models are based upon the relationship between land use characteristics and number of trips. Both *trip productions* (trips that begin at the zone) and *trip attractions* (trips that end at the zone) are estimated, usually for a series of trip purposes—home-based work trips, home-based shopping trips, home-based other trips, and non–home-based trips. Among the factors that have been found to affect the amount of tripmaking at a parcel of land are residential density, household size, automobile ownership, employment, and general location.

Two methods are used for trip generation modeling—*regression analysis* and *cross-classification analysis.* In regression analysis, a linear equation is developed relating the number of trips generated at a zone to the characteristics of the zone. In cross-classification, a table is developed indicating the number of trips generated per household as a function of household characteristics (e.g., automobile ownership and trip purposes).

A. TRIP GENERATION

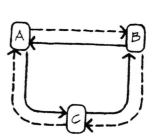

B. TRIP DISTRIBUTION

C. MODE SPLIT

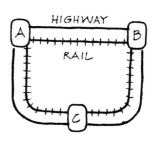

D. TRAFFIC ASSIGNMENT

Schematic travel simulation models.

Trip distribution. The process of trip distribution links together the trip productions and trip attractions to form an origin-destination pattern. A number of different methods are available, but the one used most often is the *gravity model,* based upon Newton's theory of gravitational force between two masses. As used in transportation planning, the gravity model states that the number of trips between two points is directly proportional to the size of those two places (given by trip productions and trip attractions) and indirectly proportional to the distance between the two places (usually as measured by travel time).

As initially developed, the gravity model had the following form:

$$T_{ij} = \frac{P_i * \dfrac{A_j}{d_{ij}^b}}{\displaystyle\sum_{j=1}^{n} \dfrac{A_j}{d_{ij}^b}}$$

where T_{ij} = the number of trips between i and j

$\quad P_i$ = the number of trips produced at i

$\quad A_j$ = the number of trips attracted to zone j

$\quad d_{ij}$ = the travel time between i and j

and b = an empirical constant

In the most common use the term $1/d_{ij}^b$ is replaced by F_{ij}, the *friction factor* between points i and j. An addition term, K_{ij}, (the *K factor*) is added to account for social and economic factors between the two zones. The friction and the K factors are obtained from the calibration process where simulated origin-destination patterns are compared with actual patterns.

With these factors the gravity model has the following form:

$$T_{ij} = P_i \frac{A_j * F_{ij} * K_{ij}}{\displaystyle\sum_{i=1}^{n} A_j * F_{ij} * K_{ij}}$$

Modal split. The next step in the process is to determine what percentage of trips between an origin and destination uses transit and what percentage uses automobiles. The choice of travel mode is a function of many factors. These factors include characteristics of the trip, such as purpose; characteristics of the alternative modes that are available, such as travel time, cost, and convenience; and characteristics of the individual, such as access to an automobile, age, and income. Many different mode choice models have been developed since the proper forecasting of transit use is a critical element of the transportation planning process.

A mode choice model that has gained wide acceptance is the *logit mode split model.* In this model the impedance or disutility travel of a particular mode is computed by a linear equation such as the following:

$$I_{ijm} = IV_{ijm} + C_1 * OV_{ijm} + \frac{CT_{ijm}}{C_2} + C_3$$

Where: IV_{ijm} is the actual time spent traveling in a vehicle between points i and j

OV_{ijm} is the time spent out of the vehicle (walking to a transit stop or parking lot, waiting for a transit vehicle or a transfer, and walking from the transit vehicle or a parking place to a final destination)

CT_{ijm} is the cost of travel (transit fare or auto operating cost)

C_1 represents the importance that a traveler places on out-of-vehicle time relative to in-vehicle time (travelers usually feel that out-of-vehicle time is up to three times as bothersome as in-vehicle time). As such the term $C_1 * OV_{ijm}$ is generally interpreted as a measure of the inconvenience of travel by mode m between the two points. A high value means that a lot of time is spent waiting or walking while a low value means these times are relatively short. The parameter C_2 represents the value of time for the particular traveler, since it is used to convert the cost of travel to the same units as the other terms in the equation (i.e., time). A high value for C_2 means that the traveler places a high value on saving time in travel compared to saving money. With a high value on time, the term CT_{ijm}/C_2 becomes small in relation to the other terms. A low value of time has the reverse result, with cost being most important in the equation. C_3 is sometimes called a *bias coefficient* and is used to represent other characteristics of mode m, such as comfort and privacy, which would contribute to impedance. The parameters C_1, C_2, and C_3 are obtained through the calibration process.

Given the impedances of the alternative mode choices between two points, the probability of choice of a particular mode can be computed. This relationship is illustrated by the curve as shown in the following figure. In this curve the probability that transit will be chosen is given as an S-shaped curve (called a *logistic curve;* hence, the name Logit Mode Split Model). If the transit and auto modes both have equal impedances, the probability that transit will be chosen is p = .5. If the automobile has a lower impedance than transit, then the probability that transit will be used will decrease. At the ends of the curve it flattens out to represent *captive riders* for either transit or automobile. A captive rider is a person who has only one of the modes available and therefore does not have a choice. Travelers can be either *auto-captive* (no alternate transit service exists) or *transit-captive* (no auto available, nondrivers, etc.). The curve can be represented mathematically as:

$$P_t = \frac{e^{I_{ijt}}}{e^{I_{ijt}} + e^{I_{ija}}}$$

Where: P_t is the probability that transit is chosen

I_{ijt} and I_{ija} are the impedances of transit and auto

e is the base of natural logarithms; e = 2.7183.

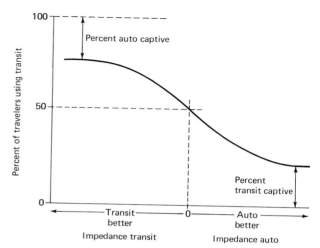

Logit mode split curve.

After trips have been split into transit and auto trips, they have to be converted to vehicle trips. This is done for automobile trips by dividing the number of *automobile person-trips* by an estimated *auto occupancy rate*. The auto occupancy rate can be determined through existing patterns. Auto occupancy can also be computed as a function of parking cost, trip purpose, income, and number of trips between the two points.

Traffic assignment. The final step in the transportation modeling process is to assign the transit person-trips and automobile vehicle trips to the *transportation network*. For computer analysis, the transportation network is described as a series of *links* and *nodes*. Each link is represented by distance, travel speed, and capacity. Forecasted highway travel between an origin and destination is *loaded* on the shortest path (usually minimum travel time) over the network of transportation links between the two points. This is done for all origin destination pairs to simulate the traffic level on each link. When all traffic is assigned, the capacity of each link is compared to its forecasted traffic volume. For those zones where the traffic volume exceeds the capacity, the speed on the links is adjusted downwards (travel time on the link increases). This in turn may cause shifts in the minimum time path routing between origin and destination. Traffic is then reassigned to the modified network. The process of checking against capacity and modifying speeds is repeated until a balance is achieved.

Transit trips are assigned to the transit network through a similar process. Initially it is assumed that a high level of service is provided with a large number of vehicles, which results in a small waiting time between vehicles (*headway*). The transit trips are assigned to the minimum travel time path in the transit network. The load per transit vehicle is then compared to its capacity (i.e., the percentage of seats occupied, called the load factor, is determined). If there is a low load factor, the number of vehicles on the route are reduced, which will cause higher headways. The assignment activity is then repeated until a balance between trip demand and vehicles supplied is reached. The result of the traffic assignment process and the sequence of travel demand models is a forecasted level of service on each link in the transportation network.

Alternative Plan Development. Another major step in the planning process is the development of alternative transportation plans from design standards and an understanding of the deficiencies of the current system. A wide range of alternatives is developed to reflect different directions of growth and means to deal with transportation problems. Land use alternatives might include places to concentrate future urban development in high-density areas, in satellite cities, or in corridor areas. Alternatives could include plans that emphasize freeways, arterial highway improvements, and different types of mass transit in varying combinations. Alternative locations and lengths of facilities are also developed. In addition, a no-build alternative involving only minor improvements is defined,

to assess how well the existing transportation system can accommodate growth in travel demand.

Each alternative is developed in considerable detail; each individual link in the transportation network is described. Such detail is necessary in order to test and evaluate the plans.

Plan Test and Evaluation. The alternative plans are next tested and evaluated by using the travel demand simulation models to forecast the performance of each plan against the criteria. Developing a table that compares each of the alternative plans to the criteria makes it possible to examine the trade-offs among the alternatives in terms of costs, improvements in mobility, and impacts. As part of the evaluation process, other analyses are conducted which may look at the performance of the plan in different parts of the community, at different points in time, and for different groups of the population.

Another important aspect of the evaluation process is the careful interpretation of the information that has been developed. This would involve such activities as an examination of the effects of uncertainty upon the choice; an examination of how well each plan would work under different future conditions from those assumed in the analysis; and a look at how factors that were omitted might affect the results of the analysis.

Evaluation should involve the participation of all relevant elected and appointed officials as well as interested citizens, through advisory committees, public hearings, informational meetings, workshops, and other means. Input and reaction from the general public and officials can provide valuable information on many of the subjective elements of a plan that cannot be easily measured or forecasted.

Plan Adoption and Implementation. Following an extensive evaluation process, the final plan is developed for formal adoption by the planning agency and appropriate units of local government. The plan is formally adopted by agencies of the state and federal government as well. Plan adoption is one of the first steps of plan implementation, as it implies a commitment by agencies with the power to carry out the plan. Plans can be modified periodically as new information becomes available; the process may be repeated in its entirety or only through certain steps.

Current Transportation Concerns

The transportation planning process has been used primarily for the development of long-range, regional-scale transportation plans. This process has become well established and has been used widely throughout the United States and other countries. Transportation planning has usually been used for major investments in high-capital facilities, such as urban freeways or rail transit systems, which provide service throughout large metropolitan areas. Recently, however, there has been an increased amount of attention to other problems and issues that require a modification of the traditional planning process.

One of these areas of recent concern is the development of improved means for short-range transportation planning and the management of existing transportation systems. As it becomes more difficult to construct major new facilities such as urban freeways or rail transit systems (because of financial and environmental reasons), emphasis has shifted to the use of operational and managerial techniques for improving the efficiency of existing transportation systems. Some of these techniques are: improved freeway control systems, staggered work hours, priority treatment for buses and car pools, changes in parking rates, van pooling, better traffic signals, and restrictions in auto use. These types of techniques are not easily evaluated by the transportation planning models described above.

A second issue of concern relates to the interaction between transportation and land use. While attempts have been made to plan for land use and transportation concurrently, these efforts have been hampered by the lack of effective controls on land use in most urban areas and the lack of an urban growth policy at different levels of government. There is a need for better understanding of the relationship between transportation and land use in order to incorporate these interrelationships.

A final area of concern is the extension of transit services to all segments of the population. This includes services for the elderly and disabled as well as services beyond the range of normal transit. Also involved are related services such as taxicabs, car pools, dial-a-ride, and jitneys. These have the potential for serving the elderly and handicapped as well as low-density areas. Further information is needed to create a higher level of effectiveness for such systems.

PUBLIC FACILITIES PLANNING

There is a strong relationship between the planning of communities and the provision of public facilities. That is, the physical and economic development or redevelopment of regions, metropolitan areas, communities, neighborhoods, and even single streets requires certain public investments. At the larger scale, these involve such facilities as airports, rail lines, highway networks, and major utility plants. Although these systems are clearly regional in nature, planning for them is complicated by the fact that they usually serve a multiplicity of local government areas—each with different problems, demands, and legal prerogatives. At the smaller scale is the provision of essential public services to particular patterns of land development. For example, a new residential area requires streets and walks, waterlines, storm and sanitary sewers, public buildings (fire, police, social services), parks, and so on. (Of course, some services may be provided by public utilities with government regulation.)

Planners must have a good working knowledge of these systems, since land cannot be developed or redeveloped without appropriate public facilities. The provision of such facilities to an undeveloped area can promote land development. Increased awareness of the need for environmental control systems and demands for the preservation and enhancement of environmental quality has made the provision of major utilities a critical issue. The following sections describe the provision of public facilities and the four types (streets, water supply systems, storm drainage systems, and sanitary sewer systems) that are most closely associated with community development. These are the most expensive to construct and are also major determinants of development patterns.

The Provision of Public Facilities

Major public facility improvements serving communities are provided by governmental units; facilities serving particular land uses are often constructed by the land developer and deeded to the governmental unit. In some cases, costs for facilities serving both an individual land use and the larger community will be shared by government and the developer.

The major planning vehicle for larger facilities is the *capital improvements program.* This is a five- or six-year program for the construction and financing of new facilities called for in comprehensive or land use plans. Because major facilities are highly interrelated (a road and its bridge and utility lines are constructed simultaneously), expensive (largely financed through public borrowing), and timely (sewer lines must precede buildings), they are carefully planned as part of the local government budget process. The first year's estimates in a five-year capital program serve as the current year's capital budget.

The provision of public facilities at the smaller scale often occurs in the context of the *subdivision of land.* Formally, the subdivision of land is the legal process of dividing large parcels of undeveloped land into smaller parcels of land for development

TABLE 11-1
Types of Public Facilities for Local Development

Highways, streets, and walks
Public utilities
    Water supply
    Sanitary sewer
    Storm-water sewer
Private utilities
    Gas
    Electricity
    Telephone
Public facilities and services
    Administrative and service offices
    Fire and police stations
    Libraries
    Schools
    Parks and playgrounds
    Solid waste collection

and ownership. In the larger sense, it is the process of developing areas of land, which inevitably requires new streets, traffic control devices, waterlines, and sanitary and storm sewers. Obviously, each of these will exist as part of larger community and regional systems.

Although the process of subdivision and areal development is initiated by the private developer, it is regulated by government—at all levels but especially the local one. For example, state regulations might relate to transportation, critical areas, noise (airports), and other environmental regulations and state plans. Regional regulations might cover the same topics, plus the water, storm, and sanitary systems. Regulations at the local level involve an official map (dedicated streets), a comprehensive or land use plan, a capital improvement program, zoning ordinances, subdivision regulations, standards for required improvements (construction standards), and building codes.

Most important in the provision of public facilities are the subdivision regulations, the standards for required improvements, and the capital program. Subdivision regulations establish the legal and substantial process of subdivision and set forth design standards (relating to suitability of land, public access, conformance to plans, streets and easements, utilities, sediment control, and so forth). Standards for required improvements include the engineering standards and specifications for those public improvements the developer must provide.

Although the subdivision process varies among governmental units, it generally includes the following steps:

1. *Preapplication Meetings.* The developer meets with municipal officials (planning commission members and staff, city manager, city engineer, etc.) to discuss proposed development in terms of the municipality's requirements (i.e., comprehensive plans, zoning, subdivision process, required improvements).

2. *Preliminary Plat.* The developer prepares and submits a preliminary plat (design) that includes the proposed plan of building sites, layout of streets and utilities, and other features. The plat is reviewed by various offices (zoning, planning, engineering) for conformance with applicable regulations and approved or rejected. If it is approved, the developer can proceed with the preparation of a more detailed final plat.

3. *Final Plat.* The developer prepares and submits a final plat, which includes all of the details of the proposed development: names of the subdivision and streets, the layout of the subdivision and lots, streets, utility structures, rights-of-way, easements, and dedicated lands. It constitutes a legal document that is recorded with the registrar of deeds when approved. The transfer of dedicated land (street rights-of-way and other land donated to the governmental unit by the developer) is part of this process.

4. *Development Agreements—Required Improvements.* The developer and the local government unit agree on the plan and financing of required public improvements, such as streets (paving, curbs, and gutters), sanitary and storm sewers, waterlines, driveway approaches and sidewalks, street trees, and signs and lights. Facilities serving a larger area may be provided solely by the municipality or the cost may be shared with the developer. Improvements related directly to the particular subdivision are usually provided by the developer and deeded over to the municipality. In either case, the required improvements must be constructed in accordance with the applicable standards.

5. *Financial Guarantees.* The developer must guarantee the provision of improvements via a bond, letter of credit, or escrow account.

6. *Engineering Plans.* Final engineering plans are prepared and then approved by the municipal engineer prior to construction.

7. *Installation of Improvements.* The required improvements are constructed and must be approved and accepted by the city engineer. With this approval, building permits may be issued and construction of individual buildings within the subdivision can begin. Although the sale of lots can begin after the final plat is recorded, construction of buildings cannot begin until public improvements are in place (e.g., the road is needed to provide fire truck access to building sites, etc.).

The analysis and design of specific public facilities for a region, community, neighborhood, or subdivision is generally the responsibility of the engineer, in conjunction with the architect and urban planner. The approach is typical of engineering problems and similar to the general process of transportation planning. Future levels of demand or need under peak conditions are estimated, and facilities are arranged and sized for those situations. This process is illustrated in the following sections.

Highways and Streets

The provision of highways and streets probably contributes more than any other factor to the ultimate physical design of an urban area. The development of streets and highways should be based upon a sound transportation planning process and used to

A typical subdivision site plan by Nelson and Associates.

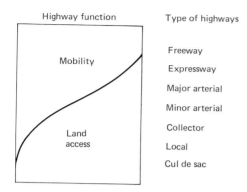

Highway function	Type of highways
Mobility	Freeway
	Expressway
	Major arterial
	Minor arterial
	Collector
Land access	Local
	Cul de sac

Functional classification of streets and highways.

enhance the overall urban environment and physical design of the community.

Highways (which can be classified according to their function and use) serve two major purposes: access to land and mobility. Different types of highways meet these functions in different ways. On one extreme is the freeway, which, as a limited access facility, provides no access to land. It is used only for mobility. On the other extreme is the *cul de sac,* which is used entirely for land access and does not permit any through movement. In between these extremes are *expressways, arterials, collectors,* and *local streets.*

It is important to develop a clear definition of the functions a highway is to perform before designing it. Arterial facilities, for example, should be designed for efficient through movements, with careful control of access points and turning movements. Local streets should be designed to prevent through travel and to provide a pleasing neighborhood within the natural terrain.

The design of streets and highways also involves the consideration of many other factors, such as basic land use information (topography, land use type, and access characteristics), traffic information (including projected traffic volumes), types of vehicles using the facility, expected operating speeds, and information about connecting roadways (their functional use, design, and operating characteristics). Highway design requires a range of environmental and community data, including noise levels, air quality, drainage patterns, neighborhood structure, locations of schools and other public institutions, pedestrian movements, and socioeconomic characteristics of the neighborhood. The consideration of environmental and community factors is especially important in the design of arterial and limited-access facilities.

The design of the highway itself involves the determination of the geometric configuration of the proposed roadway. This includes selection of a roadway *cross section, horizontal alignment,* and *vertical alignment.* A cross-section is selected according to the functional classification of the highway and its projected traffic volumes. Some typical street and highway cross sections are shown in the figure on page 275. Typical cross sections could range from a 34-foot roadway on a 60-foot right-of-way for a local street to a 92-foot roadway (two 34-foot roadways and a 24-foot boulevard) on a 120-foot right-of-way for a high-volume urban arterial street. Horizontal alignment involves the determination of the horizontal curvature of the streets, and vertical alignment involves the setting of grades and vertical curves. Horizontal curves are composed of circle curves and straight line segments, and vertical curves are composed of parabolic curves and straight line segments. They are considered together to provide a street system that blends into the physical environment and provides for adequate sight distances and safe operation.

Water Supply

Water supply is concerned with both the quantity and quality of water. Quantity involves being able to supply enough water to meet future population growth, as well as to meet the needs of fire fighting, industry, business, and other uses. Water quality concerns a supply of water that is safe for drinking and contains no undesirable odors or colors.

274

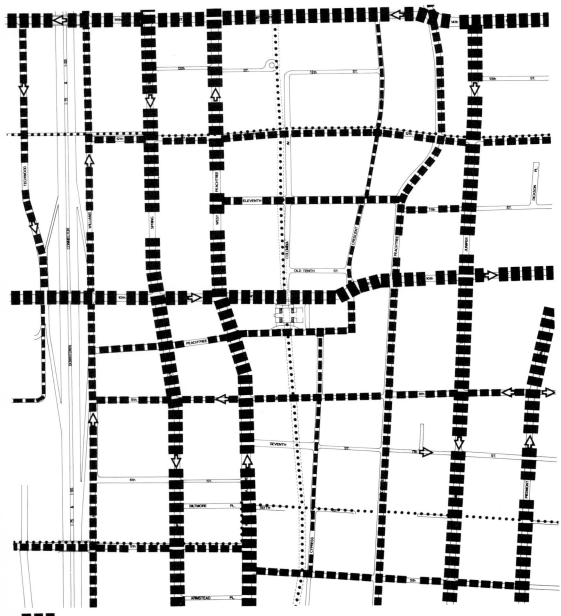

▮▮▮ Arterial Street, - One Way, 4-5 Lanes
▮▬▮ Major Collector Street, - 3-4 Lanes
▬ ▬ ▬ Local Collector Street, - 2-3 Lanes
• • • • • Bicycle Route

A typical urban-district circulation plan: the Tenth Street area, Atlanta, by Nichols, Carter, and Seay/Grant, Architects. (Courtesy of Leon Eplan and the city of Atlanta).

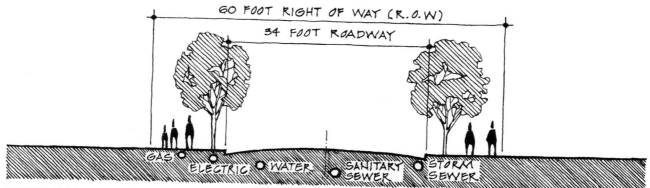

RESIDENTIAL STREET

60 FOOT RIGHT OF WAY (R.O.W)
34 FOOT ROADWAY
GAS ELECTRIC WATER SANITARY SEWER STORM SEWER

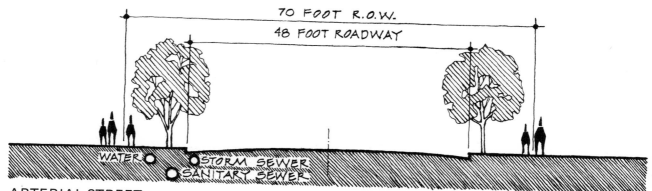

ARTERIAL STREET

70 FOOT R.O.W.
48 FOOT ROADWAY
WATER STORM SEWER SANITARY SEWER

MAJOR STREET

120 FOOT R.O.W
34 FT. ROADWAY 24 FT. BOULEVARD 34 FT. ROADWAY

Typical street cross sections.

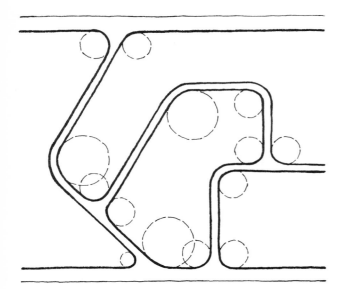

DIAGRAMMATIC ROAD PLAN: HORIZONTAL
CURVES DEVELOPED FROM ARCS OF CIRCLES.

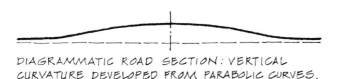

DIAGRAMMATIC ROAD SECTION: VERTICAL
CURVATURE DEVELOPED FROM PARABOLIC CURVES.

Horizontal and vertical road curves.

A water supply system involves collection, purification, and distribution of water. Water can be collected from underground sources through wells or from surface sources such as rivers, lakes, or even the seas. The first step in water purification is *sedimentation,* in which a coagulant is added to the water that causes the solids in the water to precipitate and settle out. This is followed by *filtration.* The water is passed through a sand-and-gravel filter to further remove particulates. The water is then *disinfected* through the addition of chlorine and or other chemical agents. It may receive further treatment depending upon the presence of certain impurities or its intended use.

Following treatment, the water is pumped into the distribution systems. These are usually *grid systems* with a series of closed *loops.* Water is distributed under pressure, which is mainatined by a pumping system and/or the use of water towers.

Urban Drainage Systems

The drainage of water from rain- or snowstorms can be handled by surface drainage in open channels or streams and/or by underground drainage via catch basins and storm sewers. If inadequate provision is made for the drainage of storm water, flooding and water quality problems can result, with severe economic and environmental consequences.

The two major steps in developing urban drainage systems are prediction of future storm water runoff amounts and layout and design of the drainage system. The first step involves an analysis of rainfall data and land use information to provide an estimate of the quantities and rate of flow of the water that will enter the drainage system. Runoff depends upon the duration and intensity of the storm, types of soils and surfaces over which the water will travel, slope of the land, amount of moisture in the soil, size of the catchment or drainage area, and mixture of land uses. One method used to predict runoff, the *rational method* is expressed as follows:

$$Q = C * I * A$$

where Q = rate of rainfall runoff expressed as cubic feet of water per second

C = runoff coefficient

I = rate of rainfall intensity expressed in inches of rain/hour

A = drainage area in acres.

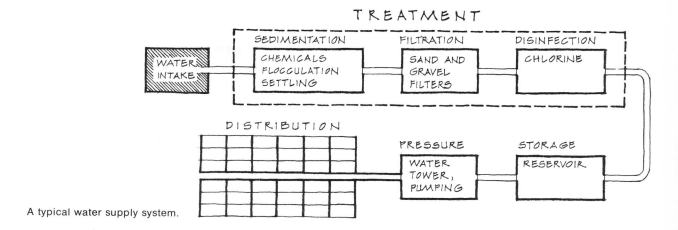

A typical water supply system.

The runoff coefficient is a number between 0 and 1 that represents the percentage of the rainfall that will result as runoff rather than being absorbed into the ground. Typical values would be 1.0 for a parking lot, 0.4 for a residential area, and 0.1 for agricultural land. The rainfall intensity term, I, is obtained from weather data and represents how rapidly the rainfall occurs. Rainfall intensity is often associated with a storm recurrence interval expressed as a number of years. The recurrence interval represents the probability of a storm of a given intensity and duration occurring. For example, from weather data it may be determined that a 50-year interval storm (one that has a probability of .02 of occurring in any one year) has a rainfall intensity rate of 4 inches per hour for a 30-minute time period.

Land use has an important effect upon the amount of storm water run off. As land is converted from rural to urban use, storm water runoff increases substantially. This occurs because of street paving, building roofs (hard surfaces), and land grading and can result in much greater risks of flooding. In addition, a certain amount of water infiltration and inflow into the drainage system from groundwater or other sources may also add to flow rates. Thus it is very important to use predictions of future land use and its effects on storm water runoff as inputs in the design of drainage systems.

The second major step is the layout and design of the drainage system. A drainage system may be an open system in the form of channels and streams or a closed system consisting of underground storm water sewers. In either case the system is laid out for the gravity flow of water through a series of tributary sewers leading to larger branches and finally to trunk line sewers. The design of such a system involves the determination of the overall layout of the collection system, pipe sizing and shape, and the location and design of inlets, manholes, and junction points. A final step may be to develop storm-water treatment facilities. These may be necessary, depending upon the water quality of the storm water as it reaches outfall points along existing streams or water bodies. This is especially important if the storm water drains an area with numerous sources of potential water pollutants.

Sanitary Sewer Systems

The design of sanitary sewer systems is similar to the design of urban drainage systems. Three major steps are involved: determination of flow amounts;

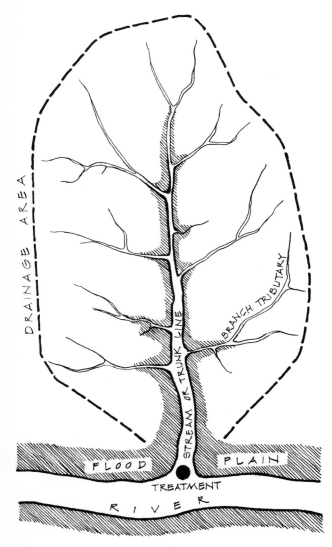

A typical storm-water stream drainage system.

sewer network system layout and design; and the design of treatment facilities. Prediction of flow amounts is made on the basis of future land use and population characteristics. Population forecasts are multiplied by a water use rate (in a range of 100 to 200 gallons per day per person) and added to es-

timated flows from industrial, commercial, and institutional uses.

Sewer network layout and design of sanitary sewers is nearly identical to that for storm water sewers. Nearly all sanitary sewers operate on gravity flow. They are designed to maintain a certain minimum velocity of flow to prevent sedimentation but to avoid a certain maximum velocity of flow to prevent scouring of the pipes.

The treatment of sewage is a multiple-step process. *Primary treatment* involves the removal of suspended solids in the sewage. The sewage is passed through screens to remove large particles and through sedimentation tanks where suspended materials will settle to the bottom. *Secondary treatment* is a biological process used to remove dissolved materials and finely suspended solids. It typically uses trickling filters or an activated sludge process. Both processes work through biological activity in which microscopic organisms obtain food from the waste water and produce carbon dioxide, water, and other stabilized materials.

Following secondary treatment, *tertiary treatment* may occur. Chemical processes are used to remove various compounds from the water, such as nitrates or trace elements, that would be harmful if they entered the effluent of the sewage treatment plant. The final step in the process is *disinfection*. Chlorination is used to kill any pathogenic bacteria which may remain in the water.

GUIDE OR ACCOMMODATE?

Transportation and public facilities constitute the basic infrastructure of urban areas; that is, such facilities provide the necessities for growth and development. Their inadequacy could be a reason for urban decline or lack of growth. How can urban planners use this infrastructure as a means of implementing planning, or more specifically, to guide growth?

Unfortunately, much of the existing functional

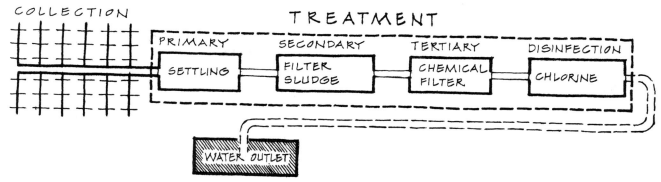

A typical sanitary sewer system.

planning has been an accommodation of predicted growth rather than a guidance of growth. The provision of transportation and public facilities has too often followed the design of residential, commercial, and industrial development. However, careful coordination of transportation and public facilities to land use planning, within a comprehensive, urban planning program, can resolve many of the problems associated with urban sprawl and unplanned development. Such coordination will require assertive actions by urban planners as well as political support by urban govenments.

FOR FURTHER READING

Transportation
Chan, Yupa. *A Review of Operational Urban Transportation Planning Models*. Report No. DOT-TSC-496. Springfield, Va.: National Technical Information Service, 1973.

Dickey, John W., et al. *Metropolitan Transportation Planning*. Washington, D.C.: Scripta: New York: McGraw-Hill, 1975.

Hutchinson, B.G. *Principles of Urban Transport Systems Planning*. New York: McGraw-Hill, 1974.

Owen, Wilfred. *The Accessible City*. Washington, D.C.: Brookings, 1972.

U.S. Department of Transportation, Federal Highway Administration. *Modal Split*. Washington, D.C.: GPO, 1970.

————. *Traffic Assignment*. Washington, D.C.: GPO, 1973.

————. *Trip Generation Analysis*. Washington, D.C.: GPO, 1975.

————. *Urban Mass Transportation Travel Surveys*. Washington, D.C.: GPO, 1972.

————. *Urban Transportation Planning: General Information*. Washington, D.C.: GPO, 1977.

U.S. Department of Transportation. Urban Mass Transportation Administration. *Urban Transportation Planning System Reference Manual*. Springfield, Va.: National Technical Information Service, 1977.

Public Works
Clark, John W.; Viessman, Warren, Jr.; and Hammer, Mark J. *Water Supply and Pollution Control*. 2d ed. Scranton, Pa.: International Textbook, 1971.

Korbitz, William E., ed. *Urban Public Works Administration*. Washington, D.C.: International City Management Association, 1976.

Water Pollution Control Federation. *Design and Construction of Sanitary Storm Sewers*. Manual of Practice no. 9. Washington, D.C.: Water Pollution Control Federation.

CHAPTER 12

Housing

Sammis B. White

The importance of planning for the housing function is self-evident. Housing accounts for the largest physical share of the built environment and occupies the most urban space. It has evolved into a complex undertaking involving many roles for different persons and agencies in both the public and private sectors. Public intervention has added new roles for the urban planner as well as reinforcing the historical roles. Ultimately, housing is also viewed as a key to neighborhood quality and preservation.

Housing is far more complex than merely physical structures that provide shelter. The *physical element* is important because it determines how well-housed the inhabitants are, what activities can occur there (e.g., cooking, eating, washing, recreation, sleeping), and the property taxes the owner pays. But housing also includes a *locational element*—the relation of each unit to such things as schools, jobs, retail areas, and parks, as well as to the quality of homes in its immediate neighborhood. And housing has a *status element*—where persons live affects what others think of them.

Because housing has so many aspects, it involves a number of actors, including individuals at all levels of government. However, planners largely deal with the local level of government, and it is on that involvement that this chapter will focus. Some planners deal with state and national housing policies and programs, and while these programs will be discussed, the planners' more limited roles are not.

The role of the government is not one of ownership, as local, state, and federal governments own little more than 1 percent of all housing in the United States. Rather, its role is largely that of intervention in the private market in an effort to produce socially desired results. This intervention ranges from laws regulating sales and rentals, to zoning ordinances regulating land uses, to programs aimed at stimulating housing rehabilitation, to subsidies that stimulate new housing construction.

Although most planners become involved in housing from the public sector, some work in the private sector. Some help translate public interventions into successful housing ventures for private individuals and corporations. Our major concerns here are why the public sector has become so involved in housing, some of the current conditions that affect the future of housing, and governmental interventions.

CONCERN FOR HOUSING

Government intervention in the housing market has been justified by the need to establish rules governing market transactions; to ensure that all persons receive a minimum level of housing; to smooth fluctuations in the economy; to redistribute income and assets; and to achieve other societal goals.[1]

Health, Safety, and Welfare

The impact of housing on the population is not entirely clear. Historically there has been conclusive evidence that very bad housing can have negative physical and mental impacts upon its inhabitants.[2] Persons living in very poor housing have usually suffered from more illnesses, had more accidents in the home, and had more pessimistic views of their lot in life and their ability to change that condition than persons in better housing. In recent times, however, with the relatively high standard of housing in the United States, there is less evidence of the negative impact of substandard housing. A higher incidence of certain illnesses seems to be linked to poor housing, but little else can be proven. Researchers are finding that many of the problems that have been linked with bad housing have had little connection with the housing itself.

Nevertheless, one of the reasons communities are concerned with housing is to make sure that it does not have negative impacts on its inhabitants. There is also a concern that housing should not be injurious to others (e.g., an individual may walk by and be struck by a falling shingle). Many local governments have instituted housing codes that seek to ensure the provision of a minimum quality of housing in order to protect both the inhabitants and others in the vicinity. These codes state the minimum conditions necessary both on the exterior and in the interior for buildings to be habitable (and even to remain standing).

The codes also create minimum housing standards in order to protect the values of the properties. If some buildings in a community are allowed to deteriorate, they may have a negative impact on nearby units and these too may be allowed to deteriorate. If this occurs, values of all properties in the area, even those that have been maintained, will fall. Those persons who have continued to maintain their homes will lose money because they will not be able to sell their units for as much as they have invested in them. In order to protect individuals from such losses and to protect the city from this erosion of its tax base, housing code enforcement is used.

Fiscal Impact

Planners and society in general are concerned with housing because of its role in financing the activities of the local units of government. The primary source of revenue for most local governments is the property tax, and the largest element of taxable real property in most communities is its residential property inventory. If the residential housing stock is in good condition and has relatively high values, a community can depend on it as a source of revenue. In turn, the community may be able to afford a high level of service provision. If the quality of housing begins to decline, however, the revenue it produces is likely to decline.

Many older communities in the United States are currently faced with declining property values, resulting in lower tax revenues. Because of inflation and higher demand for services, the communities need as many if not more tax dollars from their residential tax base. The solution usually chosen is to raise tax rates, but this can decrease property values if owners respond by doing less maintenance. Planners must try to reverse this process, so that the housing stock is not destroyed by the very government trying to provide services for it. If residential values can be maintained or increased, then a community's fiscal future becomes that much more secure.

Economic Impact

Housing plays another important role in many local economies, and in our national economy. The construction of new housing, at an average of a little under 2 million new units annually, employs 4 percent of the U.S. labor force. The investment in new housing averages over $70 billion annually. In an average year, housing construction represents 3 percent of the U.S. gross national product and 25 percent of gross investment. Rehabilitation and remodeling of housing is also big business, with homeowners spending about $30 billion in one recent year.

No wonder then that many groups, particularly the construction unions and the mortgage lending community, are interested in massive housing unit production as well as maintenance of the existing stock. These strong groups are usually quite effective in convincing Congress that it should take steps to ensure that construction activity remains at a high level.

However, construction activity is generally said to be countercyclical. That is, when the economy is booming, housing starts usually decline. When the economy is in a recession, housing starts usually increase. This cycle relates to the availability of mortgage money. When the economy is booming, other types of businesses want money for their investment, and since they can usually pay more, money is diverted from the housing industry. When the economy is slack, money finds its way into housing, since there is less competition for it.

These cycles lead to high and low periods for home builders and suppliers. The lulls force them to seek government intervention to help them out of these periods of tight money. There is some evidence that, in the long run, the number of units built is not really affected by these cycles, but it is difficult to convince unemployed construction workers that they are doing reasonably well in terms of a ten-year period.[2a] Thus, the combination of cyclical activity and the impact of construction on the national economy makes this aspect of housing a concern of planners, public officials, and citizens alike.

National Goals

Congress has set forth major goal statements for housing in two of its amendments to the *Housing Act of 1937*. The first amendment, referred to as the *Housing Act of 1949*, established as a goal "a decent home and a suitable living environment for every American family." In 1968 Congress attempted to put some strength behind this statement by declaring that "Congress reaffirms this national housing goal and determines that it can be substantially achieved within the next decade by the construction or rehabilitation of 26 million housing units, 6 million of these for low- and moderate-income families."[3]

Neither goal has been achieved. In 1978, fewer persons lived in substandard housing than in 1968, but it appears that more lived in unsuitable neighborhoods. The numerical goals stress housing alone, and that has been the focus of public policy. The goal of 2.6 million units a year, while perhaps necessary, is considerably higher than the average level of annual housing production, and, in fact, higher than the country has ever achieved. Only during the period from 1971 to 1973 did U.S. housing production exceed 2 million units a year. During the period 1974 to 1977, new construction averaged only 1.6 million units a year. However, the fact that the nation has established these goals shows that housing is of major concern to society.

CURRENT CONDITIONS

Housing in the United States has undergone a number of changes in the last 25 years. Quality has risen along with incomes, and average new housing size has nearly doubled. Home ownership has continued to increase, so that over two-thirds of heads of households are homeowners. The geographic location of the majority of new construction has switched from central cities to suburbs. Industrialized housing has come to play a significant role. Mobile homes now constitute 20 percent of annual new housing efforts.

Many of these changes have been positive. Even the positive changes, however, have had less effect in the most recent years as a new set of factors has come to influence housing. Among the most notable are high rates of inflation, dramatic increases in the cost of energy (affecting building materials as well as heat and utilities), high mortgage interest rates, a rapid rise and fall in government housing subsidy programs, increasing abandonment of inner-city housing, and decreasing neighborhood quality. These factors and others have changed the complexion of housing. Three of the most important areas are the current housing deprivation, rapid rise in the costs of new construction, and difficulties of maintaining the existing housing stock.

Housing Deprivation

Although a dozen different deprivations are discussed in the literature of housing,[4] only four of the more important areas will be explored: housing quality, neighborhood quality, cost relative to income, and racial discrimination.

Housing Quality. Decent housing has been a goal of social reformers since the turn of the century. Yet there has always been considerable difference of opinion as to what is standard or decent housing. Many communities have enacted housing codes that set some minimum standards inhabited dwellings must meet, but these standards vary from community to community.

If we were to attempt to empirically measure how much substandard housing exists in the United States, we would have even greater problems. Few communities know how much substandard housing exists (by any standard), both because it takes resources to count such units, and because it is difficult to objectively measure quality. This latter point became particularly evident during the 1960 U.S. Census of Housing. Persons from a wide variety of backgrounds were hired to evaluate the housing in this country and report their findings to the U.S. Census Bureau. These census enumerators used such varying standards to judge housing quality that the results have been dismissed as useless.

In reaction, substandard housing was defined in the 1970 Census of Housing as that which lacked all plumbing facilities or that which had more than one person per room. Obviously the latter measure says little about the physical quality of the unit or the total amount of space available in it, but the resultant statistics are the only ones currently available on a national basis. By these definitions, in 1970 the United States had 11 million substandard dwelling units. The number probably is little improved today, given the increasing costs of housing and the decline in real income since 1973.

However, although some 16 percent of the units are said to be substandard, only a small portion of these are seriously substandard. In various recent surveys of citizens in major cities, only 2 or 3 percent of the respondents have cited major problems with the physical quality of their dwelling units.[5] Although the situation may be worse in rural areas, the percentage of housing in the United States that is in dangerous condition is quite small. Housing quality, while still a concern, is no longer the major problem.

Neighborhood Quality. In the same surveys that reveal little discontent with the physical quality of dwelling units, a relatively high percentage of residents, usually city residents, expressed grave reservations about the quality of the neighborhoods in which they live. In some cities as many as one-third of the respondents felt this way. A recent estimate by the Harvard-MIT Joint Center for Urban Studies indicates that some 4 million households in otherwise good units and some 10 million households in all considered themselves to be located in undesirable neighborhoods.[6] In assessing trends in housing problems, this is one of the few that began to worsen before the early part of the 1970s, when most other housing deprivations were improving.

Neighborhood quality refers to a host of items, including the quality of the physical environment; the quality and level of provision of municipal services such as schools, police, fire fighters, and recreation facilities; and the existence of antisocial behavior such as crime, vandalism, or less serious irritants.

It appears that citizens' concerns about their neighborhood's quality are based on actual conditions, not just perceptions of change. Crime rates have increased rapidly, particularly in central cities.

Many municipal governments have been faced with increasing service costs and decreasing tax bases. They have reacted to this dilemma by reducing the level of services, particularly in areas where citizens have not had the fiscal or political power to demand better services. Once deterioration in an area begins, it is very difficult to reverse the trend. Minor problems of ten years ago have now become major.

It is very difficult to measure neighborhood quality, but more persons now see their neighborhoods declining, and living in these neighborhoods has become a major housing deprivation.

Cost Relative to Income. Another deprivation, which recently is afflicting an even greater proportion of the population, is the increasing percentage of income households must pay for housing. The accepted rule-of-thumb is that a household should not pay more than 25 percent of its income for housing; if it must pay more, there may not be enough money to cover other necessities such as food, clothing, or medical care.

In 1973 some 26 percent of the rental households in the U.S. paid more than 25 percent of their income for rent. When only households with incomes below $5,000 are considered, almost 50 percent paid greater than 25 percent of their income for housing[7]. Unfortunately no aggregate data have yet been collected on the percentage of homeowners' income going to housing, but a fair proportion of new buyers and longer-term owners, such as the elderly, whose incomes have often fallen, are likely to be paying a disproportionate share of income for housing.

The most disconcerting aspect of the cost/income problem is that, since the early 1970s, it has been getting worse. Real incomes have not been rising as fast as have the costs of housing, particularly for owner occupants. Thus, more households are devoting a greater percentage of their income to housing.[7] Even if the rule of thumb should be changed to 30 percent, a higher ratio of housing cost to income continues to plague the U.S. population, leaving fewer dollars for other basic necessities.

Racial Discrimination. A problem that transcends the others and subjects minorities in this country to a higher incidence of housing deprivation is racial discrimination. Racial discrimination affects the ability and opportunity to earn higher incomes, so that minority groups often have greater difficulty purchasing decent housing in decent neighborhoods. Racial discrimination has also resulted in the creation of an almost separate housing market for minorities.[8] Minorities are usually spatially segregated, and because they are restricted as to where they can buy or rent housing, their demand inflates the cost of the housing available to them. Also, this limited market restricts the opportunities for home ownership and its potential for producing wealth, thus further segregating the minority populations.

Racial discrimination barriers have been breaking down in the United States. The percentage of whites who said they would object to blacks of comparable income and education moving in next door dropped from 62 percent in 1942 to 21 percent in 1972.[9] A host of federal, state, and local measures aimed at reducing discrimination in housing have been instituted. For the same time period, however, there is little evidence to show that residential segregation has actually decreased. Most evidence indicates that segregation may well have increased, though perhaps not in any particular pattern or in every community.

Residential segregation seems to create unequal educational opportunities for minorities. It increases minorities' costs of living, since they usually have to pay higher mortgage interest rates and higher premiums for all types of insurance. It may affect employment opportunity. Segregation also has negative impacts on central cities in that it has made them less attractive to middle- and upper-income families and raised prices of inner-city housing, which in turn has discouraged even lower-income whites from locating there. Racial discrimination in housing has created an enormous ethical and policy dilemma.

Cost of New Construction

While the costs of new construction have not yet reached a crisis stage, many persons are concerned about the implications of the recent sharp rise. Some fear that within ten years fewer than 15 percent of all households will be able to afford a newly constructed single-family detached unit.[10] If that is the case, it would mean that so few units would be added to the stock that prices of all housing would rise, requiring all households to pay an even greater percentage of their incomes for housing. Obviously this would place a very heavy burden on low-income households, as well as limit housing opportunity for a large proportion of the population.

From 1970 to 1976, the median sales price of a new single-family detached house rose 89 percent, $23,400 to $44,200. Even worse, monthly ownership costs (mortgage, taxes, insurance, heat and utilities, etc.) for the median-priced new house rose 102 percent, from $218 a month to $441. Over the same period, median family income rose only 47 percent. And even median sales prices for existing single-family houses increased 65 percent in this period.[11]

Fewer than one-quarter of American households could afford newly constructed single-family detached homes in 1977. The rate of new construction in the last three years has averaged less than 90 percent of that of the preceding three years.[12] If employment in the housing industry is to regain former levels, or if the expected national rate of investment in housing is to occur, something must be done about the rising costs of new housing.

Maintaining Existing Housing

One of the most difficult tasks in recent years, particularly in inner-city neighborhoods, has been the maintenance of both housing and neighborhood quality. For a combination of reasons, including some of those discussed above, it has become progressively harder to attract the level of public and private investment necessary to preserve our inner-city neighborhoods. The result has been a deterioration in quality that has proven to be a very difficult trend to reverse.

A key factor in the difficulty of reversing deterioration is that of *externalities*. That is, each house affects and is affected by neighboring houses. Thus, if one home is not maintained, it has a negative impact on the housing units near it. The deterioration of a few units negatively affects the value of nearby units, discouraging repair. If a few individuals do make repairs, they may raise their values slightly, and because of externalities, also raise their neighbors' values. However, the neighbors have little incentive to make repairs, since their home values are increased most easily if they do nothing but wait for other neighbors to make repairs. In many neighborhoods, everyone realizes that it makes the most sense economically to wait for the neighbors to invest in their homes, and no one invests. The homes continue to decline in quality and value.

How to turn around these neighborhoods and the investment psychology of the owners is one of the more perplexing questions facing planners today. Most older communities have neighborhoods in which values are declining, housing is deteriorating, and owners are not maintaining their residences. The recent rise in the cost of new construction has forced more persons to think about buying and living in older homes, however, and this has expanded the volume of home repairs and remodeling. In 1975 homeowners spent $2.23 billion for materials alone for alterations to their dwellings.[13] But there is still a great need for better maintenance of existing housing.

PUBLIC INTERVENTIONS

The various interventions in housing by federal, state, and local governments have, for the most part, created the environment in which planners operate. Understanding the historical context of this intervention will help to clarify the roles of the planners.

Federal Interventions

The federal government was not involved in housing until the Depression of the 1930s (except for allowing the deduction of mortgage interest payments and property taxes from homeowners' taxable incomes, a practice started in 1913 with the creation of the federal income tax). The Depression, however, wreaked havoc with almost every aspect of housing—construction, finance, ownership, property values, maintenance, and rent/income ratios. The government decided that it must intervene in housing as it had done with the economy. Two major routes were chosen: altering housing *credit* markets and creating housing *subsidies.*

Most persons need credit to purchase housing. If money for mortgages is either not available or too expensive, only a few homes will be built or purchased. During the Depression, 50 percent of all home mortgages were in default, and new mortgage lending and home building dropped to very low levels. To remedy this, Congress created three emergency and five permanent institutions. The institutions still functioning today are the Federal Home Loan Bank Board (FHLBB) and Federal Home Loan Bank System; the Federal Deposit Insurance Corporation (FDIC); the Federal Savings and Loan Insurance Corporation (FSLIC); the Federal Housing Administration (FHA); and the Federal National Mortgage Association (FNMA). The FHLBB was created to encourage the formation of thrift institutions that would provide long-term mortgages funded from the savings of individuals. The FDIC and FSLIC were devised to help to dispel fears of financial collapse by insuring individual savings in such institutions, thereby encouraging regular savings in these institutions. The FHA was invented largely to induce these institutions to write long-term mortgage loans by insuring them against default. The FNMA was created to further encourage institutions to write mortgage loans by giving them greater liquidity through its operation as a secondary mortgage market, buying mortgages from primary lenders.[14]

The result has been a rather dramatic shift from the pre-Depression practices of 1-to 5-year-term mortgages, at high interest rates, with 50 percent down payments available from a limited number of institutions. Today, 30-year-term, 5 percent down payment mortgages, at lower interest rates, are readily available from many institutions. The total residential mortgage debt outstanding is some $650 billion.[15]

The other major change in federal involvement in housing was the creation in the *Housing Act of 1937* of what is known as *public housing*. In this act, the federal government agreed to pay the annual principal and interest on long-term, tax-exempt bonds sold by local public housing authorities to build housing for low-income persons. The local authorities owned and managed the units and charged low rates, because rents had to cover only the operating costs of the units. This subsidy program became the precedent for numerous attempts to provide decent housing to low-income households. From 1937 to 1972, however, public housing averaged only 30,000 new units a year, and it now accounts for less than 1.5 percent of the nation's housing stock.[16]

After the Depression, aside from the creation in 1944 of the Veterans Administration (VA) housing program, a program similar to FHA insurance but reserved for veterans, the federal government did little in the area of housing intervention until the passage of the aforementioned *Housing Act of 1949*. That act established the housing goals discussed earlier, greatly increased the funds for public housing, and created the Urban Redevelopment Program. The latter was an attempt to raze slums and reuse the land. The federal government would pay up to two-thirds of the project costs for such things as land acquisition, clearance, and site preparation.

In reaction to public outcry about large public expenditures for bulldozing the slums and creating vast wastelands that remained vacant for extended periods, Congress in 1954 changed the name of the program to Urban Renewal and refined and broadened the approach. Instead of just clearance, rehabilitation of existing structures became an acceptable activity. As discussed in earlier chapters, communities were required to create *workable programs* that spelled out how they would attack their overall development problems. Communities that wanted federal aid for urban renewal and related programs were responsible for adoption of a housing code and its subsequent enforcement; the use of citizen participation; development of a comprehensive community land use plan; organization and financing for the program; and creation of a relocation program for displaced families.[17]

Urban renewal has caused considerable debate. The evidence seems to show little justification for the program. It appears to have been expensive, economically inefficient, and to have had costs outweighing benefits. At the end of fiscal year 1971, this program had destroyed 538,000 units and created only 201,000 replacements, only half of which were for low- or moderate-income households. The program had done little to serve its goals of more efficient land use, increased property taxes on project and nearby land, or improved social conditions in the project and nearby areas.[17a] By June 1972 it had displaced more than 1 million persons,[18] and it had cost U.S. taxpayers in excess of $12 billion.[19] There is little wonder that it was abandoned in 1974.

The component of a workable program fared little better. The idea of tying federal aid to the adoption of such a program was abandoned by 1974, in part because communities could prohibit any federal intervention by not adopting one, and in part because delays in submission could bring other programs to a halt.

The housing code component was adopted by many communities and used somewhat indiscriminately. Over time, communities have learned to apply the code most stringently not in their worst areas, where the removal of units faced with code violations would further the shortage of low cost units, but in areas just beginning to decline, where rents are still high enough to cover the costs of the required repairs. Code enforcement is still an active weapon in a community's arsenal to promote better housing, but is it no longer relied upon to solve so many problems.

No changes occurred in the federal housing subsidy programs between 1937 and 1959. In 1959, however, the first of many federal attempts to get housing built for low-and moderate-income households was enacted. The program, referred to as *Section 202,* established below-market interest rate loans for elderly housing and was the forerunner of many housing subsidy programs created in the 1960s.[20] Most of these programs lasted only a few years and contributed little to housing production or to the solution of housing problems. Two programs, however, stand out, at least in terms of volume of units constructed—*Sections 235* and *236.*

Section 235 was a subsidy program aimed at making moderate-income households (annual incomes of $5,000 to $8,000) the owner-occupants of largely newly constructed housing. Ninety percent of the units were to be new construction, and ten percent were to be rehabilitated. Section 236 was also aimed at moderate-income households, but it was a rental program for new, quality units. Over 850,000 units were mortgaged and subsidized under these programs between 1968 and 1973. The occupants of these units have significantly better housing than they would otherwise have had.

A number of problems, especially political, were found in these programs. A record volume of subsidized housing was produced during the first part of Nixon's administration but since this construction served to antagonize his suburban constituency, Nixon placed a moratorium on housing subsidies in January of 1973. Bolstering his decision were increasing reports of scandals in these programs. Subsequent studies have shown that his decision may have had other justifications. For example, Sections 235 and 236 were found to be extremely inequitable, serving fewer than 3 percent of all eligible households. Section 236 units were

found to cost 20 percent more to construct than comparable privately financed units. Sections 235 and 236 units were expected to have foreclosure rates of six to eight times higher than the national average.[21]

In the mid-1960s Congress decided to create a more comprehensive approach to eradicating blight from impoverished neighborhoods and in 1966 created the Model Cities Program. According to the U.S. Department of Housing and Urban Development, this was not a housing program. Only 8 percent of the funds allocated under Model Cities went into the housing area, and these were used largely for counseling, assisting tenant organizations, and setting up development corporations.[22]

In view of its lack of success in redevelopment or housing subsidy programs, it is not surprising that Congress took a somewhat different approach in the *1974 Housing and Community Development Act.* As discussed earlier, this act established individual *block grants* to communities so that individually they could design and implement the housing and redevelopment programs that best fit their specific needs. One subsidy program, *Section 8*, replaced all previous programs but public housing. In the first two program years, 1975 and 1976, HUD approved over $5 billion of expenditures to some 4500 communities for use at their own discretion.[23] Over one-quarter of the funds going to metropolitan areas was spent on redevelopment-related activities (largely acquisition and clearance), one-fifth was spent on housing rehabilitation, and another fifth was spent on public works. The program has been extended until at least 1980.

The other major component of the 1974 act was the creation of three subsidy programs under Section 8: *used housing, new construction,* and *substantial rehabilitation* programs. By 1978, only the first two had proven to be of any consequence. Interestingly, they take opposite approaches to housing problems.

The used housing program relies on existing housing. Individuals qualify for the program by income, negotiate in the private housing market on their own, and, once a unit has been found that meets the housing code, receive from the government the difference between a *fair market rent* for the unit and 25 percent of their income.[24] The average subsidy per household is relatively low, since the program relies on older units. By 1976, some 85,000 units had been occupied on this basis.[25]

The new construction program is more similar to earlier housing programs. Housing units are privately owned and built, and the government commits itself to long-term leases of the units constructed. The program was slow in getting started because the rents the federal government originally set were too low to cover the costs of new construction, so that by 1976, only 20,800 units (instead of the expected 90,000 to 140,000) had been started.[26] Since then, however, rents have been revised, and Section 8 new construction has been booming in most parts of the country. Section 8 and block grants appear to be the routes the federal government will use to pursue housing goals for the next few years.

State Involvement

Most state governments have not been much involved in housing. States have created the basic laws governing real estate transactions within their boundaries, and they have passed the legislation that allows municipalities to create regulations such as zoning ordinances and building codes. Until the late 1960s, they did little else, bowing to the financial strength of the federal government.

Between 1968 and 1973, 31 states created housing finance agencies, which were used to channel federal housing subsidy dollars into the states, as well as raise additional dollars for housing in the national money markets.[27] Many of these housing finance agencies now are looking for other ways to get involved in housing, such as low-rate rehabilitation loans and low-rate mortgage loans to special groups.

Some states, such as New York, New Jersey, Connecticut, and Massachusetts, have been very active in housing for a number of years. In New York, the Urban Development Corporation (UDC) has built new towns-in-town, started new communities, and created low-and moderate-income housing, in addition to channelling a large volume of federal subsidy dollars into the state. UDC has run into some severe fiscal problems, but it represents the greatest state involvement in housing.

Local Involvement

Local governments are largely involved in housing in three ways: providing services to residents, regulating housing and land use, and locating housing subsidized by the federal government. Only the first of the three roles has been a long-term involvement.

Communities provide certain services such as schools, highways, water, sewage treatment, garbage pickup, and recreation to their residents. The levels and costs of these services help to determine the demand for housing in each community, and in turn help to determine housing values. If, for example, the level of services is low but costs (taxes) are high, as happens in some inner-city neighborhoods, there is not as much demand for housing there, and the housing is likely to be of lower quality and price than elsewhere. On the other hand, if the schools in a community are of high quality, housing demand and values are likely to be high, especially if the costs are reasonable. What level of services a community provides at what tax rates plays an important role in the distribution of housing, the demand for it, and its value, and communities make conscious expenditure decisions based on this fact.

Regulating housing and land use is a relatively new role for most communities in the United States. As we have seen, zoning, for example, did not come into general use until the 1950s. Housing codes were first discussed in the late 1800s and a few cities adopted codes around 1910, but it was not until the workable program requirement of the 1954 Housing Act that such codes became widely accepted. By 1968, about one-quarter of American municipalities had adopted some version of a housing code. Building codes date back to ancient times but have proliferated only in the twentieth century, so that half of all local governments now have them. Subdivision regulations have only become important since World War II, when large-scale subdivisions came into being.

These regulations have had varying impacts on housing and housing problems. For example, housing codes have helped to set standards, but since many communities do not have sufficient staff to enforce the codes, and many citizens cannot afford to live in units that meet the high standards of most codes, these restrictions have had limited success in resolving housing problems. Building code standards for new construction may be higher than our society can afford. The proliferation of codes themselves has made cost savings difficult in any form of industrialized building. Subdivision regulations now largely put the burden of the costs of additional infrastructure (streets, sidewalks, water, sewers, and recreation) on the new residents of a community, which is usually a more equitable approach than assessing the existing residents, but these regulations can increase the costs of construction, can help to exclude lower-income residents, and may be wasteful of resources if they overstate the infrastructure required.

PLANNERS' ROLES

The urban planner is usually called upon to deal with the spatial issues related to housing—where what types of housing should be placed, what programs can be employed at the local level to help preserve and upgrade housing, and how federal housing subsidy programs should be implemented.

Each of these tasks can in turn create a variety of roles for the planner in either the private or public sector. We focus below on the three most common areas of housing in which planners have a role—new housing development, neighborhood preservation, and subsidized housing programs.

New Housing Development

An urban planner can provide a number of services in connection with new housing development. In the private sector, planners are often asked to develop subdivision designs, either for the more traditional development of a plot of land into separate parcels or the newer planned unit developments (PUDs). The planner is asked to lay out lot lines, placement of buildings, roads, and other services and to generally map where each type of development will occur. His or her role is to make an attractive and salable layout that conforms to the various public land-use regulations.

In the public sector the planner is called upon to design those public regulations governing land development. Planners often construct zoning ordinances that dictate such things as: how land may be used (for example, for single-family residential, multifamily residential, commercial, or industrial development); at what density development may take place (by setting minimum sizes of lots necessary for development); and what size buildings can be constructed (by controlling size of front, side, and back yards, height of building, and the proportion of the lot that can be covered). Theoretically, these regulations are enacted to prevent one person's use of property from interfering with his or her neighbors' use of property. Ideally the zoning ordinance should reflect the goals and objectives a community has adopted for its future, because this ordinance is one of the main mechanisms a community can use to reach these goals.

Planners also often design the set of regulations governing subdivisions. These restrictions pertain to the way undeveloped land must be prepared. They cover such items as street widths, street construction materials, sidewalk width and placement, and the installation of sewers and waterlines. These regulations sometimes state who must pay the costs of providing these services. A community usually uses these in order to make sure that the newcomers pay for the installation of services and that the services that the community must maintain, such as roads and sewer lines, be built of such high quality that the community does not have to pay disproportionate sums for upkeep.

Planners sometimes work with public employers to help them decide what types of development should be encouraged or discouraged in the community. The planners are asked to analyze the demands for various land uses or densities of development that might be made on a community and to determine how much revenue they are likely to generate to help cover the costs of servicing them. For example, would a community benefit from more single-family development or more multifamily? What size of unit would have the greatest benefits for the community? By developing profiles of the prospective inhabitants of various housing styles and densities, planners can predict what they will demand in services and what they will be able to pay. This information can be used to develop or change the zoning ordinance.[28]

Planners may be called upon to help decide when particular parts of a community should be developed. A planner can help examine the costs and benefits of developing certain areas at various points in time. With this analysis, decision makers gain a better idea of what development they should encourage to the best advantage of the community.

Housing and Neighborhood Preservation

An area of housing that had largely been ignored until the early 1970s is that of preserving and upgrading housing and neighborhoods. Our society has been characterized as the throwaway society, where commodities are used and then discarded.

This same philosophy has seemingly been applied to older housing and neighborhoods. The federal government has actively promoted the construction of housing in newer areas in an attempt to reduce demand for inner-city, older housing. Cities themselves have tended to write off older areas, trying on the one hand to satisfy them with lower levels of services and, on the other, to tax them as heavily as possible. The result has been inner-city decline, with little thought given to the implications of this treatment.

Now, however, preserving houses and neighborhoods has become a major thrust of housing policy, for a variety of reasons, including: new interest in energy conservation; appreciation for structures with character; cost differentials that make older housing much more accessible than new; changing attitudes toward city living; greater appreciation for the housing problems of lower-income households; greater understanding of the role of established neighborhoods; and a precipitous drop in the level of new construction. Preservation efforts are referred to by a variety of names—rehabilitation, upgrading, renewal, revitalization, and stabilization—which all imply efforts to prevent areas from experiencing any further loss of quality or value and, in many cases, efforts to promote an increase in both quality and value. Some argue that the ultimate aim is "gentrification," a newly coined word referring to an attempt to change an area from low income to high income residents (the "gentry").

Planners in this area must design, implement, and evaluate various means of preserving neighborhoods. Although local planners may have been given this charge earlier, with the exception of the limited areas included in the 1966 Model Cities program, there were virtually no funds available until the institution of revenue sharing in 1974. Individual communities then became able to decide for themselves whether any federal money should be spent on preservation and, if so, in what areas and with what devices.

Many planners have had to reassess the housing conditions in their communities. They have been asked to analyze and describe the housing problems not in aggregate terms as in the past, but on a neighborhood-by-neighborhood basis. By analyzing conditions at this smaller scale, a better idea can be gained of the need for and/or possibilities of preservation. Planners can predict whether or not public funds in any number of schemes could help to turn declining neighborhoods around. Where a valid case can be made, decision makers may allocate some portion of their block grant monies to rehabilitation.

Having determined that some neighborhoods can be renewed, the planner may be asked to design programs that meet the specific needs of the target areas. He or she reviews possible types of intervention, either creating original programs or borrowing from communities that have had success. The programs that appear to be the best candidates are then designed in detail sufficient for implementation.

The planner must then evaluate the various programs in terms of the neighborhood in question. The planner should consider the probable impact of each program and try to determine whether or not the program and its results would: (1) be politically acceptable; (2) be cost effective; and (3) have a positive cost/benefit ratio. The results of this analysis help the decision makers choose what programs, if any, they will implement.

Ideally the planner would be called upon to monitor and evaluate the programs once they are made operational, but funds are not always available for this. The programs continue without the planner's direction, and they may not be functioning as efficiently or effectively as possible. As yet planning evaluation is not an established part of the work that planners in this field perform.

Low-Income Housing

Planners have played a major role in the geographic placement of subsidized low- and moderate-income housing units within a community. The federal government generally subsidizes these units and tells communities that they are eligible for such units. The communities themselves must decide whether or not they want these units and must find specific sites for them. Planners are often assigned the tasks of assessing the need for subsidized units, creating the criteria for locating these units, and preparing the applications for their funding.

The placing of these units is often problematic, particularly if they are for low income families. The United States has had a program of low-income housing subsidies since 1937, but there have been few neighborhoods that have welcomed such public housing for families. Since the late 1960s it has been virtually impossible to find any neighborhood to accept such housing. The number of public housing units has continued to grow only because they have been designated mainly for the elderly, a politically acceptable group. Currently over 40 percent of the public housing units are inhabited by the elderly.[29]

What this trend has meant is that planners have had little opportunity to deal with finding suitable locations for low-income family housing, but they have played a role in locating the more than 800,000 Section 235 and Section 236 housing units for moderate-income families. Planners assigned the task of finding suitable locations for these units try on the one hand not to concentrate them so heavily as to create new ghettos and, on the other hand, not to spread them so far apart as to antagonize too large a segment of the population.

The existing housing portion of the Section 8 program works within the confines of the established private market and has required little input from planners. The new construction portion has had some input from planners called upon to complete *Housing Assistance Plans* (HAPs) in connection with community development funds. These plans must state specifically what subsidized housing will be added where in the community to serve what objectives. Section 8 housing is a major component of these plans, and as such is a concern of the planners who are called upon to construct the HAPs.

THE FUTURE OF HOUSING

There appear to be a number of changes occurring in housing. It is difficult to specify exactly where the housing situation is headed, but we will attempt to make certain predictions regarding existing housing problems and planners' roles in dealing with them.

Housing Quality

Housing quality in this country has been improving since the end of World War II. While this trend may have leveled off or reversed slightly during the mid-1970s when housing costs began to rise faster than incomes, the overall trend toward better housing should continue. However, households will have to devote a larger percentage of income to housing. The group most harmed by this trend in housing quality is the low-income population, who cannot support any greater housing expenditure. If this group is not to suffer further setbacks, more federal subsidies must be forthcoming.

Given the vagaries of national politics, assessing this likelihood is difficult, but there has been strong support for the Section 8 program, and there appears to be increasing interest in some form of national income support. The former is tied directly to housing and should help a number of households get better housing over the next few years. The latter would give many households greater incomes, some of which could be used for housing.

Neighborhood Quality

We stated above that neighborhood quality is declining in many U.S. cities. Some neighborhoods are beyond repair, especially given the lack of interest in living in them, and others will undoubtedly follow them. But the number of forces giving new life to city neighborhoods (e.g., new interest in energy conservation, the desire to be near downtown, the appreciation for older buildings, the cost of suburban housing, and the existence of more one- and two-person households that need not worry about schools), means that some neighborhoods will

reverse their decline. More communities are investing a greater share of their community development block grants in neighborhood preservation and rehabilitation efforts. Financial institutions that previously tended to discriminate against these areas through a practice known as *redlining* are attempting to become involved. Citizen groups, which are now considered essential for neighborhood revival, are flourishing.

Overall we should not expect immediate and dramatic changes in neighborhood quality in our central cities. Too many seeds of decay have been planted, and too many of the potential investors— building owners, financial institutions, and city governments—have negative views of the future of these areas to invest much money in them. However, a growing number of neighborhoods will be revitalized or stabilized by these new forces.

Costs Relative to Income

Low-income households have historically been affected by the problem of excessive housing costs in relation to income, but currently an increasing number of households of all income levels has to pay greater than 25 percent of income for housing. Part of the reason is rising land and new construction costs, but rapidly inflating heat and utility costs are also a major factor. With all housing operating costs rising, many faster than incomes, this problem is likely to continue to worsen. More and more households are undertaking energy conservation measures, which has helped, but further steps in this direction are required. Again, for lower income households, more federal subsidies are needed and may be forthcoming. Also, some changes in construction practices may make housing less costly.

Racial Discrimination

Racial discrimination in housing has abated somewhat. Federal laws have helped, as has economic progress by minority group members. Over three-quarters of American households are now willing to accept minority group members as neighbors, and overt forms of discrimination are less often found, at least in the real estate sales market.[30] More subtle forms, however, still do exist. Yet the evidence shows an increase rather than a decrease in segregation.

What appears to be happening is that segregated housing patterns will endure because of inertia and mild preferences for living with members of one's own race.[31] Few neighborhoods are fully integrated. Though housing is becoming more open, and individuals are taking advantage of this, the basic pattern of segregation is unlikely to change in the near future.

Costs of New Construction

The rapid rise in the costs of new construction is likely to continue for a few more years, despite steps to ameliorate the situation. The basic reason for this rapid rise is demographic: the members of the baby boom of the post-World War II era are reaching the age of home buyers, and this large group is putting pressure on the new construction market. Adding to this factor is the increased interest in buying real estate as a means of warding off the effects of inflation. Since 1969 rapid inflation has been a continuing problem. While the rate is no longer 12 percent a year, it remains high enough so that most other forms of investment cannot counter its effects. This means that many households will make whatever sacrifices they can to become homeowners, and, in the process, they will continue to inflate the costs of new construction.

Some steps will be taken to help curtail the rise in new construction costs; among the more obvious are trends toward smaller homes, smaller lots, and more shared walls. With decreasing average household size, fewer Americans will need the large homes which became common in the 1960s. A decrease in size alone will reduce both construction and operating costs. Smaller homes will require smaller lots, and if walls are shared, as in a duplex or townhouse configuration, further cost savings will result. Americans seem obsessed with home ownership. They will be able to continue to achieve this goal if they are willing to accept some changes in the style, size, and lot, but without such accommodations, home ownership will almost certainly become more remote.

Planners' Functions

Few major changes should occur in the roles planners play with regard to housing. Planners will continue to operate largely at the local level. They will continue to be involved in the public regulation of housing and land use; in the private responses to those regulations; in the design and evaluation of local, particularly neighborhood, housing programs; and in the implementation of federal programs, most notably those concerning subsidized housing units.

While their basic roles may not change, the tasks of planners may become more demanding. As the regulation of land use becomes increasingly critical, planners will have to become more sophisticated in dealing with both environmental and legal issues. With the growing interest in neighborhood housing, they will have to become better acquainted with housing market operations; the variety of possible programmatic interventions; and the means of achieving the necessary alliance of lenders, community residents, and city officials. With new federal subsidy attempts, planners will have to learn how to adapt such units to communities that traditionally have resisted such interventions.

NOTES

1. William G. Grigsby, Sammis B. White, et al., *Re-thinking Housing and Community Development Policy* (Philadelphia: University of Pennsylvania Press, 1977), pp. 13–17

2. Alvin Schorr, *Slums and Social Insecurity* (Washington, D.C.: GPO 1963), p. 8.

2a. Sherman J. Maisel, "The Relationship of Residential Financing to Expenditures on Residential Construction," in *Housing and Economics,* Michael A. Stegman, ed. (Cambridge, Mass.: M.I.T. Press, 1970), pp. 39–50.

3. "The Housing and Urban Development Act of 1968," in National Housing Policy Review, *Housing in the Seventies* (Washington, D.C.: GPO, 1974), p. 18.

4. See, for example, William G. Grigsby and Louis Rosenburg, *Urban Housing Policy* (New York: APS Publications and Center for Urban Policy Research, Rutgers University, 1975), pp. 37–57.

5. See, for example, Grigsby and Rosenburg, *Urban Housing Policy,* pp. 61–63; and "Housing: A Bigger City Role in Helping Low Income Residents," *Nation's Cities* (August 1971), pp. 17–18.

6. Bernard J. Frieden and Arthur Solomon, *The Nation's Housing: 1975–1985* (Cambridge, Mass.: Joint Center for Urban Studies of M.I.T. and Harvard University, 1977), p. 95.

7. Ibid., p. 97

8. J. B. Lansing, C. W. Clifton, and J. N. Morgan, "New Homes and Poor People: A Study of the Chain of Moves," in *Housing in America: Problems and Prospects,* Daniel Mandelker and Roger Montgomery, eds. (Indianapolis: Bobbs-Merrill, 1973), pp. 244–64.

9. National Opinion Research Center, cited in National Academy of Sciences, *Segregation in Residential Areas* (Washington, D.C.: National Academy of Sciences, 1973). It also appears in *The Urban Predicament,* William Gorham and Nathan Glazer, eds. (Washington, D.C.: Urban Institute, 1976), p. 121.

10. Frieden and Solomon, *Nation's Housing,* p. 116.

11. National Housing Policy Review, *Housing in the Seventies,* pp. 7–9.

12. *Wall Street Journal,* 19 January 1977, pp. 1, 3; and U.S. Department of Housing and Urban Development *Statistical Yearbook 1974-75* (Washington, D.C.: Gpo, 1976), p. 242.

13. Frieden and Solomon, *Nation's Housing,* p. 109.

14. Ibid., p. 8.

15. *Economic Report of the President: 1977* (Washington, D.C.: GPO, 1977), p. 237.

16. National Housing Policy Review, *Housing in the Seventies,* p. 9.

17. John C. Weicher, "Urban Renewal: National Program for Local Problems," in *Perspectives of Housing and Urban Renewal* by Irving Welfeld et al. (New York: Praeger, 1974), pp. 200–201.

17a. Ibid., pp. 188–190, 208-220.

18. National Housing Policy Review, *Housing in the Seventies,* p. 157.

19. Weicher, *"Urban Renewal,"* p. 185.

20. National Housing Policy Review, *Housing in the Seventies,* pp. 14–17.

21. Ibid., p. 94, 106–7, 112–13.

22. Chester W. Hartman, *Housing and Social Policy* (Englewood Cliffs, N.J.: Prentice-Hall, 1975), p. 106.

23. U.S. Department of Housing and Urban Development, *Second Annual Report: Community Development Block Grant Program* (Washington, D.C.: GPO, 1976), p. 6.

24. Fair market rent is the term used to describe what HUD has determined as the minimum rent at which each size household should be able to procure housing which meets housing code standards in each community. It supposedly should cover maintenance on units, give landlords a fair return, and not be inflationary.

25. Comptroller General of the United States, *Report to the Congress: Major Changes Are Needed in the New Leased Housing Program* (Washington, D.C.: GPO, 1977), p. i.

26. Ibid.

27. Michael A. Stegman, "Housing Finance Agencies: Are They Crucial Instruments of Government?" *Journal of the American Institute of Planners (JAIP)* 40 (September 1974):308.

28. See, for example, George Sternlieb et al., *Housing Development and Municipal Costs* (New Brunswick, N.J.: Center for Urban Policy Research, Rutgers University, 1973).

29. Hartman, *Housing and Social Policy,* p. 123.

30. Gorham and Glazer, *The Urban Predicament,* p. 121.

31. The best discussion of this is Thomas Schelling. "On the Ecology of Micromotives," *The Public Interest* 25 (Fall 1971):61–98. See also Gorham and Glazer, *The Urban Predicament,* pp. 153–54.

FOR FURTHER READING

Frieden, Bernard, and Solomon, Arthur. *The Nation's Housing: 1975-1985*. Cambridge, Mass.: Joint Center for Urban Studies of M.I.T. and Harvard University, 1977.

Grigsby, William G., and Rosenburg, Louis. *Urban Housing Policy*. New York: APS Publications and Center for Urban Policy Research, Rutgers University, 1975.

Hartman, Chester W. *Housing and Social Policy*. Englewood Cliffs, N.J.: Prentice-Hall, 1975.

Kain, John, and Quigley, John. *Housing Markets and Racial Discrimination: A Microeconomic Analysis*. New York: National Bureau of Economic Research, 1975.

Mandelker, Daniel, and Montgomery, Roger, eds. *Housing in America: Problems and Prospects*. Indianapolis: Bobbs-Merrill, 1973.

National Housing Policy Review. *Housing in the Seventies*. Washington, D.C.: GPO, 1974.

Solomon, Arthur. *Housing the Urban Poor*. Cambridge, Mass.: M.I.T., 1974.

Stegman, Michael A., ed. *Housing and Economics: The American Dilemma*. Cambridge, Mass.: M.I.T., 1970.

Sternlieb, George. *Housing*, Vol. 3. New York: AMS Press, 1976.

CHAPTER 13

Historic Preservation

Wayne O. Attoe

Historic preservation as a distinct kind of urban planning is relatively recent in origin even though there has long been a concern, since the second century B.C., with the subject. This has to do with a complex set of organizational, methodological, professional, and economic factors that have asserted the urgency for such planning and initiated a vocabulary in the late nineteenth century. The urgency was the alarm that arose when the scope of demolition and other forms of destruction of historical buildings and areas became apparent. The vocabulary was necessary to provide a set of criteria and methods for historic preservation. This chapter deals with these recent trends as well as provides a framework within which historic preservation can be integrated into comprehensive urban planning practice.

Despite its long history, *historic preservation*—the practice of keeping older buildings intact—remains a troublesome aspect of urban planning. For one thing, notable buildings from the past do not necessarily occur in neat clusters, so new construction and new street layouts must be carefully fitted in and around isolated structures identified for preservation. Another problem concerns the rights of owners: under which circumstances should an owner be forced to preserve a building when demolition and new construction could yield a greater profit? Also, who pays for rehabilitation and maintenance of historic buildings? Another, more political problem is the question of who decides which buildings are to be preserved. Should the decision be made by experts in architectural or local history, by owners, and/or by neighborhood residents? Yet the difficulties associated with historic preservation are not insurmountable. In fact, preservation is one of the major tools available to planners attempting to plot sound physical, social, economic, political, and aesthetic development.

DEFINITIONS

Clarification of the terminology related to historic preservation is necessary, for the field includes varied and overlapping approaches. The term *historic preservation* is typically used in the United States as an umbrella expression encompassing a wide variety of strategies for dealing with existing buildings and urban settings. In Britain, *conservation* is the umbrella term and historic preservation refers more specifically to historically significant buildings.

Restoration

The most conservative form of preservation activity is *restoration.* It involves returning buildings to their original condition. The treatment of *San Francisco,* a Louisiana plantation built in the 1850s, exemplifies the process. The building had both been modified and allowed to deteriorate over a period of years. Restoration included replacement of the features that had been destroyed and removal of elements that had been added.

One of the difficulties in restoration work is deciding on the period to which the building is to be returned. For example, an eighteenth-century house to which extensive alterations were made in the nineteenth century could be restored to its original form by removing all subsequent additions and by correcting all other changes, or it could be restored to its nineteenth-century condition, which might make it more useful in modern terms. Would the building be more significant in its (now substandard) eighteenth-century form or as a nineteenth-century adaptation?

Other considerations relate to utility. How can we restore a building to an earlier condition but still incorporate necessary amenities like bathrooms, electricity, central heating, and insulation? How can we restore a community but still provide the highways, shopping facilities, community centers, and parking lots demanded by twentieth-century citizens?

Some restorations are undertaken to create architectural and community-scale museums. At these places, visitors can experience a version of life at an earlier time. Williamsburg, Virginia, is one example. It provided

San Francisco, a Louisiana plantation, 1850.

... an opportunity to restore a complete area and free it entirely from alien or inharmonious surroundings as well as to preserve the beauty and charm of the old buildings and gardens of the city and its historic significance.[1]

One of the criticisms of museum towns and similar efforts to freeze the physical fabric (and even lifestyles) of towns is that what is preserved is romanticized and antiseptic and, hence, false. It is not a real indication of life and environment in another era.

Colonial Williamsburg ... is altogether too tidy to be wholly convincing; the availability of heated comfort stations, in contrast to the miserable "necessary houses" of other times, is just one reminder of how we arrange to approach history in our terms.[2]

The discomforts of Colonial Williamsburg have been removed to create a more attractive experience for visitors. Actors are hired to play the parts of craftspersons and townspeople in an idealized version of eighteenth-century life in Virginia.

In addition to problems of authenticity, a major obstacle to restoration is cost. Duplicating construction details from a distant past is a painstaking and expensive process. Introducing modern conveniences like electricity and plumbing without destroying the sense of authenticity adds to the expense.

Rehabilitation and Renovation

Rehabilitation and *renovation* are the strategies employed to make decrepit buildings usable again. Since all buildings deteriorate, they all must be rehabilitated to a certain extent if they are to continue to be useful. Rehabilitation and renovation allow more latitude with regard to historical accuracy than does strict restoration. The theory behind *rehabbing* acknowledges that standards of living and patterns of housing, commerce, and work change, and, therefore, buildings must be adapted to the society. But while some changes are necessary, so too are historical continuity and a solid sense of place.

Whole sections of cities have undergone rehabilitation in a conscious or sometimes an inadvertent part of the planning process. Georgetown, in Washington, D.C, was once a slum, but it is now a prestigious upper-middle-class community. German Village in Columbus, Ohio, has a similar history.

The two apparently contradictory goals of historical preservation (saving the past but adapting to

Renovation: German Village, Columbus, Ohio.

the future) are often resolved through differing treatments of interior and exterior. Interiors of buildings are often changed drastically to accommodate contemporary requirements for comfort, safety, and utility, while exteriors are left in their original state (except for fresh paint, new roofing, and so forth). *Old Sacramento,* a historic section of California's capital city, exemplifies this approach.

Adaptive use is a less rigorous type of preservation. Some buildings are no longer needed or no longer practical for the purposes for which they were built, so they can be *adapted* to serve new uses while at the same time maintaining their original form and character. Ghirardelli Square in San Fran-

cisco is a classic example. There, a nineteenth-century chocolate factory has been adapted for use as a shopping and entertainment center to service and capitalize upon the presence of thousands of tourists visiting nearby Fisherman's Wharf. The overall form of the factory buildings was retained, but the site was radically altered to accommodate underground parking and new plazas to connect the shops and restaurants created in existing structures and new buildings.

Near Ghirardelli Square an old cannery was similarly adapted, but in an even more fundamental way. Only the exterior walls of the buildings were retained. The interior was entirely rebuilt. This points

Adaptive use: Ghirardelli Square, San Francisco.

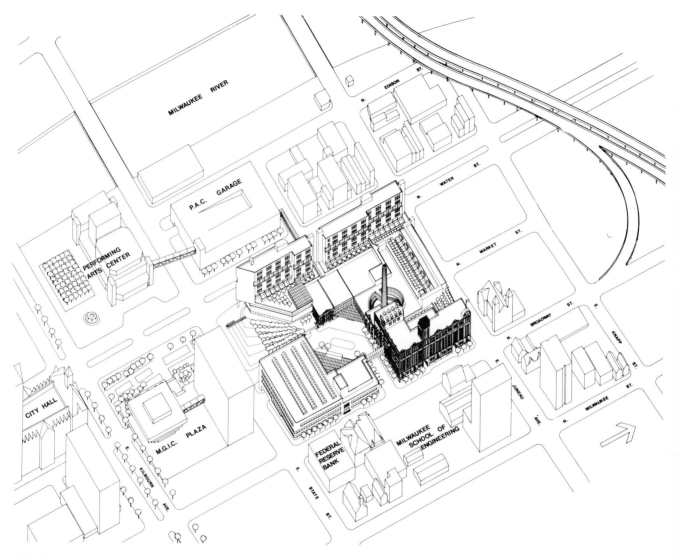

Adaptive reuse and redevelopment: Blatz Brewery Project Proposal, Milwaukee, by the Milwaukee Redevelopment Corporation and the ELS Design Group. (Courtesy of Steve Dragos)

up one of the important strategies used in historic preservation at the urban scale: the interior and exterior of a building can and sometimes should be dealt with as two very different problems. One can shelter activities, while the other can contribute to the character of the urban fabric or townscape.

Other examples of adaptive use include warehouses converted to offices, shops, and restaurants; markets converted to housing and stores; supermarkets and storefronts to churches; and grain elevators to housing.

HISTORIC PRESERVATION

Conservation

The goal of *conservation* is not so much to recapture a sense of the past as it is to preserve what exists presently and to direct change in the future. Conservation is used to keep attractive and workable places from being destroyed or modified in an inappropriate fashion. For example, town centers of numerous villages and cities in Europe have been designated as *conservation areas*. They are places in which no physical changes are allowed unless the changes are deemed to be in keeping with the existing local character:

> Every local planning authority shall from time to time determine which parts of their area are areas of special architectural or historic interest . . . the character or appearance of the whole of which it is desirable to preserve or enhance.[3]

While the general goal of conservation areas is primarily preservation of the physical fabric of town centers and notable architectural forms, sometimes a more specific goal is the stabilization of population and a concomitant lifestyle: i.e., the inhibition of social change. For example, an urban neighborhood may have little architectural significance because numerous others like it exist, but a policy of conservation can ensure that decay of building fabric, transiency of residents, and/or the pressure of increasing land values and property taxes will not dramatically change the area. The assumption behind conservation of both physical and social patterns in cities is that some parts of the urban environment work well just as they are, so it is desirable that they remain unchanged. Agencies must intervene to protect them from destructive external pressures.

Sometimes conservation measures originate in government policy, as part of a master plan for development. In other cases, residents initiate protective legislation. In Milwaukee, Wisconsin, residents of the *Water Tower Trust Area* developed an ordinance to guard against the intrusion of incompatible and nonconforming uses (specifically, a growing medical center).

Replication

Imitation, or *replication,* is not widely used at the urban scale, but it is appropriate in some situations. For example, in circumstances of utter destruction, new construction in imitation of what previously existed is sometimes a feasible policy. St. Malo, France; the Old Town section of Warsaw, Poland; and parts of Nuremberg and Rothenburg, Germany, were rebuilt after World War II as replicas of their prewar forms. This policy makes sense when the towns have symbolic importance, where the urban fabric was exemplary, or where the town's economy is dependent upon tourism. Usually, the exteriors of such replicas are authentic reproductions, and the interiors are modified according to contemporary standards of comfort and safety.

Another kind of imitation is used when it is necessary to fill in gaps between existing buildings. When a historic district has a particular architectural character, it is often required that any new construction imitate features of nearby buildings so that it will not be obtrusive. These features may include height, massing, setbacks, overall dimensions, materials, fenestration, color, and style. A new bank in the historic town of Burford, England, exemplifies this practice. It is not a case of replication but of imitation. The distinction has to do with whether the work is a strict copy or is simply sympathetic to the spirit of the place.

Relocation

Relocation is another approach to preservation. It is not widely used, but in some circumstances, moving buildings from one location to another makes sense. Relocation is used sometimes for economic reasons; it may be less expensive to purchase a used structure and move it than to construct a new building. More often the motive is aesthetic, part of an effort to create a coherent physical setting. By accumulating a group of buildings of similar character and style, one can begin to create a sense of unified place, which can become a neighborhood.

Conservation areas: Thaxted, England.

Encroachments: Water Tower Trust Area, Milwaukee.

One such area is being developed in San Francisco. This *Heritage area* is emerging through the relocation of old Victorian houses from nearby redevelopment areas, to fill in vacant lots among existing Victorian structures.

SCALES OF PRESERVATION ACTION

Preservation as an aspect of urban planning occurs at a variety of scales and in varied circumstances. Thus, it is not always possible to talk about preserva-

Replication: Barclay's Bank, Burford, England.

tion simply in relation to buildings or neighborhoods. Streetlights, manhole covers, historic sites, parks, and facades are as eligible for preservation as individual buildings, because they also are often significant ingredients of town form and character. When we look beyond built elements to natural areas, places that are ecologically crucial or desirable recreational sites, it becomes clear that the issue of preservation is not restricted to isolated structures.

Natural Areas

As adequate supplies of fresh water become critical, as air pollution increases, and as demand for recreational areas exceeds supply, preservation of natural areas becomes an unavoidable issue in urban planning. The preservation of natural areas is integral to historic preservation, for its goal is retention of the historic ecological balance that has made urbanization possible. Aquifers must be preserved, as well as areas of vegetation that affect air quality, rivers and lakes that are sources of food and sites for recreation, and watersheds that deter erosion. While

the preservation of natural areas has seldom been treated as a facet of historic preservation, it is now a critical issue. The *natural past* is as important in planning for humane environments as is the *built past.*

Among the most dramatic efforts toward preservation of natural areas are those of the British National Trust and those in areas like Hawaii, where maintenance of ecological balance is crucial to guarantee a continuing water supply. Founded in 1895, the British National Trust is a nonprofit, quasi-governmental association empowered to purchase or accept as gifts places that are valuable to the nation because of their natural beauty, historic associations, or unique qualities. Currently the Trust owns nearly 500,000 acres of natural areas throughout Britain, as well as 200 country houses, archeological sites, nature reserves, and farms. These are held in perpetuity and in most cases are open to the public. In Hawaii, lands are conserved by state law because they are the sole source of the islands' water supply. Almost daily rain in the mountains is contained by vegetation and gradually seeps through porous soil and rock to create a pool of fresh water under each island. Preservation of this delicate natural system is obviously crucial.

Towns and Villages

One of the most remarkable types of historic preservation is the practice of protecting whole towns. Towns are just as much objects as are single buildings, and they are just as vulnerable to the pressures for change. The preservation of period-piece towns will guarantee opportunities for future generations to experience urban spaces and forms unique to particular regions and historic periods.

To date, most of the preservation efforts at this scale have been the product of private initiative.

Williamsburg has been restored with the support of John D. Rockefeller, Jr.; West Wycombe, England, by the Royal Arts Society and then the National Trust; Lacock, also in England, by the National Trust; and Deerfield, Massachusetts, by Deerfield Academy and the Deerfield Foundation. Nantucket, Massachusetts, exemplifies public instead of private interest in preservation at a large scale: "There is hereby established in the town of Nantucket an Historic Nantucket District, which shall include the land and waters comprising the town of Nantucket."[4] Preservation at this scale provides a sense of the integration of all aspects of urban life: houses, workplaces, churches, schools, shops, farms, civic buildings, and transport.

Preservation: Lacock, England, by the National Trust.

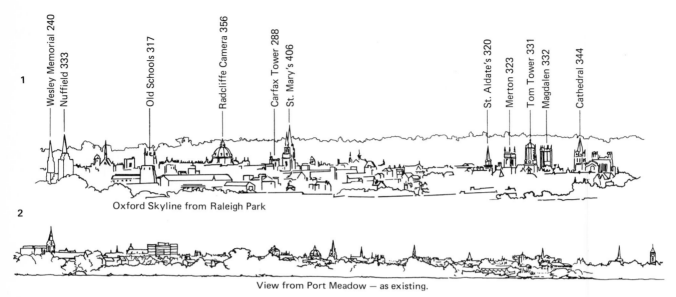

Oxford Skyline from Raleigh Park

View from Port Meadow — as existing.

Skyline: Oxford, England. (*High Buildings in Oxford,* 1975, Courtesy of the City Architects and Planning Officers Department, Oxford)

Skylines

Skyline preservation takes two forms. One involves height restriction. In Washington, D.C., and in some capital cities in the United States, construction near capitol buildings is restricted to heights that will preserve the visual impact of these structures. Elsewhere, most notably in Oxford, England, the entire skyline, rather than a single profile, is preserved. Proposals for new construction in Oxford must demonstrate that new buildings will not seriously change the city's silhouette, which is characterized by church and chapel spires and domes.

> Every building within approximately three-quarters of a mile radius from the central intersection shall be carefully examined in its relation to the townscape as well as the landscape and may be rejected on either account.[5]

Districts

Even in urban settings that have not survived *in toto* as period pieces, where growth and change have continually occurred, "pockets of the past" may remain. These are districts that have a physical coherence or that have strong *edges* that create an identity. They are preserved as examples of living and building patterns of the past. German Village (in Columbus, Ohio) was settled by Germans who built their homes in a style unlike that of neighboring areas. The area of modest brick homes is thus distinct. In other cities, other styles give districts their special identities: *Federal* buildings in Boston's Beacon Hill, *Georgian* in Georgetown, and *Victorian* in San Francisco's Heritage area.

Particularly in Europe, it is strong boundaries rather than stylistic similarity that provide a sense of edge to districts. Remnants of medieval city walls, moats, or fortifications do this, as can highways, railroad rights-of-way, and grade and land use changes.

Neighborhoods

The conservation of neighborhoods is often no different from that of districts, but the terms imply a dis-

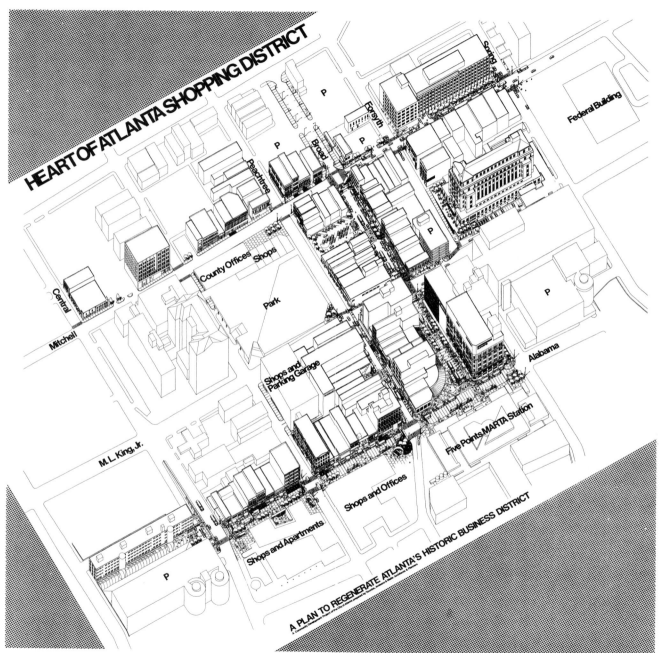

Regeneration of a historic business district: Atlanta, by Toombs, Amisano, and Wells. (Courtesy of city of Atlanta)

tinction that is worth noting. *District* relates only to the physical fabric of the city, while *neighborhood* applies also to a way of life. Also, districts are often characterized by mixed uses (commercial, residential, etc.), while neighborhoods are primarily residential. The goal of neighborhood preservation is to protect a lifestyle and a particular socioeconomic profile in an area as much as to preserve a collection of buildings. Where there are no strong physical boundaries, socioeconomic characteristics of residents, land value, and political jurisdiction are other bases for establishing neighborhood boundaries.

Streetscapes

Sometimes it is worthwhile to preserve the fronts of buildings and the street and sidewalks. For example, late Victorian storefronts found in the United States are often elaborate essays in intricate masonry detailing and contribute a unique character to the streets on which they front. By contrast, they are often undistinguished inside. Streetscape preservation, then, refers to protecting facades (with period streetlamps and other street furniture) but allowing interiors to be modified according to need. A legal technique for accomplishing this is the *facade easement,* under which owners relinquish the right to modify their building *faces* without approval.

Buildings

While the protection of individual buildings dates back to at least the second century B.C., only in the last one hundred years or so has the practice begun to seriously affect urban planning and development. As long as preservationists concentrated on isolated monuments, like the Colosseum in Rome or a castle in Germany, the impact of preservation on urban form and systems was negligible. However, as preservation activities have grown, those involved have identified not just monuments but many more modest buildings for protection. Many preserva-

tionists believe that examples of virtually *every* building type should be preserved. They contend that protection should not be restricted to architectural gems. Hence, one can imagine planners forced to preserve not only a Victorian water tower, a Georgian theater, or a Federal-style house, but also the first cinema in town, a prototypical gasoline station, a fast food outlet, a "typical" duplex or bungalow, and ubiquitous row houses. Such a long list of individual buildings makes planning even more difficult because they do not necessarily cluster in neat groupings. One of the reasons that plans for rebuilding London's Covent Garden area were abandoned was that the many listed (protected) buildings were scattered so randomly throughout the area that it was impossible to impose any new physical order upon the district while keeping them all intact.

Fragments and Objects

When it is not economically feasible to preserve whole buildings, it sometimes makes sense to retain fragments of buildings. A church tower might be incorporated in new construction to preserve an important part of a skyline. A city gate may be retained though adjacent city walls are demolished to accommodate twentieth-century traffic. More common, however, is the preservation of facades. The ZCMI Department Store in Salt Lake City, Utah, retained its distinctive facade as an example of nineteenth-century commercial building when a new facility was constructed.

The preservation of facades signifies two facts about the history and art of architecture. First, in many cases in the past, design effort and expenditures concentrated on external appearance, not on internal functional considerations. Venturi, Brown, and Izenour call the resulting buildings *decorated sheds.*[6] Second, buildings sometimes become advertisements. The facade becomes identified with the service performed and reinforcement of that relationship can enhance business.

Facade: the ZCMI Department Store, Salt Lake City.

Although they often have less visual impact than buildings (because of their size), objects can play an important part in giving character to places in the city. The Victorian streetscape is more convincing as a period piece if lighting fixtures and benches are compatible in style. In some cases historic objects are more important than the buildings around them. Funiculars, ferry boats, and cable cars (like those in San Fransicso) are things of interest in themselves. They are simultaneously attractions for tourists and needed transportation facilities.

CRITERIA FOR HISTORIC PRESERVATION

A decision to institute a policy of historic preservation is made on the basis of a number of motives and criteria. Political and economic considerations are of utmost importance if a preservation plan is to be successfully implemented, but first it is necessary to have a firm basis for deciding which aspects of the

urban landscape are historically significant. The following criteria are typically used in making such decisions.

Aesthetic

Buildings and districts within cities are sometimes preserved because they represent special achievements within a particular historic style. While it is difficult to prove that one building is more beautiful than another, some buildings seem to epitomize a certain style of construction, decoration, landscaping, or urban design. The frame of reference for these decisions varies. In some cases a building is judged against similar buildings in the area; in other cases judgment will be made with reference to masterpieces elsewhere in the world.

The *New Town* section of Edinburgh, Scotland, and much of Bath, England, are identified as unique examples of Georgian town planning and architecture, and for that reason they have been preserved.

HISTORIC PRESERVATION

Georgian Edinburgh, by reason of its homogenous character and extensive area, forms, with Bath, one of the two most outstanding examples of the town planning of its period. It is not only a precious architectural possession of Scotland and Britain, it is one of the treasures of Europe's cultural heritage.[7]

Typical

Even buildings that are not extraordinary as examples of architectural design are sometimes preserved as representatives of a special class or type of building. For example, in Milwaukee, Wisconsin, a gasoline service station was given landmark status because it is representative of a chain of similar stations that flourished after 1917 in the Midwest. This particular station is not the only one of its kind, nor is it the best of its type, but it is representative. Other sorts of building programs, structural techniques, and architectural styles are preserved because they exemplify the way things were, rather than because they are special achievements.

Scarcity

Buildings that are one-of-a-kind or that are the last remaining examples of a building or stylistic type

are also considered for preservation. Bath's sinuous Lansdown Crescent is unique. So are the Victorian water towers in Chicago and Milwaukee. Strong opposition developed at the University of London in reaction to plans to demolish a Georgian square, because, in addition to its strong university associations, the square was one of the last Georgian squares in Bloomsbury.

> The university has a special responsibility to preserve our architectural heritage and, since Woburn Square is one of the last examples of Georgian architecture in Bloomsbury [we ask] the University to halt the imminent demolition and prepare new plans that will preserve at least the existing facades and the gardens.[8]

Historical Role

Buildings and urban settings that have been the sites for significant historical events are preserved to provide a symbolic tie between those earlier events and the current events of our own lives. Physical setting is a vehicle that helps relate past events that affect us to events now determining our future. Without a sense of the physical context, our under-

Clinton Street Station, Wadhams Oil Company, Milwaukee. (Courtesy of Steven Jensen, HABS)

Water tower, Chicago.

standing of such events is limited to verbal records and graphic images. The battlefield at Gettysburg, Pennsylvania, is important in the planning of the town of Gettysburg because of its historic significance. On a smaller scale, the Alamo in San Antonio, Ford's Theater in Washington, D.C., Independence Hall in Philadelphia, and Mission Dolores in San Francisco all have been preserved because of their associations with historic events.

Charles Dickens's house in London; Abraham Lincoln's in Springfield, Illinois; and countless other residences, schools, and public buildings are preserved because they are associated with famous people. When such buildings are scattered around the countryside, they have little overall impact upon urban planning; but when they form a group, as in Haworth, England, the consequences can be considerable.

Haworth was the Yorkshire home of the famous Brontë children, who achieved fame as writers in the nineteenth century. Four buildings are at the core of Brontë associations in Haworth: the parsonage where they lived; the church where their father was minister; the Black Bull Inn where brother Branwell retreated; and *Top Withens,* said to be the model for *Wuthering Heights.* Tourists began arriving as early as 1850, even while Charlotte was still alive. A hundred years later, the parsonage is a museum at-

Mission Dolores, San Francisco.

tracting 65,000 visitors a year, and that represents only a fraction of all visitors to Haworth. The main street in Haworth, which is narrow and one of the steepest in England, began to develop monumental traffic jams. Local authorities finally intervened to accommodate the crush of tourists. Houses were torn down and replaced by parking lots and public toilets. Traffic on the main street was restricted and a bypass constructed to route vehicles around the town.

Some buildings are preserved because they are the work of a particular architect. Whether good, bad, or indifferent, any building by Christopher Wren, William Butterfield, or Frank Lloyd Wright will have a strong chance for protection. Oak Park, Illinois, has walking tours of Wright's works. Planners in the city of London have to work around the remaining Wren churches (even those that have been bombed out).

Enhancement of Adjacent Areas

Sometimes buildings or groups of buildings are preserved because an investment in them will affect nearby areas. For example, in a deteriorating neighborhood, investing in street improvements and in rehabilitating buildings can arrest deterioration and encourage owners nearby to invest in improving their own buildings. The Martin Luther King, Jr., Historic District in Atlanta, Georgia, is an example.

To be effective this strategy requires not only an investment of money, but also some public relations work. People need to be convinced through verbal commitments, as well as through investment, that decline in an area is actually being turned around.

Superlative

A few buildings have been protected because they can be talked about in terms of superlatives. They are the most, or first, or longest or biggest. St. Peter's Church, now in *Old World Wisconsin,* is an example. The building is in no way distinguished, but it endured four moves and considerable modification over a period of 135 years simply because it was the first cathedral in Milwaukee.

MOTIVES FOR PRESERVATION

Protect Our Legacy

The museum approach to preservation implies a belief that unless bits of the past are protected by law, natural processes of change will modify or even obliterate them. Relics of the past are seen as having didactic value, too. Instead of reading about scale in an eighteenth-century whaling town, one can, because of preservation action, experience such a town. In a period of declining craftsmanship it is important to be able to experience firsthand the work of early craftspeople.

Ensure Variety in the Urban Fabric

There are two aspects to the motive of ensuring variety. One is aesthetic. By preserving the past we can be assured that our cities will not become monotonous, homogenous places where everything looks like everything else. Preserving buildings from various periods guarantees visual variety.

The other aspect is strategic. Politically and economically we need variety in cities because social groups have different needs and aspirations and, of course, because people's ability and desire to pay also varies. Furthermore, we cannot afford new accommodations for everyone, so it is a wise policy to take care of what we have inherited.

Economic

Historic buildings can appreciate in value if properly cared for and, therefore, are often a sound investment. This depends also on other factors: what is happening nearby; the city's long-range plans; and the support for preservation action in a particular area. Investors in Georgetown and German Village have profited from preservation.

Haworth Hill Village, England.

War Memorial: Dresden, East Germany.

Other historic buildings are preserved or rehabilitated because of the potential income they will produce. Ghirardelli Square is more profitable as a tourist attraction than it was as a chocolate factory. Hundreds of thousands of people visit the Vieux Carré in New Orleans, Louisiana. Creation of the Nantucket historic district was in part motivated by potential profits from tourism:

> The purpose of this act is to promote the general welfare of the inhabitants of the town of Nantucket through the preservation and protection of historic buildings, places and districts of historic interest; through the development of an appropriate setting for these buildings, places and districts; and through the benefits resulting to the economy of Nantucket in developing and maintaining its vacation-travel industry through promotion of these historic associations.[9]

In some instances it is less costly to rehabilitate or adapt an existing building to a new use than it is to construct the equivalent new space.

Symbolic

Buildings or groups of buildings sometimes become associated with groups of people so that they are physical manifestations of a group's identity. The symbolic motive for preservation relates to the view that to destroy the building is in some sense to destroy the group.

Another symbolic motive for preservation is seen in memorials. In London, Coventry, Berlin, Dresden, and countless other European cities, bombed-out churches are preserved as monuments to the dead and as reminders of tragic times.

METHODS OF PRESERVATION

Legal Methods

Lists of Historic Buildings and Areas. The earliest instance of listing buildings for preservation at a national scale occurred in France in 1840. When lists become law, buildings identified are guaranteed some degree of protection, though the extent will depend upon the provisions of the law. In some countries buildings are graded according to significance, scarcity, and quality. Buildings of Grade I will be assured of protection, and buildings of Grades II and III will have less stringent preservation requirements associated with them. In England and Wales there are approximately 4,400 Grade I and 111,300 Grade II buildings. An additional 137,000 were listed as Grade III, but these are being reevaluated in response to an unexpected side effect of grading:[10] it was found that the lowest grade is "often an invitation to demolition," since both developers and local authorities feel it is only a half-hearted attempt at protection.[11] It is expected that by 1985 statutory lists for England and Wales will enumerate 250,000 buildings.[12]

The listing of areas and even whole towns is a logical extension of protecting buildings through legislation. Preservationists are now concerned with not just individual scattered buildings but whole town centers, or substantial parts of them.[13] The Council for British Archaeology established the following criteria for determining which areas or towns should be listed:

1 Town plan well preserved: "a complex of streets and open spaces, unchanged for centuries in their form and scale"

2 Town with historic bridge crossing and approaches

3 Town with a waterfront

4 Town wall, ditch or gate well preserved

5 Castle site or precinct well preserved

6 Major ecclesiastical or precinct well preserved

7 Towns characterized by a number of buildings worthy of preservation[14]

Obviously, in newer countries somewhat different criteria are necessary to determine which towns or areas are worthy of protection.

The National Register of Historic Places.
The first modern effort by the U.S. government to gather drawings, photographs, and written data on historic architecture was initiated in 1933. The Historic American Buildings Survey, as it is called, was given permanence by the Historic Sites Act of 1935, which declared as national policy the preservation for public use of historic sites, buildings, and objects. Aside from the chartering of the private National Trust for Historic Preservation by Congress in 1949, however, national support of historic preservation was for more than thirty years limited to protecting a few hundred especially significant properties in the National Park System and the National Historic Landmarks program. As local programs of preservation sprang up around the country in larger cities and communities, the inadequacy of the federal policy began to be recognized. The Historic Preservation Act of 1966 extended the federal government's concern to states and localities through grants and planning requirements, and the National Register of Historic Places was created.

The National Register includes publicly and privately owned districts, sites, buildings, structures, and objects deemed worthy of preservation because of their significance in American history, architecture, archeology, and culture. A cumulative listing is published each February in the *Federal Register,* with monthly supplements throughout the year. Properties may be nominated to the National Register in several ways. The following example illustrates nominations arising from local initiative. Cream City has established a Landmarks Commission, as have a dozen other cities and four counties in the state. Every year the Commission, at the urging of members and other interested citizens, examines a number of properties said to have important historical associations or architectural merit. These are documented and discussed at public meetings. Recently the Commission has added seven properties to its list of local landmarks. The State Historic Preservation Officer (SHPO) is notified of the additions. The SHPO's office, part of the State Historical Society (its counterpart in an adjacent state is part of the Department of Resources and Parks), has prepared the state historic preservation plan and an inventory of individual sites. This year the SHPO has done detailed research on many properties in the inventory and now has as well the information from Cream City's Landmarks Commission. Several properties, including two from Cream City, are deemed worthy of inclusion in the National Register, although they are primarily of state or local significance. The State Historic Preservation Review Board approves the nominations, and they are submitted to the National Park Service in the U.S. Department of the Interior. Notice of the proposals is published in the *Federal Register* so that comments may be received while the Park Service evaluates the nominations for conformance to prescribed criteria. The state has chosen well, and its nominations are approved and listed in the National Register.

The National Register provides recognition and procedural safeguards for listed properties, but it does not defend them from change and adversity. Private properties may be listed without receiving the consent of their owners, but the owners are not thereby prevented from modifying or demolishing their buildings. However, any undertakings executed, licensed, or financially assisted by the federal government that affect properties on or eligible for the National Register must be reviewed by the Advisory Council on Historic Preservation. The Advisory Council's comments must then be incorporated in the decision-making process, but they are not binding upon the users or providers of federal funds. The National Register does offer one unalloyed benefit: the properties listed on it may be acquired or developed for public use with federal grants-in-aid from the Historic Preservation Fund, to which a total of $500 million has been tentatively appropriated for fiscal years 1978 to 1981.[15]

Zoning *Special district zoning* accommodates a special set of uses that deviate from conventional patterns. For example, in a single-family area, *historic zoning* might allow for conversion of historic mansions to two- or three-unit dwellings in order to make the cost of maintaining them reasonable.

Usually when a historic district with special zoning is identified, it is necessary to create a commission to administer the area, and, in particular, to make judgments about the appropriateness of proposed modifications to buildings.

Overlay zoning is a set of requirements in addition to those already designated in an existing ordinance. Development must conform to both sets of requirements or to the more restrictive of the two.

Incentive zoning as discussed earlier, provides advantages for developers who offer amenities in exchange for special privileges. In the case of historic buildings, a developer who preserves a historic property may be allowed to build elsewhere at higher density or at a higher use than existing zoning would allow.

Variances. In order to promote and accommodate preservation, it is sometimes necessary to give *variances* from existing zoning restrictions. For example, a variance might be allowed for a building in a residential area to enable it to be more productive economically. If he or she is allowed to use the building for office or limited commercial purposes, the owner can afford to preserve and maintain it.

Easements and Deed Restrictions. Owners of buildings can agree to give a *facade easement* as a condition of their ownership. This says in effect that the public face of the building belongs to the public and must be preserved. What happens elsewhere in the building is not affected by the facade easement. Similarly, restrictions can be written into deeds whereby changes to buildings are prohibited without permission of a designated authority (such as a historic district commission).

Demolition Control. Special ordinances also may prohibit demolition of historic structures without permission of a designated authority. Typically in the United States there is a limit to the period of time that demolition can be stayed, thus assuring the owner that his rights are not entirely lost.

Design Guidelines. In some instances creation of historic districts includes design guidelines for new construction. This process recognizes the fact that there are often vacant lots and buildings of no historical significance within the boundaries of the district. Design guidelines specify restrictions for new construction. Requirements may pertain to style, height, proportions, setbacks, materials, and fenestration.

Economic Methods

Grants. Government grants to help cover the cost of restoration or rehabilitation are much more common in Europe than in North America. They are part of a policy that recognizes the cultural significance of historic buildings as well as their importance to the tourism industry. Otherwise private sources of grants are sometimes available, although these are most often in the form of loans or revolving funds.

Revolving Funds. Through revolving funds, capital acquired through grants or loans is used to purchase and rehabilitate structures that are then sold. (As a condition of sale, deed conditions can be attached to restrict new owners' options for modification of the building facade.) The amount of the original loan with interest is returned to the revolving fund, to be used to purchase and improve other structures. Through this mechanism a small amount of capital can have a long-range impact.

Tax Incentives. Under certain circumstances tax rates may be reduced for historic properties, or assessments may be made according to existing use rather than to highest and best use. Another technique is to allow investments in rehabilitation to replace a portion of one's tax payment or a special assessment for neighborhood improvements.[16]

Development Rights Transfer. Many urban landmarks are smaller and have a lower use than is otherwise allowed under local zoning ordinances. The *development rights transfer* permits an owner to sell the rights to the difference between the actual size and use of the building and the maximum size and highest use that the property could sustain if developed in accordance with the local zoning ordinance. The rights are usually transferred to a new building being built nearby. The owner of the historic building benefits through outright compensation and through lower taxes (since the new tax will be based on actual use instead of on highest and best use).

Penalties. Ordinances and other laws can include provisions for penalizing owners who demolish, despoil, or neglect buildings identified as historically significant. For example, in Britain,

> A person found guilty is liable on summary conviction to a fine of up to £250 or a 3-months term of imprisonment or both; or on conviction on indictment, to a term of imprisonment of up to 12 months, or to a fine which takes into account any financial benefit likely to accrue from the offence or both.[17]

The latter penalty was created in response to situations in which owners were happy to pay a small fine for demolishing a listed building because they could anticipate sizable profits through sale or alternative use.

PROBLEMS AND CONFLICTS

Historic preservation is as controversial as any other facet of urban planning. Efforts to accomplish preservation goals often conflict with other goals for urban life and form. The following questions inevitably arise in conjunction with attempts to preserve parts of the urban fabric.

1. *Who decides what is preserved and for how long? Experts in architecture or history? Owners of buildings? Politicians?* In many cases decisions are

made by a group of experts, appointed by politicians, who listen closely to owners. In other cases experts act on behalf of the public good, in spite of any objections by owners and officials.

2. *How can we reconcile preservation of historic structures with other imperatives, such as making buildings energy-efficient or constructing new mass transportation systems?* Adaptation of historic buildings to new uses or for greater energy efficiency is often possible. But when a building literally stands in the way of progressive development, compromise (often costly) is required. Demolition is no longer seen as the only resolution of such problems.

3. *Who pays for preservation and who profits from it?* Precedents for sharing the costs and benefits of preservation are now so diverse that the issue is not *who,* but *which* method shall be applied. Options vary from exclusively governmental responsibility to solely private initiative to combinations of the two.

4. *How extensive should restrictions on changes in historic buildings be?* One of the important steps in the designation of historic buildings and areas is identification of their special significance. Are they important as urban form, as interiors, as period pieces? The modifications allowed should be based upon the ways in which the building is seen to be significant.

5. *What rights do owners and renters have with regard to tenure?* In most cases owners and occupants retain their rights. However, restrictions on subsequent changes may be imposed, and value

and costs may change as a by-product of preservation orders. Whether there is compensation for losses or whether profits are somehow shared has been determined on a case-by-case basis.

6. *What rights and responsibilities do other citizens have? Can they force owners to preserve and care for historic buildings?* Legislation and court rulings have now established that in some instances the public good takes precedence over individuals' rights to modify or demolish buildings that are seen as important local or national heritages.

THE PLACE OF HISTORIC PRESERVATION IN URBAN PLANNING

Historic preservation is an established and accepted facet of planning in Europe. While there are continuing discussions regarding the *extent* of preservation, there is general agreement that the part of the built environment that has been inherited is important both as cultural history and as an amenity. In the oldest settlements of North America, there is also agreement about the importance of saving notable inheritances from the past. Elsewhere, however, there is no consensus. This is true particularly of newer areas where historical events are too recent to seem significant. But even in these areas the trend now is towards preservation. Pressures from both private groups and central government make preservation an indisputable concern of planners.

NOTES

1. John D. Rockefeller, Jr., "The Genesis of the Williamsburg Restoration," *National Geographic* 71 (April 1937):401.
2. Bill Moyers, *Newsweek,* 16 December 1974, p. 108.
3. Great Britain, *Civic Amenities Act, 1967.*
4. Massachusetts, *Acts* (1970), chap. 395, sec. 4.
5. Oxford, England, City Architect and Planning Officer, *High Buildings in Oxford,* 1962, p. 6.

6. Robert Venturi, Denise Scott Brown, and Steven Izenour, *Learning from Las Vegas* (Cambridge, Mass.: M.I.T., 1972).
7. Sir Robert Matthew, John Reid, and Maurice Lindsay, eds., *The Conservation of Georgian Edinburgh* (Edinburgh: University of Edinburgh Press, 1972), p. 10.
8. *Times* (London), 21 February 1969, p. 2.
9. Massachusetts, *Acts* (1970), chap. 395, sec. 4.

10. Donald W. Insall, *The Care of Old Buildings Today* (London: Architectural Press, 1972), p. 12.

11. Greater London Council, *The Work of the Historic Buildings Board* (London: Greater London Council, n.d.), p. 24.

12. Insall, *Care of Old Buildings*, p. 12.

13. "Towards a National Classification," *Architects' Journal* (18 January 1967), p. 139.

14. Ibid., p. 139–41.

15. For the statutory basis of this discussion, refer to the National Historic Preservation Act of 1966, P.L. 89-665, and its major amendment, the National Historic Preservation Fund Act of 1976, Title II of P.L. 94-422. Executive Order No. 11593 of 13 May 1971, "Protection and Enhancement of the Cultural Environ-

ment," sets out some general responsibilities of federal agencies. The requirements of the National Park Service and the Advisory Council on Historic Preservation may be found in Title 36 of the *Code of Federal Regulations;* see Part 60, "National Register of Historic Places," and Part 800, "Procedures for the Protection of Historic and Cultural Properties."

16. The Historic Structures Tax Act, Sec 2124 of the Tax Reform Act of 1976, P.L. 94-455, is the first clear federal tax incentive for preservation. It benefits those who rehabilitate National Register properties and limits certain deductions and depreciation rates formerly available to those who demolished and redeveloped the site of a National Register building.

17. Insall, *Care of Old Buildings*, p. 15.

FOR FURTHER READING

Cantacuzino, Sherban, ed. *Architectural Conservation in Europe.* New York: Whitney Library of Design, 1975.

Civic Trust. *Financing the Preservation of Old Buildings.* London: Civic Trust, 1971.

Fawcett, Jane, ed. *The Future of the Past: Attitudes to Conservation, 1174-1974.* London: Thames & Hudson, 1976.

Insall, Donald W. *The Care of Old Buildings Today.* London: Architectural Press, 1972.

McNulty, Robert H., and Kliment, Stephen A. *Neighborhood Conservation.* New York: Whitney Library of Design, 1976.

National Trust for Historic Preservation in the United States. *Economic Benefits of Preserving Old Buildings.* Washington, D.C.: Preservation Press, National Trust for Historic Preservation, 1976.

Papageorgiou, Alexander. *Continuity and Change.* London: Pall Mall, 1971.

United Nations. Economic and Social Council. *The Conservation of Cities.* Paris: UNESCO, 1975.

Ward, Pamela, ed. *Conservation and Development in Historic Towns and Cities.* Newcastle-upon-Tyne, England: Oriel, 1968.

CHAPTER 14

Fiscal Planning and Management

James C. Snyder

Some would argue that urban planning is effective only when it is integrated with fiscal matters. The basis for this belief is that most private and public undertakings in the realm of the built environment are constrained by economic and fiscal realities. Regardless of the severity of such constraints, urban planners have become involved in fiscal management and planning systems. This chapter discusses such matters within the context of local government management—which is so important to the implementation of all types of plans.

THE FISCAL SITUATION

Finance is an integral part of the overall management and planning function.[1] The relatively recent inclusion of fiscal planning in the larger contexts of urban planning and local government finance has occurred largely because of the increasing complexity and severity of financial problems in local government and the growing trend to integrate the planning process into the overall function of local government management.

The Fiscal Crunch

Local governments are increasingly finding that the demand for public goods and services exceeds the supply. Increasing population, income, and urbanization, along with rising expectations, have resulted in a need for more extensive local government activity. The depth and scope of public services has expanded dramatically in recent decades, and it appears that this trend will continue over the long run. In addition, inflation (particularly public worker wage inflation) has led to higher costs of production. Yet local government revenue structure and production capacity have remained relatively unchanged. The federal government, through the income tax, and the states, through sales and income taxes, have expanding revenue bases and generally have been able to provide adequate services without significant increases in tax rates. Local governments, however, rely heavily on the property tax, the revenue of which lags behind economic growth. Thus, local governments have had to raise tax rates. All these factors have produced a fiscal crunch, and local governments simply cannot finance the desired level of public service. The problem is further compounded by the fragmentation and overlapping of local political jurisdictions, which leads to the segregation of persons by income and wealth, disparities in fiscal capacity, diseconomies of scale, and a lack of overall planning and management of public resources. All of this produces confusion for citizens about the benefits they receive from their tax dollars and uncertainty by government about revenue and expenditure decisions. Most recently, public attention has been focused on fiscal issues via California's Proposition 13 tax revolt and similar movements in a number of states. Thus, the planning and management of fiscal resources has become one of the major concerns of local government officials.

Planning and Finance

There appears to be a general trend towards increased fiscal management and planning in local government. This can be seen in the historical development of the functions of planning and finance.[2]

Before World War II, planning responsibilities resided in independent commissions of citizens, which were presumably free of political influence. The commissions were usually established by ordinance and composed of several members appointed by the mayor and council, but they were to represent the community at large rather than the mayor and council. Each commission usually hired a professional staff to ascertain the public interest,

to make plans for the future based on that interest, and to recommend plans to the legislative body. Plans were focused on the physical elements of land use, transportation, and certain public facilities, combined in a long-range master plan. There was no direct relationship between the planning commission staff and the rest of local government, and the only relationship to finance was through recommendations for public capital improvements. Thus, the master plans were usually advisory. This type of planning was subjected to heavy criticism, because its structural remoteness from the rest of local government usually resulted in little effectiveness, and the emphasis on physical elements was too narrow.

In the 1940s a new concept of planning emerged. Planning was identified as a staff function of the mayor, manager, or city council. This concept has facilitated the integration of planning into the overall management system of local government and encouraged closer ties between planning and other departments such as finance. The emphasis of planning efforts has shifted from the relatively narrow physical master plan to comprehensive concerns as broad as the functions of local government. In addition, planning has become concerned with policy and program analysis. Planning can fit into a variety of current organizational structures. In the typical municipality, the voters elect a mayor, city council and other officials such as the clerk, treasurer, and assessor. The city council serves as the legislative body. The mayor can fill several different positions. He or she may serve as the presiding officer of the council (a "weak" mayor), or as the chief executive officer (a "strong" mayor). A council-manager structure uses a city manager, who is appointed by the council and/or mayor. The council and mayor are responsible for all city policy, while the city manager is responsible for administration. City operations are distributed among functional line departments; each line department has a department head responsible to the executive mayor or the city manager. Of course, there is much variation among local government organizational structures. The planning unit can be a line department or a semi-independent commission, with its own staff, advising or reporting to the mayor and council. Sometimes the commission sits as an advisory body while the staff is a line department. This variety of arrangements has led to confusion and considerable debate about to the best place for a planning unit.

Local government finance developed in a quite different way.[3] In the early 1900s there was very little actual financial management. The main concern was to prohibit illegal spending. Financial functions were distributed among several independent officials: the treasurer, tax collector, and controller. Each was a check on the others. Centralization of these financial functions came with the emergence of strong mayor and city manager forms of government in the 1920s and 1930s. Financial functions often were placed in a single department that reported directly to the mayor or manager. This comprehensiveness and centralization of power allowed for the development of central management of financial matters.

Despite their differences, the functions of planning and finance have become increasingly centralized under the chief executive and within the overall management process. Both financial and planning operations have line and staff functions. Line functions are those tasks related to the actual production and delivery of service, and staff functions involve formulating policy and advising the manager, mayor, and city council. For example, the finance department distributes bills and collect payments as a line function and formulates alternative fiscal policies as a staff function. Likewise, the planning department reviews subdivision proposals as a line function and develops alternative land use policies as a staff function.

Most importantly, there is a particularly strong relationship between the policy components of finance and planning. Most decisions with future consequences have financial implications. For example, the implementation of a land use plan requires large capital investments that must be programmed by the finance department. The recognition of this inherent relationship between policy levels of planning and finance has led to the emergence of fiscal planning. It has become apparent that planning without regard to financial consequences and financing without the benefit of planning are unproductive. Therefore, the trend now is to combine major components of the planning and finance functions into units of planning and budget, management and budget, policy analysis, or similar arrangements.

As finance and planning become integral parts of the central management function, planners and related professionals must fully understand fiscal matters and financial personnel must learn to appreciate the planning process. The extent to which the planner can affect fiscal matters will depend on the structure and process of management within his or her unit of local government. However, the planner should at the least be well versed in the basic principles of economics and public finance; the basic processes of fiscal planning and budgeting in local government; and revenue instruments, intergovernmental relations (grants and aids), debt financing, and accounting systems.

MANAGEMENT

Planning and management may be viewed as the same process. That is, rather than look at planning and finance as separate functions, the planning and management process should be applied to all the functions of local government, all of which have financial aspects.

Management is such a broad and general concept that precise definitions are impossible. A. W. Steiss refers to management as "the art of getting things done," involving "the direction, coordination, and control of resources to achieve some purpose or objective."[4] M. J. Munson describes management as that "which keeps the various activities of the organization coordinated and continuously striving towards fulfillment of the organization's internal and external purposes."[5] Management can also be looked at as a decision process. Munson states that "the management function will consist of decisions determining what the organization's purposes are, what the organization is going to do to fulfill those purposes, how the organization is going to do these things, and who in the organization is going to do them."[6]

A management system is an interrelated group of decision processes; the planning function is an integral part of the management system, not a separate element. The elements of the system can be described as broad categories of tasks. Munson uses the following categories:

1. *Strategic planning* involves the formulation of overall goals and objectives and the selection of policies that apply to the acquisition and expenditure of resources.

2. *Management planning* involves the formulation of programs of activities that are designed to accomplish goals and objectives within policy constraints.

3. *Operational control* involves the conduct of specific program tasks in order to affect objectives.[7]

The accompanying figure shows these three categories grouped into a conceptual functional hierarchy (not an organizational chart).

Strategic planning involves determining goals, objectives, and policies for the organization. Once determined, these are passed on to the management planning unit. This is not to say that management planning has no effect on the formulation of goals and policies. Alternate goals and policies may originate at any level, but the decisions are made at the strategic planning level. Specific individuals in the organization may have responsibilities in several of the functional categories. For example, a mayor might sit with the city council for strategic decisions while serving as chief administrative officer for management planning decisions.

Management planning involves selecting the operations that will be required to accomplish the objectives and policies of the organization. The output of management planning is essentially a plan of programs to be implemented. The operational control function translates the programs into a series of tasks and then implements the tasks. Ideally, these tasks result in the achievement of the goals and objectives of the organization.

The process of management is continuous. Changes occur in the environment because of the effects of the organization's activities and because of other external factors. The organization should continuously assess the changing of the environment to suitably alter its goals, objectives, policies, programs, and tasks.

For example, a city may be organized so that the strategic planning function is the responsibility of the city council, the management planning function falls to the city manager and his or her planning staff, and operational control rests with the line departments. The city council continually assesses the city environment to identify problems. Often these problems are issues brought to light by indi-

The management system.

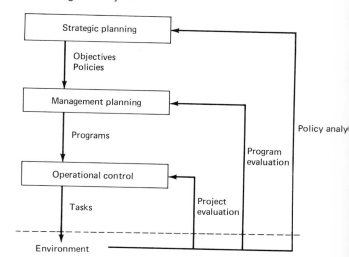

viduals or groups in the environment or within the management system.

One such issue might be traffic congestion in the central business district. The city council recognizes the problem and adopts the strategic goal of "solving the CBD traffic problem." The manager and his planning staff are directed to analyze the problem. The staff conducts the appropriate analysis and articulates the problem as one of inadequate traffic control and insufficient parking space. They explore alternative ways of providing better traffic control and more parking space, among them the provision of additional off-street parking, better traffic signals, and stronger enforcement of existing parking regulations.

The council reviews and accepts or rejects these alternatives. It actuates the acceptable policies through legislation and administrative directives to the city manager. For example, the council might alter the budget by a legislative amendment to allocate resources for acquiring land, constructing parking lots, and designing traffic signal systems. The manager and staff would then determine the operations and sequence of operations required to implement these policies. Each set of activities would constitute a program design. The programs would be directed to the relevant line departments (such as public works, streets, and police) to carry out the appropriate tasks. After some period of time, an evaluation would take place at each management level. The city council evaluates the effectiveness of its policies; the manager evaluates the effectiveness of the programs; and the line departments evaluate the effectiveness of program tasks.

Evaluation is essential to the continuous process of management. The results of the evaluation of policies, programs, and operational tasks allow for a new round of decision making. Has the problem been solved? If not, how has it been affected? Should policies, programs, and/or tasks be altered? Are more resources required? This process of incremental, continuous adjustment of the organization is *management*.

THE FISCAL PLANNING SYSTEM

The fiscal management system is approached here as a subsystem of the overall process of management—as a series of specific fiscal activities that are symbiotically related to individual elements of the management process. The accompanying figure shows both the general management and the fiscal planning processes.[8] The management side includes the three management phases previously described, articulated as the processes of generating objectives, policies, plans, and programs; implementation; and evaluation. The fiscal planning side shows the fiscal elements of that management process and the relationship of fiscal to general elements.

The strategic planning phase includes the financial elements of basic economic research and fiscal policy analysis. Basic economic research provides projections of future population, employment, income (estimates of demand for public goods and services), and other economic parameters necessary for fiscal policy analysis. Fiscal policy analysis includes two activities: (1) the estimation of potential economic and financial consequences of overall public policy alternatives being considered at the strategic planning level; and (2) the formulation and evaluation of specific alternative financial policies relevant to public goals and objectives.

Thus the strategic planning phase produces public policies, including specific financial policies, for the management planning phase. One such policy might involve "the improvement of the quality of existing neighborhoods and housing stock through the mechanisms of selective area code enforcement and rehabilitation." This policy would have been selected from alternative policies because the policy analysis showed it to be best in terms of satisfying goals and objectives, and the estimated consequences of this alternative (including economic and financial consequences) appeared to match the desired consequences most closely. Analyzing the economic and financial consequences is part of the fiscal policy analysis. Likewise, a specific fiscal policy may be formulated consistent with and supportive of overall policies; e.g., "the financing of housing development programs primarily from community development block grant funds and other categorical grant program funds."

The financial activities involved in the management planning phase include the formulation of long-range fiscal plans; capital, service, and revenue programs; and the capital and operating budget. Long-range financial planning involves conducting a fiscal outlook study to project future levels of required expenditures and revenues, as well as formulating expenditure and revenue plans to ensure a balanced budget. This financial plan must be

scaled to the comprehensive plan; in fact, they are simply two parts of the same plan. The financial plan is then translated into shorter-range, more detailed capital, service, and revenue programs. These programs must be integrated into the overall programs of the local government. That is, the financial programs represent the financial articulation of the capital facilities, services, and revenues required to carry out the programs of local government over a period of five or six years. They also serve as guidelines for the formulation of the operation and capital budgets, which allocate dollars to specific programs for one-year periods.

As programs are implemented, control is required to ensure that expenditures are not exceeding budgeted amounts and that the revenues are not

The fiscal management and planning system.

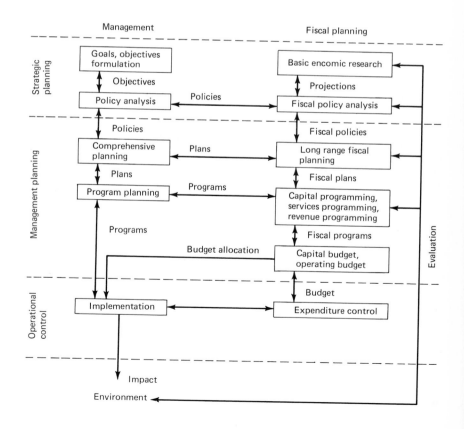

below projected estimates. Although some flexibility is built into the budgets, major variations may require readjustments in budgets, programs, plans, policies, and/or goals and objectives.

Basic Economic Research

Basic economic research, in the context of local governmental financial planning, involves the estimation of future levels of demand for public goods and services. The local government is the producer; the citizen is the consumer. Therefore, the fiscal impact of alternative public policies depends heavily on the future economic composition of the city. Policy formulation relative to capital investment (such as extension of public utilities, construction of roads, and land acquisition); service program development (health, education, and recreation); and revenue (taxes, user charges, and grants) depends on estimates of future levels of population, income, land use, and other economic variables. For example, the policy for new school construction will depend on the projected school-age population over the lifespan of the school facility. Likewise, the financial resources required for the extension of water and sewer lines will depend on the projected area and density of new physical development. The fiscal impact of a property tax rate reduction will depend on the future size of the tax base.

Fiscal Policy Analysis

Fiscal policy analysis involves the formulation and evaluation of alternative fiscal policies and the estimation and evaluation of the economic and financial consequences of alternative general policies. For example, a local government might want to formulate a consistent policy relative to the amount and quality of future growth. Policy analysis would involve estimating the effects of existing policies on past and future growth and the formulation and evaluation of alternative growth policies. The economic and financial consequences of particular growth

policies would also be included. Local government decision makers should know the probable public and private economic and financial consequences of each policy before adopting a set of policies. Basic economic projections and analysis techniques allow for such analyses.

At a more specific level, individual alternatives (e.g., new developments, zoning changes, annexations) may be evaluated in terms of cost and revenue consequences to the governmental unit. This limited type of analysis is termed cost-revenue or fiscal impact analysis.

In addition to the general policies, fiscal policy analysis deals with the formulation and evaluation of specific fiscal policies. A local government may have goals and objectives relative to economic growth, stability, equity, and efficiency, which are articulated as expenditure and revenue policy. For example, a city might want to reduce reliance on the property tax as a major revenue source because of the apparent inequity and inefficiency of that tax. Fiscal policy analysis would formulate and evaluate alternative revenue sources, including local income and sales taxes.

Analysis might be directed at estimating the economic impacts of alternative budget allocations. For example, policy analysis might explore the extent to which a city should be debt financing, using funds for matching federal or state grants, or supporting quasi-governmental activities.

Long-Range Fiscal Planning

Long-range fiscal planning occurs at the management planning stage of the overall management system. It parallels the comprehensive planning process. The long-range fiscal plan has three functions:

1 It provides financial dimension to the comprehensive plan.

2 It identifies the sequence of actions required to carry out fiscal policies.

3 It generates the necessary inputs to the capital, service, and revenue programs.

Long-range fiscal planning starts with the basic economic projections and adopted fiscal policies from the strategic planning phase of management. The development of a fiscal plan must coincide with the development of the comprehensive plan because the overall plan of capital improvements and services must be financially feasible.

The primary element of the fiscal plan is the fiscal outlook study, which compares future expected levels of revenues and expenditures; identifies potential fiscal problems; and formulates actions to overcome problems. The following list describes the sequence of fiscal planning activities:

1 Inventory of activities by category

2 Analysis of service standards

3 Analysis of methods of operation

4 Analysis of cost factors

5 Estimation of future expenditures

6 Estimation of future revenues

7 A combined fiscal outlook and identification of problems

8 Analysis of alternative solutions

9 Recommended set of fiscal actions, in sequence, with the probable effects, leading to a balanced budget and a sound financial state

Inventory of Activities. The inventory of activities is constructed from all existing and proposed activities included in the comprehensive plan. These items are organized on a line item or program basis with associated costs and/or revenues (data from the accounting system).

Capital and service activities are treated separately because of the tendency to finance capital items through debt and service activities through operating budgets and because expenditures for many capital items are one time only expenses. This separation yields a reasonable context for balancing the budget. A balanced budget does not strictly imply that total revenues equal total expenditures within a particular time period, but rather that total revenues equal the non-debt-financed expenditures plus the debt service. For example, a local government may finance a large capital facility via a bond issue (debt) and pay for the facility (repay the debt) over a period of years. The amount of the debt repayment, rather than the entire capital sum, is considered as the expenditure in a given year. Thus, it is possible to show a balanced budget each year while incurring higher levels of debt. The separate treatment of capital and service (or operating) activities provides a better overall picture of financial condition.

Activities are also categorized by priority. The highest priority includes the activities that are required by law and/or convention and are considered to constitute the absolute base of local government activity. Examples include fire and police protection, waste collection, and utilities. The second priority includes the additional facilities and services required to carry out previously adopted plans and programs. Examples include increases in service quality, capital elements of the comprehensive plan, and successive activities for multiyear programs. The third category includes new facilities and programs that have not previously received financial commitment and can be postponed if necessary.

Analysis of Service Standards, Methods of Operation, and Cost Factors. After the inventory of activities is constructed or revised from the previous year, each activity should be evaluated in terms of standards of service, methods of production and supply, and unit cost factors. The objective is to select the appropriate level of service and to relate unit costs to output for existing and alternative methods so that revisions can be made in the inventory.

Should the level of a particular service be increased or decreased? Limited resources often mean that an increase in the level of service for one activity requires a decrease in level of service for another. Intercity comparisons are sometimes useful, and standards are often suggested by national associations for particular functional areas. The basic process is one of setting priorities among services.

The analysis of production and supply methods involves scanning alternative methods for performing activity tasks, especially those developed from new technology that might yield increased productivity and/or efficiency. The analysis of cost factors involves identifying trends in the cost levels of the resources of production (such as labor and materials prices) and assessing unit costs for each existing activity and for alternative methods of performing those activities.

Estimation of Expenditures and Revenues.

The levels of expenditure for each fiscal year are usually estimated for future periods of five to ten years. The expenditure required for each activity by category (from the inventory of activities) is projected by adjusting the existing expenditure according to expected changes in the base of the activity and the cost of the activity.[9] For example, solid waste collection service for 10,000 households at a cost of $45 per household would yield a total expenditure of $450,000. A five-year estimate requires a projection of changes in the number of households and changes in costs over that period. Population projections yield an expected number of households. Adjustments to cost figures must be based on estimated changes in factor prices (land, labor, and capital), service standards, and productivity (changes in methods of operation or technological innovation).

Revenues are estimated in much the same way. Total revenues include taxes, user charges, administrative fees, short-term investment returns, grants, and other transfers. Taxes, the largest revenue class, are projected from existing tax rates, assuming changes only in the tax base. Tax bases generally include the value of real estate (the property tax digest), the level of consumer expenditure (the sales tax), and/or income (income taxes). The rates of change of these bases and other revenue sources can often be projected statistically.

If the estimate of the rate of change for the base is made from the estimate of other basic economic variables (such as income, population, or consumer expenditure), the revenue elasticity of the particular tax must be considered. The revenue elasticity is the percentage change in revenue relative to the percentage change in the economic variable. For example, the revenue from a local income tax may change more slowly than the level of income because of differences in taxable income and total income, or it may change faster because of a progressive tax rate. Estimates of elasticity can be derived from the analysis of historical data. They may be available to local governments from state revenue agencies.

Fiscal Outlook.

Expenditures are projected for each category of activity, assuming changes in expenditure bases and costs. Revenues are likewise projected, assuming changes in the bases but not in rates. Thus, the projections yield an estimate of what can be expected in the absence of additional changes in policy, program, plan, or activity.

These estimates can be plotted as shown. A number of such calculations and graphs are required to produce a sufficiently detailed fiscal outlook. Each expenditure and revenue fund and/or other financial entity (such as general fund, specific capital funds, trust funds, debt repayment funds, or public utilities) should be individually inspected. The appropriate consolidation of these charts provides a summary fiscal outlook.

Collectively these estimates exhibit the expected relationships between expenditures and revenues. If revenues cover expenditures, then no exceptional action is required. However, the more typical situation (given recent levels of inflation, expansion of the scope of local government services,

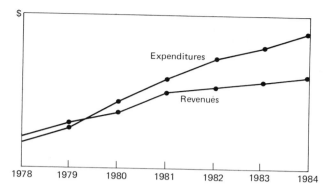

Fiscal outlook graph.

with one-year increments) of the program activities of local governments.

The capital program includes a list and description of each proposed capital project with an assignment of resources (dollar amounts) over a five-year period. This display is useful because capital projects may take more than one year to complete but, once started, represent a commitment to a certain level of expenditure. All the projects and the related expenditures make up the total capital program. Often the first year of the five-year capital program is adopted as capital budget for that fiscal year.

The capital program includes:

1 List and description of each capital project, including the purpose of the project

2 Estimation of the costs for each project over a five-year period

3 Source of funds for each project

4 Corresponding service costs for each capital project

5 Interrelationships among projects, including physical, financial, and timing

6 Priority list

7 Summary of the total capital program

The service and revenue programs are essentially similar to the capital program, including a list and description of services and revenue sources over a five-year period. They have a similar function of grouping expenditures and revenues at the level of specific activities. However, they generally are not adopted directly as budgets, but guide the formulation of the operating budget and its related tax legislation.

constrained tax bases, and recent taxpayer revolts) shows an estimated deficit in some categories, if not in the overall budget. Once the magnitude of the differences is known, alternative solutions can be formulated and evaluated. The level and composition of public services and the timing of capital improvements can be changed to affect the level of expenditures, and tax structure and tax rates can be adjusted to yield different levels of revenue. The probable impact of any such change can be estimated through an expenditure and/or revenue analysis with the changes included. Thus, alternative fiscal solutions can be evaluated in terms of fiscal impact.

The estimates, along with the subsequent fiscal actions, constitute the long-range fiscal plan. No plan should be so rigid as to preclude subsequent change; rather the process of fiscal planning is continuous to allow for adjusting the system periodically in response to changing conditions. The long-range fiscal plan is a response to future uncertainty and is designed to provide lead time for rational fiscal decisions.

Capital, Service, and Revenue Programs.

Capital, service, and revenue programs are formulated to carry out the long-range fiscal plan. In other words, fiscal programs translate the fiscal plan into shorter-range components (five-year periods

BUDGETING

Budgeting is an integral part of the fiscal planning process after the basic economic research, fiscal policy analysis, long-range fiscal planning, and programming have been completed. The term *budgeting* is often used to refer to the overall process of allocating resources as well as to the preparation of specific documents.

Today the budget is the central element of public fiscal management as well as a major element in the overall process of local government. It is both a document and a complex, collective decision process. It can be defined as the financial articulation of the activities of a governmental unit; at the local level it takes the form of an ordinance or resolution that recognizes anticipated revenues, authorizes activities, and appropriates expenditures for a one-year time period.

Budget formulation is a complex process containing elements of planning, politics, economics, and accounting. It is a planning process because it involves making decisions that have consequences for future time periods. Goals and objectives must be formulated, policies analyzed, and comprehensive plans and programs delineated before the budget can be formulated. It is not unusual for a local government to initiate the budget planning process a full year before the budget adoption.

Budgeting is a political process because it is the collective mechanism whereby decisions are made about "who gets what" in the local public sector. Budgeting is an economic process because allocating resources is a primary function of any economic system. Budgeting is therefore the public substitute for the automatic allocational mechanisms of the private market system. Finally, budgeting is an accounting process whereby revenue and expenditure information is structured to facilitate continuous inspection, evaluation, and management control. This complex process works at the local level of government largely because of the adoption of a systematic procedure, although there is a great deal of disagreement about the best procedure. A typical step-by-step budgeting process is presented here, but this process varies depending on a government's specific situation and needs.

The Budget Process

The budgeting process commonly involves four major activities:

1 Executive preparation
2 Legislative review, modification, and enactment
3 Executive implementation
4 Postaudit

The chief executive often is responsible for preparing budget estimates and a preliminary budget document. Depending on the size of the city, the executive alone may prepare the budget or he or she may rely on a budget officer, the finance department, and the planning department.

This executive budget is presented to the legislature and to the public before the fiscal year begins. The legislative body reviews the proposed budget, holds public hearings, and makes changes if necessary. The final budget is adopted with a resolution or ordinance that authorizes activities, appropriates monies, and sets tax rates.

The chief executive then administers the final budget. Changes may be necessary during the budget year because of differences between estimated and actual revenues and expenditures, emergencies, and shifting priorities. Typically, these are effected through amendments to the budget ordinance.

The postaudit is an external accounting of the actual financial activities for a budget year, which is presented to the legislative body. Each of these general activities can be broken down into a number of specific activities and set in a time sequence of a budget calendar.

The Budget Calendar. Local government budget authority (and sometimes procedure) is set by state law or local government charters or both. Detailed budget procedure is usually presented in an administrative document. This budget manual normally outlines several budget activities and a budget calendar or cycle. A budget is effective for a one-year period, either a fiscal year from July 1 to June 30 or October 1 to September 30, or the calendar year from January 1 to December 31. There is an advantage in using the same calendar used by higher levels of government.

Shown is a sample activity chart/calendar for a budget cycle on a calendar-year basis with a one-year budget preparation sequence. Each of these activities is described below, starting with the first steps of executive preparation.

Departmental Estimates. The chief executive issues a budget memorandum to all department

heads and to others with expenditure responsibilities. This communication lays the groundwork for the detailed budget requests of each department.

The memorandum includes the following items:

1 *Anticipated fiscal policy:* a summary of the overall fiscal situation, with policies that will affect specific departments, such as changes in total or particular revenues and expenditures or changes in personnel policies and salaries

2 *Capital and service programs:* a summary of anticipated activities over a five- or six-year period, including continued, discontinued, and/or new programs, with expenditure and revenue estimates

3 *Departmental activity inventory:* an activity invento-

The budget calendar.

Jan	Feb	Mar	Apr	May	Jun	Jul	Aug	Sep	Oct	Nov	Dec

Budget formulation

Basic econ. research — Estimates of demand

Fiscal policy analysis — Fiscal policies

Long range fiscal plan. — Fiscal plan

Programming — Capital program / Service program / Revenue program

Departmental estimates — Expenditure and revenue estimates

Executive review

Document prep. — Operating, capital budget

Legislative review and adoption

Budget management

Audit   Audit   Audit   Audit

Budget amendments as required

ry for each department organized by budget category, including projected service volumes, service standards, methods of operation, and cost factors

4 *Request for departmental budget request:* a standardized set of forms, designed to facilitate executive review, which is consistent with budget and accounting format

Each department head reviews the budget memorandum and completes and submits the budget request forms. The department head in effect is formulating a budget for his or her own department and planning the assignment of the resources of personnel, equipment, and supplies to the programs and activities of the department within the constraints identified in the memorandum. This task yields an estimate of the funds required by the department. The department head will have been involved in much of the previous planning process, including the formulation of the activity inventory, setting service standards, selecting methods of operation, and designing capital and service programs. The departmental requests bring all of the budgets together in a format that can be analyzed and adjusted.

Executive Review. Every local government operates in a situation of limited resources, and many operate under severe fiscal constraints. There is rarely enough revenue to allow a city to do everything it would like. Therefore, one of the major budgeting tasks for the chief executive is to balance total required expenditures with total expected revenues. (State laws usually prohibit a city from budgeting expenditures that exceed expected revenues or some percentage of expected revenues.) Department budget requests taken collectively usually exceed the estimated revenues. The executive must fit these requests into the general budget; thus the process at this stage becomes one of budget-cutting.

Department heads often submit artificially high requests in anticipation of these inevitable cuts. The extent to which this occurs depends on the constraints imposed by the budget memorandum; the extent of the overall fiscal crunch; and the working relationship between department heads and the chief executive or other designated budget officer. The chief executive must work closely with department heads when making adjustments to bring the total budget into line. A dissatisfied department head may have another chance to make proposals in the legislative review process.

In summary, the chief executive, relying on planning estimates, plans, and programs, has the responsibility for assembling the budget from the departmental requests and nondepartmental items (such as fixed costs and debt service).

Document Preparation. Once the executive budget has been formulated, it is submitted to the legislative body and the general public. Budget documents include a budget message and summary, a detailed operating budget, a capital budget, and various ordinances.

The *budget message and summary* presents a clear explanation of the important features of the budget. It covers past, present, and estimated future economic limits (growth, income), financial condition, revenue and expenditure levels; needed changes in fiscal policy; and a brief description of the operating and capital programs. Generally the summary also presents total estimated revenues by source and total planned expenditures broken down by departments or programs. This document is typically made available to the public.

The *detailed operating budget* can take a variety of forms, such as *program* or *line item,* or *unified* or *separate* capital. The typical line-item budget organizes expenditure amounts by departments, funds, and category of expenditure; for example, personnel, supplies and materials, and contractual services. The program budget is organized by program, activity, and category of expenditure.

Items requiring expenditures that are generally nonrecurring, large, of a fixed investment nature, and long-term are called capital items. These include street improvements, water and sewer lines, new buildings, purchase of land, and new major equipment. These are sometimes organized into a separate budget because they effect planning periods of more than one year. The capital budget is derived from the capital program, with each project identified and described and total costs programmed over a five-year period. The first year of the five-year estimate is the capital budget for the coming fiscal year.

The budget package generally includes the ordinances needed to adopt the budget, including appropriations, authorizations, and resolutions.

Legislative Review. The chief executive submits the budget documents to the legislative body, with a verbal presentation of the budget message. Copies are made available to the press, libraries, organizations, and interested groups and individuals. Public hearings are then scheduled and advertised. The council may review the budget as a complete body or in subcommittee. Public hearings are conducted so citizens have the opportunity to provide additional information and criticism. Department heads may also testify to clarify parts of the budget or to request a higher departmental budget. After the public hearings and the review, the legislative body may make changes in any part of the budget (within normal legal constraints).

Adoption. Once the final budget is formulated, the legislative body adopts it by resolution or ordinance. If changes have been extensive, the entire adopted budget is reprinted; if not, only the changes are printed and attached. The adoption should occur before the start of the fiscal year, but this is not always the case. The complexity, the politics involved, and delays in bureaucratic processes may postpone adoption. In such cases, legislation is adopted allowing expenditures at the previous year's level until the budget is adopted. Finally, the adopted

budget is sent to the chief executive for implementation.

Budget Management, Amendments, and Audit. The chief executive has responsibility for administering the adopted budget. Three basic mechanisms are used in this process: the allotment system, the accounting system, and financial reports. The allotment system provides a basic spending control by releasing funds to departments on a quarterly or monthly basis. This system is tied into the accounting system, which is designed to record all financial transactions and to show the total financial condition at any given time. Periodic financial reports, developed from the accounting information, are submitted to the chief executive so that he or she can periodically assess financial conditions (including the comparison of budget estimates with actual expenditures and revenues). Actual revenues may exceed or fall short of previous estimates, indicating an opportunity to increase expenditures or the need to order spending reductions. One department may be underspending while another is overspending, indicating necessary budget or activity shifts.

The budgeting/accounting system should be flexible enough to allow for routine adjustments. This flexibility is sometimes achieved by appropriating monies to a contingency fund and/or an executive emergency fund. Major adjustments generally require an amendment to the budget, however, in the form of legislation that must be passed by the council.

Part of the management system is the audit, a formal examination and verification of the accounts. There are two types: internal and external. The internal audit is conducted quarterly or semiannually by city staff or consultants to produce reports for internal management purposes. The external audit or postaudit (normally required by state law) is conducted by external certified public accountants after the fiscal year has ended. The external audit submitted to the legislative body and the regulating state agency. The legislative body reviews the audit to ensure that revenue and expenditure activities were conducted according to the intentions of the budget.

BUDGET APPROACHES

There is a great deal of variability in the budget mechanics of local governments. Legal requirements (state law, local charters) may determine the process for any particular unit. The larger the city, the more complex the process. In small cities, the entire budget might be formulated at a single meeting of the city council, where allocations are made intuitively by knowledgeable members. But in most larger cities, the fiscal planning and budgeting activities are a major management function, and a considerable full-time staff may be required.

There is a highly political side of budgeting.[10] A major part of this politics is the controversy between rational, or central, and political approaches to budgeting. The critical issue between these extremes is the extent of central control over budget formulation. The issue became important in the mid 1960s when the federal government instituted PPBS (planning, programming, budget system). Government was attempting to reform or rationalize the highly political process of budgeting by incorporating certain concepts of central planning and management to increase allocational efficiency.[11] Although PPBS was largely a failure and eventually abandoned at the federal level, it has fared better in state and local governments. Pure PPBS systems are seldom attempted, but the principles and practices developed are scattered throughout local government procedures.[12]

Several elements are dominant in the contemporary approach: concern with process, program structure, quantitative analysis, and extended time horizon.[13] The concern with process implies a systematic, rational, central management process; em-

phasis is placed on procedure and facts rather than on politics. Program structure implies a shift from the traditional line-item (salary, supplies) or departmental grouping of expenditures to groupings (programs) that reflect particular objectives. The emphasis in the former is on inputs, such as expenditures for capital and labor for a particular department, regardless of the multiple missions of the department. The latter emphasis is on both inputs and outputs for a particular activity or program, regardless of multiple departmental involvements. This structure allows the comparison of program outputs to inputs in terms of cost-benefit, cost-effectiveness, or other productivity measures. Alternate programs can then be ranked with respect to their ability to satisfy objectives, and rational expenditure decisions can be made. Quantitative analysis and an extended time horizon are by now somewhat self-explanatory parts of contemporary planning.

The opposing view of budgeting can be labeled the "leave-it-alone approach," which derives from a careful examination of actual budgetary practices and the conclusion that reform measures often do more harm than good.[14] Proponents of this approach argue that the budgeting process works primarily because of, not in spite of, its decentralized process. They see attempts to rationalize the budget process as counterproductive. In this view, budgeting is essentially a political process in an environment of uncertainty about the future consequences of current decisions and competition for resources. Legislative council members consider only a limited set of practical alternatives and accept the first one that satisfies the objectives, thereby saving time and energy.[15] Complex questions are "muddled through" by fragmenting issues and relying on the specialized knowledge of individual council members or staff experts.[16] People can coordinate themselves without resorting to an external force. Persons with different bases of power and different views of the problem can arrive at solutions through bargaining in a give-and-take format. In this "fair share" ethic, council members will "win some" and "lose some," and everyone will be satisfied somehow over the long run. Departments and agencies must compete for budget resources and in so doing will arrive collectively at a satisfactory budget allocation. Budget allocations are not made from a zero base but rather as incremental changes from previous budget allocations. All these mechanisms allow budget participants to arrive at reasonable, although not necessarily optimal, budget decisions. The imposition of rational mechanisms is thought to subvert this process.

The difference is not just between the normative (what ought to be) and the positive (what is), because advocates of both approaches believe that their view leads to better budgeting outcomes. However, the issue is no longer between extremes. No one is advocating the imposition of the major and complete changes of PPBS systems. The complexity, institutional friction, and high cost associated with massive procedural and structural change to traditional budget systems make such attempts futile.

Budgeting continues to be recognized as a highly political process. However, substantial elements of contemporary approaches have been used in state and local governments with considerable success, and the integration of some planning and finance functions has become common. Program structure has received major application in analysis if not in budget formats. Quantitative techniques are becoming the norm in program evaluation, related productivity studies, and fiscal impact studies.

Less extreme versions of contemporary budgeting, such as zero based budgeting, have gained considerable acceptance. Zero based budgeting is essentially the concept of justifying expenditures from a zero base rather than as incremental increases or decreases. President Carter instituted this method in Georgia during his term as governor and is now implementing it within the federal government. Basically, ZBB involves adopting programs as budget units, dividing each program into various service levels (e.g., 80, 90, 95, 100, 105 per-

cent of current levels), analyzing these service levels against needs, analyzing alternatives, and ranking these service levels within and across programs. Funds already committed by previous binding decisions (insurance, pensions, bond service, etc.) are not included in the analysis. Rankings or priorities are set within departments and then for the overall unit of government. Various service and funding levels facilitate trade-offs among programs. For example, an 80 percent level of one program might be a higher priority than a 100 percent level for another program. Budgets are then constructed by selecting the highest priority items, up to the service level permitted by the total budget constraint. A number of local governments are experimenting with, or have adopted, a ZBB system.

Local governments are generally beginning to take advantage of accumulated experience and expertise and to adopt more successful fiscal planning approaches. The question is no longer whether or not to adopt a contemporary approach, but rather how to use selected techniques to improve management and planning.

SUMMARY

This chapter has presented a description of a rather complete system of fiscal management and planning. As previously mentioned, this does not imply that all governmental units follow the process explicitly. However, all of the functions identified must be carried out, one way or another. This presentation might be treated as a "guide to good practice." The emphasis has been on "process" rather than organizational arrangement. Obviously, any number of institutional arrangements might facilitate good planning process.

We have seen that planning is increasingly being accepted as an integral part of the overall management process. Only in the public sector has planning, as a process, traditionally been treated as a function distinct and separate from management. The changing orientation means that planners and planning are now found in a variety of situations, rather than exclusively in planning agencies. Another important factor is the severe fiscal situation faced by many of our urban areas, which has created the demand for better fiscal management.

These two factors have combined to involve planners more directly with fiscal matters. The extent to which a planner will deal with financial planning will depend on his or her particular situation. However-

er, any urban planner should be familiar with fiscal planning and budgeting processes, as well as basic economics and public finance. Many will become proficient in the techniques of basic economic research, fiscal policy analysis, program evaluation, and the like. A smaller number will become specialists in fiscal planning and programming, and in fiscal impact analysis. It is clear that there is an increasing need for sound fiscal management, and planning is an integral part of that process.

NOTES

1. A more complete presentation of this topic can be found in James C. Snyder, *Fiscal Management and Planning in Local Government* (Lexington, Mass.: Heath, Lexington Books 1977).

2. Clyde J. Wingfield, "City Planning," in *Managing the Modern City*, James M. Banovetz, ed. (Washington, D.C.: International City Managers's Association, 1971).

3. International City Managers' Association, *Municipal Finance Administration* (Chicago: International City Managers' Association, 1962), p. 20.

4. Alan W. Steiss, *Public Budgeting and Management* (Lexington. Mass.: Heath, 1972), p. 1.

5. Michael J. Munson, "How to Keep Plans off the Shelf: An Organizational View of Planning, Management, and Implementation" (Ph.D. dissertation, University of Michigan, 1972), p. 14.

6. Ibid., p. 24.

7. The categories are taken from Munson, "How to Keep Plans off the Shelf," p. 15, and were derived from Robert Anthony, *Planning and Control Systems: A Framework for Analysis* (Cambridge, Mass.: Harvard University Press, 1965).

8. As with the management model of the previous figure the management side of this figure was derived from the works of Munson and Anthony (see note 7).

9. The expenditure and revenue estimation framework can be found in Werner Z. Hirsch, *The Economics of State and Local Government* (New York: McGraw-Hill, 1970), pp. 280–90.

10. See Aaron Widavsky, *The Politics of the Budgetary Process* (Boston: Little, Brown, 1964).

11. A good historical sketch can be found in Bertram M.

Gross, "The New Systems Budgeting," *Public Administration Review* 29 (March-April 1969), and other articles in the same issue.

12. A 1971 survey by the International City Management Association and The Urban Institute estimated that 16 percent of cities with more than 50,000 population were conducting program-type analysis. Likewise, a survey by the National Association of State Budget Officers reported that 65 percent of the states were conducting related analyses. See Harry Hatry et al., *Program Analysis for State and Local Governments* (Washington, D.C.: Urban Institute, 1976), p. 5.

13. A comprehensive treatment of contemporary budgeting approaches can be found in Steiss, *Public Budgeting and Management,* Chapters 7, 8, and 9. Also see Harry P. Hatry, "Criteria for Evaluation in Planning State and Local Programs" in *Decision-Making in Urban Planning,* Ira M. Robinson, ed. (Beverly Hills; Calif.: Sage, 1972).

14. See Wildavsky, *The Politics of the Budgetary Process;* Arnold J. Meltsner and Aaron Wildavsky, "Second Thoughts of the Reform," in *Financing the Metropolis,* John P. Crecine, ed. (Beverly Hills, Calif.: Sage, 1970); and Charles E. Lindblom, "The Science of Muddling Through," *Public Administration Review* 19 (Spring 1959).

15. The appropriate term here is "satisficing," developed by G. March and Herbert A. Simon, in *Organizations* (New York: Wiley, 1958).

16. Lindblom, "The Science of Muddling Through."

FOR FURTHER READING

Aronson, Jay Richard, and Schwartz, Eli. *Management Policies in Local Government Finance.* Washington, D.C.: International City Management Association, 1975.

Burchell, Robert W., and Listokin, David. *The Fiscal Impact Handbook.* New Brunswick, N. J.: Center for Urban Policy Research, Rutgers University. 1978.

Moak, Lennox L., and Hillhouse, Albert M. *Local Government Finance.* Chicago: Municipal Finance Officers Association, 1975.

Snyder, James C. *Fiscal Management and Planning in Local Government.* Lexington, Mass.: Heath, Lexington Books, 1977.

Steiss, Alan Walter. *Local Government Finance: Capital Facilities Planning and Debt Administration.* Lexington, Mass.: Heath, Lexington Books, 1975.

————. *Public Budgeting and Management.* Lexington, Mass.: Heath, Lexington Books, 1975.

Epilogue

This book has attempted to introduce the beginning student in urban planning, architecture, and related fields to a wide range of topics concerning urban planning. It has been concerned largely with the physical aspects or results of planning, both to illustrate the process and enable the student to approach a complicated set of issues and problems. Additional study of the social, political, and economic determinants of cities and their planning is mandatory for the serious student.

Certain pedagogical trends occurring at present may develop over the next decade or so to a stage that merits a revised edition of this book. For example:

1 Other fields and disciplines, such as architecture, social studies, and urban affairs, are expanding their education and training programs to include work formerly done exclusively by planners.

2 While there are more jobs for urban planners, there are more people looking for such jobs.

3 The profession is seeking to better define planning practice.

It is ironical that recent trends appear to be leading to a restatement of basic, traditional planning approaches in teaching. Recent years have been notable for demands by students for "marketable skills." Both students and employers want the schools to produce graduates who have useful, technical capabilities and an understanding of the context for their application. Yet they also want flexibility for future growth into the higher echelons of the planning hierarchy. The demand is for utility and flexibility.

The response by educational institutions seems to be a tightening of requirements. The institution of core course requirements instead of the "supermarket" approaches of the late 1960s and early 1970s is becoming prominent, accompanied by the discarding of secondary and "awareness-sensitivity" courses. We are witnessing a return to tighter, skills-oriented curricula.

This search for better planning skills and effectiveness has created some turmoil. Generalist educators decry these trends as a conservative effort to return to the past. Sympathetic educators argue that educational policies based on fundamental planning skills and methods have never really been tested. Many users of planning services are demanding that planners learn to communicate better through writing, speaking, and interaction with groups. These users want planners to develop the basic skills of communication and interaction that pertain to any professional field.

The next decade will see efforts to increase the substantive and technical levels of every topic in this text. Yet, we do not foresee any one of these areas to eclipse. We can predict a greater concern with the physical aspects of the built environment and a greater use of interprofessional teams to incorporate nonphysical concerns of a social, economic, or political nature into planning. Other fields will expand their efforts to contribute to urban planning. The result may be a curious covenant between urban planning and its historical relationship with architecture, as well as new covenants with landscape architecture, engineering, and design fields.

This does not mean that the many new facets of urban planning will disappear. In fact, urban planning may result in some new professions. Just as architecture was the root of urban planning, so may urban planning be the root of such fields as social welfare, health, financial, transportation, ecological, and economic development planning. Urban planning will have to deal with the new trends in growth control, decline management, neighborhood development, adaptive reuse, conservation, and revitalization.

Urban planning has undergone periods of turbulent change, but it appears to be on the brink of stability and maturity. There are likely to be much harder skills and methods developed over the next 10 to 15 years—some expositions of those included herein, and some entirely new. Urban planning is a dynamic and progressive art.

Index

Index